WESTMAR COLLE

P9-DGJ-873

COLLEGE LIBRARY

MAN
AGAINST
POVERTY:
World War III

MAN
AGAINST
POVERTY:
World War III

A READER ON THE WORLD'S
MOST CRUCIAL ISSUE

Edited by
Arthur I. Blaustein
and
Roger R. Woock

With a Preface
by John W.
Gardner
RANDOM HOUSE, New York

339.46
B645

HC
79
.P6
B55

FIRST PRINTING

Copyright © 1968 by Random House, Inc.

All rights reserved under International and Pan-American Copyright Conventions. Published in the United States by Random House, Inc., New York, and simultaneously in Canada by Random House of Canada Limited, Toronto.

LIBRARY OF CONGRESS CATALOG CARD NUMBER: 67–12753

Manufactured in the United States of America

78285

To the memory of
MARTIN LUTHER KING, JR.

Preface*

FOR MOST AMERICANS today life is reasonably comfortable. It is easy to suppose that we are safely insulated from the problems that beset this land, that they are someone else's problems, not ours.

But they are grimly and irrevocably the problems of our generation, and none of us can escape. There isn't any place to hide. The consequences of poverty, racial conflict, environmental pollution, urban decay, and other problems will affect the quality of life for everyone here today, and for everyone in this land, the comfortable and the uncomfortable. It won't be a decent life for any of us until it is for all of us.

Consider the recent turn toward violence. Where will it lead? Where *can* it lead? There are bitter and vindictive people on both sides who hope for the worst. But you and I have to believe that a saner path is possible.

Despair in the ghettos cannot be cured by savagery in the streets. Violence begets violence. It is time to speak out against those on either side who through words or actions contribute to conflagrations of bitterness and rage. They wreak more havoc than they know. They may create ruinous cleavages and paralyzing hatreds that will make it virtually impossible for us to function as a society.

This is a day of dissent and divisiveness. Everyone speaks with unbridled anger in behalf of his point of view or his party

* From a speech delivered by Mr. Gardner, then Secretary of Health, Education, and Welfare, at the University of North Carolina, Chapel Hill, October 12, 1967.

or his people. More and more, hostility and venom are the hall-marks of any conversation on the affairs of the nation.

There used to be only a few chronically angry people in our national life. Today all seem caught up in mutual recriminations —Negro and white, rich and poor, conservative and liberal, hawk and dove, Democrat and Republican, labor and manage-ment, North and South, young and old.

I've listened to them all, and at this moment I'd like to say a word not for or against any of them but in behalf of a troubled nation.

Today the first duty of responsible citizens is to bind together rather than tear apart. The fissures in our society are already dangerously deep. We need greater emphasis on the values that hold us together.

We need a greater common allegiance to the goals and binding values of the national community. A society or a nation is more than just a lot of people. A lot of people are a crowd or a population. To merit the term *society* or *nation* they have to have some shared attitudes and beliefs, and a shared allegiance. If the nation is to have any future, people have to care quite a lot about the common enterprise.

We know that many are willing to die for their country. We also have to care enough to live for it. Enough to live less comfortably than one might in order to serve it. Enough to work with patience and fortitude to cure its afflictions. Enough to forgo the joys of hating one another. Enough to make our most cherished common purposes prevail.

Today extremists of the right and the left work with purposeful enthusiasm to deepen our suspicion and fear of one another and to loosen the bonds that hold the society together. The trouble, of course, is that they may succeed in pulling the society apart. And will anyone really know how to put it together again?

The cohesiveness of a society, the commitment of large num-bers of people to live together and work together, is a fairly mysterious thing. We don't know what makes it happen. If it breaks down we don't know how one might go about repairing it.

Back of every great civilization, behind all the panoply of power and wealth is something as powerful as it is insubstantial, a set of ideas, attitudes and convictions—and the confidence that those ideas and convictions are viable.

No nation can achieve greatness unless it believes in something—and unless that something has the moral dimensions to sustain a great civilization.

If the light of belief flickers out, then all the productive capacity and all the know-how and all the power of the nation will be as nothing, and the darkness will gather.

If enough people doubt themselves and their society, the whole venture falls apart. We must never let anger or indignation or political partisanship blur our vision on that point.

In Guatemala and Southern Mexico one can observe the Indians who are without doubt the lineal descendants of those who created the Mayan civilization. Today they are a humble people, not asking much of themselves or the world, and not getting much. A light went out.

The geography and natural resources are virtually unchanged; the genetic make-up of the people is no doubt much the same. They were once a great people. Now they do not even remember their greatness. What happened?

I suspect that in the case of the Mayans, the ruling ideas were too primitive to sustain a great civilization for long.

What about our own ideas? Can they sustain a great civilization?

The answer depends on what ideas we are talking about. Americans have valued and sought and believed in many different things—freedom, power, money, equality, justice, technology, bigness, success, comfort, speed, peace, war, discipline, freedom from discipline and so on.

I like to believe that most Americans would agree on which of those values might serve as the animating ideas for a great civilization.

In my present job, I deal with a side of American society in which the existence of certain ruling ideals is visible and inescapable. I see children being taught, the sick healed, the aged cared for, the crippled rehabilitated, the talented nurtured and developed, the mentally ill treated, the weak strengthened.

Those tasks are not done by unbelieving people. Those tasks are carried forward by people who have at heart what I like to call the American Commitment.

I believe that when we are being most true to ourselves as Americans we are seeking a society in which every young person has the opportunity to grow to his full stature; a society in which every older person can live out his years in dignity; a society in which no one is irreparably damaged by circumstances that can be prevented.

All too often we have been grievously unfaithful to those ideas. And that infidelity can be cured only by deeds. Such ideas cannot be said to be alive unless they live in the acts of men, unless they are embedded in our laws, our social institutions, our educational practices, our political habits, our ways of dealing with one another. We must act in the service of our beliefs.

Every individual is of value.

The release of human potential, the enhancement of individual dignity, the liberation of the human spirit—those are the deepest and truest goals to be conceived by the hearts and minds of the American people.

And those are ideas that can sustain and strengthen a great civilization. But we must be honest about them. We must live by them. And we must have the stamina to hold to our purposes through times of confusion and controversy.

JOHN W. GARDNER
Chairman, The Urban Coalition

Acknowledgments

A GREAT NUMBER of friends and colleagues contributed to
the creation of this book. Particularly important were Professor Dan Dodson, who provided the original impetus; Henry
Goldstein; Robert W. C. Brown; Robert J. Mangum; and
William Casey, whose suggestions and arguments were very
useful.

For their patience and support we also thank Clare C.
Woock, Dorothy Dulles Bourne, Rev. Hugh Hostetler, and
Dorothy Tod; and our editor, Berenice Hoffman.

The Preface was to have been written by Senator Robert F.
Kennedy. The exigencies of his primary campaigns and the
tragic assassination made this impossible. We wish to especially thank Mr. John W. Gardner for his thoughtful remarks
on such short notice.

CONTENTS

B. Cases in Point

C. Means to an End

Part III | POVERTY IN THE WORLD

A. The Problems

B. Cases in Point

C. Means to an End

Introduction

THE PAST FIFTY YEARS have seen major technological break-throughs in one-third of the world while the other two-thirds still plow the earth with dull sticks. In the richest nation in the world, while the majority of Americans have enjoyed the benefits of unparalleled economic growth, evidence of profound human misery exists in the industrial urban ghettoes of the Watts and Harlems and among the rural poor of Appalachia.

As the gap between the "haves" and "have-nots" both in the U.S. and abroad widens, the relentless tempo of the arms race grows. This malign process has been going on since the end of World War II. While the world is spending approximately $130 billion annually for armaments and the U.S., at least an additional $30 billion annually for the Vietnam war; the "four horsemen of the Apocalypse" continue to ride the backs of the poor of Africa, Asia and Latin America. In addition, the 30 million Americans who live below the "poverty line" have seen their aspirations and allocations, built on the splendid promises of the Great Society, painfully reduced to support America's "achilles heel," the war in Southeast Asia.

In this volume the editors try to demonstrate that although the nature of the two kinds of poverty are vastly different, they do have one thing in common—they are both waiting for the Cold War to end. That the arms race stands as a stark reminder of the inequities of not only a divided world, but of divided peoples within the same country, is certainly the most dynamic and vital issue of our time. Underlying this central theme are the problems of racial injustice, equal access to opportunity for the disadvantaged, and the competence and the will of the "haves" to deal with circumstances and needs of the "have-nots."

Senators J. William Fulbright and Joseph Clark, Michael Harrington, Paul Goodman, Kenneth B. Clark, Frank Riessman, Frantz Fanon, Oscar Lewis and other educators, economists, journalists, political scientists, sociologists and psychiatrists explore the nature of poverty in the United States and the underdeveloped world. Individual case studies poignantly take the problems out of the realm of hypotheses and abstractions. Dramatic policy alternatives are presented as possible solutions to political, social and economic questions.

This collection represents a full-scale effort to view the totality of problems of institutional poverty in the U.S. and the underdeveloped world, and to see them within the context of the Cold War and the role of the United States as a world power. The selections were chosen not only to study the problems in detail but also for their ability to challenge many of our traditional assumptions and offer new alternatives.

The threat to world stability inherent in grinding poverty will severely tax the technological and human ingenuity of man. If man is to succeed, for humanitarian as well as selfish reasons, in diminishing that threat, it is obvious that a total, unconditional war against poverty must be declared; and it must be prosecuted with large sums of money, disciplined minds, social imagination and integrity . . . and it must be declared now!

PART ONE

BEYOND THE COLD WAR

INTRODUCTION

SENATOR J. WILLIAM FULBRIGHT, Chairman of the Senate Foreign Relations Committee, finds "The Great Society" to be a "sick" society. As evidence, he points to our escalating commitment in Vietnam and its effect on specific programs for domestic reform as well as the general quality of American life. Michael Harrington analyzes American power in the twentieth century. He finds its quantity awesome indeed, but is critical of the ways in which we have misused our power to the disadvantage of our own long range interests. O. Edmund Clubb describes the revolution of the "third world" against man's historical enemies, hunger and poverty. He criticizes America's military response to what he believes are basically economic and social problems.

If America is ever truly to move beyond the Cold War, the fundamental questions that economist Emile Benoit raises about the economics and politics of defense cutbacks must be considered seriously. Professor Benoit raised these basic questions about the defense budget immediately prior to our heavy and escalating commitment in Vietnam. Unfortunately the country's mood then became one of unwillingness to debate the issue of overall defense cutbacks. Nevertheless, the problems posed by Benoit can be separated from the issue of spending for Vietnam, and eventually must be faced within the context that he outlines.

Arthur I. Blaustein discusses the relationship between our foreign and domestic commitments, and indicates how the government can act to help resolve the crises of poverty at home.

| J. WILLIAM FULBRIGHT | THE PRICE OF EMPIRE* |

STANDING in the smoke and rubble of Detroit, a Negro veteran said: "I just got back from Vietnam a few months ago, but you know, I think the war is here."

There are in fact two wars going on. One is the war of power politics which our soldiers are fighting in the jungles of Southeast Asia. The other is a war for America's soul which is being fought in the streets of Newark and Detroit and in the halls of Congress, in churches and protest meetings and on college campuses, and in the hearts and minds of silent Americans from Maine to Hawaii. I believe that the two wars have something to do with each other, not in the direct, tangibly causal way that bureaucrats require as proof of a connection between two things, but in a subtler moral and qualitative way that is no less real for being intangible. Each of these wars might well be going on in the absence of the other, but neither, I suspect, standing alone, would seem so hopeless and demoralizing.

The connection between Vietnam and Detroit is in their conflicting and incompatible demands upon traditional American values. The one demands that they be set aside, the other that they be fulfilled. The one demands the acceptance by America of an imperial role in the world, or of what our policymakers like to call the "responsibilities of power," or of what I have called the "arrogance of power." The other demands freedom and social justice at home, an end to poverty, the fulfillment of our flawed democracy and an effort to create a role for ourselves in the world which is compatible with our traditional values. The question, it should be emphasized, is not whether it is *possible* to engage in traditional power politics abroad and

* From the *New York Times Magazine*, August 29, 1967. © 1967 by the New York Times Company. Reprinted by permission.

at the same time to perfect democracy at home, but whether it is possible for *us Americans,* with our particular history and national character, to combine morally incompatible roles.

Administration officials tell us that we can indeed afford both Vietnam and the Great Society, and they produce impressive statistics of the gross national product to prove it. The statistics show financial capacity, but they do not show moral and psychological capacity. They do not show how a President preoccupied with bombing missions over North and South Vietnam can provide strong and consistent leadership for the renewal of our cities. They do not show how a Congress burdened with war costs and war measures, with emergency briefings and an endless series of dramatic appeals, with anxious constituents and a mounting anxiety of their own, can tend to the workaday business of studying social problems and legislating programs to meet them. Nor do the statistics tell how an anxious and puzzled people, bombarded by press and television with the bad news of American deaths in Vietnam, the "good news" of enemy deaths—and with vividly horrifying pictures to illustrate them— can be expected to support neighborhood antipoverty projects and national programs for urban renewal, employment and education. Anxiety about war does not breed compassion for one's neighbors nor do constant reminders of the cheapness of life abroad strengthen our faith in its sanctity at home. In these ways the war in Vietnam is poisoning and brutalizing our domestic life. Psychological incompatibility has proven to be more controlling than financial feasibility; and the Great Society has become a sick society.

When he visited America a hundred years ago, Thomas Huxley wrote: "I cannot say that I am in the slightest degree impressed by your bigness, or your material resources, as such. Size is not grandeur, and territory does not make a nation. The great issue, about which hangs the terror of overhanging fate, is what are you going to do with all these things?"

The question is still with us, and we seem to have come to a time of historical crisis when its answer can no longer be deferred. Before the Second World War our world role was a potential role; we were important in the world for what we *could* do with our power, for the leadership we *might* provide, for the example we *might* set. Now the choices are almost gone: we are, almost, the world's self-appointed policeman; we are, almost, the world defender of the status quo. We are well on our way to becoming a traditional great power—an imperial nation if you will—engaged in the exercise of power for its own sake, exercising it to the limit of our capacity and beyond, filling every vacuum and extending the American "presence" to the farthest reaches of the earth. And, as with the great empires of the past, as the power grows, it is becoming an end in itself, separated except by ritual incantation from its initial motives, governed, it would seem, by its own mystique, power without philosophy or purpose.

That describes what we have *almost* become, but we have not become a traditional empire yet. The old values remain—the populism and the optimism, the individualism and the rough-hewn equality, the friendliness and the good humor, the inventiveness and the zest for life, the caring about people and the sympathy for the underdog, and the idea, which goes back to the American Revolution, that maybe—just maybe—we can set an example of democracy and human dignity for the world.

That is something which none of the great empires of the past has ever done, or tried to do, or wanted to do, but we were bold enough—or presumptuous enough—to think that we might be able to do it. And there are a great many Americans who still think we can do it, or at least they want to try.

That, I believe, is what all the hue and cry is about—the dissent in the Senate and the protest marches in the cities, the letters to the President from the student leaders and former Peace Corps Volunteers, the lonely searching of conscience by a student facing the draft and the letter to a Senator from a soldier in the field who can no longer accept the official explanations of why he has been sent to fight in the jungles of Vietnam. All believe that their country was cut out for something more ennobling than imperial destiny. Our youth are showing that they still believe in the American dream, and their protests attest to its continuing vitality.

There appeared in a recent issue of the journal, *Foreign Affairs,* a curious little article complaining about the failure of many American intellectuals to support what the author regards as America's unavoidable "imperial role" in the world. The article took my attention because it seems a faithful statement of the governing philosophy of American foreign policy while also suggesting how little the makers of that policy appreciate the significance of the issue between themselves and their critics. It is taken for granted—not set forth as a hypothesis to be proven—that any great power, in the author's words, "is entangled in a web of responsibilities from which there is no hope of escape," and that "there is no way the United States, as the world's mightiest power, can avoid such an imperial role. . . ." The author's displeasure with the "intellectuals" (he uses the word more or less to describe people who disagree with the Administration's policy) is that, in the face of this alleged historical inevitability, they are putting up a disruptive, irritating and futile resistance. They are doing this, he believes, because they are believers in "ideology"—the better word would be "values" or "ideals"—and this causes their thinking to be "irrelevant" to foreign policy.

Here, inadvertently, the writer puts his finger on the nub of the current crisis. The students and churchmen and professors who are protesting the Vietnam war do not accept the notion that foreign policy is a matter of expedients to which values are irrelevant. They reject this notion because they understand, as some of our policymakers do not understand, that it is ultimately self-defeating to "fight fire with fire," that you cannot defend your values in a manner that does violence to those values without destroying the very thing you are trying to defend. They understand, as our policymakers do not, that when American soldiers are sent, in the name of freedom, to sustain corrupt dictators in a civil war, that when the Central Intelligence Agency subverts student organizations to engage in propaganda activities abroad, or when the Export-Import Bank is used by the Pentagon to finance secret arms sales abroad, damage—perhaps irreparable damage—is being done to the very values that are meant to be defended. The critics understand, as our policymakers do not, that, through the undemocratic expedients we have adopted for the defense of American democracy, we are weakening it to a degree that is beyond the resources of our bitterest enemies.

Nor do the dissenters accept the romantic view that a nation is powerless to choose the role it will play in the world, that some mystic force of history or destiny requires a powerful nation to be an imperial nation, dedicated to what Paul Goodman calls the "empty system of power," to the pursuit of power without purpose, philosophy or compassion. They do not accept the Hegelian concept of history as something out of control, as something that happens to us rather than something that we make. They do not accept the view that, because other great nations have pursued power for its own sake—a pursuit which invariably has ended in decline or disaster—America must do the same. They think we have some choice about our own future and that the best basis for exercising that choice is the values on which this republic was founded.

The critics of our current course also challenge the contention that the traditional methods of foreign policy are safe and prudent and realistic. They are understandably skeptical of their wise and experienced elders who, in the name of prudence, caution against any departure from the tried and true methods that have led in this century to Sarajevo, Munich and Dienbienphu. They think that the methods of the past have been tried and found wanting, and two world wars attest powerfully to their belief. Most of all, they think that, in this first era of human history in which man has acquired weapons which threaten his entire species with destruction, safety and prudence and realism require us to change the rules of a dangerous and discredited game, to try as we have never tried before to civilize and humanize international relations, not only for the sake of civilization and humanity but for the sake of survival.

Even the most ardent advocates of an imperial role for the United States would probably agree that the proper objective of our foreign policy is the fostering of a world environment in which we can, with reasonable security, devote our main energies to the realization of the values of our own society. This does not require the adoption or imposition of these values on anybody, but it does require us so to conduct ourselves that our society does not seem hateful and repugnant to others.

At the present, much of the world is repelled by America and what America seems to stand for. Both in our foreign affairs and in our domestic life we convey an image of violence; I do not care very much about images as distinguished from the things they reflect, but this image is rooted in reality. Abroad we are engaged in a savage and unsuccessful war against poor people in a small and backward nation. At home—largely because of the neglect resulting from twenty-five years of preoccupation with foreign involvements—our cities are exploding in violent protest against generations of social injustice. America, which only a few years ago seemed to the world to be a model of democracy and social justice, has become a symbol of violence and undisciplined power.

"It is excellent," wrote Shakespeare, "to have a giant's strength; but it is tyrannous to use it like a giant." By using our power like a giant we are fostering a world environment which is, to put it mildly, uncongenial to our society. By our undisciplined use of physical power we have divested ourselves of a greater power: the power of example. How can we commend peaceful compromise to the Arabs and the Israelis when we are unwilling to suspend our relentless bombing of North Vietnam? How can we commend democratic social reform to Latin America when Newark, Detroit and Milwaukee are providing explosive evidence of our own inadequate efforts at democratic social reform? How can we commend the free enterprise system to Asians and Africans when in our own country it has produced vast, chaotic, noisy, dangerous and dirty urban complexes while poisoning the very air and land and water? There may come a time when Americans will again be able to commend their country as an example to the world and, more in hope than confidence, I retain my faith that there will; but to do so right at this moment would take more gall than I have.

Far from building a safe world environment for American values, our war in Vietnam and the domestic deterioration which it has aggravated are creating a most uncongenial world atmosphere for American ideas and values. The world has no need, in this age of nationalism and nuclear weapons, for a new imperial power, but there is a great need of moral leadership—by which I mean the leadership of decent example. That role could be ours but we have vacated the field, and all that has kept the Russians from filling it is their own lack of imagination.

At the same time, as we have noted, and of even greater fundamental importance, our purposeless and undisciplined use of power is causing a profound controversy in our own society. This in a way is something to be proud of. We have sickened but not succumbed, and just as a healthy body fights disease, we are fighting the alien concept which is being thrust upon us, not by history but by our policymakers in the Department of State and the Pentagon. We are proving the strength of the American dream by resisting the dream of an imperial destiny. We are demonstrating the validity of our traditional values by the difficulty we are having in betraying them.

The principal defenders of these values are our remarkable younger generation, something of whose spirit is expressed in a letter which I received from an American soldier in Vietnam. Speaking of the phony propaganda on both sides, and then of the savagery of the war, of the people he describes as the "real casualties"—"the farmers and their families in the Delta mangled by air strikes, and the villagers here killed and burned out by our friendly Korean mercenaries"—this young soldier then asks ". . . whatever has become of our dream? Where is that America that opposed tyrannies at every turn, without inquiring first whether some particular forms of tyranny might be of use to us? Of the three rights which men have, the first, as I recall, was the right to life. How, then, have we come to be killing so many in such a dubious cause?"

While the death toll mounts in Vietnam, it is mounting too in the war at home. During a single week of July 1967, 164 Americans were killed and 2,100 were wounded in city riots in the United States. We are truly fighting a two-front war and doing badly in both. Each war feeds on the other and, although the President assures us that we have the resources to win both wars, in fact we are not winning either.

Together, the two wars have set in motion a process of deterioration in American society, and there is no question that each of the two crises is heightened by the impact of the other. Not only does the Vietnam war divert human and material resources from our festering cities; not only does it foster the conviction on the part of slum Negroes that their country is indifferent to their plight—in addition, the war feeds the idea of violence as a way of solving problems. If, as Mr. Rusk tells us, only the rain of bombs can bring Ho Chi Minh to reason, why should not the same principle apply at home? Why should not riots and snipers' bullets bring the white man to an awareness of the Negro's plight when peaceful programs for housing and jobs and training have been more rhetoric than reality? Ugly and shocking thoughts are in the American air, and they were forged in the Vietnam crucible. Black Power extremists talk of "wars of liberation" in the urban ghettos of America. A cartoon in a London newspaper showed the Negro soldiers in battle in Vietnam with one saying to the other: "This is going to be great training for civilian life."

The effect of domestic violence on the chances for peace in Vietnam may turn out to be no less damaging than the impact of the war on events at home. With their limited knowledge of the United States, the Vietcong and the North Vietnamese may regard the urban riots as a harbinger of impending breakdown and eventual American withdrawal from Vietnam, warranting stepped-up warfare and an uncompromising position on negotiations. It is possible that the several opportunities to negotiate, which our government has let pass, most recently last winter, could not now be retrieved. Some eighteen months ago Gen. Maxwell Taylor said in testimony before the Senate Foreign Relations Committee that the war was being prolonged by domestic dissent. That dissent was based in part on apprehension as to the effects of the war on our domestic life. Now the war is being prolonged by the domestic deterioration which has in fact occurred, and it is doubtful that all of the war dissenters in America, even if they wanted to, as they certainly do not, could give the enemy a fraction of the aid and comfort that have been given him by Newark, Detroit and Milwaukee.

An unnecessary and immoral war deserves in its own right to be liquidated; when its effect in addition is the aggravation of grave problems and the corrosion of values in our own society, its liquidation under terms of reasonable and honorable compromise is doubly imperative. Our country is being weakened by a grotesque inversion of priorities, the effects of which are becoming clear to more and more Americans—in the Congress, in the press and in the country at large. Even the *Washington Post,* a newspaper which has obsequiously supported the Administration's policy in Vietnam, took note in a recent editorial of the "ugly image of a world policeman incapable of policing itself" as against the "absolute necessity of a sound domestic base for an effective foreign policy," and then commented:

> We are confronted simultaneously with an urgent domestic crisis and an urgent foreign crisis and our commitments to both are clear. We should deal with both with all the energy and time and resources that may be required. But if the moment ever arises when we cannot deal adequately and effectively with both, there is no shame—and some considerable logic—in making it plain beyond a doubt that our first consideration and our first priority rests with the security of the stockade.

Commenting on the same problem of priorities, Mayor Cavanaugh of Detroit said:

> What will it profit this country if we, say, put our man on the moon by 1970 and at the same time you can't walk down Woodward Avenue in this city without some fear of violence?
> And we may be able to pacify every village in Vietnam, over a period of years, but what good does it do if we can't pacify the American cities?
> What I am saying . . . is that our priorities in this country are all out of balance . . . Maybe Detroit was a watershed this week in American history and it might well be that out of the ashes of this city comes the national resolve to do far more than anything we have done in the past.

Priorities are reflected in the things we spend money on. Far from being a dry accounting of bookkeepers, a nation's budget is full of moral implications; it tells what a society cares about and what it does not care about; it tells what its values are.

Here are a few statistics on America's values: Since 1946 we have spent over $1.578 billion through our regular national budget. Of this amount over $904 billion, or 57.29 percent of the total, has gone for military power. By contrast, less than $96 billion, or 6.08 percent, was spent on "social functions" including education, health, labor and welfare programs, housing and community development. The Administration's budget for fiscal year 1968 calls for almost $76 billion to be spent on the military and only $15 billion for "social functions."

I would not say that we have shown ourselves to value weapons five or ten times as much as we value domestic social needs, as the figures suggest; certainly much of our military spending has been necessitated by genuine requirements of national security. I think, however, that we have embraced the necessity with excessive enthusiasm, that the Congress has been all too willing to provide unlimited sums for the military and not really very reluctant at all to offset these costs to a very small degree by cutting away funds for the poverty program and urban renewal, for rent supplements for the poor and even for a program to help protect slum children from being bitten by rats. Twenty million dollars a year to eliminate rats—about 1/100th of the monthly cost of the war in Vietnam—would not eliminate slum riots; but, as correspondent Tom Wicker has written, "It would only suggest that somebody cared." The discrepancy of attitudes tells at least as much about our national values as the discrepancy of dollars.

While the country sickens for lack of moral leadership, a most remarkable younger generation has taken up the standard of American idealism. Unlike so many of their elders, they have perceived the fraud and sham in American life and are unequivocally rejecting it. Some, the hippies, have simply withdrawn; and while we may regret the loss of their energies and their sense of decency, we can hardly gainsay their evaluation of the state of society. Others of our youth are sardonic and skeptical, not, I think, because they do not want ideals but because they want the genuine article and will not tolerate fraud. Others—students who wrestle with their consciences about the draft, soldiers who wrestle with their consciences about the war, Peace Corps Volunteers who strive to light the spark of human dignity among the poor of India or Brazil and VISTA volunteers who try to do the same for our own poor in Harlem or Appalachia—are striving to keep alive the traditional values of American democracy.

They are not really radical, these young idealists, no more radical, that is, than Jefferson's idea of freedom, Lincoln's idea of equality or Wilson's idea of a peaceful community of nations. Some of them, it is true, are taking what many regard as radical action, but they are doing it in defense of traditional values and in protest against the radical departure from those values embodied in the idea of an imperial destiny for America.

The focus of their protest is the war in Vietnam, and the measure of their integrity is the fortitude with which they refuse to be deceived about it. By striking contrast with the young Germans, who accepted the Nazi evil because the values of their society had disintegrated and they had no moral frame of reference, these young Americans are demonstrating the vitality of American values. They are demonstrating that, while their country is capable of acting falsely to itself, it cannot do so without internal disruption, without calling forth the regenerative counterforce of protest from Americans who are willing to act in defense of the principles they were brought up to believe in.

The spirit of this regenerative generation has been richly demonstrated to me in letters from student leaders, from former Peace Corps Volunteers and from soldiers fighting in Vietnam. I quoted from one earlier. Another letter that is both striking and representative was written by an officer still in Vietnam. He wrote:

> For eleven years I was, before this war, a Regular commissioned officer—a professional military man in name and spirit; now—in name only. To fight well (as do the VC), a soldier must believe in his leadership. I, and many I have met, have lost faith in ours. Since I hold that duty to conscience is higher than duty to the Administration (not "country" as cry the nationalists), I declined a promotion and have resigned my commission. I am to be discharged on my return, at which time I hope to contribute in some way to the search for peace in Vietnam.

Some years ago Archibald MacLeish characterized the American people as follows:

> Races didn't bother the Americans. They were something a lot better than any race. They were a People. They were the first self-constituted, self-declared, self-created People in the history of the world. And their manners were their own business. And so were their politics. And so, but ten times so, were their souls.

Now the possession of their souls is being challenged by the false and dangerous dream of an imperial destiny. It may be that the challenge will succeed, that America will succumb to becoming a traditional empire and will reign for a time over what must surely be a moral if not a physical wasteland, and then, like the great empires of the past, will decline or fall. Or it may be that the effort to create so grotesque an anachronism will go up in flames of nuclear holocaust. But if I had to bet my money on what is going to happen, I would bet on this younger generation—this generation of young men and women who reject the inhumanity of war in a poor and distant land, who reject the poverty and sham in their own country, who are telling their elders what their elders ought to have known—that the price of empire is America's soul and that the price is too high.

MICHAEL HARRINGTON	**AMERICAN POWER IN THE TWENTIETH CENTURY***

. . . THE WORLD—and I borrow here from Peter Worsley's imaginative way of speaking—is scarcely begun. The globe has, of course, existed for eons, and humans project their various histories more than 4,000 years into the past. But those inter-relationships that transcend tribe, nation, and empire, uniting the people of the earth in a common destiny—whether they like it or not—are only a century or so old. The first day of this creation took place when economics, science, and warfare put the planet together. The second day is now, and there might not be a third.

Applying such high-flown biblical imagery to politics strikes

* Excerpted from the article that originally appeared in *Dissent*, September/October 1967 issue. Reprinted by permission of *Dissent* and Michael Harrington. This essay appears in different form in *Toward a Democratic Left*, by Michael Harrington, published by Macmillan Co.

most Americans as grandiose; they leave the world-to-come to the preachers while they pragmatically reconstruct the reality that is. Until World War II the Pacific and Atlantic oceans allowed Americans to disdain foreign entanglements on principle. And being of an anti-imperialist imperialism, a power which usually dominated other lands through the subtlety of money rather than the brutality of force, America burdened its people with an excessively good conscience. For all these reasons, it is particularly important to insist within the United States that the day-to-day decisions of foreign policy involve the choice of a new order of things for the twenty-first century. So far, America is creating the world very badly—though this need not be.

America is imperialist. To the average citizen, this statement is a patent slander. If the nation has erred, he would say, it has been generous to a fault, and only a Communist could deny the charity and anti-colonialism of its historic record. But the United States has been profoundly imperialist in the decades after World War II (and before, but that is another story). Yet, the United States need not be imperialist. This notion strikes most revolutionists, and not just the Communists, as unpardonably tender-minded. To them, fat, prosperous, capitalist America cannot possibly ally itself with the downtrodden and against the international *status quo*; it is fated to be reactionary, the very headquarters of the world's counterrevolution. This trust in the country's inherent evil is, however, almost as naive as the patriotic faith in its goodness. For given a turn to the democratic Left, this nation could play a crucial and positive role in finishing the creation of the world.

Anti-utopia seems more possible than a better world. And yet, there is hope. Although there are tremendous social, political, and economic forces urging the U.S. (and the West, and the rich Communist East) to do wrong, this country could take the lead in making a democratic revolution—in finishing the creation of the world in humane fashion. This fragile hope is my point of departure.

It has been said so often that the rich nations are getting richer and the poor nations poorer that the very enormity of the fact is lost in cliché.

In the middle of the "Development Decade," proclaimed by the U.N., the Food and Agricultural Organization (FAO) announced that the developing lands were more ill-nourished in 1965 than they had been before World War II, and the Organization for Economic Cooperation and Development (OECD) estimated in 1966 that the nourishment needs in these countries will grow twice as fast as the supply during the remaining years of the century. Also in 1966, the U.N. journal *World Economic Survey* reported that the purchasing power of the Third World had declined while its net outflow of interest and profit to the wealthy powers—the tribute the poor pay to the rich—had increased by 10 percent. This outrage has been repeatedly denounced by the Secretaries General of the U.N., various Popes, the World Council of Churches, and the U.S. Secretary of Defense.

As Mr. McNamara summarized this anguished prospect in a Montreal speech in 1966, in the year 2000 half of the developing nations will have achieved a per capita income of $170 a year, assuming a continuation of present trends; the American figure would be $4,500. This tragedy is utterly rational according to the economic "laws" of the world the West has carefully created in the last century. . . .

According to the rationalizations of the time, the various countries were simply doing what they could do "best," submitting to the impersonal laws of economics. People somehow failed to realize that these "laws" were artificial constructions of Western power. Asia, Africa, and Latin America were carefully and systematically denied the benefits of the new industrialism; they were designated the hewers of wood and the drawers of water.

After World War II a new indignity was in store for the Third World. Paradoxically, the new nations suffered because the advanced lands were now less interested in exploiting them. The new mid-century technology no longer required great quantities of traditional raw materials; synthetics now substituted for old imports, and subsidized, protected agricultural sectors took care of about 80 percent of the need for primary products. Ironically, the very success of the Western welfare state, and particularly of government policies to promote full employment, made profiteering in the backward areas less attractive. For now the wealthy powers had created such stable and enormous markets that they could make more money producing for one another's affluence than by investing in underdeveloped countries.

On the world market, the demand for manufactured goods zoomed while that for primary products declined. The First Committee of the U.N. Trade and Development Conference in 1964 reported the result: between 1950 and 1962 prices paid for the exports of the underdeveloped countries went down by 7 percent and prices paid for their imports from the industrialized countries went up by 27 percent. And whenever the Third World managed to attract some public or private capital from the great powers, they paid cash on the barrelhead. The result of these trends has been, in the words of Raul Prebisch, "a regressive redistribution of income . . . between the developed and developing countries."

Profit, Priorities & Economic "Laws"

As Gunnar Myrdal has pointed out, everyone knows that it is more profitable to invest in safe projects than in risky ones—in European and American affluence rather than in Third World poverty. Given the political and social outlook of private business, available funds will go to private rather than to public enterprises, and to undertakings in the ex-colonies only when they promote a quick profit rather than balanced growth of the whole society. The priorities so skillfully built into the very structure of the international economy are often a more efficient, and subtle, way of keeping the world's poor in their unhappy place than were the gunboats and troops of the earlier imperialism. To do incalculable harm to the masses of the Third World, the Western politician or businessman need not be evil, but only reasonable and realistic.

The manmade logic of the international division of labor is so compelling that it directs the developing country to embrace the misfortune which has been visited upon it. And this is precisely what the Committee for Economic Development (CED), one of the most sophisticated and liberal business organizations in the U.S., advocated in a 1966 policy statement. The new nations, the CED said, must invest "where the increment in value of product promises to be greatest." This sounds quite sensible, and it leads to the conclusion that priority should be given to those export industries "that can earn substantial foreign exchange if they can compete with effective industries in other countries. . . ." Obviously, fledgling societies cannot compete with the advanced giant industries of Europe and America; it would be a waste to allocate resources to a modern technological sector which would, after all, only duplicate Western factories and at a much higher and noncompetitive cost.

In obedience to the "laws" of the world market, the developing country must find some export specialty that suits the needs of the big powers, for that is the only rational thing to do in a system created by, and for, these big powers. And this logic can easily override consideration of the needs of the people or the requirements for building a balanced, modern economy. But even a country that manages to escape from these inexorabilities of the international economy and invests in an advanced enterprise is victimized by the way the world is organized. Celso Furtado, a brilliant Latin-American economist, has vividly analyzed what this means:

Technology developed "organically" in the West. When the first factories needed semiskilled and unskilled operatives, peasants were expropriated and a working class was created. As mechanical ingenuity advanced, the workers were progressively withdrawn from primary and secondary occupations (agriculture, mining, and mass production) and channeled into the service and white-collar sector. At times, these transitions were accomplished by brute force; at times, mass action won concessions and ameliorations. In either case, economy and society grew up side by side with the machines and the new organization of work.

Thus, Furtado points out, the corporation is designed to fit the needs of profit-making in an advanced economy, and when one tries to transplant its technology to impoverished, developing lands, furious contradictions result. The newest machines save manpower—a blessing in the U.S. and a curse in a country with rampant underemployment. Mass production requires a huge market nonexistent in an archaic agricultural society. So, Furtado concludes, the very structure of economic life in the new nations—forced upon them in the last century—makes it difficult for them to absorb the benefits of scientific and technical progress on those rare occasions when they might have the opportunity to do so.

Thus, the rich nations specialize in activities which make work easier, goods more abundant, leisure more widespread, and living standards higher. The poor nations are left with the grubby tasks of primary production and with a stagnant or declining market; they must sell cheap and buy dear from the booming factories. In such a world, the gap separating the impoverished from the affluent will grow no matter what the U.N. General Assembly decides.

The foreign policies of the big powers operate to reinforce the logic of injustice which is part of the world created by the nineteenth century West. Thus, statesmanship has served to increase the distance between the world's haves and have-nots. And yet, the average American would argue that the U.S. possesses no colonies; that it has spent tremendous sums in the military defense of freedom around the earth and given away billions of dollars to impoverished nations. In return for all this idealism and largesse, he would conclude, the country has received little but ingratitude; how can the recipients of all this charity call the United States imperialist?

This perplexed and angry view is not described here for purposes of ridicule. No doubt, generosity is a peculiarity of the American national character, and this excellent emotion has provided the political basis for foreign aid from the Marshall Plan to the present. Yet, the results of these efforts have often been at variance with the spirit that motivated them. And this is precisely why it is so important to understand how the U.S., even when it acts out of its best instincts (and is *not* motivated by hysterical anticommunism, oil diplomacy, and the like), has intensified the very social and economic miseries it deplores.

There is a deep American political tradition which holds that a man who gives away something for nothing is probably effeminate and certainly not fit for public office. Therefore, it is often necessary for the politician to disguise noble impulses in the rhetoric of the counting house. Harry Truman's Leninism in the following statement on Point Four was probably such verbiage, designed to win support from a dubious business community for the do-gooding concepts of Point Four:

> It seemed to me that if we could encourage stabilized governments in underdeveloped countries in Africa, South America, and Asia, we could encourage the use for the development of these areas of some of the capital which had accumulated in the United States. If the investment of capital from the United States could be protected and not confiscated, and if we could persuade the capitalists that they were not working in foreign countries to exploit them, it would be to the mutual benefit of everybody concerned.

From Truman's presidency to the present, it has been U.S. policy to proceed according to this scenario: to discover some reasonable ex-colonials committed to capitalist development of their lands; to instill some social purpose in American businessmen; then, to have the American government provide the financial framework within which these two groups can make a free-enterprise idyll of peaceful progress. But the contradictory elements in this vision guaranteed its self-defeat. The U.S. indeed honestly felt committed to a democratic alternative to Communist industrialization, to abolition of the world's inequities by means of freedom rather than dictatorship. But this fine aspiration was to be pursued according to the traditional rules of world capitalism—rules which were a major source of the misery that supposedly was to be abolished.

Concretely, American foreign aid and military programs, private investment, and tariff policy were permeated and guided by the principles of the old order they were intended to challenge. While trying to be noble, the U.S. thus, unwittingly but inevitably, made money and, more often than not, worsened the plight of those it had set out to aid and whose support it sought in the Cold War. Dean Acheson, in an important speech in Cleveland, Mississippi, on the direct orders of President Truman, noted that American exports were twice as great as the imports, and that the balance of trade was *too* favorable. Therefore, Acheson concluded, American funds must go to Europe. Now it is clear that the Marshall Plan was not simply designed in order to give businessmen a stable market in the Old World.

Political, military, and even cultural considerations led to the decision to defend the continent against what was seen as the imminent threat of Communist insurrection and/or invasion. But American generosity and anticommunism also had the effect of priming the European pump; it was a type of international Keynesianism creating an effective demand for U.S. products overseas and consequently leading to higher profits.

This self-interest rationale for foreign aid persists to this day. In lobbying for the Administration's 1967 program, the Agency for International Development (AID) told Congress, "In the less developed world today, the AID program is introducing American products and performance standards to some of the great potential markets of the future. . . . The goods and services go overseas, the dollar stays here to pay for them."

In part, this is the same shamming cynicism as Harry Truman's Leninist tough talk, used to conceal decent motives; but it also has another dead serious aspect. For when there is conflict between the needs of the American corporation and those of the impoverished whom we supposedly are helping, the domestic dollar comes first. In March 1966 a Buenos Aires meeting was convened to consider what gains had been made by the Alliance for Progress. There was an immediate uproar when the Latin Americans attacked the policy of "tied" aid—which requires the beneficiary to spend his gift or loan in the United States ("The goods and services go overseas, the dollar stays here to pay for them"). The delegates pointed out that they could often get cheaper goods in Europe or Japan. Lincoln Gordon of the State Department replied for the U.S. His nation, he said, was interested in worldwide trade liberalization but "considerations of national security and structural problems within our own economy have led to the imposition of import restrictions." Plainly, the Latin American developers were to subordinate their needs to those of the American commitments in Vietnam, the balance of payment problem, and the alleged threat of domestic inflation. . . .

We have one foot in genesis and the other in apocalypse, and annihilation is always an option. The future could even conform to a half-truth found in the fantasies of Mao Tse-tung: the advanced Communist societies can benefit from international

injustice every bit as much as the corporations. This might lead
to a deal between well-heeled commissars and executives to end
the old-fashioned conflict between East and West, so that the
industrialized North could get on with the serious work of
exploiting the backward South without regard to race, class, or
political creed. An extraordinary potential exists in the world of
the late 1960s. The struggle between East and West, communism
and capitalism, which has dominated international politics since
the end of World War II, could now come to an end—and be
replaced by this conflict between the North, both Communist
and capitalist, and the South, which is poor. . . .

This fact has not escaped the notice of the Third World. Here
is Julius Nyerere's observation:

> Socialist countries, no less than capitalist countries, are pre-
> pared to behave like the millionaire—to use millions to destroy
> the other "millionaire," and it need not be a capitalist million-
> aire—it is just as likely to be a socialist "millionaire." In
> other words, socialist wealth now tolerates poverty, which is
> an even more unforgiveable crime . . . don't forget that rich
> countries . . . may be found on either side of the division be-
> tween the capitalist and socialist countries.

. . .

The theory that the advanced powers are inevitably committed to reaction implies that there is no hope of democracy
in the new nations.

The various formulations of America's (or, more precisely,
capitalism's) role and fate, from Lenin to Mao, have obvious
deficiencies. Yet, it is true that America has displayed a vested
interest in at least some of the misery and poverty of the globe,
and the defense of such ill-got gains could be (and in the past
has been) the basis of a world view and foreign policy. There
is the tragic possibility that this view might lead America to
continue to promote the gap between rich and poor nations.
The exploitation of impoverished people, however, is not a
necessity for the American economy but only a cruel con-
venience. The nation could make new international departures
without undergoing a sweeping domestic transformation. There
would be many motives for such a change, among them enlightened self-interest (the present trends hurry toward more

instability and violence which could be disastrous for the wealthy as well as for the hungry)—and that current of democratic idealism which still flows within American society.

So the U.S. embraces an *almost* imperialism. America has the potential of positive change, of helping to create a new world; yet that course would require considerable radicalization of its political life. If, as Aldous Huxley once said pessimistically, a 99 percent pacifist is a 100 percent militarist, then one can optimistically hope that an *almost*-imperialist will become anti-imperialist. . . .

The Cold War

The Cold War began with a series of crises in Eastern Europe and the Middle East (Poland, Greece, Iran, Turkey). But the real struggle was over the future of Europe. The American commitments were, of course, made in the revered name of centuries of historical, political, and religious ties; but they rested upon a crass substratum of self-interest. I am not suggesting anything subtle or Machiavellian; quite simply, Communist domination of Western Europe or capitalist domination of Eastern Europe would have decisively tipped the international balance of power. Such disequilibrium would have been intolerable enough according to the old-fashioned rules designed for nations within a single social system—but it became utterly impossible when the contending powers represented alternate ways of organizing the globe.

In *Power and Impotence, the Failure of America's Foreign Policy,* Edmund Stillman and William Pfaff wrote, "In effect, the early Cold War was a contest for the control of a prostrate, but fundamentally very rich, continent that had functioned as the center of world politics for three hundred years." There is close correspondence between material self-interest and the political and military commitment on both sides. But once one leaves the initial, European period of the Cold War and turns to the Third World, the disparity between economics and foreign policy becomes manifest.

The historians of the twenty-first century might well conclude that the Korean War was the most curious "accident" of our postwar period. That country had been partitioned in desultory fashion on the basis of proposals made by General MacArthur and sanctioned by Stalin. The Russo-Korean treaty of 1949 did not even contain a mutual assistance provision, and in January 1950 Dean Acheson suggested that both Korea and Formosa were outside of the American defense perimeter. The Chinese Communists did not maintain an ambassador in North Korea and, Robert Guillian speculated in *Le Monde* in 1966, may well have regarded the invasion of the South as a Stalinist adventure. There were even public opinion polls in the United States which showed, in the late forties, that there was no strong popular support for action against Mao. And in August 1946, five months after Winston Churchill's famous "Iron Curtain" speech, President Truman was telling Chiang that, unless he liberalized a bit, "it must be expected that American opinion will not continue its generous attitude toward your nation."

But with the Korean War the ideological hostility which was rooted in the serious conflict of interests in Europe began to take on a life of its own in Asia. The French were then able to involve the U.S. in their Indochina debacle and thus laid the basis for the tragic Vietnamese conflict of the sixties. The issue of who "lost" China began to play a role in American politics, and Chiang's pseudo China on Taiwan became a centerpiece of the nation's Asian policy. Thus, in the 1950s Chiang, Syngman Rhee, Bao Dai and Diem received a vast outpouring of American aid—and Nehru relatively little. The former group had enlisted in the cause of the "Free World"; the latter was, of course, a neutralist.

John Foster Dulles officially gave the Cold War its ideological cast: the struggle between the United States and the Soviet Union was turned into a titantic conflict between good and evil in which any challenge, no matter how remote, had to be met. A far-flung network of alliances and treaty organizations was established; it was based on conservative and reactionary powers and excluded the modernizers, non-Communist revolutionaries, and neutralists. This approach accentuated the gap between the rich and the poor, for it meant that American donations were effectively militarized and usually assigned to the indigenous friends, rather than the foes, of backwardness.

In the period of the post-European Cold War the U.S. was

ruled by domestic conservatism. A Republican, business-oriented Administration held office for two terms, the Dixiecrat-Republican coalition prevailed in Congress, and McCarthyism made it difficult to even have a debate. These were the internal reasons for the nation's reactionary foreign policy. American leadership, unable to see the need for reform at home, was of course bewildered by a world in revolutionary transition. Since the Administration—and the people—genuinely believed in their own benevolence, the only possible explanation for nationalist and anti-American movements abroad seemed to them subversion, spying, infiltration. And these demons are fought with guns and counterespionage, not with social programs. If democratic reformers came to power, the argument went, they would only create instability, a breakdown of order, and conditions which would lead to a Communist takeover. Therefore, the only true friends of the "Free World" were on the Right. In the fifties, this logic brought American support to Batista, Jiminez, Trujillo, and their like.

But this emphasis on the ideological aspect of the Dulles policy should not lead to the conclusion that justice would have been served if the nation simply had stuck to its material self-interest. In 1945, as De Gaulle bitterly recounts the fantastic incident in his memoirs, Roosevelt was in favor of independence for Indochina on the basis of the "ideology" of democracy. If the United States had persisted in its policy of cooperating with the nationalist revolutionary movement in that country, there would have been a chance of avoiding the more than two decades of bloodletting which followed the return of French colonialism.

The main point remains: the history of the Cold War shows that American foreign policy need not be the result of economic interest, and much of it has not been. Yet, it is sad to remember that most of our disinterested idealists have been reactionary, as in the case of Dulles. But even this unfortunate example proves that our role in the world does not have to be determined by cost accountants.

Another important theory seeks to demonstrate that America's reactionary stance in foreign affairs, particularly in the Third World, is an inevitable consequence of the very structure of the society. In this view, the society does not need the Cold War in order to protect its overseas profits, but rather to justify a domestic war economy which is the main bulwark against depression. . . . In his farewell message as President, Dwight D. Eisenhower said of the "immense military establishment," which was "new in the American experience," that its "total influence —economic, political, even spiritual—is felt in every city, every state house, every office of the federal government."

If America were to embark upon a genuinely democratic foreign policy, and sought to abolish the gap between rich and poor nations, this vested interest in death would be threatened. For an emphasis on international construction, massive investments of men and money in the Third World, and disarmament would reverse the priorities which have prevailed in the postwar period. Could the American economy tolerate such steps toward peace?

In theory, the answer is yes. In practice, everything depends on politics. Building an arsenal of annihilation is a congenial activity for American society. The mass unemployment of the Depression, it must be remembered, was not ended by the social and economic policies of the New Deal. Indeed, by the end of the thirties, Keynes himself wondered if any peacetime (and capitalist) government would ever intervene on the scale required by his computations. The abolition of joblessness took place during the reign of Dr. Win-the-War, not during that of Dr. New Deal.

There are solid, conservative reasons for the high esteem conferred upon spending for destruction. Government investment in socially useful projects tends to raise disturbing, ideological questions. There is always the danger that some reformer will suggest that monies be appropriated for an undertaking like TVA, and that actually redefines the lines between the public and private sectors.

A vast increase in war spending is usually accompanied by an end to social innovation. The emotion of patriotism unites the entire nation, and class differences are submerged in the common effort. In the case of a shooting conflict, the military obligingly dispenses with competitive principles and adopts uneconomic methods like cost-plus contracts. (When it is necessary in a conservative cause, or in fighting a war, America is always ready to turn its back on the myths of the market economy, but such idealism is almost never applied to truly idealistic projects.) In a cold war, particularly one run by a top executive from the Ford Motor Company, the old rules of efficiency are in force; but then military hardware has the marvelous quality of becoming obsolete almost on the day it becomes operational. The production possibilities are therefore almost infinite.

For these and many other reasons Congress will enthusiastically vote $70 billion for Defense while it haggles over a less than $2 billion appropriation for fighting poverty. It is most dangerous to think that, as peace begins to break out, it would be simple enough to transfer funds from the work of destruction to that of construction. The socialization of death is, thus far, much more generally popular than the socialization of life. And a shift of money from Defense to, say, Health, Education, and Welfare would require a basic turn toward the democratic Left within the society.

The crucial question is whether or not it is possible, without a revolution of the system itself, to substitute social for armaments spending. . . .

America, the *almost*-imperialist, could act to change the imperialist order of things. American (and Western) prosperity does not depend on the evil which is done in the international economy; this country—and the rest of the West—could actually benefit by acting humanely in the world. If the imperialist heritage of economic interest, ideology, and feeling of superiority were rooted in economic necessity, there would be no hope of overcoming it. Since it is not, there is hope—but so far, in the postwar period, this is a most modest and theoretical consolation. The statistical possibilities for doing global good require radicalized politics if they are ever to be realized. An America that cannot even provide decent housing for its own "well-off" poor is hardly going to lead in the bold measures needed to end the threat of starvation forever. . . .

Toward a New World Economy

If, however, the direction of this spiral were reversed, hopeful factors would reinforce one another. If some wealth were actually transferred from the rich nations to the poor, at least some economic compulsion toward coercion and violence would be removed. Consumption could, for instance, be gradually increased without endangering the whole modernization program. And the marvelous fact of ex-colonial people rising out of their poverty should make it politically easier in the U.S. to argue for redoubled efforts. And so, the crucial issue is political, not economic, for trends do not create new societies; they only make them possible.

In undertaking to help complete the creation of a more humane world, one must not expect too much. It will take radical new beginnings to justify modest hopes. This cruel paradox, like everything else about the contemporary international disorder, is a creation of man in history. The developing nations were deprived of capital and skills, and both of these deficiencies can be made up in part by capital and technical assistance from the advanced economies. But a heritage of backwardness is not easily overcome. Native oligarchies, tribalism, anti-modern cultures, and other reactionary trends were vigorously encouraged by the West during its imperial rule. (Africa's Balkanization to suit European needs is an obvious case in point.)

To paraphrase Keynes, the pursuit of a just world economy will guarantee not civilization itself but its possibility. And to follow this unprecedented course of action is our only chance to close the gap between the world's rich and poor. . . .

The United States must abandon its ideological hostility to the public sector in the developing nations. In saying this, I do not intend to turn the free-enterprise myth topsy-turvy or argue that nationalization is some magic, painless way to modernization. For after recent events in countries like China and Cuba, this view can no longer be seriously maintained. There is no easy road out of underdevelopment, and one must talk pragmatically about some sort of international mixed economy. The Third World cannot simply put its faith in Adam Smith or any of his heirs; for the market mechanism is a cause of, rather than a solution to, its poverty.

Thus, the democratic revolution must build on economic and social foundations unknown, and even antithetical, to those of the great European capitalist transformations of the eighteenth and nineteenth centuries. . . .

As John F. Kennedy realized when he initiated the Alliance for Progress, there is structural resistance to positive change in the developing lands; the Latin American oligarchs are the classic case in point. In its original, reformist version, the alliance sought to meet this problem by making grants contingent on policy changes in the recipient nations, such as the creation of an equitable tax system. Thus, there was hope that a revolution would proceed from the top down. "The leaders of Latin America," President Kennedy said at Bogota, "the industrialists and the landowners are, I am sure, also ready to admit past mistakes and accept new responsibilities." In retrospect, the President's confidence was either naive or ceremonial. The Latin American *status quo* is not even prepared to take a position of enlightened self-interest.

Although America must provide massive assistance precisely in order to minimize the potential for bloody conflict within the Third World, there must be an expectation of turmoil and even violence—and the U.S. must find itself sympathetic to armed revolutionists of the Left rather than, as so often in the past, to the military dictators of the Right. But this most emphatically does not mean that this country should adopt some democratic variant of the Maoist strategy and seek to foment wars of "national liberation" all over the globe. The pretension to omnipotence which led to the tragic commitment in Vietnam is as dangerous in the service of a good policy as of a bad one. And that is why it is so important to specify exactly what is proposed in this activist notion of creating a new world—and what is not proposed.

Paradoxically, one of the most vigorous actions the U.S. could take in support of the democratic revolution simply involves ceasing to do the wrong thing. For during the postwar period, America usually gave political, economic, and military support to the confirmed opponents of social change. The list of recipients is dreary and familiar: Chiang, Rhee, Bao Dai, Diem, Ky, Franco, Batista, Jiminez, Trujillo, and so on. The tragic conflicts of the sixties, as Theodore Draper has pointed out, pitted the United States against popular upheavals—in Vietnam, Cuba, and the Dominican Republic—and were a consequence of previous American policy, such as the support of French imperialism and of Cuban and Dominican dictatorship.

But it is not enough to refrain from doing evil; it is possible to establish political sympathy for revolutionary movements without sending agents to direct them. For all of the failings of the Alliance for Progress, for instance, there is no question that in the period of its inception John F. Kennedy managed to identify his Administration's policy with the aspiration for change in Latin America. And the President's speech in support of Algeria's right to independence was one of the few events of the fifties that demonstrated not all Americans were bent on subordinating democratic and anti-colonial principles to the political needs of the NATO alliance.

Indeed, the U.S. should follow the advice of the Latin Americans who met in Bogota in August 1966 (Frei of Chile, Lleras Restrepo of Colombia, Leoni of Venezuela) and restore the "Betancourt doctrine" under which this nation refuses to recognize rightist *coups d'état*. In this way, and by refusing to create and finance the armies of Latin America, the U.S. could make an enormous contribution to the cause of democratic revolution without pretending to be omnipotent. Beyond these crucial political and military acts, a public commitment by the United States to make a democratic revolution economically possible will be in itself an incitement to change. Over a century ago, Marx realized that one of the factors which made the bourgeois revolution more dynamic than any previous upheaval was the development of the means of communication; now, of course, this point is a thousand times more relevant. The American word, if it is backed up with the right deeds, could thus become a mighty force. There is the danger that America might adopt a policy of "sentimental imperialism" (the phrase is that of Arthur Schlesinger, Jr.). Instead of assuming that our military technology allows us to intervene everywhere in the world, we would then act as if our social ingenuity and political institutions were universal models. There was more than a hint of this attitude when Lyndon Johnson proposed in 1966 to build a Great Society in Asia (since he had not yet built one in the U.S., the announcement was, at a minimum, premature). Yet, by ceasing to support the rightist opponents of change, by open political sympathy extended to revolutionists (and sometimes even violent ones), and, above all, by making political democracy in the Third World an economic possibility, the United States could take a step toward the creation of a new world. . . .

O. EDMUND CLUBB | **THE SECOND WORLD REVOLUTION***

THE ESCALATION of the war in Southeast Asia highlights the persisting failure of the American policy-makers in the postwar period to comprehend the changing nature of the times in which we live. Especially marked is the failure to recognize the significance of contemporary social developments in the "third world," that zone of developing nations which lies between the Western industrialized nations and the Communist bloc. The chronic obsession of the United States over the past two decades with its self-appointed task of containing "the menace of world communism" by military measures, is now bearing its bitter fruit: we have lost contact with human realities. We have been led by our half-blinded fascination with a political chimera first to neglect and then to ignore the concerns uppermost in the consciousness of Asians, Africans, and Latin Americans.

The First World Revolution, which had its beginnings in the eighteenth century and aimed at national political independence, has about run its course. Colonialism and imperialism of the old type are dying, and will soon have disappeared from the earth. But "neo-colonialism" is more than a phrase invented by Communists for the purpose of tarring honest business entrepreneurs of the West. For the poorer emerging nations of the world, which see the gap between themselves and the industrialized countries increasing instead of narrowing, it is taking

* From *The Progressive*, June 1965. Copyright © 1965 by *The Progressive*, Madison, Wisconsin.

on a real meaning. Those nations have discovered that prosperity does not necessarily follow in the footsteps of political independence.

The hard fact is that, with the burgeoning world population, not even the basic problem of food supply has been solved by most of the developing nations. The problem is seen in all its stark reality in Asia. With a population of less than one billion in 1920, that continent will probably contain four billion persons at the end of this century. Many Asian countries have less food per capita today than they had before they achieved political independence. The U.N. Food and Agriculture Organization (FAO), reporting on food production in the year ending July 15, 1964, stated that for the fifth consecutive year the world's agricultural production had increased less, in percentage, than had population.

It is against this background of poverty and dearth that the world's problems must now be viewed. How shall the oppressive poverty of the emerging nations be overcome? They need capital in amounts which they cannot accumulate by themselves—some $10 billion to $14 billion annually in order to achieve an economic growth rate of three percent. They need technological and administrative skills. They are also sadly in need of better world trade terms, which now favor the industrialized nations over those producing primary materials. This is the situation they face, along with a great disparity in their natural resources —compared to North America particularly—in terms of arable land, forests, iron ore, coal, and petroleum reserves.

In spite of these critical circumstances, the United States is following a policy, especially in Asia, that is anachronistic and divorced from fundamentals. For the past twenty years, since the end of the war with Japan, our Asia policy has revolved around China. That policy, justified to Americans by the continued existence of Communist rule in China, is chiefly of military design. We have 50,000 troops in South Korea still, twelve years after the Korean truce.[1] There are also American troops in Japan, two decades after the end of the war in which Japan was defeated, and we occupy Okinawa as a victorious power.

[1] Fifteen years after the truce the number is still 50,000.—Eds.

The United States has long-term bases, and armed forces, in our former colony, the Philippines. We still maintain the transparent fiction that the Kuomintang right-wing faction on Formosa constitutes the rightful government of all China, and we support that refugee establishment with American money and arms and the U.S. Seventh Fleet. We contribute military aid to both Pakistan and India (thereby exacerbating the strained relations between the two); we are deeply, if imprecisely, involved in both Thailand and Laos. Our commitment in Vietnam is notoriously military.

In the final struggle, our most frightful weapons will not help. The United Nations Conference on Trade and Development (UNCTAD), held in Geneva from March to June 1964, constituted a major implicit challenge to the presumed verities of an American foreign policy centered on the concept of military containment. In that conference, attended by representatives from 120 countries, the emerging nations showed themselves united in the demand for a more equitable world economic order. In the general principles recommended by the conference, it was held that there should be "no discrimination on the basis of differences in socio-economic systems;" that all countries should cooperate in creating conditions conducive to the achievement of a rapid increase in the exports of developing countries; and that new preferential import concessions should be made by developed countries to developing countries to assure the latter "a fair and reasonable share" of the developed countries' markets.

The conference also took note of "the wide concern expressed regarding the inadequacy of the growth target of 5 percent per annum for the United Nations Development Decade," and recommended that the developing countries should mobilize their domestic resources for development—while developed countries, for their part, should assist in that economic development. It was proposed that each economically advanced country should endeavor to supply to the developing countries financial resources "of a minimum net amount approaching as nearly as possible to 1 percent of its national income . . ." This would amount to five billion dollars or more in the case of the United States.

What is proposed here, in simplified terms, is a renunciation, by the rich industrialized nations, of some of their most profitable trade advantages in favor of something on the order of a partial sharing of international wealth and markets. With the debt burden of developing countries rapidly growing beyond their capacity to pay, nations with high standards of living are being called upon to open their markets not only to primary products but to semi-processed and manufactured goods from developing nations possessing lower standards of living—which also means lower wage scales.

The Soviet Union, in accord with the UNCTAD recommendations, has removed all customs duties on imports from the developing countries of Asia, Africa, and Latin America. It is hardly to be expected that the United States will quickly follow suit. For all of the United Nations Relief and Rehabilitation Agency, the Marshall Plan, and our annual foreign-aid programs, no Administration in Washington has even begun thinking about abolishing such tariffs. It must be granted, on the American political record, that there is little likelihood of the President's proposing to Congress that we should open the protected U.S. market to the competition of Indian cotton goods, Peruvian ceramics, or Venezuelan petroleum—not to mention Chinese hog bristles or Cuban sugar. The existing structure of American economic enterprise, including profits and wages, does not permit such international altruism in other than a minor way.

Other countries have a more flexible attitude than the United States respecting economic relations with the "third world" of developing nations. Japan is one; the Soviet Union is another. Even in Stalin's time, the Soviets had begun to address themselves to the changing world economic situation. In 1938, the last year before World War II, the Soviet Union had a two-way foreign trade of only slightly more than $500 million. In 1959, its foreign trade topped the $10 billion mark. Most of that trade is still with developed countries. But the Soviet U.N. representative, in making the notification of tariff elimination to U.N. Secretary General U Thant, forecast a Soviet trade of $11 billion with the developing nations by 1980. He may have been excessively optimistic. But the Soviet direction is clear.

The other Communist giant, China, is not unaware of the importance of the economic factor. Because of its economic weakness (for it is itself a "developing nation"), it is not in a good position to compete directly with either the United States or the Soviet Union in the extension of credits, loans, and grants, and in the provision of technical aid and advanced industrial equipment to other countries. But it proposes to substitute political for economic factors in the competition for influence among the developing nations, to help establish its leadership in the third world.

We have authoritative expositions by Chinese Communist leaders in this connection. In August 1963, with particular reference to racial troubles in the United States, Mao Tse-tung called for, in effect, the formation of a world united front, to include even "enlightened elements of the bourgeoisie," against "the racial discrimination practiced by U.S. imperialism . . ." In January 1964, Peking proclaimed the doctrine of the "intermediate zone," again proposing a world united front against the United States—this time embracing political and economic elements of broader scope. And at the end of the year, Premier Chou En-lai urged that Communist countries join with other nations, and in particular with those of Asia, Africa, and Latin America, in opposition to the United States.

Next, in February of this year [1965], speaking before the Afro-Asian Economic Seminar at Algiers, the chief of the Chinese delegation, Nan Han-chen, made a report in which he traced the root cause of the present poverty and economic backwardness of the Afro-Asian countries to "the continuous aggression, control, rapacious plunder, and exploitation by imperialism, colonialism, and neo-colonialism." He noted the profits of American and British interests in oil production, the control by American and Belgian firms of valuable mines in the Congo and Southern Rhodesia, and the heavy American consumption of rare world metals. He did not fail to point up the disadvantageous terms of trade experienced by the developing nations, the high rates of interest imposed upon borrowers by the rich lending countries, and the benefits deriving to the developed nations through their control of shipping and marine insurance.

Nan offered remedies that might well attract frustrated nations. Holding up Chinese Communist policies as a pattern, he proposed in effect that developing countries should practice self-reliance, all the while practicing "friendly cooperation" with other countries, such as China. In his exposition, he permitted the easy inference that he favored denial by the underdeveloped nations of their resources to the "neo-colonialist" industrial nations—and the ultimate expropriation by the underdeveloped countries of foreign capital investments located on their soil. Nan Han-chen thus clearly exposed Peking's current strategy: the Chinese Communists would harness the frustrations and deepening angers of the hungry peoples of the world to the end that, under China's leadership, the have-nots of the world should overcome the haves, and forcibly effect an "equitable" redistribution of the world's wealth.

It is a bold strategy, and one obviously designed for implementation only over decades. China suffers many handicaps and in the end may lose out to the Soviet Union or Japan or some combination of "non-aligned" states in the contest for influence in the contested zone of the developing nations; but is there any greater assurance that the rich and powerful United States can gain the day? What, in the end, will be the fruits of an American world strategy which depends to such a great extent upon military power?

The annual world expenditure on arms is approximately $120 billion. Of this amount, the United States alone spends nearly half. As the poor, overpopulated nations of the world meet frustration in their desire for economic advancement, are they going to endure indefinitely, without protest, the sight of the United States, so much richer than they, wasting some $50 billion annually on armaments, while they are unable to scrape together one-third that sum for needed capital investment? And are they going to starve willingly, while the United States struggles with the problem of storing its food "surpluses," and seeks through many devices to keep good agricultural land out of cultivation to prevent ever greater "surpluses"?

A Second World Revolution is in the immediate offing. It will see the poor nations of the world ranged against the rich, in a demand for substantial aid for the achievement of economic progress. The poor will not necessarily endeavor to wrest wealth from the rich by violent means. But the conscience of man marches with the growing awareness of man, and there is now a forum undreamed of in the First World Revolution in which the demands of humanity can make themselves felt—the United Nations. In that forum, "communism" will increasingly be less an issue than food, ideological crusades less important than industrialization, American-designed "total victories" of less concern than compromise settlements. American policies formulated within the framework of a simplistic anticommunism are thus predestined to be rejected by the nations of the world.

Like a Titan, the United States still relies upon its physical prowess. It has built up a quasi empire of military power, founded upon a network of treaties, girdling the earth. That empire of influence compares in some outward aspects to some of the great empires of the past. But the resemblance is only superficial: The United States does not own the military strong points it occupies from Korea in a great crescent swinging south and then east to Western Europe. It wields neither political sovereignty nor suzerainty along that crescent, but leases or borrows its bases. We enjoy only a probationary status in the face of the quickened sense of nationalism that affects not only Europeans and Americans, but Japanese, Indonesians, Filipinos, Pakistani, and Latin Americans. The Canadians some time ago felt the necessity to take action to curb expanding American control over their economy. Western Europe now is developing a wariness and growing hostility to the inroads of American business firms and has begun to apply restrictions upon American investment. The movement spreads.

The tide of anti-Americanism keeps pace with rising opposition to American military policies. The hungry peoples of the world are less concerned with the Chinese bomb—so long as it is not directed at any particular country—than they are with the effects of the population explosion. With the persistence of that gnawing hunger, Communist activities increase in the Philippines, Thailand, Indonesia, the Malaysian Federation, and in India.

The use by the United States of harsh military means in an effort to stem the tide of Asian revolution evokes strong reactions from Asian peoples. They do not forget that the first nuclear bombs were American and that they were used against an Asian people. They will be increasingly critical of American efforts to solve the economic and political problems of South Vietnam by the use of bombs and napalm against North Vietnam, and noxious gas against the Vietcong in South Vietnam. It is safe to predict that at the second Afro-Asian Conference [May 1965], there will be new manifestations of resentment against the United States. The American war in Southeast Asia will provide the immediate occasion for the expression of much anti-American feeling; but the economic factor contributing to social unrest and political upheavals will be an underlying cause.

The world is in revolutionary flux and demands the greatest flexibility in contemporary statesmanship, but the United States seems content to continue to hold untenable world positions and to fight for obsolete causes. Intellectually, it is still fighting in the First World Revolution. Yet the Second Revolution has already begun. In the coming clash of cultures mixed with racial conflict there will increasingly be denial of the values that American policy-makers swear by. What strength will our "anticommunism" then be able to muster?

What should be our policy for Asia?

An effective policy would incorporate new political and economic elements to lend it strength. Here, there would be no disgrace, no "loss of face," if the United States were to borrow a leaf or two from the Soviet and Chinese—and even the Japanese and Indian—books. We might then come to a realization that the chief desire of the Asians, now that they have possessed themselves of political independence, is not to fight as foot soldiers in an American crusade against "world communism," but to attain peace and progress. And we might finally admit (especially to ourselves) that there exists a diversity in Asian as well as in European communism which is susceptible of exploitation for the profit of world order even if that exploitation is intellectually more demanding than military exercises.

The United States has made a gesture in its offer, outlined by the President in his speech at Johns Hopkins University [April 7, 1965], to provide $1 billion for "cooperation in increased development" of the Mekong River basin. Survey work for the exploitation of the Mekong potential began some years ago under U.N. auspices, and it is obvious that $1 billion for use in that general connection would be helpful and welcome. Let it be said at once, however, that such a commendable American contribution to economic progress is not by itself a substitute for solution of basic political and social problems unrelated to factors of irrigation, river transport, and fisheries. Some political solutions are required, too. American grants-in-aid are, it has been demonstrated, no guarantee of good government—or of a more equitable social system. The Mekong grant could be a significant beginning; it is not the end.

In any event, it must be realized that $1 billion, to be expended over an unspecified period of time, is notably less than the amount now being spent by the United States for support of South Vietnam's and our own military operations in the Vietnamese war.

The U.S. government, despite periodic fits and starts dating back to 1956, has not yet undertaken a fundamental reassessment of its foreign aid program. We should abandon the principle by which we refuse to accept payment in kind for the aid we provide overseas because such payment in commodities competes with our domestic producers of petroleum, synthetic rubber, and a host of light consumer goods. We should depend more on mutual trade, supplementing aid, in an economic program related to the desperate needs of the underdeveloped countries. This would require a reduction of American tariffs. It would call for certain American industries to abandon the luxury of administered prices, with government protection, in favor of competition from the products of the "cheap" labor of the developing countries.

Finally, aid grants would in due course be channeled through an international aid agency, for fairness and efficiency in distribution. Then, at long last, if substantial funds were diverted from American military expenditures to the meeting of world economic needs, there could be fruitful implementation of the promise in President Johnson's statement on March 25 of American co-operation with "wider and bolder" programs of economic development which Asian leaders could be expected to evolve in the future, for "progress and peace."

The challenge is clear and present. Is the world to arrive at the conviction that its hungry peoples, who will increasingly be asking the United States for bread, are to get from us little more than a military answer? If so, our policy with respect to the third world is headed for certain disaster. If not, we should, without further delay, begin a fundamental restructuring of our present harsh policy. For our world position deteriorates dangerously with each day that passes.

<table>
<tr><td>

**EMILE
BENOIT**

</td><td>

THE ECONOMICS AND POLITICS OF DEFENSE CUTBACKS*

</td></tr>
</table>

A VIEW is gaining ground in Washington that we need cuts in the defense budget to make possible more spending for social welfare. Two groups in particular seem eager to accept this notion: those who think a smaller defense budget would contribute to an international détente, and those who are eager to find means for larger welfare programs. A tie-in between defense cuts and a "war against poverty" was suggested in President Johnson's budget, and reflected also in a widely-quoted speech of Senator Fulbright on the adverse effects of the Cold War on American social welfare.[1] Nevertheless, there are serious pitfalls in tying the two notions together in this way.

In the first place, it is not true that large defense expenditures have prevented us from spending more on social programs. For a number of years we have been running our economy at perhaps $30 to $50 billion a year short of its potential owing to excess unemployment and under-utilized capacity. With so much slack in the economy we could have had greatly increased

* From *War/Peace Report,* June 1964. Excerpted by the Editors.
[1] "Individual Freedom and Collective Security: A Balancing of Objectives." University of North Carolina Symposium on Arms and the Man, April 5, 1964.

social expenditures without reducing defense outlays and without creating demand inflation.

Psychologically and politically as well as economically, it does not appear that the defense program is the main obstacle to increased social welfare spending. While the burden of defense constitutes a convenient rationalization for restricting social welfare, the real motive seems to be a positive congressional dislike of such expenditures. The hostility to non-defense expenditures has given rise to the myth of "runaway government spending." But the facts show a sharply declining real federal expenditure on non-defense goods and services. Expressed in 1963 prices, and on a per capita basis, such expenditures were $83 back in 1939, $75 in 1953, and only $56 in 1963. And non-defense purchases at *all* government levels—including state and local—have declined from 17 percent of gross national product (GNP) to 12 percent of GNP over the same period. Moreover, since 1953, even with defense spending included, the share of GNP absorbed by purchases of federal government alone has declined from 17.5 percent to 11.3 percent.

The defense budget as a whole must, of course, compete with other parts of the budget, and with other uses of national income, but there is no practical point in trying to compare the amount of welfare provided by an additional billion dollars in the defense program with what would be achieved if the same amount were spent on public housing or for other social purposes. Defense expenditures are importantly affected by what economists call "indivisibilities." Slightly less than sufficient defense expenditures to deter war would involve incalculable (and wholly disproportionate) losses of welfare. In such a situation the only sensible criterion for judging the level of defense expenditures is its necessity for achieving the defense program's own goal of national security. Of course, judgments on this point will differ, but we should not try to make such judgments on the basis of what else we could buy for the money. Within rather broad limits we can "afford" to have as big (or as small) a defense program as security requires. We are now spending about 9 percent of GNP on defense compared with 42 percent at the peak of World War II, and 13.5 percent in 1953. We could readily spend more. Whether we *should* is another matter.

There are also good political reasons for not tying defense and welfare expenditures together too closely. Cutting defense to free funds for welfare programs could have politically dangerous consequences. It could invite a right-wing reaction which would attack the liberal forces of the country for gambling with national security to achieve partisan social welfare benefits. Such a reaction could be particularly dangerous in the event of a new international crisis. For this reason alone, we should insist that any defense cuts should be solidly based on explicitly strategic considerations.

Such considerations do now exist. They derive from the forthcoming development within both major nuclear powers of invulnerable deterrents and the approach of a destructive capability beyond which there is no genuine military justification for more weapons.

As is well known, the atomic bomb at Hiroshima was thousands of times more destructive than earlier weapons. The hydrogen bomb further raised the destructiveness of weapons by a factor of about a thousand. We have now incorporated these explosives into missiles which raise the speed of delivery by a factor of 20-40 times, and have built automatic guidance systems into them which home them in on their targets by a fantastically complex and rapid set of computations, thereby raising their effectiveness by another large factor. We have also developed highly efficient decoys and jamming devices that make the chance of intercepting any substantial percentage of such missiles exceedingly remote. As a final step we have learned how to harden, disperse, conceal, or keep in motion the missile launchers, so that it becomes impossible to prevent a large number of them from functioning even if a first-strike attack were made by the other side. . . .

It is possible to conceive of different and more involved weapons and delivery systems, but it is hard to imagine any that would kill people more quickly, reliably and cheaply—and even if such weapons were invented they could not do anything *more* than the weapons already available, i.e., destroy the enemy population and economy. The only technologically unsettling possibility is that of a breakthrough in defense which would destroy the invulnerability of the deterrent. No effective device along these lines is on the horizon. An anti-missile-missile able to distinguish between missiles and decoys, to overcome the effects of jamming, and to explode the missiles far enough away from their objectives to do much good still looks technically impossible, especially when one considers how low a margin of failure one could tolerate. Laser technology cannot yet foresee the possibility of handling the volume of energy required for such a purpose. The problems of keeping submarines under continuous surveillance and destroying them before they could fire also appear quite hopeless, although research on underwater detection and surveillance devices continues.

Moreover, the partial test ban treaty, which seems largely intended to head off an anti-missile-missile race, and the U.N. agreement not to develop orbiting nuclear weapons, appear to indicate a genuine desire by the U.S. and the Soviet Union to discourage wasteful and disruptive efforts to develop further major weapons systems. We should not uncritically project a continuing revolution in weapons technology every few years, as Herman Kahn appears to have done.

To be sure, U.S. official policy has not yet wholly abandoned the arms race either in its qualitative or quantitative sense. There is still talk in the Pentagon about the need for continuing U.S. development of an effective anti-missile system, space weapons and other new weapons systems. Also, on the quantitative side, even Secretary McNamara has talked of U.S. policy as being a "damage-limiting policy," requiring a large number of missiles to be used against enemy missile sites and other bases, thereby limiting the damage which they could inflict. Thus, the U.S. has not entirely abandoned a "counterforce" military strategy even though it is admitted that such a strategy becomes less and less attractive as the Soviets move toward an effectively invulnerable deterrent, and as even the so-called "limited" damage they could inflict on the U.S. becomes catastrophically large.

Despite these holdovers of older modes of strategic thinking (reflecting intense controversy within the government), the new trend seems definitely toward what might appropriately be called an ending of the arms race. An ending of the arms race, it must be recognized, does not involve any reduction in actual military capabilities, but simply a freezing of the present tremendous capabilities. Ending the arms race at that point would not lessen the danger to life represented by the present weapons stocks. However, by reducing suspicion and tension it might somewhat reduce the likelihood of war by accident or miscalculation, and it would provide a more hopeful atmosphere for consideration of further steps toward world security. Moreover, a halt in the arms race would have economic effects of very considerable importance—effects which would introduce some of the same economic adjustment problems that would arise with general disarmament.

There are specific signs that the big-power arms race may be ending. The U.S. [in 1964] announced cutbacks of 40 percent in the production of enriched uranium and 20 percent in plutonium production during the coming four years. The Soviet Union . . . announced, in parallel, a promise to discontinue construction of two big new reactors for producing plutonium, to make a substantial reduction in the output of enriched uranium for nuclear weapons, and to increase the allocation of fissionable materials for peaceful uses. . . .

Beyond these moves, the U.S. is trying at Geneva to negotiate a freeze on the production of nuclear weapons and delivery vehicles. If such a freeze were established, it might bring with it savings of upwards of $5 billion a year.

Further large savings would become possible if, as the U.S. government is proposing, the freeze on retaliatory weapons is accompanied or followed by a large-scale destruction of bombers. Approximately $2 billion is assigned for the operation of the strategic retaliatory forces, and the larger part of this is for the bomber command. Also, the mutual destruction by agreement of bomber forces, or their gradual attrition through obsolescence and wear and tear, would in turn make possible further large savings in the continental air and missile defense forces now costing close to $2 billion a year, the larger part of which is devoted to anti-bomber defenses.

In the event of a complete weapons freeze (both nuclear and conventional), it seems clear that savings of upwards of $16 billion per year should be readily obtainable. We are now spending about $16.5 billion per year in procuring military equipment, as well as an additional $2.8 billion for the Atomic

Energy Commission, and presumably most of these amounts would be eliminated. It would also seem almost inevitable, once a definite standstill agreement had been reached, that there would be substantial cuts in the nearly $7 billion going into research and development (R&D). These cuts would come mainly in the final engineering and testing segments of the R&D program, which now account for a major share of the total. However, a considerable sum would probably remain available for basic and applied research required to keep abreast of current developments and to explore new frontiers of technology.

Just how far it would be possible to go in the direction of a weapons freeze without a definite arms control agreement is uncertain. Ex-Under Secretary of Defense Roswell L. Gilpatric has recently predicted that a reduction of about $13 billion in national defense expenditures would become possible by 1970 if the present détente continues, even without a formal arms agreement.[2] A full weapons freeze, which would go beyond the reduction projected by Mr. Gilpatric, seems unlikely in the absence of explicit, effectively policed arms control arrangements.

For domestic political reasons, if for no other, the U.S. would like to get some *quid pro quo* even for a freeze limited to strategic retaliatory weapons. From a strictly military viewpoint, however, it may be safe not to require one, and it might even be undesirable to pressure the Soviets for a cutoff in expenditures on their retaliatory system until they have completed their invulnerable deterrent. Until they do so, they will

[2] Roswell L. Gilpatric, "Our Defense Needs: The Long View," *Foreign Affairs*, April, 1964. In opposition, an anonymous Pentagon spokesman has recently denied any plans for any cuts in expenditure in the next five years going beyond 5 percent, and expressed himself as mystified by the current talk of the possibility of larger cuts. (*New York Times*, April 20, 1964.) The contradiction between this statement and that of Mr. Gilpatric is only apparent. Mr. Gilpatric is talking of what may be possible in the event of a continuing détente, whereas the anonymous spokesman is referring only to what has been definitely decided upon. The apparent inconsistency of the two statements reveals no more than that there is a major struggle going on within the U. S. government (as there probably is also within the Soviet government) as to whether the traditional arms race approach should be continued, or whether the realities of the new strategic situation should be recognized and the possibilities of an end of the arms race seriously explored.

be unable to agree to inspection measures indispensable for extensive arms control and disarmament agreements, since they must rely largely on concealment for the protection of their vulnerable deterrents against a pre-emptive attack. It is only as their retaliatory system approaches the invulnerability of ours that they could afford the military risks of inspection. For the time being, therefore, it may be wise to proceed toward a cutoff on a tacit basis. . . .

G. C. D. vs. Freeze

A freeze on nuclear and conventional weapons systems might have about half the economic impact of general and complete disarmament. This calculation is based on an expected cutback of more than $16 billion per year for a complete freeze, as compared to an estimated $32 billion net reduction for general and complete disarmament.[3] However, the impact of a general weapons freeze on *specialized defense industry* might be quite as severe as that of general disarmament, or even worse. The main economic difference between a freeze and disarmament is that the latter would involve not only a cutoff in weapons production but also major cutbacks in personnel of the armed forces and defense agencies. Such personnel cutbacks would add to the number of persons and communities facing severe adjustment problems, but would not necessarily add to the problems of defense industry. Indeed, with respect to industry, disarmament might have certain compensations: first, there would probably be substantial offset programs, such as U.S. contributions to international inspection and enforcement agencies, and development of enlarged civilian space and atomic energy programs; second, in recognition of the drastic changes involved, there would probably be advance government planning and acknowledged responsibility. A weapons freeze, on the other hand, especially if it is unilateral and justified as an economy measure rather than as an international agreement,

---

[3] See *Disarmament and the Economy,* edited by Emile Benoit and Kenneth Boulding, Harper & Row, New York, 1963; and Panel Report, *Economic Impacts of Disarmament,* U. S. Arms Control & Disarmament Agency, Economic Series 1, Publication 2, January, 1962.

would more likely be implemented in a way that would leave defense industry essentially to shift for itself.

The confusion in Washington about the possibilities of defense cutbacks is compounded for the public by important differences of opinion within the government on the political and public relations treatment of this theme. On the one hand, the conservative military viewpoint in the Pentagon would prefer to deny until the last moment that any substantial cuts are in prospect, and to interpret any that do occur as embodying merely changes in emphasis within the program, or as savings from improved organization. This approach springs partly from an inability to imagine that the new technological situation may make the arms race obsolete, and partly from a narrow professional view of purchasing objectives, which seem best served if defense contractors and their key personnel go on producing with unimpaired confidence in the continuation of the program until the very moment when the program does cease. There is also some fear in the Pentagon and in the State Department, as well as in Congress, of encouraging a mood of relaxation and détente which may prove premature.

On the other side, there is some disposition on the part of the President and civilian officials to give considerable—even exaggerated—publicity to actual and possible defense cuts. The reasons in this case are to provide an example for emulation by the U.S.S.R., and to strengthen the atmosphere of détente, thereby encouraging polycentrism in the Communist world, as well as the possibility of East-West agreements. There are also domestic political objectives: to win votes of the "economy bloc" and the "peace bloc" (neither of which is trivial). The executive branch can also use defense cutbacks as a means of putting political pressure on Congressmen; uncooperative politicians may find that defense facilities in *their* districts are the first ones to be eliminated.

How severe would the impact of defense cuts be? Some commentators have taken an unqualifiedly optimistic position. For example, it has been suggested occasionally that even in the event of disarmament, the requirements for minimum national forces and for international inspection and enforcement would be so large, and the expenditures on foreign aid and other forms of international competition so extravagant, that little actual reduction in expenditures would be anticipated.[4] These assumptions seem to minimize the problems to an unrealistic extent.[5]

Even more optimistic appraisals have argued that defense cutbacks will raise national income and employment by (1) releasing engineers and scientists for civilian work, thus ending bottlenecks now impeding growth, and (2) adding to total employment by the higher job-creating potential of public works as compared to defense work.[6]

Beguiling as these arguments may appear, they do not have much substance. In fact, the employment of scientists and engineers by civilian industry has on the whole been speeded up by the example of the spectacular achievements of defense R&D, and by the rapid increase in the number of people receiving technical training as a result of the arms race. Even so, within the last year or two, civilian industry has shown a decreasing capacity to absorb the scientists and engineers released as the demand for them has slackened in the defense industry. There is, therefore, little reason to believe that American industry's slow rate of growth has been caused by the lack of fundamental research and development capabilities; instead, improvements already worked out in civilian laboratories or in defense industry, or already pioneered in other countries, have been introduced into American industry only slowly. The real difficulty is the excess of industrial capacity in relation to our too-slowly-growing consumer demand. This lagging demand, in turn, has been caused by high taxes and a tendency of the government to seek surpluses in the budget.

As for the argument that non-defense spending creates more

[4] William D. Grampp, "Defense and Disarmament: Some Economic Surprises," *Michigan Business Review*, XVI, no. 1, January, 1964; "False Fears of Disarmament," *Harvard Business Review*, January-February, 1964, and *War/Peace Report*, April, 1964; "What We Must Know About Economics," *The Correspondent*, November-December, 1963.

[5] Emile Benoit, "The Economics of Coexistence and Disarmament," *The Correspondent*, November-December, 1963; "The Economic Burden of Adjustment to Disarmament," *Michigan Business Review*, XVI, no. 3, May 1964.

[6] Donna Allen, "The Economic Necessity to Disarm: A Challenge to the Old Assumptions," 2nd International Arms Control and Disarmament Symposium, University of Michigan, January 1964.

jobs, it is based on unrealistic premises, and even its technical validity is debatable. It is quite unrealistic to assume that defense cuts will automatically mean more public works expenditures. Congress just does not think or work that way. It is more likely that the defense cuts will come first, and public welfare spending will follow only after substantially increased unemployment develops. There is no assurance at all that Congress will then vote large enough public works programs to absorb all of the additional unemployment created by the defense cuts, let alone sufficient to mop up the unemployment which existed before the defense cuts came. It is likely that part of the defense savings would be used for tax cuts. Dollar for dollar these provide a substantially smaller impetus to employment than either defense or public works projects. There will also be a temptation to use some of the defense savings to reduce the national debt, which is even more deflationary.[7] Even the part of the defense savings used for public works will not necessarily be productive of more jobs than the displaced defense expenditures *on the average.* Public works may create more jobs per dollar of expenditure than weapons production (and R&D), but not more than payments to personnel in the armed forces and defense agencies—which account for a majority of defense-dependent jobs. In any case, to try to meet the unemployment problem by deliberately selecting programs that provide the most jobs per dollar of expenditure would give preference to programs with low productivity.

Cheery optimism about the economic impact of defense cuts is unwarranted if based on arguments such as the foregoing. On the other hand, suggestions that we face a major economic crisis, or that we "cannot afford to disarm," seem equally wide of the mark. A freeze on strategic weapons would involve something like 1 percent of GNP, a total weapons freeze perhaps 3 percent, and general and complete disarmament (after offsets) about 5 percent. This compares with a defense cutback

---

[7] Emile Benoit, "The Propensity to Reduce the National Debt Out of Defense Savings," Proceedings of the American Economic Association, *American Economic Review,* March 1961; also *Disarmament and the Economy, op. cit.,* chapters 8 and 15.

equal to 5 percent of GNP (in real terms) between 1953 and 1960, after the Korean War. In short, what we face is well within the range of what we have been through before without disaster or even major disturbances.

Two significant problems nevertheless remain. Our economy is undoubtedly more sensitive to deflationary influences than it was in 1945 or 1953, and we still have no really effective system for assuring that total purchasing power will be sustained when government spending (or any other type of spending) is cut. Built-in stabilizers, such as unemployment compensation, take care of only part of the problem—and only after the economy has already started an unnecessary decline. We need a renewed commitment to the goals of the Employment Act of 1946 embodied in firm policies and specific advance arrangements to cut taxes and increase non-defense spending promptly as defense expenditures are reduced.

Second, we face a very real structural problem arising from the considerable concentration of defense procurement and R&D in a limited number of areas and industries, and from intense specialization by major defense contractors. Whole communities are now heavily dependent on activities quite unlike those characteristic of civilian industry. Adjustment difficulties would therefore arise even from a limited weapons freeze; in fact, they are already beginning to become apparent in some areas.

Traditional concepts of adjustment, whether along the lines of relocating defense employes in other communities, retraining them for new skills, or converting defense facilities to civilian production, often turn out to be impracticable. Far too much has been invested in building up these communities to let them become "ghost towns"; the people involved, unlike the "defense workers" of 1940–45, consider their jobs and communities as permanent, and they are politically too sophisticated and well organized to be easily shunted aside.

But what they are doing, and their whole basis of employment, has in many cases no obvious parallel outside the defense program. The single exception is the space program which, like defense industry, utilizes a high proportion of scientists, engineers and skilled workers, sells exclusively to the government, and is based in large part on research and development on frontier problems. The objectives, the organization, the personnel requirements, and the management skills are completely different from those of traditional commercial businesses.

With these circumstances, it seems clear that novel solutions will be required to meet at least part of the problem. We will need to develop new, large-scale R&D programs, organized and financed primarily by government, since the rewards will generally be too long range and indirect to be of interest to private investors unless the government guarantees a market. Such programs would be like the space program, but directed to terrestrial goals. Among the possible objectives of such a program would be: industrial exploitation of the oceans, unconventional energy sources, mass rapid transit, urban renewal, desalinization of water, weather control, population control, basic improvement in human nutrition through synthetic food supplements and new means of food production, elimination of mankind's remaining serious diseases, and rapid diffusion of literacy, basic skills, and even advanced education through teaching machines, etc. The Telstar program and government participation in a commercial supersonic jet transport plane provide examples of the sort of business-government partnerships on which such programs might be based.

Easy Transition

With such programs to work on, many existing contractors could make the transition to non-defense work quite easily, and the extraordinary human and organizational resources which have been developed as a by-product of the defense effort could be preserved to promote the goals of human welfare.

A final advantage of such a program is that it would preserve a standby R&D capacity for the defense system. Such capacity might be extremely important in the event of a technological breakthrough, or of a breakdown in a weapons freeze or disarmament agreement. Even in the event of a properly-enforced disarmament agreement, it is likely that for a good many years the nation would wish to maintain its ability to rebuild a national defense system in the event the treaty broke down. It would be possible to do this only by mounting bold new programs of the type here advocated. Otherwise the talents and organizations now employed in the defense industry would wither away.

Because of the important contribution to national security which such a standby capacity would have, it would seem reasonable for defense appropriations to finance a substantial part of the initial costs of launching such programs. In the long run the nation could count on recovering far more than its investment in the form of increased productivity, broadened energy supplies, better health, new and improved products and services, and even rising tax revenues from the greater tax base. Most important, the cause of world peace would be served as these programs helped raise living standards in the underdeveloped countries. And the provision of plentiful opportunities for defense companies to apply their existing organizations to meeting new challenges would do more than anything else to dissipate lurking economic fears of arms cuts.

ARTHUR I. BLAUSTEIN | THE TWO WARS

ABOUT A YEAR and a half ago I was asked, during the course of an interview, what had become a standard question, "Is the war in Vietnam hurting the War on Poverty?" Having been inured in the past three years to imperceptive and insensitive questions I felt compelled to respond, half-seriously, in another vein. My answer was, "We will probably never win the war in Vietnam because the middle class in Saigon simply does not support the pacification program in the rural areas, but we will probably win the 'war' at home because the middle class in suburbia basically does support the pacification program in the ghettoes." I then went on to point out that a nation's foreign policy is usually consistent with its domestic policy, and therefore I was gravely concerned about the direction of, and repressive institutional response to, the unrest in our urban areas.

What is the relationship between the two wars and what have we learned about both in the past several years? Four years ago Lyndon Johnson promised the American people the Great Society, i.e., butter; three years ago it became "butter and bullets," two years ago "bullets and butter," and last year "bombs and oleomargarine." This year, faced with a policy of "bombs and pure corn oil," most of the voices that are indispensable to a healthy and creative government went into opposition over the conduct of the war. In addition, the poor, particularly the blacks, were growing more restive. Their plight and frustrations were accurately documented and publicized by the President's Commission on Civil Disorders, which had the temerity to actually take its role seriously. Shortly after this, the President, looking over his shoulder at the historians (not to mention the pollsters and primary results), wisely decided to remove himself from the more mundane debate over policies. Like his previous decisions, this one must be evaluated within the general context of our foreign policy and the reasons for the diverse opposition toward it. The gist of the argument is something like this: The events in Southeast Asia may make a difference in the total world picture, but not the decisive difference needed to justify a war which will brutally reduce a country to rubble; which will require more than a million American troops and will render heavy casualties over another five years; which will kill, maim and hopelessly displace far more Vietnamese than a Communist regime would have liquidated—and which will not result in a definite outcome. The disproportion between ends and means has grown so absurd, the consequent deterioration of American foreign and domestic policy so extreme, that one cannot consider the war merely a mistaken initiative to be amended eventually, but to be tolerated meanwhile.

With the exception of a handful of critics, however, notably Walter Lippmann, Senator J. William Fulbright, and William Pfaff, the central focus of the debate essentially remains an argument over method. This is unfortunate, for it is the policy of "globalism" and its underlying assumptions that is really the heart of the issue—a policy that is effectively being undermined by events in Vietnam. It is therefore curious that globalism is still accepted as a legitimate goal of our foreign policy, in the name of some unspecified commitment to a doctrine of world-wide moral conversion.

It is this very doctrine that should be challenged. This vague and messianic notion, with deep roots in American attitudes dating back to Woodrow Wilson, was the cornerstone of John Foster Dulles' policy and more recently has been blindly pursued with righteous vigor by Dean Rusk (under *both* the Kennedy and Johnson Administrations. This brand of Pax Americana, which is steeped in sentimentality and intellectual complacency, must be seriously and openly debated if those who shape American foreign policy are ever to adopt realistic alternatives.

It is also clear that beyond agreeing that we should get out of Vietnam, the New Left theoreticians and the dis-established New Deal liberals have little enough in common. But it is not at all clear that they have formulated what they expect or want of foreign policy. It is also possible that an incoherent opposition, mobilized to elect a new president, could be worse than the Johnson Administration in the long run, if there is no clear-cut presentation of objectives.

Essentially there are two vital lessons to be learned from the Vietnam tragedy. They are:

1. That foreign policy is basically a means by which our nation is protected, and should not be used as a tool, militarily, to prevent reform or revolution in the underdeveloped world. The fact is that nations and societies work out their own fates, and true national success (like national failure) is primarily dependent on the character of the society itself. We are faced with a stalemate in Vietnam, in spite of our superior fire power, not because the Vietcong are braver fighters (although they may be more committed), but because of the intractable nature of internal Vietnamese politics.

2. That a refocused American policy cannot completely abandon a commitment to values or to moral influence in international affairs, but it should be more cautious in its expectations and should realize that its primary obligation is to defend

the international conditions which secure a civilized and reasonable balance between nations. This means limiting conflicts, not enlarging them. We are not on a crusade. There will always be conflict, but it is our ability to control the level of conflict that is important.

In the future we should work toward strengthening the established institutions and the mechanisms of international mediation and legality, not breaking them. It means dealing with the ideological attacks of others in terms of what those nations actually do and can do to harm us, rather than adding our voice to the clamor of rhetoric and hysteria which embitters international relations. In Vietnam, for example, we set in motion a totally irrational pattern of escalating troops while at the same time escalating rhetoric and expectations.

We should also keep in mind that disorders in the Third World, which is now going through profound upheaval, are inevitable. Tomorrow we could very well have our own Algeria in Brazil or Venezuela, and unless we are prepared to solve the problems of poverty and insurrection by unilateral repression or brutal destruction, we must direct our efforts toward neutralizing conflicts by constructing the kind of international machinery that has the competence and tools to isolate and control future Vietnams. *This, therefore, is the vital issue.* The U.S. must get over the militaristic hangover of "gunboat diplomacy" and seriously think and act within the context of international security.

The proper agency for dealing with possible world disruptions resulting from national revolutions should be the United Nations, which represents international democracy, not a politically and morally isolated United States playing the dumb cop. We have never really taken seriously Franklin Delano Roosevelt's early warning that "The United Nations is not the place to go to end wars, but the place to go to end the beginnings of wars."

Meanwhile on the home front whatever did happen to the Great Society and the "war on poverty"? The tragic assassination of Martin Luther King, Jr., and the Riot Commission Report (see pages 176–184) merely serve to underline what has been abundantly clear for some time. The old white self, hesitant for a moment after Birmingham and Selma, reasserted itself after

Watts, Newark and Detroit. "Law and order," the clinical definition for keeping minorities in their place in a democracy,
became the white preoccupation. So far as the Negro, Puerto
Rican, Mexican-American, Indian and poor white was concerned, life was a temporary hope for justice, but conditions are
now returning to normal—normal meaning pacification with the
threat of repression.

Most of the anticipated progress in developing new programs
(and meeting raised expectations) in housing, education, health,
manpower, welfare, and community action fell victim to the
budgetary necessities of the Vietnam War. It should also be
noted that many Congressmen, particularly the Republican-
Dixie coalition, were relieved to hold these projects hostage.
The programs were given impressive names, new agencies were
created and an awful lot of administrators were hired; but the
fact remains that they never delivered the services to the poor
people. The public relations value of names like "Model Cities,"
"Headstart," "Jobs in the Ghetto," "JOBS," etc., were unques-
tionable; they all made the headlines.

But by and large the "War on Poverty" was manipulated
much the way the British dealt with the natives in the colonies.
Every time the natives became restive the British would squirt
them with some welfare money and buy off the leadership in
order to tranquilize the troublemakers. As the long hot summers
move into the long cold winters Congress seems to languish, as
though expecting the urban problems and the dashed expectations to somehow disappear. One senses that nothing has
changed, that men are going through the old, tired motions without any real capacity for learning from the past. It should be
emphasized that my criticism is directed neither at the original
intent nor the design of these projects, but at the unfortunate
fact that they were never allowed to grow out of the planning
and administrative stage and into the program phase so that
they could have a meaningful impact on the grass-roots level.

Martin Luther King fully well realized the madness of the
times. King himself said, "There is nothing except a tragic death
wish to prevent us from reordering our priorities, so that the
pursuit of peace will take precedence over the pursuit of war."
He also knew that time was running out for the moderates. It

was for these reasons that he planned a non-violent, direct-action demonstration. At this time it is not really necessary to reiterate all the proposals for economic opportunity and social justice; they are all too familiar to anyone who has read the headlined pieties of the past few years. However, I will suggest one specific proposal that if adopted could symbolically signify a meaningful departure from the sterile and empty promises of the past.

The President should immediately establish an Economic Conversion Commission (which could be known as the Martin Luther King Commission). It would be responsible for taking appropriate action to facilitate conversion from a war to a peace economy. It would also be a fitting memorial to the first American leader of stature who dramatically pointed out the logical and cruel connection between the war in Vietnam and the "war on poverty." The Commission would be charged with the primary responsibility of implementing the "Recommendations for National Action" of the Riot Commission Report. Among other responsibilities the Commission could prepare schedules of private and public investment patterns and the employment and income effects to be expected therefrom. This could well be an excellent opportunity to declare that the government must become the employer of the last resort, assuring a job to everyone who wants to work. Short of this, every inducement should be extended to industry to become the employer of the first resort. Toward this end there should be: tax exemptions for corporations that build in or near slum areas, insurance protection for businesses in high-risk ghetto areas, and additional manpower-training programs and guarantees against loss (re worker dropouts) for companies that make a special effort to hire the unemployed.

In effect this action would serve notice that the United States is willing to prepare itself to "wage peace." It would be significant in that only through this kind of intelligent planning and meaningful commitment, not pious rhetoric, is it possible for us to make a satisfactory transition to a just society for all Americans. It would also indicate to a nervous and watchful world that America is willing to take an important step toward recovering her sanity.

PART

TWO

POVERTY
IN THE
UNITED
STATES

A. THE PROBLEMS

INTRODUCTION

IN JUNE OF 1963 President Kennedy, speaking to the American nation, said:

> The Negro baby born in America today, regardless of the section of the nation in which he is born, has about half as much chance of completing high school as the white baby born in the same place on the same day, one-third as much chance of becoming a professional man, twice as much chance of becoming unemployed, about one-seventh as much chance of earning $10,000 a year, a life expectancy which is seven years shorter, and the prospects of earning only half as much.

In addition to the Negro, the roster of the disadvantaged includes Puerto Ricans, Mexican-Americans, Indians, and white Caucasians. Our health service has failed to reach every American. All our social programs together have failed to eliminate delinquency, crime, alienation and poverty. Our expanding economy has failed to produce enough jobs. Our school system has failed to prevent drop-outs.

Michael Harrington, who first made America aware of poverty in the midst of plenty, begins by looking at "The Rejects," the economic underworld of unemployed and unemployable "other Americans." Alan Batchelder examines the special economic burden Negro Americans carry in terms of lack of education, unemployment, and low earning power. Paul Goodman focuses attention on the school drop-out. He suggests that our problem is not so much the drop-out as it is what he has dropped out of—the public school—which he describes as "The Universal Trap." Senator Joseph S. Clark finds that most ancient

and appalling result of poverty—starvation—is not a stranger
to the poor in the United States. The evidence of hunger and
starvation in Mississippi reported to the Senate Subcommittee
on Employment, Manpower and Poverty is incontrovertible.
Psychiatrist Robert Coles focuses on the relationship between
psychiatry as a helping profession and the poor. He offers a
trenchant commentary on the failure of the profession to deal
with the problems of the economically disadvantaged.

**MICHAEL
HARRINGTON**

THE REJECTS*

IN NEW YORK CITY, some of my friends call 80 Warren Street
"the slave market."

It is a big building in downtown Manhattan. Its corridors
have the littered, trampled air of a courthouse. They are lined
with employment-agency offices. Some of these places list good-
paying and highly skilled jobs. But many of them provide the
work force for the economic underworld in the big city: the
dishwashers and day workers, the fly-by-night jobs.

Early every morning, there is a great press of human beings
in 80 Warren Street. It is made up of Puerto Ricans and
Negroes, alcoholics, drifters, and disturbed people. Some of
them will pay a flat fee (usually around 10 percent) for a day's
work. They pay 50¢ for a $5 job and they are given the address
of a luncheonette. If all goes well, they will make their wage.
If not, they have a legal right to come back and get their half-
dollar. But many of them don't know that, for they are people
who are not familiar with laws and rights.

But perhaps the most depressing time at 80 Warren Street is
in the afternoon. The jobs have all been handed out, yet the

* Excerpted from Chapter 2 of *The Other America: Poverty in the
United States* by Michael Harrington. Reprinted with the permission of
The Macmillan Company. Copyright © 1962 by Michael Harrington.

people still mill around. Some of them sit on benches in the larger offices. There is no real point to their waiting, yet they have nothing else to do. For some, it is probably a point of pride to be here, a feeling that they are somehow still looking for a job even if they know that there is no chance to get one until early in the morning.

Most of the people at 80 Warren Street were born poor. (The alcoholics are an exception.) They are incompetent as far as American society is concerned, lacking the education and the skills to get decent work. If they find steady employment, it will be in a sweatshop or a kitchen.

In a Chicago factory, another group of people are working. A year or so ago, they were in a union shop making good wages, with sick leave, pension rights, and vacations. Now they are making artificial Christmas trees at less than half the pay they had been receiving. They have no contract rights, and the foreman is absolute monarch. Permission is required if a worker wants to go to the bathroom. A few are fired every day for insubordination.

These are people who have become poor. They possess skills, and they once moved upward with the rest of the society. But now their jobs have been destroyed, and their skills have been rendered useless. In the process, they have been pushed down toward the poverty from whence they came. This particular group is Negro, and the chances of ever breaking through, of returning to the old conditions, are very slim. Yet their plight is not exclusively racial, for it is shared by all the semi-skilled and unskilled workers who are the victims of technological unemployment in the mass-production industries. They are involved in an interracial misery.

These people are the rejects of the affluent society. They never had the right skills in the first place, or they lost them when the rest of the economy advanced. They are the ones who make up a huge portion of the culture of poverty in the cities of America. They are to be counted in the millions.

Each big city in the United States has an economic underworld. And often enough this phrase is a literal description: it refers to the kitchens and furnace rooms that are under the city; it tells of the place where tens of thousands of hidden people labor at impossible wages. Like the underworld of crime, the economic underworld is out of sight, clandestine.

The workers in the economic underworld are concentrated among the urban section of the more than 16 million Americans denied coverage by the Minimum-Wage Law of 1961. They are domestic workers, hotel employees, bus boys, and dishwashers, and some of the people working in small retail stores. In the most recent Government figures, for example, hotel workers averaged $47.44 a week, laundry workers $46.45, general-merchandise employees $48.37, and workers in factories making work clothing $45.58.

This sector of the American economy has proved itself immune to progress. And one of the main reasons is that it is almost impossible to organize the workers of the economic underworld in their self-defense. They are at the mercy of unscrupulous employers (and, in the case of hospital workers, management might well be a board composed of the "best" people of the city who, in pursuing a charitable bent, participate in a conspiracy to exploit the most helpless citizens). They are cheated by crooked unions; they are used by racketeers.

In the late fifties I talked to some hospital workers in Chicago. They were walking a picket line, seeking union recognition. (They lost.) Most of them made about $30 a week and were the main support of their families. The hospital deducted several dollars a week for food that they ate on the job. But then, they had no choice in this matter. If they didn't take the food, they had to pay for it anyway.

When the union came, it found a work force at the point of desperation. A majority of them had signed up as soon as they had the chance. But, like most of the workers in the economic underworld, these women were hard to keep organized. Their dues were minuscule, and in effect they were being subsidized by the better-paid workers in the union. Their skills were so low that supervisory personnel could take over many of their functions during a strike. It required an enormous effort to reach them and to help them, and in this case it failed.

An extreme instance of this institutional poverty took place in Atlanta, Georgia, among hospital workers in mid-1960. Men who worked the dishwashing machines received 68¢ an hour; women kitchen helpers got 56¢; and the maids 55¢ an hour. If these people all put in the regular two thousand hours of work a year, they would receive just over $1,000 for their services.

The restaurants of the economic underworld are somewhat like the hospitals. The "hidden help" in the kitchen are an unstable group. They shift jobs rapidly. As a result, a union will sign up all the employees in a place, but before a union certification election can occur half of those who had joined will have moved on to other work. This means that it is extremely expensive for the labor movement to try to organize these workers: they are dispersed in small groups; they cannot pay for themselves; and they require constant servicing, checking, and rechecking to be sure that the new workers are brought into the union structure. . . .

When the hotels, the restaurants, the hospitals, and the sweatshops are added up, one confronts a section of the economy that employs millions and millions of workers. In retailing alone, there are 6 million or 7 million employees who are unorganized, and many of them are not covered by minimum wage. For instance, in 1961 the general-merchandise stores (with an average weekly wage of $48.37) counted over 1,250,000 employees. Those who made work clothes, averaging just over $45 a week, totaled some 300,000 citizens, most of them living in the other America of the poor.

Thus, in the society of abundance and high standards of living there is an economically backward sector which is incredibly capable of being exploited; it is unorganized, and in many cases without the protection of federal law. It is in this area that the disabled, the retarded, and the minorities toil. In Los Angeles they might be Mexican-Americans, in the runaway shops of West Virginia or Pennsylvania, white Anglo-Saxon Protestants. All of them are poor; regardless of race, creed, or color, all of them are victims.

In the spring of 1961, American society faced up to the problem of the economic underworld. It decided that it was not worth solving. Since these workers cannot organize to help themselves, their only real hope for aid must be directed toward the intervention of the federal government. After the election of President Kennedy, this issue was joined in terms of a minimum-wage bill. The AFL–CIO proposed that minimum-wage coverage should be extended to about 6,500,000 new workers; the Administration proposed new coverage for a little better than 3 million workers; the conservatives of the Dixiecrat-Republican coalition wanted to hold the figure down to about 1 million.

There was tremendous logrolling in Congress over the issue. In order to win support for the Administration approach, concessions were made. It does not take much political acumen to guess which human beings were conceded: the poor. The laundry workers (there are over 300,000 of them, and according to the most recent Bureau of Labor statistics figures they averaged $47.72 a week) and the hospital workers were dropped from the extension of coverage. The papers announced that over 3 million new workers had been granted coverage—but they failed to note that a good number of them were already in well-paid industries and didn't need help.

In power politics, organized strength tells. So it was that America turned its back on the rejects in the economic underworld. As one reporter put it, "We've got the people who make $26 a day safely covered; it's the people making $26 a week who are left out." Once again, there is the irony that the welfare state benefits least those who need help most. . . .

POVERTY*

ALAN BATCHELDER

THE SPECIAL CASE

OF THE NEGRO

PRESUMABLY, a Negro family receiving $2,400 annually would experience, because of such low income, discomfort identical with that experienced by a white family in exactly the same

* From the *American Economic Review*, May 1965.

circumstances. Why, then, a special *economics* paper on Negro poverty? Because at least four economic considerations distinguish Negro from white poverty. As Wordsworth observed of the echo, "Like—but oh how different."

First, $1,000 buys less for a poor Negro than for a poor white. Second, the demographic cross section of the Negro poor is unlike that of the white poor. Third, poor Negroes suffer, though the general weal and poor whites benefit, from secular changes in urban renewal, education medians, agriculture, manufacturing location, technology, and social minimum wages. Fourth, discrimination operates against Negroes to restrict access to education and to the jobs that can provide an escape from poverty. These considerations will be discussed in turn.

When considering American Negro affairs, one must remember that social and economic conditions of Negroes are most responsive to changes in unemployment rates. In 1900, 90 percent of American Negroes lived in the South, most on farms. The few urban Negroes were totally excluded from manufacturing and from all but menial and laborious jobs. The situation changed to the Negro's advantage only during German nationalism's wars. Wartime labor shortages induced managers of large manufacturing corporations to admit Negroes to the production jobs that permitted Negroes to make relative income gains.

During peacetime, the Negro position remained the same or deteriorated. When labor markets softened between 1949 and 1959, the income position of Negro men relative to that of white men fell in every section of the country. Rising productivity cut the number of white and Negroes living in poverty, but the incidence of poverty among Negroes rose between 1950 and 1962 from two to two and a half times the white rate.

The past decade's many admonitions and laws opposing discrimination could, by themselves, not raise the Negro's relative economic position in the face of rising unemployment. If Negroes are to approach economic and civil equality in the future, unemployment rates must fall.

Full employment affects all Negroes. Attention now turns to

the characteristics distinguishing poor Negro from poor white Americans.

The Negro Dollar: Second-Class Money

When citing statistics of poverty, the portion of Negro families receiving incomes below a particular figure, e.g., $3,000, is often compared with the portion of white families receiving incomes below $3,000. Such comparisons implicitly assume the Negro's $3,000 buys as much as the white's $3,000. It does not.

American cities have two housing markets: the city-wide white market and the circumscribed Negro market. Because supply is restricted, Negroes "receive less housing value for their dollars spent than do whites. . . . Census statistics indicate that . . . nonwhite renters and home owners obtain fewer standard quality dwellings and frequently less space than do whites paying the same amounts."

Landlords are sometimes judged greedy extortionists for charging Negro tenants higher rents than whites. But they are operating in a market of restricted supply; high Negro rents reflect supply and demand relationships, not conspiratorial landlord greed. Since 15 percent of the consumption expenditures of urban Negro families is for shelter, real income is significantly reduced by relatively high rents.

Poor urban Negroes also pay more than whites for identical consumer durables bought on credit. The difference may be due to white reluctance to sell to Negroes, to Negro immobility, or to the sellers' assumption that poor Negroes are poorer risks than poor whites. Whatever the cause, real income suffers.

Poor Negro families average a half person larger than poor white families. Consequently, per capita real income of poor Negroes is even further below per capita real income of poor whites with the same money income.

If, then, $3,000 in Negro money buys only as much as $2,800 or even $2,500 in white money and is distributed over more people, one should keep in mind appropriate reservations when comparing percentage of whites with percentage of Negroes below some income level.

Differences in Demographic Characteristics

The Negro poor differ secondly from the white poor in demographic characteristics. If we remember that Negro numbers will be understated, uniform dollar incomes can be used to identify nonwhite (not Negro) and white poor. Defining as poor, families with incomes under $3,000 and individuals living independently with incomes under $1,500 in 1959, four social-economic variables distinguish the nonwhite from the white poor.

First, the nonwhite poor are concentrated in the South. In 1960, 72 percent (52%)[1] of poor nonwhite families, only four of ten (27%) poor white families, lived in the South.[2] The 32 point difference in Southern concentration resulted because, in 1960, the proportion of nonwhites was double the proportion of whites living in the South.

Second, low-income is more of a rural phenomenon for whites than for nonwhites: 18 of every 100 (4%) poor white families, 12 of every 100 (3%) poor nonwhite families lived on farms in 1960. Most rural nonwhites are poor. Fully 84 percent (79%) of nonwhite, only 44 percent (65%) of white, farm families were poor in 1959, but nonwhites have withdrawn from farming more completely than have whites.

Third, the aging of husbands is a much more important cause of white than of nonwhite poverty. In 1959, 29 percent of poor white families but only 13 percent of poor nonwhite families were headed by a man older than 64 years. Among unrelated individuals, 40 percent of the white poor, only 26 percent of the nonwhite poor were past 64.

Fourth, nonwhite poverty, far more than white, is associated with families headed by women. American Negro women have always borne exceptionally heavy family responsibility. In 1910, for every 100 employed white men, there were 20 gainfully employed white women; for every 100 employed Negro men, there were 67 employed Negro women. Even in 1959, only 8

---

[1] The figures in parentheses refer to individuals living independently.

[2] See U.S. Bureau of the Census. *U.S. Census of Population: 1960,* Supplementary Reports, *Low Income Families: 1960,* PC(S1)-43, February 24, 1964.

percent of white families but 21 percent of nonwhite families were headed by women, and three-fourths of these nonwhite families were poor in 1959. Consequently, 32 percent of all poor nonwhite families, only 19 percent of all poor white families, were headed by women in 1959. So much for demographic differences involving regional residence, urban residence, age of men, and female heads of families.

Six Forces

Urban Renewal, Shrinking the Supply of Dwellings. The third difference between the Negro poor and the white poor is the collection of some six forces afoot today that enrich the affluent members of society and even poor whites while injuring poor Negroes. One of these forces is urban renewal. It replaces slums with aesthetically attractive, commercially profitable structures, some of which provide low-income housing superior to that which the private market could provide.

Yet urban renewal seems to effect a net reduction in housing supply for poor Negroes. L. K. Northwood found "The supply of housing has been reduced in areas formerly occupied by Negro families . . . 115,000 housing units were . . . planned to replace 190,500 . . . *a net loss of 75,000.*" Because many urban Negroes live in slums, 60 percent of the persons dispossessed by urban renewal demolition have been Negroes.

The long-run tendency to reduce the supply of low-cost housing is aggravated in the short run because time must elapse between demolition of old and dedication of new buildings. During short runs as long as five years, urban renewal reduces housing supply by demolition uncompensated by new construction.

Poor whites may move elsewhere; poor Negroes must face reduced supply. Reduced supply should raise prices, and there is evidence that Negroes displaced by urban renewal pay rent 10 percent higher after relocation than before.

Education: The Illiterate Fall Farther Behind. The second force benefitting the rest of society but injuring poor Negroes is rising education norms. Improved education is manifested in rising median school years completed. In 1950 Negro medians for men and for women past age twenty-four lagged white medians by 2.8 years. By 1960, Negro medians had pushed up a year and a third. So had white medians. Average Negroes remained in the same relative position, but rising educational medians increased the comparative disadvantage of the 2,265,000 nonwhite functional illiterates (less than five years of school) making up 23.5 percent of the 1960 nonwhite population past age twenty-four.

Many poor whites are illiterate, but figures on school years completed understate the number of illiterate Negroes and the size of their educational disadvantage. Understatements result for Negroes because so many attended inefficient segregated Southern schools. Testing poor Negro literacy, Illinois departments of public aid recently sampled able-bodied Negroes aged sixteen to sixty-four receiving public assistance (*not* a random sample of all Negroes). Each person was asked his school attainment; each took the New Stanford Reading Test. Of persons educated in Illinois, 3 percent were functionally illiterate; 35 percent tested as illiterate. Of persons educated in Mississippi, 23 percent were functionally illiterate; 81 percent, four of five adults, tested as illiterate.

Of nonwhites living North or West in 1960, 41 percent had been born in the South. These educationally deprived poor Southern Negroes are increasingly disadvantaged in regions where the median education of the local labor force and the quality of local schools rise each year.

Left ever farther behind rising national educational norms, poor Negro families are ever less qualified to compete for jobs or to help their children acquire the education required to escape poverty. Improving education benefits the general public but injures poor Negroes moving from the South to the North and West.

Agriculture: End of an Exodus. The third force benefitting most Americans but particularly injuring poor Negroes has been agricultural change. Since 1945, the mechanization of cotton culture has revolutionized Southern agriculture. There has also been persistent change in crops grown and livestock raised. These changes raised agricultural productivity and expelled hand labor from Southern farms. In 1930, there were 882,000 Negro farms (with 4,680,500 residents). In 1950, there were 559,000 (with 3,167,000 residents); in 1959, only 265,000 (with 1,482,000 residents).

The economy benefits as productivity rises. The effect on Negroes is less favorable. As whites left, the white farms that averaged 130 acres in 1930 grew to average 249 acres in 1959. But Negro farms showed little growth. They averaged 43 acres in 1930, 52 acres in 1960; the remaining Negro farmers remained poor.

Change has not resulted in larger, more prosperous Negro farms. Change has expelled from Southern farms the most ill-educated Americans.

Looking ahead, the Negro reservoir is nearly exhausted. The number of rural farm Negroes in 1960 was only 47 percent the number in 1950. The Negro exodus can never again approach the scale reached during the 1950s. Poor Negroes are already committed to the city.

Manufacturing Migration: Jobs Out of Reach. The fourth change benefitting the general public and injuring poor Negroes has been manufacturing migration. Since 1950, Southern manufacturing has expanded more rapidly than Northern. From 1950 to 1960, the number of manufacturing jobs grew 28 percent in the South, only 12 percent in the North. Because most poor Negroes live in the South, and because Negroes' wartime income gains were based on accession of Negroes to production jobs in manufacturing, Negroes are particularly affected by shifts in manufacturing employment.

Manufacturing's Southern migration to new markets and new sources of raw material has distributed American resources more efficiently. It has taken jobs to poor whites but not to poor Negro men. Between 1950 and 1960, the number of jobs in Southern manufacturing rose by 944,000. Of these 944,000 jobs, 12,000 went to Negro women (proportionately fewer than to white women); none went to Negro men.

Manufacturing: Technological Change Blocks the Exits. During wartime, rural Southern Negroes proved themselves in manufacturing and developed vested interests in the growth of unskilled and semi-skilled manufacturing jobs.

Today, technological change benefits all by raising productivity. It also changes America's occupational cross section. In 1880 textile mechanization replaced skilled workers with unskilled rural immigrants. Negroes would prefer such changes today, but in 1964 skilled workers replaced unskilled.

In recent years, the occupations that during war gave Negroes a chance to get ahead have not grown as rapidly as the number of Negroes seeking work. Between 1947 and 1964, as male employment rose 10 percent, the number of manufacturing production jobs rose only 5.5 percent. Between 1950 and 1960, male employment rose 6.9 percent; the number of semi-skilled jobs in manufacturing rose only 4.1 percent.

Most unfavorable for aspiring unskilled poor Negroes, the number of men's laboring jobs in manufacturing fell 20 percent (by 200,000) between 1950 and 1960.

These changes in America's occupational cross section result from technological developments that raise society's affluence. Poor whites are relatively free to enter other occupations, but, as present trends continue, manufacturing, the Negro's past ladder to escape from poverty, will offer fewer exits from poverty for Negroes handicapped by rural Southern origins.

The Rising Social Minimum Wage and the Able-Bodied Unemployed. Many Negroes transplanted from farms to cities are unable to obtain steady work. Long's argument that America's social minimum wage rises above the marginal revenue product of society's least productive members applies especially to urban Negroes with rural Southern antecedents. Law and respectable custom press upward on the social minimum wage. The general welfare benefits as many low-income persons receive more money and employers increase efficiency to offset higher costs. But the first increase in the minimum causes the discharge of the least able persons employed. Successive increases cause the discharge of successively more able persons among the less able employed.

It is the function of the market to choose technology appropriate to available resources as reflected in flexible resource prices. But the market does not operate below the social minimum. Weighed down with their heritage from the Southern Way of Life, able-bodied Negroes with marginal revenue products below the social minimum wage must either find employers paying below the minimum or depend on transfers.

So much for six forces benefitting the general public but especially hurting poor Negroes.

Peroration

Because of discrimination in education and employment, there is one last important difference between the Negro and white poor. Logic rather than statistics suggests its existence and its implications. To begin, assume the innate ability distribution of Negroes is identical with that of whites. Next assume the inexorable winnowing out of those least able to earn is the dominant cause of white poverty, but is only a partial cause of Negro poverty. It follows that poor whites are the least able whites, but that poor Negroes include those least able as well as many of middling to superior ability. These able Negroes are poor because of racial discrimination; society denied them access to the channels in which their earning ability could be developed and used.

The economist then concludes that the marginal efficiency of social capital invested in educating and finding work for the Negro poor could be much higher than the marginal efficiency of social capital similarly invested in the white poor. However, we know that the conversion of the poor Negro's potential into dollar product is very difficult in American society. The potential is latent in the Negro poor. Since Southern [as well as Northern] segregated Negro schools have placed poor Negroes at a greater disadvantage than poor whites, since racial discrimination keeps qualified Negroes from demanding jobs, since weak labor markets remove the inducement that historically has been most important in helping Negroes score economic gains, it follows that improved education, reduced discrimination, or a 3 percent unemployment level would bring the Negro poor nearer the realization of their latent potential.

PAUL
GOODMAN

THE UNIVERSAL
TRAP*

(I)

A CONFERENCE of experts on school drop-outs will discuss the backgrounds of poverty, cultural deprivation, race prejudice, family and emotional troubles, neighborhood uprooting, urban mobility. It will explore ingenious expedients to counteract these conditions, though it will not much look to remedying them— that is not its business. And it will suggest propaganda—e.g., no school, no job—to get the youngsters back in school. It is axiomatic that they ought to be in school.

After a year, it proves necessary to call another conference to cope with the alarming fact that more than 75 percent of the drop-outs who have been cajoled into returning, have dropped out again. They persist in failing; they still are not sufficiently motivated. What curricular changes must there be? how can the teachers learn the life-style of the underprivileged?

Curiously muffled in these conferences is the question that puts the burden of proof the other way: What are they drop-outs from? Is the schooling really good for them, or much good for anybody? Since, for many, there are such difficulties with the present arrangements, might not some better arrangements be invented? Or bluntly, since schooling undertakes to be compulsory, must it not continually review its claim to be useful? Is it the only means of education? Isn't it unlikely that *any* single type of social institution could fit almost every youngster up to age sixteen and beyond? (It is predicted that by 1970, 50 percent will go to college.)

But conferences on drop-outs are summoned by school professionals, so perhaps we cannot hope that such elementary

* From Chapter I of *Compulsory Mid-Education* by Paul Goodman. Copyright © 1964 by Paul Goodman. Reprinted by permission of Horizon Press.

questions will be raised. Yet neither are they raised by laymen. There is a mass superstition, underwritten by additional billions every year, that adolescents must continue going to school. The middle-class *know* that no professional competence—i.e., status and salary—can be attained without many diplomas; and poor people have allowed themselves to be convinced that the primary remedy for their increasing deprivation is to agitate for better schooling. Nevertheless, I doubt that, *at present or with any reforms that are conceivable under present school administration,* going to school is the best use for the time of life of the majority of youth.

(II)

Education is a natural community function and occurs inevitably, since the young grow up on the old, toward their activities, and into (or against) their institutions; and the old foster, teach, train, exploit, and abuse the young. Even neglect of the young, except physical neglect, has an educational effect—not the worst possible.

Formal schooling is a reasonable auxiliary of the inevitable process, whenever an activity is best learned by singling it out for special attention with a special person to teach it. Yet it by no means follows that the complicated artifact of a school system has much to do with education, and certainly not with good education.

Let us bear in mind the way in which a big school system might have nothing to do with education at all. The New York system turns over $700 millions annually, not including capital improvements. There are 750 schools, with perhaps fifteen annually being replaced at an extra cost of $2 to $5 millions each. There are 40,000 paid employees. This is a vast vested interest, and it is very probable that—like much of our economy and almost all of our political structure, of which the public schools are a part—it goes on for its own sake, keeping more than a million people busy, wasting wealth, and pre-empting time and space in which something else could be going on. It is a gigantic market for textbook manufacturers, building contractors, and graduate schools of Education.

The fundamental design of such a system is ancient, yet it has not been altered—although the present operation is altogether different in scale from what it was, and therefore it must have a different meaning. For example, in 1900, 6 percent of the seventeen-year-olds graduated from high school, and less than ½ percent went to college; whereas in 1963, 65 percent graduated from high school and 35 percent went on to something called college. Likewise, there is a vast difference between schooling intermitted in life on a farm or in a city with plenty of small jobs, and schooling that is a child's only "serious" occupation and often his only adult contact. Thus, a perhaps outmoded institution has become almost the only allowable way of growing up. And with this pre-empting, there is an increasing intensification of the one narrow experience, e.g. in the shaping of the curriculum and testing according to the increasing requirements of graduate schools far off in time and place. Just as our American society as a whole is more and more tightly organized, so its school system is more and more regimented as part of that organization.

In the organizational plan, the schools play a noneducational and an educational role. The noneducational role is very important. In the tender grades, the schools are a baby-sitting service during a period of collapse of the old-type family and during a time of extreme urbanization and urban mobility. In the junior and senior high school grades, they are an arm of the police, providing cops and concentration camps paid for in the budget under the heading "Board of Education." The educational role is, by and large, to provide—at public and parents' expense—apprentice-training for corporations, government, and the teaching profession itself, and also to train the young, as New York's Commissioner of Education has said (in the Worley case), "to handle constructively their problems of adjustment to authority."

The public schools of America have indeed been a powerful, and beneficent, force for the democratizing of a great mixed population. But we must be careful to keep reassessing them when, with changing conditions, they become a universal trap and democracy begins to look like regimentation.

(III)

Let me spend a page on the history of the compulsory nature of the school systems. In 1961, in *The Child, the Parent, and the State,* James Conant mentions a possible incompatibility between "individual development" and "national needs"; this, to my mind, is a watershed in American philosophy of education and puts us back to the ideology of Imperial Germany, or on a par with contemporary Russia.

When Jefferson and Madison conceived of compulsory schooling, such an incompatibility would have been unthinkable. They were in the climate of the Enlightenment, were strongly influenced by Congregational (town-meeting) ideas, and were of course makers of a revolution. To them, "citizen" meant society-*maker,* not one "participating in" or "adjusted to" society. It is clear that they regarded themselves and their friends as citizens existentially, so to speak; to make society was their breath of life. But obviously such conceptions are worlds removed from, and diametrically opposed to, our present political reality, where the ground rules and often the score are predetermined.

For Jefferson, people had to be taught in order to multiply the sources of citizenly initiative and to be vigilant for freedom. Everybody had to become literate and study history, in order to make constitutional innovations and be fired to defend free institutions, which was presumably the moral that history taught. And those of good parts were to study a technological natural philosophy, in order to make inventions and produce useful goods for the new country. By contrast, what are the citizenly reasons for which we compel everybody to be literate, etc.? To keep the economy expanding, to understand the mass communications, to choose between indistinguishable Democrats and Republicans. Planning and decision-making are lodged in top managers; rarely, and at most, the electorate serves as a pressure group. There is a new emphasis on teaching science . . . but the vast majority will never use this knowledge and will forget it; they are consumers.

Another great impulse for compulsory education came from the new industrialism and urbanism during the three or four decades after the Civil War, a time also of maximum immigration. Here the curricular demands were more mundane: in the grades, literacy and arithmetic; in the colleges, professional skills to man the expanding economy. But again, no one would have spoken of an incompatibility between "individual development" and "national needs," for it was considered to be an open society, abounding in opportunity. Typically, the novels of Horatio Alger, Jr., treat schooling as morally excellent as well as essential for getting ahead; and there is no doubt that the immigrants saw education-for-success as also a human value for their children. Further, the school system was not a trap. The 94 percent who in 1900 did not finish high school had other life opportunities, including making a lot of money and rising in politics. But again, by and large this is not our present situation. There is plenty of social mobility, opportunity to rise—except precisely for the ethnic minorities who are our main concern as drop-outs—but the statuses and channels are increasingly stratified, rigidified, cut and dried. Most enterprise is parceled out by feudal corporations, or by the state; and these determine the requirements. Ambition with average talent meets these rules or fails; those without relevant talent, or with unfortunate backgrounds, cannot even survive in decent poverty. The requirements of survival are importantly academic, attainable only in schools and universities; but such schooling is ceasing to have an initiating or moral meaning.

We do not have an open economy; even when jobs are not scarce, the corporations and state dictate the possibilities of enterprise. General Electric swoops down on the high schools, or IBM on the colleges, and skims off the youth who have been pre-trained for them at public or private expense. (Private college tuition runs upward of $6,000, and this is estimated as a third or less of the actual cost for "education and educational administration.") Even a department store requires a diploma for its salespeople, not so much because of the skills they have learned as that it guarantees the right character: punctual and with a smooth record. And more generally, since our powers-that-be have opted for an expanding economy with a galloping standard of living, and since the powers of the world are in an arms and space race, there *is* a national need for many graduates specifically trained. Thus, even for those selected, the purpose is irrelevant to citizenly initiative, the progress of an open society, or personal happiness, and the others have spent time and effort in order to be progressively weeded out. Some drop out.

(IV)

It is said that our schools are geared to "middle-class values," but this is a false and misleading use of terms. The schools less and less represent *any* human values, but simply adjustment to a mechanical system.

Because of the increasing failure of the schools with the poor urban mass, there has developed a line of criticism—e.g., Oscar Lewis, Patricia Sexton, Frank Riessman, and even Edgar Friedenberg—asserting that there is a "culture of poverty" which the "middle-class" schools do not fit, but which has its own virtues of spontaneity, sociality, animality. The implication is that the "middle class," for all its virtues, is obsessional, prejudiced, prudish.

Pedagogically, this insight is indispensable. A teacher must try to reach each child in terms of what he brings, his background, his habits, the language he understands. But if taken to be more than technical, it is a disastrous conception. The philosophic aim of education must be to get each one out of his isolated class and into the one humanity. Prudence and responsibility are not middle-class virtues but human virtues; and spontaneity and sexuality are not powers of the simple but of human health. One has the impression that our social-psychologists are looking not to a human community but to a future in which the obsessionals will take care of the impulsives!

In fact, some of the most important strengths that have historically belonged to the middle class are flouted by the schools: independence, initiative, scrupulous honesty, earnestness, utility, respect for thorough scholarship. Rather than bourgeois, our schools have become petty-bourgeois, bureaucratic, time-serving, gradgrind-practical, timid, and *nouveau riche* climbing. In the upper grades and colleges, they often exude a cynicism that belongs to rotten aristocrats.

Naturally, however, the youth of the poor and of the middle class respond differently to the petty-bourgeois atmosphere. For many poor children, school is orderly and has food, compared to chaotic and hungry homes, and it might even be interesting compared to total deprivation of toys and books. Besides, the wish to improve a child's lot, which on the part of a middle-class parent might be frantic status-seeking and pressuring, on the part of a poor parent is a loving aspiration. There is here a gloomy irony. The school that for a poor Negro child might be a great joy and opportunity is likely to be dreadful; whereas the middle-class child might be better off *not* in the "good" suburban school he has.

Other poor youth, herded into a situation that does not fit their disposition, for which they are unprepared by their background, and which does not interest them, simply develop a reactive stupidity very different from their behavior on the street or ball field. They fall behind, play truant, and as soon as possible drop out. If the school situation is immediately useless and damaging to them, their response must be said to be life-preservative. They thereby somewhat diminish their chances of a decent living, but . . . the usual propaganda—that schooling is a road to high salaries—is for most poor youth a lie; and the increase in security is arguably not worth the torture involved.

The reasonable social policy would be not to have these youth in school, certainly not in high school, but to educate them otherwise and provide opportunity for a decent future in some other way. How? . . . In my opinion, the wise thing would be to have our conferences on *this* issue, and omit the idea of drop-out altogether. But the brute fact is that our society isn't really interested; the concern for the drop-outs is mainly because they are a nuisance and a threat and can't be socialized by the existing machinery.

Numerically far more important than these overt drop-outs at sixteen, however, are the children who conform to schooling between the ages of six to sixteen or twenty, but who drop out internally and daydream, their days wasted, their liberty caged and scheduled. And there are many such in the middle class, from backgrounds with plenty of food and some books and art, where the youth is seduced by the prospect of money and status, but even more where he is terrified to jeopardize the only pattern of life he knows.

It is in the schools and from the mass media, rather than at home or from their friends, that the mass of our citizens in all classes learn that life is inevitably routine, depersonalized, venally graded; that it is best to toe the mark and shut up; that there is no place for spontaneity, open sexuality, free spirit. Trained in the schools, they go on to the same quality of jobs, culture, politics. This *is* education, mis-education, socializing to the national norms and regimenting to the national "needs."

John Dewey used to hope, naïvely, that the schools could be a community somewhat better than society and serve as a lever for social change. In fact, our schools reflect our society closely, except that they *emphasize* many of its worst features, as well as having the characteristic defects of academic institutions of all times and places.

(V)

Let us examine realistically half a dozen aspects of the school that is dropped out *from.*

1. There is widespread anxiety about the children not learning to read, and hot and defensive argument about the methods of teaching reading. Indeed, reading deficiency is an accumulating scholastic disadvantage that results in painful feeling of inferiority, truancy, and drop-out. Reading is crucial for school success—all subjects depend on it—and therefore for the status success that the diploma is about. Yet in all the anxiety and argument, there is no longer any mention of the freedom and human cultivation that literacy is supposed to stand for.

In my opinion, there is something phony here. For a change, let us look at this "reading" coldly and ask if it is really such a big deal except precisely in the school that is supposed to teach it and is sometimes failing to do so.

With the movies, TV, and radio that the illiterate also share, there is certainly no lack of "communications." We cannot say that as humanities or science, the reading matter of the great majority is in any way superior to the content of these other media. And in the present stage of technology and economy, it is probably *less* true than it was in the late nineteenth century—the time of the great push to universal literacy and arithmetic—that the mass teaching of reading is indispensable to operate the production and clerical system. It is rather our kind of urbanism, politics, and buying and selling that require literacy. These are not excellent.

Perhaps in the present dispensation we should be as well off if it were socially acceptable for large numbers not to read. It would be harder to regiment people if they were not so well "informed"; as Norbert Wiener used to point out, every repetition of a cliché only increases the noise and *prevents* communication. With less literacy, there would be more folk culture. Much suffering of inferiority would be avoided if youngsters did not have to meet a perhaps unnecessary standard. Serious letters could only benefit if society were less swamped by trash, lies, and bland verbiage. Most important of all, *more* people might become genuinely literate if it were understood that reading is not a matter of course but a *special useful art with a proper subject matter, imagination and truth,* rather than a means of communicating top-down decisions and advertising. (The advertising is a typical instance: when the purpose of advertising was to give information—"New shipment of salt fish arrived, very good, foot of Barclay Street"—it was useful to be able to read; when the point of advertising is to create a synthetic demand, it is better not to be able to read.)

2. Given their present motives, the schools are not competent to teach authentic literacy, reading as a means of liberation and cultivation. And I doubt that most of us who seriously read and write the English language ever learned it by the route of "Run, Spot, Run" to *Silas Marner.* Rather, having picked up the rudiments either in cultured homes or in the first two grades, we really learned to read by our own will and free exploration, following our bent, generally among books that are considered inappropriate by school librarians!

A great neurologist tells me that the puzzle is not how to teach reading, but why some children fail to learn to read. Given the amount of exposure that any urban child gets, any normal animal should spontaneously catch on to the code. What prevents? It is almost demonstrable that, for many children, it is precisely going to school that prevents—because of the school's alien style, banning of spontaneous interest, extrinsic rewards and punishments. (In many underprivileged schools, the I.Q. steadily falls the longer they go to school.) Many of the backward readers might have had a better chance on the streets.

But let me say something, too, about the "successful" teaching of reading and writing in the schools. Consider, by contrast, the method employed by Sylvia Ashton-Warner in teaching little Maoris. She gets them to ask for their *own* words, the particular gut-word of fear, lust, or despair that is obsessing the child that day; this is written for him on strong cardboard; he learns it instantaneously and never forgets it; and soon he has an exciting, if odd, vocabulary. From the beginning, writing is by demand, practical, magical; and of course it is simply an extension of speech—it is the best and strongest speech, as writing should be. What is read is what somebody is importantly trying to tell. Now what do our schools do? We use tricks of mechanical conditioning. These do positive damage to spontaneous speech, meant expression, earnest understanding. Inevitably, they create *in the majority* the wooden attitude toward "writing," as entirely different from speech, that college teachers later try to cope with in Freshman Composition. And reading inevitably becomes a manipulation of signs, e.g., for test-passing, that has no relation to experience.

(Until recently, the same discouragement by schoolteachers plagued children's musical and plastic expression, but there have been attempts to get back to spontaneity—largely, I think, because of the general revolution in modern art and musical theory. In teaching science, there is just now a strong movement to encourage imagination rather than conditioned "answers." In teaching foreign languages, the emphasis is now strongly on vital engagement and need to speak. Yet in teaching reading and writing, the direction has been the contrary; even progressive education has gone back to teaching spelling. These arts are regarded merely as "tools.")

3. The young rightly resist animal constraint. But, at least in New York where I have been a school-board Visitor, most teachers—and the principals who supervise their classes— operate as if progressive education had not proved the case for noise and freedom of bodily motion. (Dewey stresses the salutary alternation of boisterousness and tranquillity.) The seats are no longer bolted to the floor, but they still face front. Of course, the classes are too large to cope with without "discipline." Then make them smaller, or don't wonder if children escape out of the cage, either into truancy or baffled daydream.

Here is a typical case: an architect replacing a Harlem school is forbidden by the board to spend money on soundproofing the classrooms, even though the principal has called it a necessity for the therapy of pent-up and resentful children. The resentment, pent-up hostility, is a major cause of reactive stupidity; yet there is usually an absolute ban on overt expression of hostility, or even of normal anger and aggression.

Again, one has to be blind not to see that, from the onset of puberty, the dissidence from school is importantly sexual. Theoretically, the junior high school was introduced to fit this change of life; yet astoundingly, it is sexless. My own view, for what it's worth, is that sexuality is lovely, there cannot be too much of it, it is self-limiting if it is satisfactory, and satisfaction diminishes tension and clears the mind for attention and learning. Therefore, sexual expression should be approved in and out of season, also in school, and where necessary made the subject of instruction. But whether or not this view is correct, it certainly is more practical than the apparent attempt of the schools to operate as if sexual drives simply did not exist. When, on so crucial an issue, the schools act a hundred years out of date, they are crucially irrelevant.

But the following *is* something new:

Trenton, May 24 (AP)—A state health official believes some overanxious New Jersey parents are dosing their children with tranquilizers before sending them to school . . . the Health Department pediatrician assigned to the State Education Department said the parents apparently are trying to protect the children from cracking under pressure for good grades.

4. Terrible damage is done to children simply by the size and standardization of the big system. Suppose a class size of twenty is good for average purposes; it does *not* follow that thirty-five is better than nothing. Rather, it is likely to be positively harmful, because the children have ceased to be persons and the teacher is destroyed as a teacher. A teacher with a ten-year-old class reading at seven-year level will have to use the content as well as the vocabulary of *Dick and Jane* since that is the textbook bought by the hundred thousands. The experience of a wise principal is that the most essential part of his job is to know every child's name and be an available "good father," so

he wants a school for 400. Yet the city will build the school for 2,000, because only that is practical, even though the essence is entirely dissipated. The chief part of learning is in the community of scholars, where classwork and social life may cohere; yet social engineers like Dr. Conant will, for putative efficiencies, centralize the high schools—the "enriched" curriculum with equipment is necessary for the national needs.

A program—e.g., to prevent drop-out—will be, by an attentive teacher, exquisitely tailored to the children he works with; he will have a success. Therefore his program must be standardized, watered down, for seventy-five schools—otherwise it cannot be financed—although now it is worthless. But here is an unbeatable anecdote: An architect is employed to replace a dilapidated school but is forbidden to consult the principal and teachers of the school about their needs, since his building must conform to uniform plans at headquarters, the plans being two generations out of date. As a functionalist, the architect demurs, and it requires an *ad hoc* assembly of all the superintendents to give him special permission.

Presumably all this is administratively necessary, but then it is also necessary for bruised children to quit. Our society makes a persistent error in metaphysics. We are so mesmerized by the operation of a system with the appropriate name, for instance, "Education," that we assume that it *must* be working somewhat, though admittedly not perfectly, when perhaps it has ceased to fulfill its function altogether and might even be preventing the function, for instance education.

5. Especially today, when the hours of work will sharply diminish, the schools are supposed to educate for the satisfaction of life and for the worthwhile use of leisure. Again, let us try to be realistic, as a youngster is. For most people, I think a candid self-examination will show that their most absorbing, long, and satisfactory hours are spent in activities like friendly competitive sports, gambling, looking for love and lovemaking, earnest or argumentative conversation, political action with signs and sit-ins, solitary study and reading, contemplation of nature and cosmos, arts and crafts, music, and religion. Now none of these requires much money. Indeed, elaborate equipment takes the heart out of them. Friends use one another as

resources. God, nature, and creativity are free. The media of the fine arts are cheap stuff. Health, luck, and affection are the only requirements for good sex. Good food requires taking pains more than spending money.

What is the moral for our purposes? Can it be denied that in some respects the drop-outs make a wiser choice than many who go to school, not to get real goods but to get money? Their choice of the "immediate"—their notorious "inability to tolerate delay"—is not altogether impulsive and neurotic. The bother is that in our present culture, which puts its entire emphasis on the consumption of expensive commodities, they are so nagged by inferiority, exclusion, and despair of the future that they cannot enjoy their leisure with a good conscience. Because they know little, they are deprived of many profound simple satisfactions and they never know what to do with themselves. Being afraid of exposing themselves to awkwardness and ridicule, they just hang around. And our urban social arrangements—e.g., high rent—have made it impossible for anybody to be decently poor on a "low" standard. One is either in the rat-race or has dropped out of society altogether.

6. As a loyal academic, I must make a further observation. Mainly to provide Ph.D.s, there is at present an overwhelming pressure to gear the "better" elementary schools to the graduate universities. This is the great current reform, genre of Rickover. But what if the top of the ladder is corrupt and corrupts the lower grades? On visits to seventy colleges everywhere in the country, I have been appalled at how rarely the subjects are studied in a right academic spirit, for their truth and beauty and as part of humane international culture. The students are given, and seek, a narrow expertise, "mastery," aimed at licenses and salary. They are indoctrinated with a national thoughtlessness that is not even chauvinistic. Administrators sacrifice the community of scholars to aggrandizement and extramurally sponsored research.

Conversely, there is almost never conveyed the sense in which learning is truly practical, to enlighten experience, give courage to initiate and change, reform the state, deepen personal and social peace. On the contrary, the entire educational system itself creates professional cynicism or the resigned conviction

that Nothing Can Be Done. If this is the University, how can
we hope for aspiring scholarship in the elementary schools?
On the contrary, everything will be grades and conforming, getting ahead not in the subject of interest but up the ladder. Students "do" Bronx Science in order to "make" M.I.T. and they
"do" M.I.T. in order to "make" Westinghouse; some of them
have "done" Westinghouse in order to "make" jail.

| JOSEPH S. CLARK | STARVATION IN THE AFFLUENT SOCIETY* |

GLORIA PALMER, a round-eyed, solemn-faced little girl of ten,
stood shyly outside her slum home in Washington, D.C., and
shifted her six-months-old baby brother from one arm to another, while two other tots leaned against her and stared up at
the two United States Senators. Curiosity and childish baffle-
ment were written across their faces. They did not know what
Senators were or why they should be asking questions, nor did
they recognize Senator Robert Kennedy or me. As we talked
in front of the dilapidated and condemned tenements on Defrees
Street, five blocks away could be seen the gleaming white dome
of the Capitol.

I asked Gloria—one of eleven children of Wilhelmina Palmer
—what she had eaten for lunch. "We didn't have any lunch,"
said Gloria quietly, and added, "But we have black-eyed peas
for supper a lot." I asked her little brother, George, aged seven,
"What did you have for lunch yesterday?" George replied,
"Soup." "And what did you have for breakfast?" "Soup,"
George said.

A community action worker, who accompanied Senator Kennedy and me on this personal inspection of slums in the shadow
of the Capitol, commented: "There are hundreds of others in

* From *The Progressive*, October 1967. Copyright © 1967 by *The Progressive*, Madison, Wisconsin.

this neighborhood who are hungry, kids and adults who get up in the morning hungry and who go to bed at night hungry. It's been that way ever since I've been here, years and years."

When Senator Kennedy remarked that Gloria should have been in school during this neighborhood visit of our Senate Subcommittee on Employment, Manpower and Poverty, my thoughts suddenly whirled back two weeks to another group of youngsters who were also hungry and also not in school.

This time the subcommittee, which I serve as chairman, was walking along the dusty, sun-scared country roads of the Mississippi Delta. Here in ramshackle homes of one or two rooms holding families of eight and ten, we encountered children who were not sent to school by their mothers because they had no shoes. Later on, doctors suggested to us a more shocking reason: "bloated stomachs, chronic sores of the upper lip, and extreme lethargy—all tragic evidence of serious malnutrition."

In Belzoni, heart of the Delta, a mother of four told me that she and her brood had bologna sandwiches for breakfast and this would be the big meal of their day. Other times they have rice or grits, she told me in an infinitely tired voice, "but we never have any milk or fruit or fresh meat." Over and over again I was told that the staple diet for Belzoni's poor was beans, rice, margarine, lard, meal, peanut butter, raisins, powdered milk, and one can of meat for each person in the family per month. The can lasts, at the most, a week and a half.

The children we saw were visibly underweight, their bodies spotted with sores and untreated lesions.

Mrs. Ollie May Chapman and her nine children live in a tar-paper shack in Belzoni. On the day she was interviewed the family had gone without breakfast; for lunch they had soup made from a meat bone and cornmeal bread. For supper they would have beans—and a rare treat, a can of peaches.

We found a mother of fifteen children nursing a three-day-old child which she had delivered herself. There was no food in the house, she said, and no money. She didn't know what she would do.

Near Greenville, Mississippi, I came across a tumbledown collection of shacks ironically called Freedom City, housing the families of displaced plantation workers. Surviving, somehow, in this appalling squalor were forty-eight children who subsisted entirely on grits, rice, soybeans, and "whatever is donated," plus the customary one can of meat per month. Eggs, milk, and fruit juice, the mothers told me, were unknown.

There is no way in which you can prepare yourself for the overpowering effect of hunger and starvation seen close up. No matter how familiar you may be with the facts and figures of malnutrition, nothing can avert the feeling of stunned, disbelieving horror at the sight of little children with swollen bellies, shriveled limbs, and open sores that disfigure the small, bewildered faces and weakened bodies.

One reaches desperately for comparisons to give some semblance of reality to an experience that is essentially unreal and irrational. The mind rejects the evidence that innocent children *can and do* starve in this most abundant and fruitful of all nations, or go hungry in the Delta which contains 6 million acres of the richest land on the continent. The visitor reaches for analogies. Senator Kennedy remarked that what he saw on our visit to the Mississippi Delta was as bad as anything he encountered in Latin America. A former British Army doctor with extensive experience in Africa told us that what he saw in Mississippi was comparable only to what he had observed in primitive parts of Kenya. Another doctor who worked for the World Health Organization in Asia told me, "I've been in India and I've seen famine and starvation. What we have seen in Mississippi and places in the North is slow starvation."

Yes, the North, too, allows its citizens, including its children, to waste away with hunger and to starve. Hunger, we discovered, is no respecter of area or region. No state is free of hunger any more than any state is free of poverty and deprivation. There is hunger, for example, in prosperous Illinois, which admits that 1,281,100 people, or 12 percent of the state's population, have incomes below the poverty line.

The subcommittee recently reported that in a small Appalachian town, near the border between Virginia and Tennessee, five small children tore apart and devoured a chicken before it could be cooked. It was the first meat the family had eaten in three months.

"In the San Joaquin Valley of California," our report continued, "fifty yards off a seldom-traveled road, a migrant family of seven, the youngest child not yet two, were living in a pick-up truck abandoned by a small stream. They had had no breakfast and did not know where they would find food for lunch. In other years they could have fished, but the stream had dried up."

As such specific cases as these came increasingly to the attention of the subcommittee, we were struck by the discovery that these instances could not be projected against an overall picture of malnutrition and hunger in the United States. The fact is we simply do not know the extent or severity of malnutrition in this country today. Newspapermen were shocked when the U.S. Surgeon General told the subcommittee that we know more about malnutrition in Pakistan and other poor countries than in the United States. He said such studies have not been made in this country and, if they were to be made, he was not sure which agency should make them.

How vague our information is can be judged by the fact that the subcommittee was forced to report, after soliciting the best opinion available, that "estimates of the number of American citizens in serious need of food vary from as few as 400,000 to more than 4,000,000." Twelve years ago a federal study estimated that 23 percent of America's poor—those with incomes under $3,000—had "poor diets." In 1955 that meant 7,500,000 Americans had insufficiently nutritious diets.

Nor do we know with any degree of accuracy the minimum cost of an adequate diet. An Office of Economic Opportunity official told me a tentative conclusion had been reached that an average of $16 a month or $192 a year would provide one person with a "minimum low standard diet—enough to hold body and soul together."

On the basis of other figures compiled by the Department of Agriculture, it seemed more realistic to assume an annual minimum food cost per individual of $225, about twenty-one cents a meal.

Manifestly what is needed before the government can deal decisively with hunger and malnutrition is a comprehensive and incisive study of the problem. We must know the number of Americans who suffer from malnutrition and, next, what can be done to correct their inadequate diets.

Let us return to Mississippi because here surveys and studies have been made, and possibly they may provide clues to the nationwide dimensions of the hunger problem.

A study this year by the Department of Agriculture covered 509 poor families in two wealthy Delta counties. At least 60 percent of these families had diets providing less than two-thirds of the *minimum* dietary requirements recommended by the National Research Council. Moreover, these family diets were seriously deficient in milk, vegetables, and fresh fruits. The value of all the meals consumed by the average individual in the study was a miserable four dollars a week, or fifty-seven cents a day, including the foods distributed free by the federal government.

A spot-check study in seven Delta counties was made by the Mississippi Council on Human Relations and reported to us by its Executive Director, Kenneth L. Dean. Here are brief excerpts from the report:

> Using an economic standard, Mississippi is the poorest state in the republic. The fact that we receive more Office of Economic Opportunity poverty program funds per capita than any other state, and that during the month of March, 1967, 405,000 people received food assistance, indicate that there is a widespread problem of poverty that could, at any given moment, turn into acute hunger or a slow starvation if federal programs are not upgraded in keeping with population trends. . . .
>
> The most acute problem of hunger, and the most common situation, is the middle-aged mother, without a husband, in a small two-room shack, caring for somewhere between four and fifteen children. Most of the children will be of school age but many will not be attending school. . . .
>
> The diet of such a family usually consists of a breakfast of grits, molasses, and biscuit. For lunch the adults will eat nothing, and the children who are at home will be given a piece of bread and a drink of Kool-aid or water. The evening meal usually consists of boiled beans and corn bread. Sometimes boiled rice, dry peanut butter, or a canned meat substitute from the commodity program will supplement the evening meal.

These people, while not starving in the extreme sense of the word, are suffering from acute hunger. This hunger could be called starvation in that people's bodies actually are being denied proper sustenance, which causes the mortality rate of the [Negro] children to be much higher than that of whites, and which also shortens the life span of adults considerably. Medical doctors who work among these people say they never know the depth of their hunger for, from the time of birth on, they never have enough to eat.

Any consideration of hunger, in Mississippi or elsewhere, must take cognizance, as does the council's report, of the distribution of surplus foods. One-fifth of Mississippi's entire population is now being fed through the federal food distribution programs. But the too-seldom-recognized fact is that surplus foods were never intended to comprise full meals or adequate diets. Nevertheless, they have become almost the only source of food for hundreds of thousands of Americans. The meaning of this for nutrition and health can be perceived in the fact that the total value of the commodities distributed amounts to about $5 per person per month. They consist chiefly of flour, cornmeal, dry milk, and shortening. Only recently was the one can of meat per person per month added to the diet.

Appalling as this situation was, it became worse when a shift from surplus commodities to food stamps in just eight Mississippi counties in one year's time deprived 36,000 poor residents of their commodity allotments. The result simply had to be more hunger and more malnutrition since these people could not afford to buy food stamps to exchange for groceries.

By far the most impressive testimony on hunger was given to the Senate subcommittee by a group of six doctors who made a first-hand investigation of malnutrition and starvation in the Delta. Sponsored by the Field Foundation, the doctors comprised a distinguished panel of medical experts: Dr. Joseph Brenner, Medical Department, Massachusetts Institute of Technology; Dr. Robert Coles, Harvard University Health Service; Dr. Alan Mermann, Department of Pediatrics, Yale University; Dr. Milton J. E. Senn, Sterling Professor of Pediatrics, Yale University; Dr. Cyril Walwyn, Medical Adviser to Friends of the Children of Mississippi and a private practitioner in Mississippi;

and Dr. Raymond Wheeler, a private practioner of Charlotte, North Carolina.

Their report emerged as a unique document, unique in its fusion of professional and humanitarian shock and profound concern. Here is part of their findings on hunger among the Delta's children:

> We saw children whose nutritional and medical condition we can only describe as shocking—even to a group of physicians whose work involves daily confrontation with disease and suffering. In child after child we saw evidence of vitamin and mineral deficiencies; serious untreated skin infections and ulcerations; eye and ear diseases; also unattended bone diseases; the prevalence of bacterial and parasitic diseases as well as severe anemia with resulting loss of energy and ability to lead a normally active life; diseases of the heart and lung—requiring surgery—which have gone undiagnosed and untreated; epileptic and other neurological disorders; severe kidney ailments that in other children would warrant immediate hospitalization; and finally, in boys and girls in every county we visited, obvious evidence of severe malnutrition, with injury to the body's tissues—its muscles, bones, and skin as well as an associated psychological state of fatigue, listlessness, and exhaustion.
>
> We saw homes with children who are lucky to eat one meal a day—and that one inadequate so far as vitamins, minerals, or protein are concerned. We saw children who don't get to drink milk, don't get to eat fruit, green vegetables, or meat. They live on starches—grits, bread, Kool-aid. They are living under such primitive conditions that we found it hard to believe we were examining American children in the twentieth century.
>
> In some we saw children who are hungry and who are sick —children for whom hunger is a daily fact of life and sickness, in many forms, an inevitability. *We do not want to quibble over words, but "malnutrition" is not quite what we found, the boys and girls we saw were hungry—weak, in pain, sick, their lives are being shortened; they are, in fact, visibly and predictably losing their health, their energy, and their spirits. They are suffering from hunger and disease and directly or indirectly they are dying from them—which is exactly what "starvation" means.*

The charge of starvation was supported by all six of these eminent doctors.

In their individual testimony before the Senate Subcommittee, the doctors presented other observations and conclusions, some of them almost heartbreaking.

DR. WHEELER: "Only one of the [Delta] families I visited ever had milk at all and this was reserved for 'the sickliest' ones. One mother summed up the question of diet in a single, poignant sentence: 'These children go to bed hungry and get up hungry and don't ever know nothing else in between.' Thin arms, sunken eyes, lethargic behavior, and swollen bellies were everywhere to be seen."

DR. BRENNER: "What is it that makes these Negro children so vulnerable to diseases that ordinarily are no longer considered killers in the United States? These children are vulnerable because their bodily resistance is so low they don't have ability to cope with infections the way healthy children have. The main cause of lack of resistance is malnutrition. The food available to them lacks the vital components that are necessary to build healthy bodies that can develop resistance against disease. . . . I would estimate that among the many families that I saw and I visited, with 150 or 160 children, at least three-quarters of them get less than the vital amount of animal protein per day—at least three-quarters, and I think I am being very conservative. Increasing evidence has come from different countries to suggest that infants both before birth and after birth, deprived of the kinds of foods which are necessary for normal bodily growth, suffer not only visible damage to their bodies but also to the central nervous system, to the brain."

DR. COLES: "I would like to speak briefly about the psychiatric aspect of my work . . . I am describing in detail what it means for a child and his or her parents to be sick, more or less all the time, and hungry, more or less regularly. From all that one can learn, the aches and sores of the body become, for a child of four or five, more than a concrete physical factor of life; they bring in the child's mind a reflection of his worth and a judgment upon him and his family by the outside world. They ask themselves and others what they have done to be kept from the food they want or what they have done to deserve the pain they feel.

"In my experience with families in the Delta, their kind of life can produce a form of withdrawn, sullen behavior. I have seen some of the families I knew in the South go North and carry with them that state of mind and I am now working with them in Boston. They have more food, more welfare money, and, in the public hospitals of the Northern city, certain medical services. But one sees how persistently sickness and hunger in children live on into adults who doubt any offer, mistrust any goodness or favorable turn of events.

"I fear that we have among us now in this country hundreds of thousands of people who have literally grown up to be and learned to be tired, fearful, anxious, and suspicious . . . The children need food, the kind of food that will enable their bones to grow, their blood to function as it should, their vital organs to remain healthy, and their minds to stay alert. It is inconceivable to us that children at this stage of American history, and in the context of American wealth, continue to live like this in Mississippi, in Alabama, in Kentucky, in West Virginia, in the Southwest, and, indeed, carry this condition of life to all of our Northern cities."

Later I asked Dr. Coles, a vital young psychiatrist who has not become insensitized by repeated trips into the most poverty-stricken areas of the Deep South and Appalachia, how many children suffering from malnutrition live in the Delta region today.

"There is no way, at present, of knowing for certain," he replied. "There are thousands and thousands of children in the Delta we didn't see, out of sight, out of reach, out of mind, out of access to white doctors and Negro doctors. There must be betwen 50,000 and 100,000 children suffering from malnutrition in the Delta."

Dr. Coles agreed on the use of the word "starvation" rather than "malnutrition." "The kind of starvation we observed," he said, "is the kind of starvation in which the body is slowly consuming itself. The body is victimized by diseases which definitely can shorten life. We saw severe malnutrition, hunger, and starvation in the sense that the body is irretrievably going downhill."

I am convinced from what I saw that among the great number of Negroes who have moved from the Deep South to Northern ghettos are some who knew starvation in the South as children, and that this bitter experience makes some of them potential recruits for the riots in cities.

I wish to reemphasize, as would the doctors, that hunger, malnutrition, and slow starvation are not confined to the Deep South nor to any other part of the country. There is, certainly, widespread hunger and malnutrition in all the Negro ghettos, north and south.

Washington, D.C., for example, is no better nor any worse than any other American city, although undoubtedly, as the center of federal government, it should be better. One-third of the population of the nation's capital exists at little more than subsistence level.

Under the District of Columbia's Headstart program, for example, 4,200 children recently received physical examinations. Between 40 and 50 percent of these youngsters were found to have low hemoglobin counts, a condition (when not caused by infection) reflecting a food deficiency which produces nutritional anemia.

Deficient diets among Washington children are also indicated in the School Free Lunch Program which provides free lunches in elementary and secondary schools *only on application by the family, certifying need.* Nationally, a total of 11 percent of all schoolchildren receive free school lunches, but in Washington they are provided to 51 percent of all school youngsters.

Another index of deficient diets in the nation's capital is found in Public Assistance payments, which provide a maximum of $417 a month for a family of thirteen, including $228 for food, which comes to nineteen cents a meal for each member of the family.

The subcommittee's disclosures—preliminary as they are— of hundreds of thousands, perhaps millions, of hungry Americans have had two early results. The first was an unexpected public response; the second was the subcommittee's success in effecting a quick change in the Department of Agriculture's food stamp policies and in moving emergency legislation through the Senate.

Perhaps we should have anticipated the public's warm, sympathetic response to the revelations of hunger, but actually members of the subcommittee were surprised by the letters and telephone calls they received from concerned citizens. Some of the letters contained checks; mostly the writers inquired (as did the callers) where money and collections of food and clothing could be sent. Frequently the letters combined expressions of heartfelt solicitude with indignant comments on the affluent society that allowed penury and hunger to persist.

The way in which the food stamp program operated, particularly the cash payments required of poor families, was seen by the subcommittee as a major obstacle to alleviating hunger. Time and again, in Mississippi and in Washington, the subcommittee was told that many families could not afford the $2 per person a month that would buy them desperately needed food stamps worth much more when exchanged for commodities. A family of six, for example, would have to pay $12 a month for coupons exchangeable for $72 worth of food. Many families, we were told, went "months on end without seeing $12 all together."

Finally, after an impatient exchange of letters between the subcommittee and Secretary of Agriculture Orville Freeman, and appeals to the White House, the Department of Agriculture was induced to cut the cost of food stamps from $2 to fifty cents. This meant that the family of six that previously paid $12 for $72 worth of food would now pay $3. With other members of the subcommittee, I hope that even the fifty cents charge can be eliminated and stamps be made available to the needy free of cost.

In addition, the subcommittee persuaded Sargent Shriver's Office of Economic Opportunity to institute an emergency $1,000,000 four-month Food Stamp Loan Program in twenty counties in seven Southern states. This provides the needy with cash loans ranging from $2 to $12 a month, depending on the size of the family. It now makes possible the purchase of food stamps by thousands of families that previously could not afford them. By the end of the year it is expected that 30,000 families (with an average of four to a family) will have obtained OEO loans for food stamps in these Deep South counties.

Emergency legislation was the next step, and for once the normally laggard machinery of the U.S. Senate moved with dispatch. On Friday, July 21, Senator John Stennis, Mississippi Democrat, introduced a bill proposing a $10,000,000 appropriation to provide, on an emergency basis, "food and medical services to any individual in any state whenever such action is required to prevent the loss of such individual's life or to avoid suffering caused by lack of food or medical attention." By late afternoon, seven other Senators and I, all members of the Labor and Public Welfare Committee, had joined as co-sponsors of the bill and had pledged the speediest possible action on the proposal.

On the following Tuesday the bill was unanimously approved by the full committee but not before the $10,000,000 appropriation was increased to $25,000,000 for the first year and $50,-000,000 for the second, and an amendment added to initiate the first comprehensive study in the nation's history "of the incidence and location of serious hunger and malnutrition and health problems incident thereto. . . ." The bill sailed through the Senate the next day without a single dissenting vote.

I am hopeful that the new war on poverty legislation—which includes additional funds of $2.8 billion approved by the Senate Committee on Labor and Public Welfare for a series of improving amendments to the existing Economic Opportunity Act —will make a major contribution toward the abolition of poverty and hunger. By strengthening the Job Corps, the Neighborhood Youth Corps, adult work-training, aid to small business, community action programs, assistance to migrant workers, rural loans, Headstart, and VISTA—by making these programs more effective, I believe we can do much to raise American living standards and begin the long-overdue eradication of poverty, hunger, and malnutrition.

As the long hot summer of 1967, with its unprecedented civil disorders, bloodshed, and looting, recedes into history, the nation and its leaders find themselves reassessing their goals and priorities. Remembering the devastated neighborhoods, the burned-out homes and shops, in nearly thirty cities across the country, I found the words of the philosopher Seneca, 2,000 years ago, echoing meaningfully down to our day: "A hungry people listens not to reason, nor cares for justice, nor is bent by any prayers."

Now, as never before, reason and justice dictate that we devote our purpose and our nation's resources to the goal that there shall no longer be hungry people in an America of overflowing abundance.

ROBERT COLES

PSYCHIATRISTS AND THE POOR*

PSYCHIATRISTS have to know a lot about what their patients are thinking and about what they themselves are thinking. In the United States they are called in consultation on so many problems that one would suppose they know a good deal more than they sometimes do. The demands upon them are enormous, and some of them inappropriate. Unlike the work of their friends in many other fields, their work is still to be satisfactorily defined, and information badly needed by others from them is sometimes simply not to be had at all.

Psychiatrists should not be particularly blamed for their predominantly middle-class clientele or for their increasing concern with the certification of their position in medical centers and wealthy suburbs. Although some people think of them as gods, there is ample proof to the contrary. Psychiatrists are all clearly human, and in America clearly doctors. Whatever general criticism can be made of them is also applicable to others in American professional life. Lawyers are now beginning to see how hard it is for the poor to obtain "equal protection under the law," and for the first time our highest courts are prodding them in this regard. Educators are troubled by their failure to reach

* From *Atlantic Monthly*, July 1964. Copyright © 1964, by the Atlantic Monthly Company, Boston, Massachusetts. Reprinted by permission.

millions of potentially educable, even gifted children. The fact that money purchases the best medical care and that the want of it frequently consigns one to the worst is a fact of life throughout the nation. When psychiatric goods and services follow similar patterns of distribution, they are simply conforming to the way our society is set up.

There have been important advances in what is now called social psychiatry. Before the term came into popular professional use, Anna Freud had done her moving and courageous work with English children under the Nazi blitz, establishing the practical value of psychoanalytic advice in a serious social crisis. In America a few bold spirits were intent on finding out how our isolated and rejected Indians survived individually, with their separate culture. In the thirties, Sol Ginsberg, a compassionate New York psychiatrist, studied the reactions of the unemployed to their grim and unnerving lot; and years before the 1954 Supreme Court decision, Erik Erikson had described the effects of segregation on the Negroes in America.

These pioneering efforts were followed by three major studies which stand out as landmarks: the Yale study by A. Hollingshead and F. C. Redlich of the relationship between social class and mental illness, and the two studies which have come from the social psychiatry unit of the Cornell Medical School—the Stirling County Study of Psychiatric Disorder and Sociocultural Environment and the Midtown Manhattan Study, whose findings were published in book form under the title *Mental Health in the Metropolis*. These carefully documented researches have all been concerned with the relationship of class—social and economic background—to mental illness, and with the incidence of mental illness in cities and towns. What we learn from these reports is revealing about psychiatrists, their patients, and our society. There is, in fact, a self-scrutiny, an honest self-appraisal in these investigations which represents the very best tradition of scholarly research.

The Yale study, published under the title *Social Class and Mental Illness*, concerns itself with the relationship between social class and both psychiatric symptoms and care, and is a sociological and psychiatric study of New Haven. It was done with scrupulous concern for statistical validity. The class structure of the city was analyzed and described. The patterns of mental illness and its treatment are shown. The book reveals that poor people tend to have a higher incidence of diagnosed psychoses, the most serious form of mental disease, and also receive radically different forms of medical and psychiatric care for their difficulties. Whereas the wealthy and the well-to-do are more likely to be treated with individual psychotherapy, purchased privately or secured at clinics which largely provide for the middle classes, the poor are usually sent to hospitals and, once there, receive the less humane treatment of electric shock or drugs.

The authors of the Yale study are not content merely to emphasize these cold-blooded facts and the influence of money on psychiatric diagnoses and treatment. They examine the interesting relationship of the psychiatrist, as a middle-class citizen, to the large number of poor patients he may be called to see and subsequently—persuaded by forces in his own life—reject or diagnose in ways reflecting more about his life than their illness. These two social scientists, Dr. Hollingshead and Dr. Redlich, have the courage and honesty to face directly the serious differences between psychiatry and the rest of medicine. An infection is an infection, and rich or poor respond to the same dosage of penicillin. Mental illness is not so easy to treat, and the psychiatrist cannot depend upon pills, vaccines, or intravenous solutions, all nicely free of biases of personality and prejudices of class.

In a sense, most of the findings of the Yale study confirm the difficult problems of psychiatry as a profession under heavy demands in American life. The calls for it are everywhere; the respect for its capabilities is sometimes even too generous. The hopes for its future ability to cure mental illness and even change future generations through its understanding of child behavior and growth are certainly high. Yet, as Redlich and Hollingshead point out at the end of their book, there are too few good therapists, meeting all too many patients; the poor, the culturally or socially exiled, are frequently hard for many psychiatrists to understand, hence suitably treat; large numbers of patients therefore find their way to those sad and sometimes outrageous back wards of state institutions. Or they may run the risk of inadequate evaluation and hasty, basically faulty treatment. Such are the troubles with which the poor and their society, including its psychiatrists, must cope.

The apathy of the poor needs no psychiatric study for its proof, nor do their widespread dependency, their common lack of tidiness, thrift, and respect for the legal and moral codes embraced by their "betters." What is needed, the Yale investigators emphasize, is careful studies of incidence, of prevalence of disease in communities, of attempted correlation of such occurrence with as large a number of environmental facts as possible. The more we know of the external forces involved in mental illness, the more we understand the obviously complex connection between individual and social pathology.

The Cornell unit in social psychiatry has taken up where its brother group in New Haven suggested the need was greatest. Its work is both extensive and impressive. Its intention, exemplified by such studies as the Yorkville one in Manhattan and the Stirling County one in Nova Scotia, has been to find out how many people actually are mentally ill in a large city, or a small town, or a village, and who those people are, by race, religion, occupation, education, marital status, and a host of significant social and economic variables.

One of their crucial findings ties in all too neatly with the Yale study: social disorganization is associated with a significantly higher incidence of mental illness. And, in any case, the incidence of mental illness may well be higher than the statistics indicate. Among the poor it frequently goes unrecorded or unrecognized. Indeed, the gist of the Cornell studies is that psychiatric symptoms bear substantial relationship to various social, cultural, and economic conditions. Worse, among large numbers of poor these symptoms abound and tend to be handed down to children as a kind of grim social inheritance, making it harder and harder for each generation to escape the bondage rising out of the hopelessness and shallowness of life in the rural or city slum.

What these statistics and research studies with their abstractions tell us, all too many testify to in their daily lives—lives hobbled with joblessness, with uselessness, with arbitrary unkindness or contempt at the hands of others. Millions in such straits know constant mental hurt, emotional suffering, despair of the soul without any possibility of help. Their troubles are both real and imaginary—hunger breeds suspicion, hate breeds fear and retaliatory hate—and relief for both kinds of troubles is often inadequate. It is an ironic sorrow for many well-intentioned people in the social sciences that they know these facts and are unable to do much to correct them.

The irony revealed by both the Yale and Cornell studies is that psychiatrists are frequently out of touch with the conditions which help create their potentially sickest patients. The incidence of paranoid schizophrenia among Negroes is high, probably an example of social reality kindling medical ruin. How many Negroes in the South can go to strictly segregated psychiatric facilities and feel secure and wanted enough to discuss their innermost thoughts and fears? We talk about segregation, by custom, law, or fact; we easily denounce it. A state of affairs which renders a mentally disturbed Negro, wherever he lives, unable to seek or secure competent medical and psychiatric care is a personal tragedy, not an abstract injustice, for millions of individuals—and not the least for the doctors concerned.

I have seen some segregated Negro "state hospitals" in the South, and all too many seriously disturbed Negro children, youths, and adults in Northern cities. The mother of one of the Negro children who is pioneering desegregation in his state had received the care of that state's mental hospital system. Curious, I went there for a visit. She had called the place "that hell." I found her description a bit subdued. The real hell for anyone, especially when troubled, is loneliness. It is hellish to be mentally ill, additionally so to be confined and largely ignored, particularly at the hands of white officials who have little respect for one's basic human dignity. "Maybe I could talk with *some* white doctors; I'm not saying I can't," the mother said, "but I sometimes wonder—and anyway, even if I could, they never have wanted to talk with me." She suffered from periodic depressions, crippling while they lasted. She could be reached, be helped, at least in theory. Her name is indeed legion, just as the Cornell social sicentists suggested when they gave one of their books the title *My Name Is Legion*.

Those pockets of poverty whose existence is increasingly acknowledged are also pockets of many kinds of psychopathology, mostly untreated. In some instances—with migratory farm workers, Indians, and many of the Appalachian whites—the people are not merely poor, not only beyond the reach or even ken of medical or psychiatric attention, but are really striking examples of what social scientists call "subcultures." They mean by such a term groups of people living significantly apart from the rest of us in habits, customs, and beliefs, so that even though we speak a common language, even though we share a national history and citizenship with them and need the same goods and services, they see a different world or have different assumptions about our world.

Such people may confuse, then alarm, and finally anger us, doctors included. Their experience has not been ours. We are provoked by their laziness or various forms of easy living. They, in turn, are at a loss to understand, given what is possible for them, what we would have them do. "I tried," a white hillbilly told me, and he repeated the words, "I tried to get a job for a long time here, and then I even went up to Chicago, but there wasn't anything to do, and so we figured we'd rather die here where our kin come from."

There was no question in my mind that two of his children needed the help of a child psychiatrist. One was irritable, still wet the bed at ten, was much too mean to herself (picking at her scalp) and to her all too many brothers and sisters as well. Another child, a boy of twelve, was deeply, deadly silent and had been so for a long time. Regional sentimentality aside, it is a hard life the poor live anywhere, and one filled with high risks for diseases of the body and mind. This is so in Appalachia, in spite of those lovely pictures of quaint rural pathways along fetching hills whose inhabitants, always smiling, sing their specially pure ballads and appear to be our last nostalgic contact with our pioneer ancestors.

What do they do, these millions of our poor? What happens to their neuroses and psychoses? They live with them and die with them or of them. In cities, violence, vagrancy, alcoholism, addiction, apathy, high suicide rates, high murder rates, high delinquency rates bespeak the hopelessness which becomes depression, the doubts which become paranoia, the confusions which

MAN AGAINST POVERTY

become addiction, the frantic attempt to make sense of a sense-less world which becomes drunkenness or sudden irrational ferocity. In rural areas, on farms or reservations, the same human scene can be found: retarded children, epileptic children kept, and their limitations accepted, not as possible challenges to be overcome, but as the grim reminders of an all-too-familiar fate; disgruntled, liquored parents venting their frustrations and discouragement in angry feuds and spells of silence or inaction which in many of us would warrant immediate hospitalization.

The solutions to some of these problems will come in part with the recognition of them, followed by laws which authorize more money and more trained personnel to deal with them. As for the problem of the limited relationship between psychiatrists and some of the neediest of our mentally ill, the Yale and Cornell studies emphasize the necessity to look closely at the training of psychiatrists and those in associated professions. They suggest changes in training programs, a fresh look at how to get more suitably trained and better motivated recruits.

· · ·

Yet, even with more planning and some new professional flexibility from social scientists, there will remain serious prob-lems for both the poor and our American psychiatrists. Psychia-trists cannot solve many difficulties really created by unfair social and economic conditions, and they had better know that. . . .

The public must become more informed about just what psychiatrists can and what they cannot do. The flashy, the glib, the dogmatic, and sometimes even the absurd and commercial have plagued and tarnished some areas of American psychiatry, as they have touched American life generally, fulfilling Freud's premonition of just such a possibility. For the most part, Ameri-can psychiatrists are dedicated, serious, and socially concerned citizens. If, like others, they have not freed themselves of all of the contaminants supplied by their culture, they have at least been willing to examine their own limitations while learning facts that are hard to live with, or, for that matter, live by.

The poor neither know about us nor can they afford our expensive care. And often we do not know about the poor and seem little concerned about getting to know them. These are the facts, plain to see but not so easy to change. Nevertheless, the medical profession and its several specialties will have to serve the large numbers who need them most and can afford them least. To do this will require effort in changing curricula and effort in living up to the old but sometimes forgotten ideals of what a doctor should be. The Yale study is even more explicit: doctors largely come with middle-class views when they approach the poor and usually have little interest in going beyond those views, many of them unsympathetic or outright antagonistic to lower-class people and their kind of living. I have seen many bright young men and women who will never get to college, let alone medical school, because of who they are and their environmental handicaps.

Some of them might become doctors and psychiatrists if they could get financial assistance and continue their education. And then they might help their own people and their profession to achieve an urgently needed mutual understanding.

B. CASES IN POINT

INTRODUCTION

ALTHOUGH many Americans have been exposed to sociological analyses and statistics about poverty, these treatments have not dealt with the actual human experience of being poor. In this section the reader will find a closer look at the "other America." It becomes abundantly clear that poverty is not just unemployment statistics, average annual incomes, or comparative rates of infant mortality, but rather human beings: suffering, going hungry, dying needlessly, and very likely seeking desperate solutions.

Kenneth Clark in "The Cry of the Ghetto" lets the poor of Harlem speak for themselves; about their fears, their agonies, and their hates. They provide a vivid introduction to those who live outside the boundary of "The Great Society."

Impoverished peoples are found in all regions of the United States. Harry Caudill's "The Permanent Poor" is a moving account of rural poverty in Kentucky, Tennessee, and West Virginia, that province known as Appalachia. Paul Jacobs provides a chilling description of a typical day in the life of a California "stoop laborer." To better understand these workers, Jacobs himself hires out as a day laborer. The American Indian, frequently overlooked in the United States, is graphically described by Stan Steiner in a shocking account of this most deprived minority group. The August 1965 riot in the Watts district of Los Angeles was the forerunner of 1967 violence in Newark and Detroit. Novelist Thomas Pynchon visited Watts a year after the uprising and reports on the generally unchanged conditions.

KENNETH B. CLARK	THE CRY OF THE GHETTO*

A LOT OF TIMES, when I'm working, I become as despondent as hell and I feel like crying. I'm not a man, none of us are men! I don't own anything. I'm not a man enough to own a store; none of us are.
—Man, age about 30

You know the average young person out here don't have a job, man, they don't have anything to do. They don't have any alternative, you know, but to go out there and try to make a living for themselves. Like when you come down to the Tombs down there, they're down there for robbing and breaking in. They want to know why you did it and where you live, but you have to live. You go down to the employment agency and you can't get a job. They have you waiting all day, but you can't get a job. They don't have a job for you. Yet you have to live. I'm ready to do anything anyone else is ready to do—because I want to live—I want to live. No one wants to die. I want to live.
—Drug addict, male, age 30

If a man qualifies, it should be first come, first serve. You understand what I mean? Regardless of whether we're black or white, we all have families! It should be first come, first serve. But that's not how they do you! If you're black, you're automatically turned down on a lot of jobs. They'll take your application, but no sooner than you walk out of the office, or wherever it is, they take the application and put it in the wastebasket, and tell you they'll let you know in a couple of weeks.
—Man, age about 24

* From *Dark Ghetto* by Kenneth B. Clark. Copyright © 1965 by Kenneth B. Clark. Reprinted by permission of Harper & Row, Publishers.

No one with a mop can expect respect from a banker, or an attorney, or men who create jobs, and all you have is a mop. Are you crazy? Whoever heard of integration between a mop and a banker? —Man, age about 38

The way the Man has us, he has us wanting to kill one another. Dog eat dog, amongst us! He has us, like we're so hungry up here, he has us up so tight! Like his rent is due, my rent is due. It's Friday. The Man wants sixty-five dollars. If you are three days over, or don't have the money; like that, he wants to give you a dispossess! Take you to court! The courts won't go along with you, they say get the money or get out! Yet they don't tell you how to get the money, you understand? They say get the money and pay the Man, but they don't say how to get it. Now, if you use illegal means to obey his ruling to try to get it—which he's not going to let you do—if you use illegal means to pay your bills according to his ruling—he will put you in jail.
—Man, age 31

They are raising the rents so high, like that, with a job, the menial jobs that we have or get, the money we will receive—we won't be able to pay the rent! So where we going to go? They are pushing us further, and further, and further—out of Harlem.
—Man, age 31

If you could get onto the ninth floor of the Tombs, you would see for yourself. They are lying there like dogs, vomiting and what not, over one another. It is awful. It smells like a pigpen up there. If you look, you'll see nothing but Spanish. And the black man. You'll seldom see a white man. When you do, he is from a very poor group. They are twenty years old, looking like they were forty. —Drug addict, male, age about 37

I want to go to the veins.
You want to do what?

I want to go to the veins.
You want to go to the veins; you mean you want to get high?
Yeah.
Why do you want to get high, man?
To make me think.
You can't think without getting high?
No.

Discrimination is even in the school I attend right now. I know my teacher is very prejudiced because I have certain questions that have to be answered for my knowledge, but he will never answer. He would always call on a little white boy to give the answer. I told him one night, to his face, that if he didn't want to answer my questions just tell me and I would leave. There are always other teachers. He didn't say anything. He just looked at me and figured I was going to—so he said, "Well, maybe next time." There is no next time—this is the time and I'm not taking second best from any white man.　　　　—Boy, age 17

Well, the gang, they look for trouble, and then if they can't find no trouble, find something they can do, find something they can play around. Go in the park, find a bum, hit him in the face, pee in his face, kick him down, then chase him, grab him and throw him over the fence.　　　　—Boy, age 15

The conditions here are the way they are because of white domination of this community, and when that changes, as is being attempted here, by these [Black] Nationalists, or by any other nationalist groups, or by the Muslims; when they can unite and change these conditions, change the white domination for black domination, the conditions will change. —Man, age 28

Why in the hell—now this is more or less a colored neighborhood—why do we have so many white cops? As if we got to have somebody white standing over us. Not that I am prejudiced or anything, but I can't understand why we have to have so many white cops! Now if I go to a white neighborhood, I'm not going to see a lot of colored cops in no white neighborhood, standing guard over the white people. I'm not going to see that; and I know it, and I get sick and tired of seeing so many white cops, standing around. —Woman, age 38

My wife was even robbed coming back from the store. They tried to snatch her pocketbook, and she came upstairs crying to me. What could I do? Where was the police? Where is the protection? —Man, age about 50

The white cops, they have a damn sadistic nature. They are really a sadistic type of people and we, I mean me, myself, we don't need them here in Harlem. We don't need them! They don't do the neighborhood any good. They deteriorate the neighborhood. They start more violence than any other people start. They start violence, that's right. A bunch of us could be playing some music, or dancing, which we have as an outlet for ourselves. We can't dance in the house, we don't have clubs or things like that. So we're out on the sidewalk, right on the sidewalk; we might feel like dancing, or one might want to play something on his horn. Right away here comes a cop. "You're disturbing the peace!" No one has said anything, you understand; no one has made a complaint. Everyone is enjoying themselves. But here comes one cop, and he'll want to chase everyone. And gets mad. I mean, he gets mad! We aren't mad. He comes into the neighborhood, aggravated and mad.
—Man, age about 33

Last night, for instance, the officer stopped some fellows on 125th Street, car No. ———, that was the number of the car, and because this fellow spoke so nicely for his protection and his rights, the officer said, "All right, everybody get off the street or inside!" Now, it's very hot. We don't have air-conditioned apartments in most of these houses up here, so where are we going if we get off the streets? We can't go back in the house because we almost suffocate. So we sit down on the curb, or stand on the sidewalk, or on the steps, things like that, till the wee hours of the morning, especially in the summer when it's too hot to go up. Now where were we going? But he came out with his nightstick and wants to beat people on the head, and wanted to—he arrested one fellow. The other fellow said, "Well, I'll move, but you don't have to talk to me like a dog." I think we should all get together—everybody—all get together and every time one draws back his stick to do something to us, or hits one of us on the head, take the stick and hit *him* on *his* head, so he'll know how it feels to be hit on the head, or kill him, if necessary. Yes, kill him, if necessary. That's how I feel. There is no other way to deal with this man. The only way you can deal with him is the way he has been dealing with us.

—Man, about 35

Everything is a big laugh in this dump unless you kill a cop. Then they don't laugh. I had a cop walk up to me a couple of days ago. You know what he said? "Move over." They have the street blocked up and he's going to tell me you can go around them. I said, "Hell if I do." He said, "What did you say?" I said, "Hell if I do." He said, "I'll slap your black ass." I told him, "That's one day you'll know if you're living or dying." He just looked at me. I said, "Why don't you say it? You want to say nigger so bad."

—Man, age 21

The flag here in America is for the white man. The blue is for justice; the fifty white stars you see in the blue are for the fifty white states; and the white you see in it is the White House. It represents white folks. The red in it is the white man's blood —he doesn't even respect your blood, that's why he will lynch you, hang you, barbecue you, and fry you. —Man, age about 35

A stereotyped Negro you see him in the movies or on TV, walking down the levee with a watermelon in his hand, his shiny teeth, and his straw hat on his head. That's the one you see on television, yassuh, yassuh, and the showboys come in Stepin

Fetchit, because that's what every Negro is associated with. To me, the middle-class Negro and the upper-class Negro is one that's trying to get away from that stereotype. They're the ones trying to get away.   —Man, age 18

I don't see why we've got to always look up to the white man's life. That's what we've been exposed to, you know. Be like the white man. I think we have to have criteria of our own. They had "Amos and Andy" on radio, they were done by white men. You hear the fellows saying, "Oh, I'm going to get me a white broad." We should form our own criteria. We should try and have some more people like Martin Luther King, like James Baldwin. We can send some draftsmen to school, some engineers; people can come back and build a city for Negroes to live in, or you know, not just for Negroes but for Negroes and anyone else who wants to live there. Why do we always have to get up—come up to the white man's level? We struggle like the devil to get up there, and we hardly ever do it. Why can't we form our own level?   —Girl, age 15

I have been uncomfortable being a Negro. I came from the South—Kentucky, on the Ohio River line—and I have had white people spit on me in my Sunday suit.   —Woman

The main thing is to know just where he comes from, knowing about his race. The main thing. He will then disregard every time he turns on the television that he sees a white face. That won't mean anything to him; it will be just another program because he will know that the conditions of the way of this world are based on only the white man's psychology, that makes these things. It won't be because this man is better fitted than he is on the television; it is because he dominates, he capitalizes, he corrupts.   —Man, age 35

First stop wearing the white man's clothes. Dress in your ancestral clothes. Learn your history and your heritage. This is part

KENNETH B. CLARK

115

of my culture and I'm proud. Wear your clothes! Put on your *abdaba*, your *dashiki* and your *fella*. You can do it.
—Woman, age about 45

The Honorable Elijah Mohammed teaches, but the only thing is, some of our people still don't take that old blue-eyed, hook-nosed picture of Christ off their wall—take it down and step on it. These people have been exploiting us for years.
—Man, age about 35

Hear me now, hear me. Thy kingdom come, thy will be done, on earth as it is in Heaven. The kingdom is ours, black man's kingdom. We want our own God, our own paradise, our own joys on this earth, and if we are not getting that, then something must be wrong somewhere, so with all of your Gospel and all your preaching, if you cannot benefit the children, it has no value.
—Man, age about 50

Churches don't mean us no good. We've been having churches all our lives under the same conditions, and look at the condition we're still in. The church must not have meant anything. See, when you go to church you don't learn how to read and write, and count, at church. You learn that in school. See what I mean? So what good the churches doing us? They are not doing us any good! You could build some factories or something in Harlem and give our people some work near home. That would do us more good than a church. —Man, age about 45

The preacher is a hustler. He creates a system for people to believe in that makes faggots, homosexuals, and lesbians out of the population of the black people, and this is exactly what whitey wants him to do. If you keep the damn preachers out of it, we'd solve our whole problem, just like the NAACP and the CORE over here in Brooklyn now; they don't want no part of the medicine, so that's it. But I'm a U-Pad member of the National Black Nationalists, and that's all I have to say. I don't go with this. His members that are here can believe him, they can fall behind or whatsoever. The only thing he wants—you never see a rabbi ride in a Cadillac, you never see a Jew rabbi, a charity rabbi, ride in nothing. They walk—They're doing a big enough job in the church, we don't need any leaders out here. In fact, we need to get rid of preachers like this because they are the very first ones who are going to sell us down the creek like he has done, like ministers have been doing over and over again. And incidentally, there was a big crook over in Brooklyn who sold everybody out on the picket line.

—Man, age 35

We don't want any bloodshed if we can help it, but if there has to be a little bloodletting, well and good. But this is only the beginning—what happened here today. Our next big step is the Harlem Police Department—we want black captains and we're going to have them. I've been fighting for dozens of years here in Harlem, where the so-called leaders play—Uncle Tom—play politics and let the people starve. You have district leaders here that draw a big fat salary. You can't hardly walk the street for trash. You have captains here—district captains and what not—all kinds of leaders here in Harlem. You never see them until election. —Woman, age about 30

I think there's a great lack of offensive direction and most of the adults have, more or less, succumbed to the situation and have decided, what the hell can I do? This is the attitude; that we can do nothing, so leave it alone. People think you're always going to be under pressure from the white man and he owns and runs everything, and we are so dependent on him that there's nothing I can do. This is the general impression I've gotten from most of the adults in Harlem. —Girl, age 15

It's got to get better. It can't get worse—it's got to get better, and they'll open up. They have to open up because they will find themselves going down all over the world, not only here.

It's not just us picketing that forced them to do this; all over the world people are talking about American imperialism, and it's forcing them to do all these things. Because whether I walk the line or not, whoever walks the line that has a black face is walking the line for me. Whether they are walking in Alabama, Arizona, Mississippi, or wherever they're walking. And there isn't anything for the Man to do but begin giving us an equal chance if he wants to save himself, because he's going down and we're the only ones that are holding him up.

—Man, age about 45

All right, so you get into the school and you get your rights, but in the whole scope of the black man in America, how can you accomplish anything by doing this? Yes, all right, you are accepted into Woolworth's; you fought and got your heads beat in. But what do your children think of you? Do you have any economic or political power? The people like you who're going into Greenwood, Mississippi, say, where the people are living—you are all dependent. It's unthinkable. The people have nothing. At this point they are living on things that are being sent to them from New York, Chicago, and other places in the United States. Do you know how much money we spend on foreign aid while here in the United States we people are starving?

—Man, age 18, and girl, age 15

When the time comes, it is going to be too late. Everything will explode because the people they live under tension now; they going to a point where they can't stand it no more. When they get to that point. . . . They want us to go to Africa, they say.

That would be the best thing they would want in the world because then they could get all of us together. All they would have to do is drop one bomb and we're dead.—Men, ages 30 to 35

I would like to see the day when my people have dignity and pride in themselves as black people. And when this comes about, when they realize that we are capable of all things, and can do anything under the sun that a man can do, then all these things will come about—equality, great people, presidents—everything.   —Man, age 19

I would like to be the first Negro president. —Boy, age about 17

HARRY M.
CAUDILL

THE PERMANENT

POOR* The Lesson

of Eastern Kentucky

The Cumberland Plateau of Kentucky is one of the great natural resource regions of the American continent. Industrialists bought up its great wealth three-quarters of a century ago and soon after 1900 commenced the large-scale extraction of its timber and minerals. When the development of the eastern Kentucky coalfields began, mining was largely a manual pursuit. Mining machines were displacing mules and ponies, and electricity was making it possible to do an increasing number of tasks with electric power rather than muscle power. Nevertheless, some of the undercutting of coal, much of the drilling, and practically all of the loading into cars were done by armies of grit-blackened miners. Industrial wages enticed thousands of mountaineers to turn from the plow and hoe to the pick and shovel. Hordes of Negroes were induced away from the cotton rows of Georgia, the Carolinas, Tennessee, Mississippi, and Alabama and forsook plantation life for the mines. Shiploads of Europeans were brought to the southern coalfield. The extraction of the region's mineral wealth was undertaken in the atmosphere of a tremendous industrial boom.

The Depression destroyed the coalfield's prosperity, but the

* From *Atlantic Monthly*, June 1964. Copyright © 1964, by the Atlantic Monthly Company, Boston, Massachusetts. Reprinted by permission.

Second World War revived it, and for a few years the boom returned and the miner was again a useful and honored citizen. The coal industry depended upon his skill and courage, and steel production, electric-power generation, and other basic industries were dependent upon coal. The collapse of the war and of the postwar boom is now history, and we have an opportunity to reflect upon the social, political, and economic consequences that result when a modernized industry is able to cast aside three-quarters of its workmen within the span of a decade.

In the postwar years technologists were able to design and manufacture machines of remarkable power and efficiency. Their genius was nowhere better demonstrated than in the coal industry. Devices were developed for boring directly back into the face of the coal seam, and chewing out immense quantities of the mineral, thus eliminating the need to undercut or blast the seam. Simultaneously, the conveyor belt displaced the tracks, mining locomotives, and strings of cars in many mines. Roof bolting made its appearance. This method of supporting the roof eliminated the need for wooden props and proved most effective. A single mechanical loading machine could load more coal than two dozen hardworking shovelers.

Machines were costly, but investment capital was plentiful. The mine operators borrowed from the banks and mechanized and automated the mines and tipples to a remarkable degree. Big, amply financed operations bought up their small competitors. Many inefficient and nearly worked-out pits suspended operations altogether. Thus in a few years the fragmented and archaic coal industry became surprisingly modern and technologically advanced. The operators were delighted. Corporations that were bankrupt only a few years before now basked in a sustained new prosperity. For example, Consolidation Coal Company, which had been in receivership, paid off all its obligations and acquired a controlling interest in Chrysler Corporation.

While a new optimism pervaded the offices of the automated and mechanized companies, disaster befell thousands of the men who had depended for so long upon the old industry. By the thousands they found the scrip offices and payroll windows closed in their faces. Mining companies for which they and their fathers had worked, in some instances for two generations, simply vanished altogether. Some three-fourths of eastern Kentucky's miners found themselves without work. They had become the victims of a materialistic social order which venerates efficiency and wealth above all other things and largely disregards social and human consequences. When they were no longer needed, their employers dropped them as a coal miner might have thrown away the scrip coins of a bankrupt company.

The legions of industrial outcasts were left with three choices. They could leave the area and find work elsewhere if employment of any kind could be found. Many thousands followed this course, and the population of the mining counties subsided dramatically. A third of the people fled from the shadow of starvation.

They could remain within the region and attempt to live by mining coal from the thin seams not monopolized by the big and highly efficient operations. These men could operate small "dog-hole" mines with little equipment and trifling capital, pitting their arms and backs against the tireless machines of their big competitors. They were goaded to desperation by the fact that in a camp house or a creek shanty a wife and five to ten children depended upon them for clothes and bread. They had been educated for the mines at a time when little formal education was required for that calling. Thus, in the contest with the big coal corporations they could contribute little except their muscles and their will. Thousands entered these small mines, often "gang working" as partners and sharing the meager profits at paydays.

In the third situation was the miner who for one reason or another could not or would not leave the area, and found that however hard he toiled in the small mines his income was too meager to provide for the needs of his household. He and his family became charges of the government. Federal and state agencies came to his relief with a wide variety of cash and commodity doles. He was confined to a kind of dull, bleak reservation-existence reminiscent of that imposed by military fiat on the reservation Indians of the Western plains.

Living by welfare, without work and without purpose save

existence, these numerous mountaineers settled down to while away the years and await developments.

The men who left the region for the great cities of the North and Middle West did not always find smooth sailing. The rapid process of industrial modernization which had first, and so dramatically, waved its wand across the eastern Kentucky coalfield had penetrated into the immense industrial complexes of the nation's cities. Assembly lines which had traditionally required hundreds of swarming workmen were reorganized, and wonderfully efficient machines were introduced into the automobile and other great manufacturing industries. In many instances, these machines were guided by sensitive electronic masters which, with belts of punched plastic and electric current, could impose unerring and immediate obedience.

In some respects, to be sure, eastern Kentucky is unique. Its people were dependent for fifty years on but a single industry, and, remarkably, they were an industrial people living in a rural rather than an urban setting. The coal industry, like extractive industries generally, invested little of its profits back in the region and allowed its communities to maintain schools of only the most rudimentary sort. It created an environment which left its workmen almost totally dependent upon their employers for bread and leadership, then provided only a small measure of the former and practically none of the latter. Nevertheless, the collapse of coal as a mass hirer of men left in the Kentucky mountains a splendid case study of the social and political implications arising from the displacement of men by machines.

Government at all levels was wholly unprepared for the dramatic developments that ensued. To be sure, these developments were a logical outgrowth of the continuing industrial revolution, which, once set in motion, appears to be destined to carry us inevitably toward a day when a few people and many machines will do the work for a leisurely population of consumers. But between the first spinning jenny and the distant utopia lie many pitfalls, some of which yawn before us today.

In short, government in our democratic society proved practically bankrupt of ideas when confronted with this new challenge. Hoping against hope that expansion in other industries would eventually absorb the displaced miners, government agencies waited. When the stranded miner had exhausted his unemployment insurance benefits and his savings, when he had come to the ragged edge of starvation and was cloaked in bewilderment and frustration, government came to his rescue with the dole. It arranged to give him a bag of cheese, rice, cornmeal, beef, butter, and dried milk solids at intervals, and in most instances to send him a small check. Having thus contrived to keep the miner and his family alive, the government lost interest in him. Appropriations were made from time to time for his sustenance, but little thought was given to his spirit, his character, his manhood. He was left to dry-rot in the vast paleface reservation created for his perpetuation in his native hills.

And, inevitably, he fell prey to the politicians who dispense the bread and money by which he lives. Coal mining and thirty years of subservience to the scrip window had already done much to impair the mountaineer's ability to adapt well to rapidly changing circumstances. He had dwelt too long as a kind of industrial serf in company-owned houses, on company-owned streets, in company-owned towns. For too long the company had buffered him from the swift-flowing social and economic tides swirling in the world outside his narrow valleys. When his employers cast him aside, he still possessed only a single valuable remnant of his birthright—the ballot. He was essential to the politicians because he could vote, so he was placed in a sort of suspended animation in which he came fully to life only at election time. He became increasingly dependent upon the political machines that ran his counties. He accepted the food doles and the welfare checks and ratified the arrangement by voting for the men and women who thus sustained him. The politicians expanded their operations into other fields where public funds could make the difference between life and death. In all too many counties they captured the school systems, thereby acquiring large new sums to be dispensed as patronage. The positions of schoolteacher, bus driver, lunchroom director, truant officer, and a multitude of others were treated as so many plums to be dispensed to the acquiescent, the obedient, and the meek. The union of school politics and welfare politics resulted in a formidable prodigy indeed. Its power was quickly recognized at Frankfort and Washington. New political pacts were made, and a wide range of state jobs were placed at the disposal of the local overlords. Thus their power became virtually complete.

Today in many eastern Kentucky counties political machines of remarkable efficiency are to be found. Their effectiveness surpasses Tammany Hall at its best. In a typical county the school board and state agencies control the biggest payrolls. The politicians who run them can also reach and influence the many small merchants, automobile dealers, and service-station operators with whom they do business. Thus they are masters of the majority of those who still work for a living.

The state and federal governments act as tax-collecting enterprises, which funnel vast sums into the hands of merciless and amoral local political dynasties. The county machines dispense the funds so as to perpetuate themselves and their allies at Frankfort and Washington. Increasingly, these omniscient organizations manage to gather into their hands funds and gifts from private charities, including even the American Red Cross. Taxpayers in fifty states, oblivious to what their dollars buy, pay little heed to this ominous course of events.

These developments raise a disquieting question which Americans have never confronted before:

How fares the American concept of government of the people, by the people, and for the people when a clear majority become permanently dependent upon and subservient to their elected leaders?

Indeed, can democratic government survive at all in such a setting?

The situation in eastern Kentucky is new to the American scene, but much of the pattern is as old as Rome.

In ancient Italy the social order was remarkably healthy so long as the populace consisted, in the main, of freeholding farmers and self-employed artisans and artificers. The scene darkened when Roman armies conquered distant territories and sent home multitudes of captives. The rich bought up the small plots of farmers and cultivated the resultant plantations with the labor of slaves. Other slaves were set to work in mass manufactories. Because of their great numbers, their carefully planned organization, and their specialization, they were able to produce far more cheaply than their self-employed, free competitors. The corporations that ran these huge enterprises provided grain, leather goods, cloth, and weapons for the empire. The free men and women flocked to the towns and cities to cluster in slums. To keep them orderly the government fed them, clothed them, and entertained them with games. An astoundingly complex system of doles and subsidies was perfected to sustain the idled millions of Roman citizens. In idleness the Roman decayed. He became bitter, vengeful, irresponsible, and bloodthirsty. The mutterings of Roman mobs came to speak more loudly than the voice of Caesar. Rome withered within, long before alien armies crashed through her walls.

These ancient events cast shadows of portent for us today. The machine is a far more profitable servant than any slave. It is untiring, wears out slowly, and requires no food or medication. Technological progress is inexorable and moves toward perfection. What will be the final consequences of it all for the American ideals of equality, liberty, and justice?

We are in the throes of a rapidly quickening new technological revolution. Fifty years ago 700,000 American coal miners were able to mine less coal than 140,000 dig today. Experts tell us that coal production may double by 1980 without any increase in the number of miners. Automobile production increases year by year, but the number of workmen declines. In every field of manufacturing, sensitive, accurate, unfailing steel monsters crowd men and women from workbench and turning lathe, from well and mine. On the land the number of farmers decreases as farms are consolidated into giant tracts. Tractors and mechanical cotton pickers and threshers have rendered the farm laborer as obsolete as the coal miner of 1945.

New turns of the technological wheel are in sight. In twenty years nuclear power may render all fossil fuels obsolete, valued only for their chemical derivatives. If this occurs, new legions of workmen will follow the coal miner into abrupt obsolescence.

On the material side, this revolution undoubtedly represents only progress. It brings us more and more goods for less and less work, thus bringing to fruition one of mankind's ancient dreams.

But what of man's social, spiritual, and political aspects? Is it possible we are moving rapidly forward on the one hand and going backward to barbarism on the other?

What is to become of the jobless miner who takes his family to a Chicago housing development, there to press in upon a one-time automobile assembler from Detroit and a discarded tool and die maker from Pittsburgh? What results when these men and their wives and children are joined by a Negro from Mississippi whose job as a cotton picker was taken over by a machine, or by a white hill-farmer from Tennessee whose ninety acres could not produce corn in competition with the splendidly mechanized farms of Iowa? Are the mushrooming housing developments of the great cities to become the habitations of millions of permanently idled people, supported by a welfare program as ruinous as the one devised by the Caesars? Are whole segments of American citizenry to be consigned to lifetimes of vexatious idleness, resentment, and bitterness? Are these centers to become vast new slums out of which will issue the ominous rumblings of titanic new mobs?

And what torrents of new bitterness will be added to the nation's bloodstream when computers send multitudes of white-collar workers into abrupt idleness in the mortgaged houses of suburbia?

In my opinion these questions pose the foremost issue of our time.

It strikes me that our scientists may develop the explosive power to send a few Americans to Mars while, simultaneously, our society prepares a vastly greater explosive power among disillusioned millions of Americans who remain behind on our own battered planet.

The industrialists who run the eastern Kentucky coalfield laid careful plans for the creation and use of mining machines but cast aside their mining men as lightheartedly as one might discard a banana peel. Most of the victims of this callous treatment accepted their fate resignedly. Some did not, however, and in the winter of 1962–63 the hills in four eastern Kentucky counties resounded with gunfire and nocturnal explosions. For several months a situation bordering on anarchy prevailed across a wide region. Tipples and mines were blasted. Automobiles, power lines, and mining machines were destroyed. Such acts were committed by desperate men seeking to strike at a social and economic order which had rejected them.

Today the challenge of eastern Kentucky is a great national challenge. If we can triumph over it, the solutions we find will offer hope to the entire nation. Increasingly, the agony of eastern Kentucky is but a part of the misery that afflicts great cities, mill towns, and mining regions everywhere. The pain grows out of the evil paradox of mass idleness in the midst of booming production.

Liberty, like a chain, is no stronger than its weakest part. If the freedom and well-being of a part of the people are lost, the freedom and well-being of all are mortally imperiled. If the nation writes off our Southern highlands as unworthy of rescue and rehabilitation, then the nation as a whole is unworthy of survival. As an optimist and a liberal I believe that the nation will rise to the challenge of the depressed and backward Appalachian region, and that in so doing, it will find many of the answers that democracy requires for survival throughout the nation.

A population equivalent to the present population of New York State is being added to the nation every four or five years. Technology eliminates some 40,000 jobs each week. These facts tell us that we must successfully master new frontiers of social justice, and do so in a hurry, or become another nation of regimented serfs.

A social and political crisis of the first magnitude will confront America before the end of another decade. Substitutes for such presently accepted goals as full employment will have to be found. Fresh definitions of the concepts of work, leisure, abundance, and scarcity are imperatively needed. Economic theories adequate to an infant industrial revolution are wholly unsatisfactory when applied to a full-fledged scientific revolution such as that which now engulfs us. The complexity and interdependence of the scientific–industrial nation call for national planning and action. Government must and will intervene more and more in the nation's industrial life. The destiny toward which we move is a national economy under the law. A radical change in public attitude toward law and government is necessary if the general welfare is to be achieved without the total sacrifice of individual liberty. Having bargained for the benefits of technology on all fronts, law is our only means of assuring that it serves the common good.

In 1963 the American economy brought unprecedented prosperity to some 80 percent of the people. Simultaneously, a segment of the population as numerous as the inhabitants of Poland consisted of paupers, and 5.5 percent of the nation's breadwinners were without jobs. Clearly a new tack must be taken soon unless America the Beautiful is to become a crazy quilt of bustle and sloth, brilliance and ignorance, magnificence and squalor.

For more than a dozen years the prevailing political ideology has implemented a *de facto* return to the Articles of Confederation. This doctrine holds that action at the state or local level is admirable while any direct effort by Washington to deal with social or economic malaise is un-American and dangerous. The result is a growing paralysis of the national government as an instrumentality of the public will. This reasoning has brought tremendous outpouring of federal grants-in-aid to states and communities, under circumstances which entail much waste and, often, minimal benefits.

In eastern Kentucky, and in many other depressed areas, the state government will not act effectively to combat poverty and economic decline because it is allied to or controlled by the interests that produced the problems. Thus, state officials talk piously about reform but strenuously oppose any real effort to attack the status quo. They respond to the political machines nurtured by welfare grants and founded on impoverished and dependent citizens. It is not too much to expect that, as matters now stand, federal funds trickling through state treasuries will finance the rebuilding of new political machines in practically every state—machines more odious than those once bossed by Crump, Pendergast, and Hague.

Common sense and past experience argue strongly for a system of federally administered public works. Only in America are able-bodied men permitted to loaf in idleness amid a profusion of unperformed tasks. Should not the thousands of jobless Kentucky coal miners be set to work reforesting the wasted hills, building decent consolidated schoolhouses and roads, and pro-

viding decent housing in lieu of the dreadful shacks that now
dot every creek and hollow? And why not a modernized version
of TVA—a Southern Mountain Authority—to develop the immense hydro- and thermal-power potential of the Appalachian
South for the benefit of the entire nation, and to stop the hideous
waste of the land now being wrought by the strip- and auger-
mining industries? What of the possibility of an educational
Peace Corps to break the old cycle of poor schools, poor job
preparation, poor pay, and poor people?

Unless the nation can profit from the terrible lesson eastern
Kentucky so poignantly teaches, new multitudes of once prosperous Americans may find themselves slipping inexorably into
an economic mire that breeds poverty, despair, dependency,
and, eventually, revolution.

<table>
<tr><td>PAUL
JACOBS</td><td>MAN WITH
A HOE, 1964*</td></tr>
</table>

THE PARK on the border of the Skid Row area in this California farm town is filled with men (and one or two women)
sprawled out on the grass or sitting under the few trees. Some
of them are sleeping, their mouths open, their stubbled faces
pressed into the ground; others are merely staring off into space.
Here and there a bottle is being passed around a group, each
man taking a deep swig before handing it on to the next. I
count about a hundred of these near-derelicts from where I sit
on a bench at the edge of the park. Later, as I walk by, they
look at me incuriously. No one hails me as "Sir," and no one
tries to make a touch. In my dirty pants, torn sweatshirt, and
straw workhat, an old beachbag in my hand, I look like just
another farm worker living on Skid Row.

On my way through the park to find a cheap hotel or flop-

* From *Commentary*, July 1964. Copyright © 1964 by Paul Jacobs.
Reprinted by permission.

house for a few nights, the eyeglass case I have in my shirt pocket begins to feel uncomfortable, so I stop to take it out and put it into the bag. As I do I am struck by the fact that very few of these people in the park seem to wear glasses; in fact, I can spot only three who are either wearing glasses or have eyeglass cases in their pockets. And yet, nearly everyone in the park is in the age group that would normally need glasses.

Just on the outskirts of the Skid Row area, I find a hotel where I can get a room for $2 a night. Most day-haul farm workers would spend only a dollar, or at most $1.50, but I have learned how terribly depressed I get in the dirty, gray flophouses that are the only homes so many farm workers know. Skid Row not only houses bums, outcasts, and voluntary exiles from society, but blurs at the edges to take in the old and the poor as well. For where else can a badly paid worker find a place to sleep for $2 or less?

I pay the $2 in advance—all rent in such "hotels" is paid in advance, either by the day, the week, or the month—and take the key to the room in which I will be staying for the next few days before going on to spend a couple of weeks in a migrant workers' camp in the San Joaquin Valley. The room is about what I expect: peeling walls, a window with a tattered shade overlooking a dark airshaft, a broken bureau with a plastic doily on top, one wooden chair, a closet built into a corner, and overhead, a light bulb swinging on a chain. There is no lamp by the bed—who reads in such a room at night?

My next stop is the farm labor office on the other side of the Skid Row area. Walking down a street past tong houses, Chinese shops and restaurants, Filipino barber shops and social clubs, and Mexican bars, I notice a small store with the word "Shoeshine" crudely lettered across the window; obviously, though, it isn't shines the three gaudily dressed Mexican women inside are selling. One of them catches my eye as I go by and shouts, "Hey, sport, come on in!"—waving her arm to show me the curtained recess at the back. Such girls service the Skid Row community, including fringe groups like the Filipinos. The most skilled of all the farm workers in Skid Row—they generally harvest asparagus, Brussels sprouts, and the early grape crop—many of these Filipinos have been in the area for more than twenty years without their families, and these women represent their only sexual contacts. Because they have no wives and the law once prohibited intermarriage, the Filipinos reportedly suffer from a high rate of venereal disease. Yet they tend to be neater and cleaner than their neighbors on Skid Row, and when they dress up in their big-brimmed hats, wide-seated pants, and heavily padded jackets, they remind one of sporty gangsters in a 1930s movie.

It is early afternoon by now, and the farm labor office—whose hours are from 5 A.M. to 2 P.M.—is very quiet. Two men are sitting behind a counter (there are no chairs or benches on my side of the counter). I announce that I want to register for farm work, and wait while one of them checks to see if I have registered before at this office. Satisfied that my name isn't listed in any of his files, he motions me behind the counter to his partner's desk. "Can I see your social security card?" the man at the desk says. I take out my wallet, now thin and flabby without the thick bundle of credit cards I've left back home in San Francisco, and show him the social security card.

"Were you in the Army, Paul?" He uses my first name as a matter of course, even though I am at least ten years older than he is and he has never seen me before. I say that I was, giving him the little photostat of my Army discharge I carry with me on these trips. Then he asks me what kind of farm work I've done, and I tell enough of the right lies to get a green card from him with my new occupational title printed on it: "Farm hand, general."

"Is there much work?" I ask. "No," he answers, "the asparagus is about finished, but if you'll do stoop labor, you can work until the freeze in the fall. Be here tomorrow morning at 5 A.M. to get on the bus."

For the rest of the afternoon and evening, I walk around Skid Row, going from one dingy card room to another, where $2 will get you into a game of draw poker, low-ball poker, or pan. The games are run by the house, which takes a chip from each pot in exchange for supplying the chairs and tables and a man to keep an eye on the betting. As for the players, they are a mixed group of Mexicans, Filipinos, whites, and Negroes; and there are even a few young fellows who look as though they go to college and just come down to Skid Row for the cards.

I eat my dinner in one of the many grimy restaurants in the neighborhood. The floor is littered with napkins, the counter is greasy, and sugar is spilled around the rack holding the condiments. A pleasant Mexican waitress serves me watery tomato rice soup, fatty lamb stew with potatoes and rice, diced beets, and one slice of canned pineapple. The meal costs eighty-five cents, and I buy a nickel cigar on my way out. Again I wander the streets, indistinguishable from the other men shifting a frayed toothpick around in their mouths.

It is nightfall now. Skid Row is crowded; the bars are jammed with beer and sweet-wine drinkers; the drunks stagger into the street and collapse in the alleys. For many of these men, Skid Row is the end point of some personal tragedy—perhaps a divorce, or alcoholism, or unexpected unemployment. Then the police cars make their appearance. They cruise slowly around the area, circling it like keepers in a zoo. One of them pulls up to the corner where I'm standing talking with three asparagus cutters, and the officer behind the wheel looks at me. "Hello, there," he says. As I return the greeting, I notice him remarking to his partner, "That's a new face around here." He will keep my face in mind—just in case.

Back at the hotel three very old men and one middle-aged farm worker are sitting in a row in the lobby, dozing intermittently through a rerun of an *I Love Lucy* show on TV. I watch too for a while and then walk upstairs to my room. It is hot and stuffy. Undressing, I wonder what the temperature in the room gets to be during the summer when the valley becomes a furnace, made habitable for most of its residents only by air-conditioners.

The work day begins at night. At 4 A.M., wakened by the body noises of the man in the next room, I struggle out of my narrow, lumpy bed. As I wash, I can hear him washing; I brush my teeth, but he doesn't; and neither of us shaves. Outside it's still dark. In my dirty work clothes, I eat breakfast—a "short stack with bacon"—at the counter of a nearby all-night restaurant. After finishing the heavy pancakes soaked in thick syrup and drinking two mugs of coffee, I buy a box lunch from the Chinaman at the cash register to take with me out to the fields.

For fifty-five cents I get three sandwiches of dry, thinly sliced roast beef with a piece of lettuce on soggy white bread, an orange, and a small Danish pastry.

Outside, crowds of men are heading toward the farm labor office where the contractors' buses pull in to pick up their loads of day-haul workers. In the office, under a sign that says, "Do not spit, sit, or lie on the floor," I line up with about twenty-five other men, moving slowly toward the desk at which work is being assigned. Everybody is wearing some kind of hat or cap for protection against the hot sun, and the soiled, ragged clothes which are the day laborer's uniform and stigma. In my hand, I hold the green registration card that will get me on the bus if there is work to be had. The only jobs listed on the board today are cutting asparagus, and short-handled-hoe work on tomatoes or beets. Asparagus is cut by crews and is a comparatively skilled job—much more desirable than such stoop labor as hoe work. But I've never done any asparagus cutting and so I have to take tomatoes or beets.

"Don't send anybody in who won't work short-handle hoe!" one of the three men behind the counter of the employment office shouts angrily after one of the workers has refused the job. Because short-handle hoe work is back-breaking and pays badly, there is often difficulty in finding enough men to fill the contractors' quotas.

"Beets or tomatoes, Paul?" asks the young man at the desk. I choose tomatoes, even though they pay only $1.00 an hour as against $1.10 for beets. But beets, I know, are much harder to work.

By 5:15 A.M. the big yard next door is jammed with men waiting to be assigned to a contractor's bus. Only one or two of the huge California farms do their hiring directly; most of the others deal with the labor contractors who set a flat price for supplying the workers to handle a particular job. The contractor then pays the workers out of this flat fee, naturally keeping enough for himself to make a profit. Some of the contractors are decent employers, but some are known as chiselers, to be avoided if at all possible. Even so, the difference between the best and the worst is only a matter of small degree; most farm workers are subjected to conditions long banished from modern industry.

More than half the men in the loading yard are Mexicans. Somehow, their Spanish sounds more educated than the English of the whites and Negroes greeting their friends and talking about how they made out yesterday. One slightly tipsy Negro is jumping around playing a guitar very badly; the more everyone ignores him, the harder he strives to get their attention. The asparagus crews are the first to be assigned to buses; they all have cheap plastic goggles on their hats which they will later use to keep the heavy dust out of their eyes. Finally, from the back end of the yard I see a contractor coming for my group. He is recognizable immediately by his baseball cap, his leather jacket, his boots and, most of all, his assured manner. He stops to kibitz a bit with the man from the employment office, and it becomes obvious that the relationship between them is much different from the one each of them has with us. Even though we farm workers are formally the clients of the state employment service, the real clients are the contractors, for they are permanent while we are only temporary; we are dependent upon both of them; and besides, they are social equals and we are their social inferiors. It is to the contractor, who needs it least, and not to the worker, who needs it most, that the state gives the benefit of its publicly supported employment service: the state is the instrument that provides the contractors with a good income and the growers with a pool of extremely cheap labor.

We board an old bus, painted blue, with the name of the contractor stenciled on the outside. In front of me, two Mexicans are chatting in Spanish, and across from them another Mexican sits alone. There are also eight other men in the bus—three Negroes and five whites, including myself. We sit and doze in the chill dark air, and then, at 6 A.M., when the buses in front of us start leaving the lot, our driver, who is Mexican, comes back with six more workers—three young white men, a Negro, and two Mexicans. Only one of the group, I notice, is wearing glasses. A few minutes later, we swing out of the lot and drive out on the highway.

By this time it is daylight and I can see the interior of the bus more clearly. On the dashboard is stenciled "Speed Limit 45 m.p.h.," the maximum speed the state law allows farm buses to travel. I know these buses are supposed to be inspected by the state, but this one must have had its inspection a long time ago. The rear-view mirror is broken in half and the speedometer doesn't work at all. On the floor is a fire extinguisher, but it doesn't appear to be in very good working order either. Next to the driver is a large old-fashioned milk can filled with water. Once we get on the highway, the driver starts speeding, and we go barreling along until the contractor catches up to us in his pickup truck and signals the driver to stop. The driver gets out and I hear the contractor tell him in Spanish to slow down because the police are on the highway.

The driver gets back in the bus and begins going more slowly. But soon he is accelerating again, and in a few minutes we are moving at about the same speed as before. Some thirty-five minutes later, we turn off the highway and drive another three or four miles to a huge field with tomato plants growing in long straight furrows. Leaving our lunches on the seats, we file out of the bus, and the driver hands each of us a brand new hoe, about fifteen inches long with a head that is set back at an angle toward the handle.

In the field waiting for us is the contractor, talking with a stocky Nisei in his early forties. The Nisei tells us, in perfect English, to thin out the plants which are now about three inches high and growing close together. We are to chop out the row, leaving only one or two of the plants in each cluster, nipping off the weeds growing around them, and making sure that there is a space of from four to nine inches between the remaining plants. We station ourselves at every other furrow so that when we get to the end of the field, each of us can come back along the next row.

To chop at the tomato plants with a fifteen-inch hoe requires bending over almost double, and in only a few minutes, the sweat is pouring down my face. I soon fall behind almost all of the workers in the field: the end of the furrow seems a million miles away, and it takes me a half hour to get there. The bus driver, who is now acting as straw boss, keeps an impatient eye on me. He complains that I am not thinning the plants enough, and he tries to show me how to move my feet so that I can stay bent over. But the Nisei foreman tells me to take my time and do the job properly. As I get to the end of the row, the muscles in my back, thighs, and calves ache from the strain. Working my way back on the next furrow, I am acutely conscious of the straw boss watching and checking on me. By now, I am streaming sweat and in agony from the bending over. In the next furrow, an elderly man is working almost as slowly as I am, muttering to himself, "This here work's too hard, this here work's too hard."

"You ever done this kind of work before?" I ask him. "Sure," he answers, "I never done nothin' but farm work all my life, but this here's too hard. I'm too old to be bending over like this." Then, as I watch, he opens his pants and begins to urinate, never breaking the rhythm of his work, one hand hoeing, the other holding his organ with the urine dribbling through his fingers and down onto his pants.

And so the day moves on, with the sun rising in the sky and the heat rising in the field. The furrows extend into an eternity of tiny tomato plants and dirt, and the short-handled hoe is an instrument of torture. At last we take a break for lunch, after which a few of the men walk out into the field to defecate, scraps of newspaper stuck in their back pocket. Then hoeing again until shortly before four, when we quit and are driven a few miles to the labor camp, a small group of battered shacks in which crews are housed when they are working by the week. We line up at the contractor's office and are paid eight dollars for the day.

On the drive back to town the men talk more than they have all day, mostly about which bar serves the best beer for the money. In front of me, there is a discussion of how to beat the blood bank system. Selling blood is a good way to supplement your income. The only problem is that you can't give blood more than once every few months, and the date on which you sell the blood is marked on your fingers in ink that becomes visible under fluorescent light and won't wash off even with strong detergents. But one of the men has discovered that you can erase the ink by rubbing tobacco very, very hard over your fingers for a long time.

The bus stops on the street where the farm labor office is located, and we pile out. All around us, buses and trucks are pulling in to discharge their cargoes. Some of the men head for their rooms to wash off the dust and dirt; others make for a bar to get a beer or two first. Then there is the lamb-stew dinner again, and again the walk along the streets, the stopping on corners, the surveillance by the police, and maybe, if a couple of guys get together, the buying of a "jug" to knock off before bed. At 4 A.M., the work day will start again.

If you want to and have the strength to make it, you can go out to the fields six days a week and earn $48. Stoop labor is available in California for eight or nine months of the year, so you might, putting in six days a week, earn up to $1,700— $600 more than the average wage of a farm worker in 1962. If you get sick, you earn nothing, and when the work season is over, you receive no unemployment insurance. Thus eventually you have to move on to another town, looking for another job which offers exactly the same conditions. And since you can never save enough to escape from Skid Row, it is easy to slip just a notch or two down to the bum level. At $1 an hour for back-breaking labor performed under the worst physical conditions, what possible incentive is there to work?

All this—when the government subsidizes crops and livestock, and when it has been estimated that doubling the wages of stoop labor might increase the retail price of tomatoes by a *penny* a can or a pound.

STAN
STEINER

THE AMERICAN INDIAN* GHETTOS IN THE DESERT

WHERE THE OLD U.S. 66 winds and unwinds through the lava beds, west of Albuquerque, New Mexico, a hitchhiker flagged my car. He was a young man from the Pueblo de Acoma: "The City in the Sky." And as we drove through the black-rock country that spreads out from the highway we got to talking about

* From *The Nation,* June 22, 1964.

how little work there was thereabouts and how hard it was to
farm such land.

"How do you earn a living?" I asked.

"Living?" he smiled. "I just live."

He got out at a crossroads to nowhere, laughingly waved
goodby, and walked off toward the Pueblo de Acoma, some
twenty miles away.

Surveying unemployment figures among Indians in the winter
of 1962–63, the House Committee on Interior and Insular
Affairs found that at the Pueblo de Acoma, of 1,380 adults
between the ages of eighteen and fifty-five years, 197 were then
working. The unemployment rate: 89.6 percent. Cash income
of these Pueblo Indians for the previous year was estimated at
$500 to $1,000 *per family*. In answer to the question, how many
of the residents had "completed an apprenticeship or other training program" during that past year, the reply was a terse,
"None." Jerry P. Garcia, Governor of Pueblo de Acoma, when
asked, "How is the morale of the Indian people?" said merely,
"They want employment."

Similarly, the United Pueblo Agency of the Bureau of Indian
Affairs found that of 13,711 adults on eighteen New Mexican
pueblos, 3,212 were employed; half of these temporarily. Unemployment rate: 77 percent. Income of these tranquil and
ancient people, believed to be among the oldest inhabitants of
the country, was said to average from $750 to $1,000 yearly
per family. The Hopis, too, whose idyllic reputation as the
"Peaceful People" has won for their legends the status of a
perennial Christmas Book, reported a somewhat less than idyllic
unemployment rate of 71.7 percent.

To the north, on the Blackfeet reservation of Montana, the
House committee uncovered a "permanent unemployment" rate
of 72.5 percent with approximately 1,500 of the 2,000 Blackfeet
jobless. The yearly income: "less than $500 per family."

On the plains of the Dakotas, the Sioux reservations reported:
the Pine Ridge Sioux had 1,225 of 3,400 tribal adults employed
(yearly income per family: $105), the Sisseton Sioux had 543
of 835 employed (income: $600), the Rosebud Sioux had
1,276 of 2,996 employed (income: $1,000) and the Standing

Rock reservation listed 380 of 880 "heads of households" as employed (income: $190). Down in Mississippi, on the Choctaw reservation, 170 of the 1,225 adults had jobs. Unemployment rate: 86.1 percent.

The Navajos, the most populous of American Indian tribes, numbering upward of 96,000, fared not much better. Of 33,734 Navajos in the labor force of Arizona, 23,334 were listed, in August, 1963, as unemployed. The Indian Bureau was reluctant even to estimate the "median annual cash income," fearing it was too low to be "meaningful." If this economic quagmire had engulfed the Dineh, "The People," as the Navajos proudly call themselves, it had no less bogged down their linguistic cousins, the Apaches. The San Carlos and Fort Apache reservations reported that 2,170 of 3,390 Apaches—61 percent—were out of work.

The "oil millionaires" offered statistics as dismal. In the mythology of the oil-rich Indians, so credulously celebrated in after-dinner jokes and romantic tales, none are supposedly wealthier than the Creek, Cherokee, Chickasaw, Choctaw and Seminole. But when the House Indian Unemployment Survey investigated some 19,000 adults in these Five Civilized Tribes, approximately 10,000 were listed as jobless. The annual income per family—*including* the fabled oil lease and royalty disbursements—came to $1,200.

Each year in Washington there is a ceremonial wringing of hands over "the Indian problem." It took place this year in the East Room of the White House, where tribal leaders presented President Johnson with an appeal from the National Congress of Indians that stated: "Unemployment is our major concern. Almost one-half of the employable American Indians are without jobs. On some reservations three-fourths are unemployed. Indian reservations are indeed pockets of poverty."

Unemployment among the Indians is thus *ten times* the national average. Their family incomes, though reports are frequently inconclusive and difficult to verify, are generally estimated to be from one-third to one-fifth of the national average. Indian poverty is so widespread and so intense that it tends to fall outside national calculations on the problem. Perhaps this partially explains why studies such as the Conference on Economic Progress report, *"Poverty and Deprivation in the*

U.S.," do not as a rule delve into it. Chronic unemployment of the majority of a people that is not due to technological change, nor to depressed areas in the economy, appears to be beyond measure, or remedy, by methods that are applied elsewhere. Especially is this so on the reservations, where poverty, as the Sioux Chief, Standing Bear, had said, is but one of the conditions that have "dehumanized" his people.

"Statistics permit us to walk untouched through the world of extremely low-income groups, uneducated children, substandard housing, disease and hopelessness," wrote Congressman George F. Senner, Jr., (D., Ariz.) in *The Navajo Times* this winter. But the conditions of the nearly 400,000 Indians—of an estimated 600,000—who live on the neglected reservations cannot be ignored. "We cannot avoid the truth," Senner wrote, "no matter how impersonally it may be presented."

It has been calculated, for example, that 90 percent of the Indians live in substandard housing. But substandard, when applied to the reservation Indian, is actually a euphemism for a rural slum of shacks and one-room huts. The wickiups of grass, logs and canvas of the Apaches, the earth and log hogans of the Navajos, the sod igloos of the Eskimos and the adobes of the Pueblo Indians may house legends of enchantment, but the living conditions of the occupants are less than enchanting to Public Health Service doctors.

Dr. Carruth J. Wagner, Chief of the Division of Indian Health, of the PHS, has testified that "The burden of disease is heavy [among Indians] and much of it is associated with the hazards and rigors of the environment in which these Indian beneficiaries live. . . . The one-room structure is occupied by an average of four or five people. This serious overcrowding promotes the transmission of disease."

He reported that the average "death age" of an Indian is forty-two years (thirty years for the Alaskan native and about thirty-one years for the Arizona Indians), compared to an average of sixty-two years for the general population.

The death rate of Indian babies is three times higher (for Alaskan natives six times higher) than the national average. Of 1,000 Indian babies born alive, forty-three die before their first birthday, Dr. Wagner said, and "many [of these deaths are] associated with the home environment." Moreover, infant mortality accounts for 21 percent of all Indian deaths, compared to 6 percent for the general population.

Speaking of specific disease rates, Dr. Wagner estimated the incidence of tuberculosis to be seven times higher among Indians (fifteen times higher among Alaskan natives). Tuberculosis death rates are four times higher among Indians (seven times higher among Alaskan natives). And the death rate from infectious diseases such as dysentery, gastroenteritis, influenza and pneumonia averages from two to five times higher than those of the rest of the population.

These disease and death rates continue despite the expanded Public Health Service care and treatment of the past few years. Dr. Wagner indicated his dismay, as have others in the field, that unalleviated poverty, subsistence diets and chronic unemployment frustrate the efforts of government and tribal health officials. "Nutritional deficiencies are associated with many of the illnesses and diseases," the Indian Health chief said; "Malnutrition of babies results in long periods of hospitalization and premature, unnecessary death."

Approaching another aspect of the problem, the Public Health Service studied sanitation conditions among 42,506 Indians in eleven states. "The unsafe water supply is a very common cause of many of the diseases," the survey found. More than 81.6 percent of the Indians haul their drinking water, many from "distances of a mile or more," and from "irrigation ditches and ponds." "Potentially contaminated water" sources supplied more than 77 percent of this water. On several reservations the entire water supply was condemned. "Many families have to get along on one to three gallons of water a day, when the poorest non-Indian rural family has double and triple this amount." And of the Indians surveyed, 78.1 percent were found to "use unsatisfactory excreta disposal facilities."

Confronted with this appalling bill of particulars, the late Congressman Hjalmar C. Nygaard (R., N.D.) blandly said: "I hope some day these problems can be solved."

Indian education is the one field where government officials and tribal councils have reached some agreement. Educators in the Bureau of Indian Affairs point with pride to figures showing that, in 1963, 88.4 percent of all Indian children between the ages of six and eighteen years were enrolled in schools. More than half of these were in local public schools. Even allowing for the discrepancy between statistics and facts in reservation school enrollments, it does seem that the educational situation has been substantially improved since World War II, and especially in the past few years.

Within this aura of rising hopes, however, it should be noted that 3.7 percent of Indian children are dismissed as "unknown." In Oklahoma these "unknown" children total 20.7 percent and on the Montana reservations they total 14.1 percent.

Even more serious, as it reflects the relationship between Indian poverty and education, is the discrepancy between elementary-school enrollment and that of the vocational and high schools, where job training is to be had. In these later years the drop-out rate is estimated to be 60 percent!

The chairman of the Navajo Tribe, Raymond Nakai, has emphasized the concern of Indian leaders, not only because of the rudimentary education offered Indian children, but because training in job skills is so often aborted by the dead-end economics of reservation life. "However high the quality of vocational training," Nakai has said, "it will only aggravate the worker's frustration if the vocation for which he has been trained is barred to him because of his present economic and reservation condition." Or, he added, because "racial discrimination stands in his path."

Still others, like Martin Vigil of Tesuque Pueblo, head of the All Pueblo Council of New Mexico, are skeptical of the congratulations the Indian educators award themselves. "There are thousands of Indian children who have no school," Vigil has said; "The level of Indian education is the fifth grade, while that of the white man's is the tenth grade. Is that right? Is this getting the Indian ready for the space age?"

In a comprehensive study of "the Indian problem," Ralph Nader, editor of *The Harvard Law Record*, offered this rather bleak view: "Notwithstanding the improvements in Indian education, the school day is often extraordinarily short, the quality of teaching is inferior and there are still many children not enrolled." In spite of the "gradual improvements," to which it paid judicious tribute, *The Harvard Law Record,* in 1956, editorially commented that the "American Indians are by far the worst-fed, worst-clad and worst-housed group in the United States. These people, recipients of the poorest educational and medical services in the country, are in a state of social and psychological maladjustment. This is a situation of which the American public is only dimly aware."

The American Indian "may be technically free," Attorney General Robert F. Kennedy told the convention of the National Congress of American Indians at Bismarck, North Dakota, last summer, "but he is the victim of social and economic oppressions that hold him in bondage. He is all too likely to become the victim of his own proud anger, his own frustrations, and—most humiliating of all—the victim of racial discrimination in his own land.

"Will the injustice go on?" the Attorney General rhetorically asked his Indian audience.

Kennedy's reply was hopeful. "I believe there are signs of a change," he said, "clear signs of a turning of the tide." There had been in fact "signs" of something new in the approach to Indian needs ever since the late President Kennedy established a Special Task Force early in his administration. The Task Force, in 1961, set forth three major goals for the Indians: maximum economic self-sufficiency, full participation in American life and equal privileges and responsibilities of citizenship. The then newly appointed Commissioner of Indian Affairs, Philleo Nash, hailed these goals as "an important shift in program emphasis."

Somewhat reserved Oliver La Farge [America's most respected writer on Indian life] endorsed this hopeful prognosis, but suggested that "major changes must be taken *now.*" Just before his death [1963], La Farge returned to this theme and—feeling that "On the positive side there is little that is striking" by way of "major changes"—said that the situation called for "the vigor and determination of Paul Bunyan, and his ox Babe, yes, and Bunyan's goad and his axe."

The impatience here voiced, and expressed with still greater force by tribal leadership, nonetheless recognized a change of approach. La Farge himself wrote of the possibility of "bold new advances." What buoyed these hopes was not merely the task force's report. It was also the reaction to Commissioner Nash's stated belief that henceforth the economic development of the reservation Indian "of course is a job which will have to be accomplished by the Indians themselves. If the plans are worth the paper they are written on they must be basically *Indian* plans, reflecting Indian thinking." Similar was the statement of Attorney General Kennedy that the new Administration's "firm policy has been to consult with tribal groups and work with them in determining every phase of federal action in their behalf—in marked contrast to the long-standing custom of the past, when the wishes of the tribal organizations were all too often ignored."

Traditionally the non-Indian, whether in government or business, has sought to make the Indian over in the white man's image. When this could not be done through the "policy of extermination" of "the War Camp" (*New York Times,* July 7, 1876), it has been attempted through the humane persuasions of paternalism. But since that too proved ineffective, legal means have been found—as for example, the reservation "Termination Acts" of the Eisenhower Administration.

Equally traditionally, the Indian has viewed these policies with little enthusiasm. Reluctant to give up his beliefs, or his way of life, in spite of the "fight, coax or run" programs of the nineteenth century Bureau of Indian Affairs, he has been treated as incorrigible, and relegated to social oblivion.

The Indian's poverty was not a social accident, nor a historical aberration. It was the inevitable result of policy. The friend of the Indian, or the dedicated public servant, discovered that whatever he accomplished to improve the condition of the Indians in one field was too often nullified by a decline in another. The plight of the Indian was endemic to his economic and social status.

"We cannot expect good health and the desire for education if there is poor housing, unemployment and dire poverty," said Robert Burnette, a Rosebud Sioux and director of the National

Congress of American Indians. "So we believe all of these things go hand in hand." Walter Wetzel, Chief of the Blackfeet, has said: "We must seek a new policy." And this new policy, if it is to succeed, must, in the opinion of many tribal councils, deal with fundamental problems in a comprehensive way and from an Indian point of view. The Kiowa, Amos Hopkins-Dukes, who heads the Tribal Indian Land Rights Association, speaks for the younger leaders when he says: "If the U.S. is to grow and improve its Indian policy, the U.S. will have to be willing to let the American Indians grow also—as Indian people."

Another Indian leader recently startled officials by suggesting that if Indian poverty was really in the forefront of the "war on poverty," then a government loan of at least $200 million to the tribes, for industrial and resource development—by the tribes—might be a "good start." But, he added, the tribes would have to be free to use such funds "as they see fit." This was a practical application of Robert Burnette's sardonic comment: "The government must allow the Indians to make a few of their own mistakes."

The variety of present-day approaches to "the Indian problem" is in itself encouraging. The Tribal Indian Land Rights Association has evolved a plan to apply the original provisions of the Allotment Act of 1887, not to break up the reservations, but to enable nonreservation Indians to claim federal lands which, it contends, are theirs by legal right. Suits based on treaty rights have long concerned the Indians Rights Association and similiar groups. "Indian Health Year" has been proclaimed by the Association on American Indian Affairs, in cooperation with the Public Health Service. And the Bureau of Indian Affairs is concentrating on the Area Redevelopment Act, the "Youth Job Training Corps," educational expansion and the Public Housing Act.

The most immediately pertinent programs, however, are those aimed at expanding industries that might employ Indians. The Association of American Indian Affairs has been singularly, if modestly, successful in its campaign to relocate small industries on or near reservations. The Bureau of Indian Affairs, for its part, has brought nineteen new plants into Indian population areas since 1961; they are said to provide more than 1,000 jobs.

Federal work projects, as urged by the National Congress of American Indians, have proved to be another job source. Under an accelerated program, projects begun on some eighty-eight reservations employ a fluctuating Indian labor force of 2,700 to 5,700. However, these projects are of a service character: improvements of roads, soil conservation, reforestry, building of community centers, etc. They are more likely to offer temporary and emergency employment than to assure long-term economic opportunity.

Unfortunately, between the many programs and their fulfillment, there is what might be called a "capital gap." Commissioner Nash has noted: "A common characteristic of under-developed communities, on reservations and off, at home and abroad, is lack of capital." In the Indian communities the "gap" is increased by the reluctance of private industry to invest plants and equipment in areas often far from markets and where available labor is poorly trained and untested. Furthermore, non-Indian interests have a historic itch for Indian lands and resources, which even now are mostly leased to non-Indians. Hoping for direct ownership, such interests have ever been willing to drive the reservation Indians to the economic wall. Private and public capital has thus been doled out sparingly. "And the reservations are starved for both kinds," Nash has said.

In the face of this economic and industrial backwardness, a development program that might have meaningful results would appear to require goals substantially larger than any we have yet projected. A few years ago, Oliver La Farge suggested that a program of federal loans and aid for reservation self-help might take the form of an American Indian Point Four Program—with a budget at least as large as those extended to underdeveloped countries overseas. More recently, a somewhat scaled-down version—"Operation Bootstrap"—has been proposed.

Since the government has from 1787 on, and before the present Administration came into office, appropriated more than $2.25 billion for its less than successful Indian programs, an investment of Point Four dimensions is not wholly unreasonable.

A moral obligation to the Indians is implicit in all these considerations. But leaving morality quite aside, there is the consideration of the relentless cost to the nation incurred by failure to lift the bondage of perpetual poverty from these proud, intensely patriotic and undefeatable people.

| THOMAS PYNCHON | JOURNEY INTO THE MIND OF WATTS* |

THE NIGHT OF MAY 7 [1966], after a chase that began in Watts and ended some fifty blocks farther north, two Los Angeles policemen, Caucasians, succeeded in halting a car driven by Leonard Deadwyler, a Negro. With him were his pregnant wife and a friend. The younger cop (who'd once had a complaint brought against him for rousting some Negro kids around in a more than usually abusive way) went over and stuck his head and gun in the car window to talk to Deadwyler. A moment later there was a shot; the young Negro fell sideways in the seat, and died. The last thing he said, according to the other cop, was, "She's going to have a baby."

The coroner's inquest went on for the better part of two weeks, the cop claiming the car had lurched suddenly, causing his service revolver to go off by accident; Deadwyler's widow claiming it was cold-blooded murder and that the car had never moved. The verdict, to no one's surprise, cleared the cop of all criminal responsibility. It had been an accident. The D.A. announced immediately that he thought so, too, and that as far as he was concerned the case was closed.

But as far as Watts is concerned, it's still very much open. Preachers in the community are urging calm—or, as others are putting it: "Make any big trouble, baby, the Man just going to come back in and shoot you, like last time." Snipers are sniping but so far not hitting much of anything. Occasional fire

* From the *New York Times Magazine*, June 12, 1966. Copyright © 1966 by the New York Times Company. Reprinted by permission.

bombs are being lobbed at cars with white faces inside, or into empty sports models that look as if they might be white property. There have been a few fires of mysterious origin. A Negro Teen Post—part of the L.A. poverty war's keep-them-out-of-the-streets effort—has had all its windows busted, the young lady in charge expressing the wish next morning that she could talk with the malefactors, involve them, see if they couldn't work out the problem together. In the back of everybody's head, of course, is the same question: Will there be a repeat of last August's riot?

An even more interesting question is: Why is everybody worrying about another riot—haven't things in Watts improved any since the last one? A lot of white folks are wondering. Unhappily, the answer is no. The neighborhood may be seething with social workers, data collectors, VISTA volunteers and other assorted members of the humanitarian establishment, all of whose intentions are the purest in the world. But somehow nothing much has changed. There are still the poor, the defeated, the criminal, the desperate, all hanging in there with what must seem a terrible vitality.

The killing of Leonard Deadwyler has once again brought it all into sharp focus; brought back long-standing pain, reminded everybody of how very often the cop does approach you with his revolver ready, so that nothing he does with it can then really be accidental; of how, especially at night, everything can suddenly reduce to a matter of reflexes: your life trembling in the crook of a cop's finger because it is dark, and Watts, and the history of this place and these times makes it impossible for the cop to come on any different, or for you to hate him any less. Both of you are caught in something neither of you wants, and yet night after night, with casualties or without, these traditional scenes continue to be played out all over the south-central part of this city.

Whatever else may be wrong in a political way—like the inadequacy of Great Depression techniques applied to a scene that has long outgrown them; like an old-fashioned grafter's glee among the city fathers over the vast amounts of poverty-war bread that Uncle is now making available to them—lying much closer to the heart of L.A.'s racial sickness is the coexistence of two very different cultures: one white and one black.

While the white culture is concerned with various forms of systematized folly—the economy of the area in fact depending on it—the black culture is stuck pretty much with basic realities like disease, like failure, violence and death, which the whites have mostly chosen—and can afford—to ignore. The two cultures do not understand each other, though white values are displayed without let-up on black people's TV screens, and though the panoramic sense of black impoverishment is hard to miss from atop the Harbor Freeway, which so many whites must drive at least twice every working day. Somehow it occurs to very few of them to leave at the Imperial Highway exit for a change, go east instead of west only a few blocks, and take a look at Watts. A quick look. The simplest kind of beginning. But Watts is country which lies, psychologically, uncounted miles further than most whites seem at present willing to travel.

On the surface anyway, the Deadwyler affair hasn't made it look any different, though underneath the mood in Watts is about what you might expect. Feelings range from a reflexive, angry, driving need to hit back somehow, to an anxious worry that the slaying is just one more bad grievance, one more bill that will fall due some warm evening this summer. Yet in the daytime's brilliance and heat, it is hard to believe there is any mystery to Watts. Everything seems so out in the open, all of it real, no plastic faces, no transistors, no hidden Muzak, or Disneyfied landscaping, or smiling little chicks to show you around. Not in Raceriotland. Only a few historic landmarks, like the police substation, one command post for the white forces last August, pigeons now thick and cooing up on its red-tiled roof. Or, on down the street, vacant lots, still looking charred around the edges, winking with emptied Tokay, port and sherry pints, some of the bottles peeking out of paper bags, others busted.

A kid could come along in his bare feet and step on this glass—not that you'd ever know. These kids are so tough you can pull slivers of it out of them and never get a whimper. It's part of their landscape, both the real and the emotional one: busted glass, busted crockery, nails, tin cans, all kinds of scrap and waste. Traditionally Watts. An Italian immigrant named Simon Rodia spent thirty years gathering some of it up and converting a little piece of the neighborhood along 107th Street into the famous Watts Towers, perhaps his own dream of how things should have been: a fantasy of fountains, boats, tall openwork spires, encrusted with a dazzling mosaic of Watts debris. Next to the Towers, along the old Pacific Electric tracks, kids are busy every day busting more bottles on the steel rails. But Simon Rodia is dead, and now the junk just accumulates.

A few blocks away, other kids are out playing on the hot blacktop of the school playground. Brothers and sisters too young yet for school have it better—wherever they are they have yards, trees, hoses, hiding places. Not the crowded, shadeless tenement living of any Harlem; just the same one- or two-story urban sprawl as all over the rest of L.A., giving you some piece of grass at least to expand into when you don't especially feel like being inside.

In the business part of town there is a different idea of refuge. Pool halls and bars, warm and dark inside, are crowded; many domino, dice and whist games in progress. Outside, men stand around a beer cooler listening to a ball game on the radio; others lean or hunker against the sides of buildings—low, faded stucco boxes that remind you, oddly, of certain streets in Mexico. Women go by, to and from what shopping there is. It is easy to see how crowds, after all, can form quickly in these streets, around the least seed of a disturbance or accident. For the moment, it all only waits in the sun.

Overhead, big jets now and then come vacuum-cleanering in to land; the wind is westerly, and Watts lies under the approaches to L.A. International. The jets hang what seems only a couple of hundred feet up in the air; through the smog they show up more white than silver, highlighted by the sun, hardly solid; only the ghosts, or possibilities, of airplanes.

From here, much of the white culture that surrounds Watts—and, in a curious way, besieges it—looks like those jets: a little unreal, a little less than substantial. For Los Angeles, more than any other city, belongs to the mass media. What is known around the nation as the L.A. Scene exists chiefly as images on a screen or TV tube, as four-color magazine photos, as old radio jokes, as new songs that survive only a matter of weeks. It is basically a white Scene, and illusion is everywhere in it, from the giant aerospace firms that flourish or retrench at the whims of Robert McNamara, to the "action" everybody mills along the Strip on weekends looking for, unaware that they, and their search which will end, usually, unfulfllled, are the only action in town.

Watts lies impacted in the heart of this white fantasy. It is, by contrast, a pocket of bitter reality. The only illusion Watts ever allowed itself was to believe for a long time in the white version of what a Negro was supposed to be. But with the Muslim and civil-rights movements that went, too.

Since the August rioting, there has been little building here, little buying. Lots whose buildings were burned off them are still waiting vacant and littered with garbage, occupied only by a parked car or two, or kids fooling around after school, or winos sharing a pint in the early morning. The other day, on one of them, there were ground-breaking festivities, attended by a county supervisor, pretty high school girls decked in ribbons, a white store owner and his wife, who in the true Watts spirit busted a bottle of champagne over a rock—all because the man had decided to stay and rebuild his $200,000 market, the first such major rebuilding since the riot.

Watts people themselves talk about another kind of aura, vaguely evil; complain that Negroes living in better neighborhoods like to come in under the freeway as to a red-light district, looking for some girl, some game, maybe some connection. Narcotics is said to be a rare bust in Watts these days, although the narco people cruise the area earnestly, on the lookout for dope fiends, dope rings, dope peddlers. But the poverty of Watts makes it more likely that if you have pot or a little something else to spare you will want to turn a friend on, not sell it. Tomorrow, or when he can, your friend will return the favor.

At the Deadwyler inquest, much was made of the dead man's high blood alcohol content, as if his being drunk made it somehow all right for the police to shoot him. But alcohol is a natural part of the Watts style; as natural as LSD is around

Hollywood. The white kid digs hallucination simply because he is conditioned to believe so much in escape, escape as an integral part of life, because the white L.A. Scene makes accessible to him so many different forms of it. But a Watts kid, brought up in a pocket of reality, looks perhaps not so much for escape as just for some calm, some relaxation. And beer or wine is good enough for that. Especially good at the end of a bad day.

Like after you have driven, say, down to Torrance or Long Beach or wherever it is they're hiring because they don't seem to be in Watts, not even in the miles of heavy industry that sprawl along Alameda Street, that gray and murderous arterial which lies at the eastern boundary of Watts looking like the edge of the world.

So you groove instead down the freeway, maybe wondering when some cop is going to stop you because the old piece of a car you're driving, which you bought for $20 or $30 you picked up somehow, makes a lot of noise or burns some oil. Catching you mobile widens the Man's horizons; gives him more things he can get you on. Like "excessive smoking" is a great favorite with him.

If you do get to where you were going without encountering a cop, you may spend your day looking at the white faces of personnel men, their uniform glaze of suspicion, their automatic smiles, and listening to polite putdowns. "I decided once to ask," a kid says, "one time they told me I didn't meet their requirements. So I said: 'Well, what are you looking for? I mean, how can I train, what things do I have to learn so I *can* meet your requirements?' Know what he said? 'We are not obligated to tell you what our requirements are.' "

He isn't. That right there is the hell and headache: he doesn't have to do anything he doesn't want to do because he is the Man. Or he was. A lot of kids these days are more apt to be calling him the *little* man—meaning not so much any member of the power structure as just your average white L.A. taxpayer, registered voter, property owner; employed, stable, mortgaged and the rest.

The little man bugs these kids more than the Man ever bugged their parents. It is the little man who is standing on their feet and in their way; he's all over the place, and there is not much they can do to change him or the way he feels about them. A Watts kid knows more of what goes on inside white heads than possibly whites do themselves; knows how often the little man has looked at him and thought, "Bad credit risk"—or "Poor learner," or "Sexual threat," or "Welfare chiseler"—without knowing a thing about him personally.

The natural, normal thing to want to do is hit the little man. But what, after all, has he done? Mild, respectable, possibly smiling, he has called you no names, shown no weapons. Only told you perhaps that the job was filled, the house rented.

With a cop it may get more dangerous, but at least it's honest. You understand each other. Both of you silently admitting that all the cop really has going for him is his gun. "There was a time," they'll tell you, "you'd say, 'Take off the badge, baby, and let's settle it.' I mean he wouldn't, but you'd say it. But since August, man, the way I feel, hell with the badge—just take off that gun."

The cop does not take off that gun; the hassle stays verbal. But this means that, besides protecting and serving the little man, the cop also functions as his effigy.

If he does get emotional and say something like "boy" or "nigger," you then have the option of cooling it or else—again this is more frequent since last August—calling him the name he expects to be called, though it is understood you are not commenting in any literal way on what goes on between him and his mother. It is a ritual exchange, like the dirty dozens.

Usually—as in the Deadwyler incident—it's the younger cop of the pair who's more troublesome. Most Watts kids are hip to what's going on in this rookie's head—the things he feels he has to prove—as much as to the elements of the ritual. Before the cop can say, "Let's see your I.D.," you learn to take it out politely and say, "You want to see my I.D.?" Naturally it will bug the cop more the further ahead of him you can stay. It is flirting with disaster, but it's the cop who has the gun, so you do what you can.

You must anticipate always how the talk is going to go. It's something you pick up quite young, same as you learn the different species of cop: the Black and White (named for the color scheme of their automobiles), who are L.A. city police and in general the least flexible; the L.A. county sheriff's department, who style themselves more of an elite, try to maintain a certain distance from the public, and are less apt to harass you unless you seem worthy; the Compton city cops, who travel only one to a car and come on very tough, like leaning four of you at a time up against the wall and shaking you all down; the juvies, who ride in unmarked Plymouths and are cruising all over the place soon as the sun goes down, pulling up alongside you with pleasantries like, "Which one's buying the wine tonight?" or, "Who are you guys planning to rob this time?" They are kidding, of course, trying to be pals. But Watts kids, like most, do not like being put in with winos, or dangerous drivers or thieves, or in any bag considered criminal or evil. Whatever the cop's motives, it *looks* like mean and deliberate ignorance.

In the daytime, and especially with any kind of crowd, the cop's surface style has changed some since last August. "Time was," you'll hear, "man used to go right in, very mean, pick maybe one kid out of the crowd he figured was the troublemaker, try to bust him down in front of everybody. But now the people start yelling back, how they don't want no more of that, all of a sudden the Man gets very meek."

Still, however much a cop may seem to be following the order of the day read to him every morning about being courteous to everybody, his behavior with a crowd will really depend as it always has on how many of his own he can muster, and how fast. For his mayor, Sam Yorty, is a great believer in the virtues of Overwhelming Force as a solution to racial difficulties. This approach has not gained much favor in Watts. In fact, the Mayor of Los Angeles appears to many Negroes to be the very incarnation of the little man: looking out for no one but himself, speaking always out of expediency, and never, never to be trusted.

The Economic and Youth Opportunities Agency (EYOA) is a joint city-county "umbrella agency" (the state used to be represented, but has dropped out) for many projects scattered around the poorer parts of L.A., and seems to be Sam Yorty's native element, if not indeed the flower of his consciousness.

Bizarre, confused, ever in flux, strangely ineffective, EYOA hardly sees a day go by without somebody resigning, or being fired, or making an accusation, or answering one—all of it confirming the Watts Negroes' already sad estimate of the little man. The Negro attitude toward EYOA is one of clear mistrust, though degrees of suspicion vary, from the housewife wanting only to be left in peace and quiet, who hopes that maybe the Man is lying less than usual this time, to the young, active disciple of Malcolm X who dismisses it all with a contemptuous shrug.

"But why?" asked one white lady volunteer. "There are so many agencies now that you *can* go to, that *can* help you, if you'll only file your complaint."

"They don't help you." This particular kid had been put down trying to get a job with one of the larger defense contractors.

"Maybe not before. But it's different now."

"Now," the kid sighed, *"now.* See, people been hearing that *'now'* for a long time, and I'm just tired of the Man telling you, *'Now* it's OK, *now* we mean what we say.' "

In Watts, apparently, where no one can afford the luxury of illusion, there is little reason to believe that now will be any different, any better than last time.

It is perhaps a measure of the people's indifference that only 2 percent of the poor in Los Angeles turned out to elect representatives to the EYOA "poverty board." For a hopeless minority on the board (7 out of 23), nobody saw much point in voting.

Meantime, the outposts of the establishment drowse in the bright summery smog: secretaries chat the afternoons plaintively away about machines that will not accept the cards they have punched for them; white volunteers sit filing, doodling, talking on the phones, doing any kind of busy-work, wondering where the "clients" are; inspirational mottoes like SMILE decorate the beaverboard office walls along with flow charts to illustrate the proper disposition of "cases," and with clippings from the slick magazines about "What Is Emotional Maturity?"

Items like smiling and Emotional Maturity are in fact very big with the well-adjusted, middle-class professionals, Negro and white, who man the mimeographs and computers of the poverty war here. Sadly, they seem to be smiling themselves out of any meaningful communication with their poor. Besides a nineteenth century faith that tried and true approaches—sound counseling, good intentions, perhaps even compassion—will set Watts straight, they are also burdened with the personal attitudes they bring to work with them. Their reflexes—especially about conformity, about failure, about violence—are predictable.

"We had a hell of a time with this one girl," a Youth Training and Employment Project counselor recalls. "You should have seen those hairdos of hers—piled all the way up to here. And the screwy outfits she'd come in with, you just wouldn't believe. We had to take her aside and explain to her that employers just don't go for that sort of thing. That she'd be up against a lot of very smooth-looking chicks, heels and stockings, conservative hair and clothes. We finally got her to come around."

The same goes for boys who like to wear Malcolm hats, or Afro haircuts. The idea the counselors push evidently is to look as much as possible like a white applicant. Which is to say, like a Negro job counselor or social worker. This has not been received with much enthusiasm among the kids it is designed to help out, and is one reason business is so slow around the various projects.

There is a similar difficulty among the warriors about failure. They are in a socio-economic bag, along with the vast majority of white Angelenos, who seem more terrified of failure than of death. It is difficult to see where any of them have experienced significant defeat, or loss. If they have, it seems to have been long rationalized away as something else.

You are likely to hear from them wisdom on the order of: "Life has a way of surprising us, simply as a function of time. Even if all you do is stand on the street corner and wait." Watts is full of street corners where people stand, as they have been, some of them, for twenty or thirty years, without Surprise One ever having come along. Yet the poverty warriors must believe in this form of semimiracle, because their world and their scene cannot accept the possibility that there may be, after all, no surprise. But it is something Watts has always known.

As for violence, in a pocket of reality such as Watts, violence is never far from you: because you are a man, because you have been put down, because for every action there is an equal and opposite reaction. Somehow, sometime. Yet to these innocent, optimistic child-bureaucrats, violence is an evil and an illness, possibly because it threatens property and status they cannot help cherishing.

They remember last August's riot as an outburst, a seizure. Yet what, from the realistic viewpoint of Watts, was so abnormal? "Man's got his foot on your neck," said one guy who was there, "sooner or later you going to stop *asking* him to take it off." The violence it took to get that foot to ease up even the little it did was no surprise. Many had predicted it. Once it got going, its basic objective—to beat the Black and White police—seemed a reasonable one, and was gained the minute the Man had to send troops in. Everybody seems to have known it. There is hardly a person in Watts now who finds it painful to talk about, or who regrets that it happened—unless he lost somebody.

But in the white culture outside, in that creepy world full of pre-cardiac Mustang drivers who scream insults at one another only when the windows are up; of large corporations where Niceguymanship is the standing order regardless of whose executive back one may be endeavoring to stab; of an enormous priest caste of shrinks who counsel moderation and compromise as the answer to all forms of hassle; among so much well-behaved unreality, it is next to impossible to understand how Watts may truly feel about violence. In terms of strict reality, violence may be a means to getting money, for example, no more dishonest than collecting exorbitant carrying charges from a customer on relief, as white merchants here still do. Far from a sickness, violence may be an attempt to communicate, or to be who you really are.

"Sure I did two stretches," a kid says, "both times for fighting, but I didn't deserve either one. First time, the cat was bigger than I was; next time, it was two against one, and I was the one." But he was busted all the same, perhaps because whitey, who knows how to get everything he wants, no longer has fisticuffs available as a technique, and sees no reason why everybody shouldn't go the Niceguy route. If you are thinking maybe there is a virility hangup in here, too, that putting a Negro into a correctional institution for fighting is also some kind of neutering operation, well, you might have something there, who knows?

It is, after all, in white L.A.'s interest to cool Watts any way it can—to put the area under a siege of persuasion; to coax the Negro poor into taking on certain white values. Give them a little property, and they will be less tolerant of arson; get them to go in hock for a car or color TV, and they'll be more likely to hold down a steady job. Some see it for what it is—this come-on, this false welcome, this attempt to transmogrify the reality of Watts into the unreality of Los Angeles. Some don't.

Watts is tough; has been able to resist the unreal. If there is any drift away from reality, it is by way of mythmaking. As this summer [1966] warms up, last August's riot is being remembered less as chaos and more as art. Some talk now of a balletic quality to it, a coordinated and graceful drawing of cops away from the center of the action, a scattering of the Man's power, either with real incidents or false alarms.

Others remember it in terms of music; through much of the rioting seemed to run, they say, a remarkable empathy, or whatever it is that jazz musicians feel on certain nights; everybody knowing what to do and when to do it without needing a word or a signal: "You could go up to anybody, the cats could be in the middle of burning down a store or something, but they'd tell you, explain very calm, just what they were doing, what they were going to do next. And that's what they'd do; man, nobody had to give orders."

Restructuring of the riot goes on in other ways. All Easter week this year, in the spirit of the season, there was a "Renaissance of the Arts," a kind of festival in memory of Simon Rodia, held at Markham Junior High, in the heart of Watts.

Along with theatrical and symphonic events, the festival also featured a roomful of sculptures fashioned entirely from found objects—found, symbolically enough, and in the Simon Rodia tradition, among the wreckage the rioting had left. Exploiting textures of charred wood, twisted metal, fused glass, many of the works were fine, honest rebirths.

MAN AGAINST POVERTY

In one corner was this old, busted, hollow TV set with a rabbit-ears antenna on top; inside, where its picture tube should have been, gazing out with scorched wiring threaded like electronic ivy among its crevices and sockets, was a human skull. The name of the piece was *The Late, Late, Late Show*.

C. MEANS TO AN END

INTRODUCTION

THERE ARE NO MAGIC SOLUTIONS or painless formulas for ridding the United States of poverty. There is no single answer —but this does not imply that there are no answers, or that any plan or program is as good as any other. The reader will find in this section suggestions that range from the specific and local to the sweeping and nationwide, from limited day-to-day programs to new massive campaigns for attack on the problems of poverty.

"The Triple Revolution," endorsed by a number of leading economists and social scientists, provides an innovational perspective for viewing three crucial problems of American society: cybernation, weaponry, and human rights. "The Freedom Budget" offers a blueprint for government spending in the amount of $168 billion over the next ten years, which, its proponents claim, would virtually eliminate poverty by the end of those ten years.

The President's Commission on Civil Disorders produced an alarming and thorough report. It documented all the injustices and pointed its finger at the squalid conditions that are a way of life for millions of slum dwellers in our urban ghettos. It urged in no uncertain terms that the federal government reorder its priorities and make available massive aid for our cities. Finally, and of critical importance, it placed the onus of responsibility for racism squarely on the shoulders of white America.

In September of 1966, President Johnson appointed the National Advisory Commission on Rural Poverty. He charged the commission with the responsibilities of making a comprehensive study and appraisal of economic trends in rural life and how they relate to community problems in rural areas. "The People Left Behind" is a general evaluation and summary of the recommendations of the commission. It is obvious that we have only begun to scratch the surface in dealing with the problems of the rural poor. The commission's report could well be entitled "The Other, Rural America."

Martin Luther King, Jr., in "A New Kind of Power," analyzes Black Power, gives his reasons for its growth, and interprets it as a positive attempt by black people to "amass the political and economic strength to achieve their legitimate goals."

Based on the successful experience of ACTION-Housing in Pittsburgh, Bernard Loshbough defines the role of community action programs in urban renewal and discusses how these programs can contribute to the overall objectives of the "war on poverty." Although this article was written two years ago, it is particularly relevant today in that it gets right at the heart of the vital issue of what constitutes a viable community action program. In spite of the fact that a single, standard model applicable to all communities has not evolved, Loshbough does illustrate, through the Pittsburgh project, all the necessary resources that must be harnessed and utilized in order to develop a well-balanced program. He analyzes the need for more meaningful coordination and communication between neighborhood people on the one hand and federal, state, and local agencies on the other; that need is to this day the major problem facing planners, administrators, indigenous participants and Congress.

Frank Riessman and Arthur Pearl present their widely acclaimed plan for providing para-professional careers for the poor, particularly in the helping professions of medicine, law, education, and social service. A startling and yet feasible program to force American leaders to come to grips with the real nature of poverty is outlined by Richard Cloward and Frances Piven; their proposal, if effectively carried out, would drive local welfare programs to financial ruin.

Roger Woock examines the failures of both "compensatory" programs and urban school desegregation programs to solve the educational problems of minority group youngsters. He suggests that the alternative of community-operated schools, although not a panacea, might provide a better educational framework.

THE TRIPLE
REVOLUTION*

THIS STATEMENT is written in the recognition that mankind is at a historic conjuncture which demands a fundamental re-examination of existing values and institutions. At this time three separate and mutually reinforcing revolutions are taking place:

The Cybernation Revolution: A new era of production has begun. Its principles of organization are as different from those of the industrial era as those of the industrial era were different from the agricultural. The cybernation revolution has been brought about by the combination of the computer and the automated self-regulating machine. This results in a system of almost unlimited productive capacity which requires progressively less human labor. Cybernation is already reorganizing the economic and social system to meet its own needs.

The Weaponry Revolution: New forms of weaponry have been developed which cannot win wars but which can obliterate civilization. We are recognizing only now that the great weapons have eliminated war as a method for resolving international conflicts. The ever-present threat of total destruction is tempered by the knowledge of the final futility of war. The need of a "warless world" is generally recognized, though achieving it will be a long and frustrating process.

* Written and published by the Ad Hoc Committee on the Triple Revolution. Reprinted by permission.

The Human Rights Revolution: A universal demand for full human rights is now clearly evident. It continues to be demonstrated in the civil rights movement within the United States. But this is only the local manifestation of a worldwide movement toward the establishment of social and political regimes in which every individual will feel valued and none will feel rejected on account of his race.

We are particularly concerned in this statement with the first of these revolutionary phenomena. This is not because we underestimate the significance of the other two. On the contrary, we affirm that it is the simultaneous occurrence and interaction of all three developments which make evident the necessity for radical alterations in attitude and policy. The adoption of just policies for coping with cybernation and for extending rights to all Americans is indispensable to the creation of an atmosphere in the U.S. in which the supreme issue, peace, can be reasonably debated and resolved.

The Negro claims, as a matter of simple justice, his full share in America's economic and social life. He sees adequate employment opportunities as a chief means of attaining this goal: The March on Washington [1963] demanded freedom *and* jobs. The Negro's claim to a job is not being met. Negroes are the hardest-hit of the many groups being exiled from the economy by cybernation. Negro unemployment rates cannot be expected to drop substantially. Promises of jobs are a cruel and dangerous hoax on hundreds of thousands of Negroes and whites alike who are especially vulnerable to cybernation because of age or inadequate education.

The demand of the civil rights movement cannot be fulfilled within the present context of society. The Negro is trying to enter a social community and a tradition of work-and-income which are in the process of vanishing even for the hitherto privileged white worker. Jobs are disappearing under the impact of highly efficient, progressively less costly machines.

The U.S. operates on the thesis, set out in the Employment Act of 1964, that every person will be able to obtain a job if he wishes to do so and that this job will provide him with resources adequate to live and maintain a family decently. Thus job-holding is the general mechanism through which economic resources are distributed. Those without work have access only to a minimal income, hardly sufficient to provide the necessities of life, and enabling those receiving it to function as only "minimum consumers." As a result, the goods and services which are needed by these crippled consumers, and which they would buy if they could, are not produced. This in turn deprives other workers of jobs, thus reducing their incomes and consumption.

Present excessive levels of unemployment would be multiplied several times if military and space expenditures did not continue to absorb 10 percent of the gross national product (i.e., the total goods and services produced). Some 6 to 8 million people are employed as a direct result of purchases for space and military activities. At least an equal number hold their jobs as an indirect result of military or space expenditures. In recent years, the military and space budgets have absorbed a rising proportion of national production and formed a strong support for the economy.

However, these expenditures are coming in for more and more criticism, at least partially in recognition of the fact that nuclear weapons have eliminated war as an acceptable method for resolving international conflicts. Early in 1964 President Johnson ordered a curtailment of certain military expenditures. Defense Secretary McNamara is closing shipyards, airfields, and Army bases, and Congress is pressing the National Space Administration to economize. The future of these strong props to the economy is not as clear today as it was even a year ago. . . .

Proposal for Action

As a first step to a new consensus it is essential to recognize that the traditional link between jobs and incomes is being broken. The economy of abundance can sustain all citizens in comfort and economic security whether or not they engage in what is commonly reckoned as work. Wealth produced by machines rather than by men is still wealth. We urge, therefore, that society, through its appropriate legal and governmental institutions, undertake an unqualified commitment to provide every individual and every family with an adequate income as a matter of right.

This undertaking we consider to be essential to the emerging economic, social and political order in this country. We regard it as the only policy by which the quarter of the nation now dispossessed and soon-to-be dispossessed by lack of employment can be brought within the abundant society. The unqualified right to an income would take the place of the patchwork of welfare measures—from unemployment insurance to relief—designed to ensure that no citizen or resident of the U.S. actually starves.

We do not pretend to visualize all of the consequences of this change in our values. It is clear, however, that the distribution of abundance in a cybernated society must be based on criteria strikingly different from those of an economic system based on scarcity. In retrospect, the establishment of the right to an income will prove to have been only the first step in the reconstruction of the value system of our society brought on by the triple revolution.

The present system encourages activities which can lead to private profit and neglects those activities which can enhance the wealth and the quality of life of our society. Consequently, national policy has hitherto been aimed far more at the welfare of the productive process than at the welfare of people. The era of cybernation can reverse this emphasis. With public policy and research concentrated on people rather than processes, we believe that many creative activities and interests commonly thought of as noneconomic will absorb the time and the commitment of many of those no longer needed to produce goods and services.

Society as a whole must encourage new modes of constructive, rewarding and ennobling activity. Principal among these are activities such as teaching and learning that relate people to people rather than people to things. Education has never been primarily conducted for profit in our society; it represents the first and most obvious activity inviting the expansion of the public sector to meet the needs of this period of transition.

We are not able to predict the long-run patterns of human activity and commitment in a nation when fewer and fewer people are involved in production of goods and services, nor are we able to forecast the over-all patterns of income distribution that will replace those of the past full-employment system.

However, these are not speculative and fanciful matters to be contemplated at leisure for a society that may come into existence in three or four generations. The outlines of the future press sharply into the present. The problems of joblessness, inadequate incomes, and frustrated lives confront us now; the American Negro, in his rebellion, asserts the demands—and the rights—of all the disadvantaged. The Negro's is the most insistent voice today, but behind him stand the millions of impoverished who are beginning to understand that cybernation, properly understood and used, is the road out of want and toward a decent life.

The Transition[1]

We recognize that the drastic alternations in circumstances and in our way of life ushered in by cybernation and the economy of abundance will not be completed overnight. Left to the ordinary forces of the market such change, however, will involve physical and psychological misery and perhaps political chaos. Such misery is already clearly evident among the unemployed, among relief clients into the third generation and more and more among the young and the old for whom society appears to hold no promise of dignified or even stable lives. We must develop programs for this transition designed to give hope to the dispossessed and those cast out by the economic system, and to provide a basis for the rallying of people to bring about those changes in political and social institutions which are essential to the age of technology.

The program here suggested is not intended to be inclusive but rather to indicate its necessary scope. We propose:

1. A massive program to build up our educational system, designed especially with the needs of the chronically under-

---

[1] This view of the transitional period is not shared by all the signers. Robert Theobald and James Boggs hold that the two major principles of the transitional period will be (1) that machines rather than men will take up new conventional work openings and (2) that the activity of men will be directed to new forms of "work" and "leisure." Therefore, in their opinion, the specific proposals outlined in this section are more suitable for meeting the problems of the scarcity-economics system than for advancing through the period of transition into the period of abundance.

educated in mind. We estimate that tens of thousands of employment opportunities in such areas as teaching and research and development, particularly for younger people, may be thus created. Federal programs looking to the training of an additional 100,000 teachers annually are needed.

2. Massive public works. The need is to develop and put into effect programs of public works to construct dams, reservoirs, ports, water and air pollution facilities, community recreation facilities. We estimate that for each $1 billion per year spent on public works 150,000 to 200,000 jobs would be created. $2 billion or more a year should be spent in this way, preferably as matching funds aimed at the relief of economically distressed or dislocated areas.

3. A massive program of low-cost housing, to be built both publicly and privately, and aimed at a rate of 700,000–1,000,-000 units a year.

4. Development and financing of rapid-transit systems, urban and interurban; and other programs to cope with the spreading problems of the great metropolitan centers.

5. A public power system built on the abundance of coal in distressed areas, designed for low-cost power to heavy industrial and residential sections.

6. Rehabilitation of obsolete military bases for community or educational use.

7. A major revision of our tax structure aimed at redistributing income as well as apportioning the costs of the transition period equitably. To this end an expansion of the use of excess profits tax would be important. Subsidies and tax credit plans are required to ease the human suffering involved in the transition of many industries from man power to machine power.

8. The trade unions can play an important and significant role in this period in a number of ways:

a. Use of collective bargaining to negotiate not only for people at work but also for those thrown out of work by technological change.

b. Bargaining for perquisites such as housing, recreational facilities, and similar programs as they have negotiated health and welfare programs.

c. Obtaining a voice in the investment of the unions' huge pension and welfare funds, and insisting on investment policies which have as their major criteria the social use and function of the enterprise in which the investment is made.

d. Organization of the unemployed so that these voiceless people may once more be given a voice in their own economic destinies, and strengthening of the campaigns to organize white-collar and professional workers.

9. The use of the licensing power of government to regulate the speed and direction of cybernation to minimize hardship; and the use of minimum wage power as well as taxing powers to provide the incentives for moving as rapidly as possible toward the goals indicated by this paper.

These suggestions are in no way intended to be complete or definitively formulated. They contemplate expenditures of several billions more each year than are now being spent for socially rewarding enterprises, and a larger role for the government in the economy than it has now or has been given except in times of crisis. In our opinion, this is a time of crisis, the crisis of a triple revolution. Public philosophy for the transition must rest on the conviction that our economic, social and political institutions exist for the use of man and that man does not exist to maintain a particular economic system. This philosophy centers on an understanding that governments are instituted among men for the purpose of making possible life, liberty, and the pursuit of happiness and that government should be a creative and positive instrument toward these ends.

Change Must Be Managed

The historic discovery of the post-World War II years is that the economic destiny of the nation can be managed. Since the debate over the Employment Act of 1946 it has been increasingly understood that the federal government bears primary responsibility for the economic and social well-being of the country. The essence of management is planning. The democratic requirement is planning by public bodies for the general welfare. Planning by private bodies such as corporations for their own welfare does not automatically result in additions to the general welfare, as the impact of cybernation on jobs has already made clear.

The hardships imposed by sudden changes in technology have been acknowledged by Congress in proposals for dealing with the long- and short-run "dislocations," in legislation for depressed and "impacted" areas, retraining of workers replaced by machines, and the like. The measures so far proposed have not been "transitional" in conception. Perhaps for this reason they have had little effect on the situations they were designed to alleviate. But the primary weakness of this legislation is not ineffectiveness but incoherence. In no way can these disconnected measures be seen as a plan for remedying deep ailments but only, so to speak, as the superficial treatment of surface wounds.

Planning agencies should constitute the network through which pass the stated needs of the people at every level of society, gradually building into a national inventory of human requirements, arrived at by democratic debate of elected representatives.

The primary tasks of the appropriate planning institutions should be:

To collect the data necessary to appraise the effects, social and economic, of cybernation at different rates of innovation.

To recommend ways, by public and private initiative, of encouraging and stimulating cybernation.

To work toward optimal allocations of human and natural resources in meeting the requirements of society.

To develop ways to smooth the transition from a society in which the norm is full employment within an economic system based on scarcity, to one in which the norm will be either nonemployment, in the traditional sense of productive work, or employment on the great variety of socially valuable but "nonproductive" tasks made possible by an economy of abundance; to bring about the conditions in which men and women no longer needed to produce goods and services may find their way to a variety of self-fulfilling and socially useful occupations.

To work out alternatives to defense and related spending that will commend themselves to citizens, entrepreneurs and workers as a more reasonable use of common resources.

To integrate domestic and international planning. The technological revolution has related virtually every major domestic problem to a world problem. The vast inequities between the industrialized and the underdeveloped countries cannot long be sustained.

The aim throughout will be the conscious and rational direction of economic life by planning institutions under democratic control.

In this changed framework the new planning institutions will operate at every level of government—local, regional and federal—and will be organized to elicit democratic participation in all their proceedings. These bodies will be the means for giving direction and content to the growing demand for improvement in all departments of public life. The planning institutions will show the way to turn the growing protest against ugly cities, polluted air and water, an inadequate educational system, disappearing recreational and material resources, low levels of medical care, and the haphazard economic development into an integrated effort to raise the level of general welfare.

We are encouraged by the record of the planning institutions both of the Common Market and of several European nations and believe that this country can benefit from studying their weaknesses and strengths.

A principal result of planning will be to step up investment in the public sector. Greater investment in this area is advocated because it is overdue, because the needs in this sector comprise a substantial part of the content of the general welfare, and because they can be readily afforded by an abundant society. Given the knowledge that we are now in a period of transition it would be deceptive, in our opinion, to present such activities as likely to produce full employment. The efficiencies of cybernation should be as much sought in the public as in the private sector, and a chief focus of planning would be one means of bringing this about. A central assumption of planning institutions would be the central assumption of this statement, that the nation is moving into a society in which production of goods and services is not the only or perhaps the chief means of distributing income.

The Democratization of Change

The revolution in weaponry gives some dim promise that mankind may finally eliminate institutionalized force as the method of settling international conflict and find for it political and moral equivalents leading to a better world. The Negro revolution signals the ultimate admission of this group to the American community on equal social, political and economic terms. The cybernation revolution proffers an existence qualitatively richer in democratic as well as material values. A social order in which men make the decisions that shape their lives becomes more possible now than ever before; the unshackling of men from the bonds of unfulfilling labor frees them to become citizens, to make themselves and to make their own history.

But these enhanced promises by no means constitute a guarantee. Illuminating and making more possible the "democratic vistas" is one thing; reaching them is quite another, for a vision of democratic life is made real not by technological change but by men consciously moving toward that ideal and creating institutions that will realize and nourish the vision in living form.

Democracy, as we use the term, means a community of men and women who are able to understand, express and determine their lives as dignified human beings. Democracy can only be rooted in a political and economic order in which wealth is distributed by and for people, and used for the widest social benefit. With the emergence of the era of abundance we have the economic base for a true democracy of participation, in which men no longer need to feel themselves prisoners of social forces and decisions beyond their control or comprehension.

THE "FREEDOM

BUDGET" IN BRIEF*

THE "FREEDOM BUDGET" stems from seven basic principles:

1. Freedom on the American scene must include what Franklin D. Roosevelt called "freedom from want." This can be achieved, not by the power of any one group, but by the power of a fully-employed U.S. economy plus the power of the aroused conscience of the American people.

2. "Freedom from want" for an increasing majority of our citizens is not good enough; it must embrace all. Our economy is rich enough, and should be just enough, to reject as intolerable the ghetto within stone's throw of the duplex apartment; the alien worlds of slums and suburbs; the unemployment rate four times as high in some localities as in the nation at large; the millions receiving substandard wages despite many thousands of millionaires; the low-income farmers despite luxury restaurants; the poverty among 34 million and the deprivation among another 28 million, in a land where median family income is now close to $7,000, and where the families in the top income fifth have about eight times as much income as the families in the lowest income fifth. We have already received tragic warning that there is no prospect for domestic tranquility in a nation divided between the affluent and the desperately poor.

3. The U.S. economy has the productive power to abolish "freedom from want" by 1975, not by pulling down those at the top but by lifting those at the bottom, if we start *now* and do our best. What we have the power to do, we will in fact do, if we *care* enough about doing it. The real issue is neither economic nor financial, but moral.

4. Our economy is now too abundant for the poverty or

* From *A "Freedom Budget" for All,* A. Philip Randolph Institute, October 1966.

deprivation still afflicting almost a third of a nation to be explained mainly by the personal characteristics of the victims. True, personal deficiencies have a bearing upon the economic condition of many individuals. But it is even more true that deficiencies in nationwide policies and programs, evidencing a default in the national conscience, spawn and perpetuate these personal deficiencies. Just as malaria has been stamped out more by clearing swamps than by injecting quinine, the main attack upon poverty and deprivation must deal more with the nationwide environment than with the individual. Beyond this, the modern technology has advanced to the point where every American should enjoy "freedom from want," regardless of personal characteristics.

5. While "freedom from want" by 1975 will require action at all levels, private and public, the leadership role must be taken by our federal government. It alone represents all the people. Its policies and programs exert the most powerful single influence upon economic performance and social thinking. We accept this principle without question during a total war against external enemies. A "war against poverty" establishes the same principle on the domestic front.

6. A war against want cannot be won with declarations of intent. It cannot be won with token or inadequate programs which identify areas of need, but apply policies and programs which only scratch the surface. It demands specific quantitative goals, fully responsive to the need, and commitment to their attainment.

7. This war against want must be color blind. Negroes will benefit most, relative to their numbers, because, for reasons not of their making, want is most heavily concentrated among them. But in absolute numbers, the vast majority of those yearning for release from want are white. And those already free from want, both white and nonwhite, cannot enjoy fully the benefits of economic progress and the blessings of democracy until "freedom from want" becomes universal throughout the land.

Founded upon these principles, the seven basic objectives of the "Freedom Budget" are these:

1. *To restore full employment as rapidly as possible,* and to

maintain it thereafter, for all able and willing to work, and for all whom adequate training and education would make able and willing. This means an unemployment rate below 3 percent by early 1968, and preferably 2 percent. Full 40 percent of all U.S. poverty is due directly to inadequate employment opportunity, and involuntary unemployment is corrosive of the human spirit.

2. *To assure adequate incomes for those employed.* About 20 percent of all U.S. poverty is among the working poor (including their dependents) who receive substandard wages. In addition, millions of farm families and others in rural areas have substandard incomes. Treatment of these problems depends primarily upon federal legislation.

3. *To guarantee a minimum adequacy level of income to all those who cannot or should not be gainfully employed.* About 40 percent of all U.S. poverty is among those who cannot or should not work because of age or other disabling factors. More than 13 percent of all U.S. poverty is among families headed by women who should not work. Until, under federal auspices, we achieve such a guaranteed income, there should be immediate and vast improvements in all Social Security and welfare programs, with much larger federal participation.

4. *To wipe out the slum ghettos, and provide a decent home for every American family, within a decade.* Foul housing is both cause and consequence of poverty. It breeds resentment and unrest. Housing and urban renewal, on a scale matching the need, would also make the largest single contribution to job creation in the face of job displacement by technological trends elsewhere in the economy. It would accent the types of jobs most suitable for absorbing those now most vulnerable to unemployment.

5. *To provide, for all Americans, modern medical care and educational opportunity up to the limits of their abilities and ambitions, at costs within their means.* The shortage of personnel and facilities upon enactment of Medicare (which helps *only* the aged portion of the population) speaks for itself. Many schools in our great cities are a shambles.

6. *To overcome other manifestations of neglect in the public sector, by purifying our airs and waters, and bringing our trans-*

portation systems and natural resource development into line with the needs of a growing population and an expanding economy. This, too, would provide the types of jobs most suited to reducing unemployment. Along with housing and urban renewal, it would immensely improve the living conditions even of those who already enjoy "freedom from want" in a more limited sense.

7. *To unite sustained full employment with sustained full production and high economic growth.* This is essential, in order that "freedom from want" may be achieved, not by robbing Peter to pay Paul, but under conditions which bring progress to all.

The Key Role of Our Federal Government

The "Freedom Budget" sets forth the above seven basic objectives in specific and quantitative terms. It sets time schedules for their accomplishment. It establishes their feasibility by means of a balance sheet of all our needs and resources, with due allowance for all of our other private and public undertakings and aspirations as a nation and a people.

In this way, the "Freedom Budget" is a call to action. But the response to this call must take the form of national programs and policies, with the federal government exercising that leadership role which is consistent with our history, our institutions, and our needs. The six prime elements in this federal responsibility are now set forth.

1. *Beginning with 1967, the President's Economic Reports should embody the equivalent of a "Freedom Budget."* These reports should quantify ten-year goals for full employment and full production, for the practical liquidation of U.S. poverty by 1975, for wiping out the slum ghettos, and indeed for each of the seven basic objectives set forth in the "Freedom Budget." With due allowance for private and public performance at other levels, but with a firm determination by our federal government to close the gaps, all major federal economic, financial, and social policies—including the federal budget—should be geared to attainment of these ten-year goals, starting at once in realistic magnitudes.

2. *The bedrock civilized responsibility rests with our federal*

government to guarantee sustained full employment. The government should at once and continuously lead in organizing and financing enough job-creating activities to close the gap between full employment and employment provided at other public and private levels. None of these federally-created jobs need to be made-work, because our unmet needs in the public sector are large enough to absorb beneficially this federal effort. Training programs, to be effective, must be synchronized with job creation.

3. *The federal government should exert the full weight of its authority toward immediate enactment of a federal minimum wage of $2 an hour, with coverage extended to the uppermost constitutional limits of federal power.* This would be a moderate start toward eradication of substandard living standards among millions of those employed.

4. *A new farm program, with accent upon incomes rather than prices, should focus upon parity of income for farmers and liquidation of farm poverty by 1975.* More than 43 percent of all farm families now live in poverty, contrasted with only 13 percent of all nonfarm families.

5. *To lift out of poverty and also above deprivation those who cannot or should not be employed, there should be a federally-initiated and supported guaranteed annual income, to supplement rather than to supplant a sustained full-employment policy at decent pay.* The anti-poverty goal alone involves lifting almost all multiple-person families above $3,130 by 1975. Pending this, there should be immediate and vast improvements in all Social Security and welfare programs, with greatly enlarged federal contributions to all of them, including old-age insurance and assistance, general public assistance, special-purpose public assistance, unemployment insurance, and workmen's compensation.

6. *Fiscal and monetary policies should be readjusted to place far more weight upon distributive justice.* The massive federal tax reductions in recent years tended to redistribute income with undue concern for those high up in the income structure, and inadequate concern for those lower down. State and local taxes and indirect taxes are so regressive—they bear with such excessive weight upon low-income people—that we should make the federal income tax much more progressive than now. The

decision to rely so heavily upon tax reduction and so little upon increased domestic spending to stimulate the economy was undesirable; it lowered our capacity to serve some of the greatest priorities of our national needs which depend upon public spending and are hardly helped by tax reduction. The current monetary policy does little to curb the excesses in the economy, and places a severe handicap upon activities of utmost urgency, especially housing. The sharply rising interest rates help those most who need help least, and hurt those most who need help most, because it is the lower income people who depend most upon borrowing. We cannot afford to neglect equity and social considerations in fiscal and monetary policies which transfer billions of dollars every year from some to others. Improved income distribution also helps the whole economy.

REPORT OF THE NATIONAL ADVISORY COMMISSION ON CIVIL DISORDERS— SUMMARY

No AMERICAN—white or black—can escape the consequences of the continuing social and economic decay of our major cities.

Only a commitment to national action on an unprecedented scale can shape a future compatible with the historic ideals of American society.

The great productivity of our economy, and a federal revenue system which is highly responsive to economic growth, can provide the resources.

The major need is to generate new will—the will to tax ourselves to the extent necessary to meet the vital needs of the nation.

We have set forth goals and proposed strategies to reach those goals. We discuss and recommend programs not to commit each of us to specific parts of such programs but to illustrate the type and dimension of action needed.

The major goal is the creation of a true union—a single society and a single American identity. Toward that goal, we propose the following objectives for national action:

· Opening up opportunities to those who are restricted by racial segregation and discrimination, and eliminating all barriers to their choice of jobs, education and housing.

· Removing the frustration of powerlessness among the disadvantaged by providing the means for them to deal with the problems that affect their own lives and by increasing the capacity of our public and private institutions to respond to these problems.

· Increasing communication across racial lines to destroy stereotypes, to halt polarization, end distrust and hostility, and create common ground for efforts toward public order and social justice.

We propose these aims to fulfill our pledge of equality and to meet the fundamental needs of a democratic and civilized society—domestic peace and social justice.

Pervasive unemployment and underemployment are the most persistent and serious grievances in minority areas. They are inextricably linked to the problem of civil disorder.

Despite growing federal expenditures for manpower development and training programs, and sustained general economic prosperity and increasing demands for skilled workers, about two million—white and nonwhite—are permanently unemployed. About ten million are underemployed, of whom 6.5 million work full time for wages below the poverty line.

The 500,000 "hard-core" unemployed in the central cities who lack a basic education and are unable to hold a steady job are made up in large part of Negro males between the ages of 18 and 25. In the riot cities which we surveyed, Negroes were three times as likely as whites to hold unskilled jobs, which are often part time, seasonal, low-paying and "dead end."

Negro males between the ages of 15 and 25 predominated among the rioters. More than 20 percent of the rioters were unemployed, and many who were employed held intermittent, low status, unskilled jobs which they regarded as below their education and ability.

The Commission recommends that the federal government:

· Undertake joint efforts with cities and states to consolidate existing manpower programs to avoid fragmentation and duplication.

· Take immediate action to create 2,000,000 new jobs over the next three years—one million in the public sector and one million in the private sector—to absorb the hard-core unemployed and materially reduce the level of underemployment for all workers, black and white. We propose 250,000 public sector and 300,000 private sector jobs in the first year.

· Provide on-the-job training by both public and private employers with reimbursement to private employers for the extra costs of training the hard-core unemployed, by contract or by tax credits.

· Provide tax and other incentives to investment in rural as well as urban poverty areas in order to offer to the rural poor an alternative to migration to urban centers.

· Take new and vigorous action to remove artificial barriers to employment and promotion, including not only racial discrimination but, in certain cases, arrest records or lack of a high school diploma. Strengthen those agencies such as the Equal Employment Opportunity Commission, charged with eliminating discriminatory practices, and provide full support for Title VI of the 1964 Civil Rights Act allowing federal grant-in-aid funds to be withheld from activities which discriminate on grounds of color or race.

The Commission commends the recent public commitment of the National Council of the Building and Construction Trades Unions, AFL-CIO, to encourage and recruit Negro membership in apprenticeship programs. This commitment should be intensified and implemented.

Education

Education in a democratic society must equip children to develop their potential and to participate fully in American life. For the community at large, the schools have discharged this responsibility well. But for many minorities, and particularly for the children of the ghetto, the schools have failed to provide the educational experience which could overcome the effects of discrimination and deprivation.

This failure is one of the persistent sources of grievance and resentment within the Negro community. The hostility of Negro parents and students toward the school system is generating increasing conflict and causing disruption within many city school districts. But the most dramatic evidence of the relationship between educational practices and civil disorders lies in the high incidence of riot participation by ghetto youth who have not completed high school.

The bleak record of public education for ghetto children is growing worse. In the critical skills—verbal and reading ability —Negro students are falling further behind whites with each year of school completed. The high unemployment and underemployment rate for Negro youth is evidence, in part, of the growing educational crisis.

We support integration as the priority education strategy; it is essential to the future of American society. In this last summer's disorders we have seen the consequences of racial isolation at all levels, and of attitudes toward race, on both sides, produced by three centuries of myth, ignorance and bias. It is indispensable that opportunities for interaction between the races be expanded.

We recognize that the growing dominance of pupils from disadvantaged minorities in city school populations will not soon be reversed. No matter how great the effort toward desegregation, many children of the ghetto will not, within their school careers, attend integrated schools.

If existing disadvantages are not to be perpetuated, we must drastically improve the quality of ghetto education. Equality of results with all-white schools must be the goal.

To implement these strategies, the Commission recommends:

· Sharply increased efforts to eliminate de facto segregation in our schools through substantial federal aid to school systems seeking to desegregate either within the system or in cooperation with neighboring school systems.

· Elimination of racial discrimination in Northern as well as Southern schools by vigorous application of Title VI of the Civil Rights Act of 1964.

· Extension of quality early childhood education to every disadvantaged child in the country.

· Efforts to improve dramatically schools serving disadvantaged children through substantial federal funding of year-round compensatory education programs, improved teaching, and expanded experimentation and research.

· Elimination of illiteracy through greater federal support for adult basic education.

· Enlarged opportunities for parent and community participation in the public schools.

· Reoriented vocational education emphasizing work-experience training and the involvement of business and industry.

· Expanded opportunities for higher education through increased federal assistance to disadvantaged students.

· Revision of state aid formulas to assure more per student aid to districts having a high proportion of disadvantaged school-age children.

The Welfare System

Our present system of public welfare is designed to save money instead of people, and tragically ends up doing neither. This system has two critical deficiencies:

First, it excludes large numbers of persons who are in great need, and who, if provided a decent level of support, might be able to become more productive and self-sufficient. No federal funds are available for millions of men and women who are needy but neither aged, handicapped nor the parents of minor children.

Second, for those included, the system provides assistance well below the minimum necessary for a decent level of existence, and imposes restrictions that encourage continued dependency on welfare and undermine self-respect.

A welter of statutory requirements and administrative practices and regulations operate to remind recipients that they are considered untrustworthy, promiscuous and lazy. Residence requirements prevent assistance to people in need who are newly arrived in the state. Regular searches of recipients' homes violate privacy. Inadequate social services compound the problems.

The Commission recommends that the federal government, acting with state and local governments where necessary, reform the existing welfare system to:

· Establish uniform national standards of assistance at least as high as the annual "poverty level" of income, now set by the Social Security Administration at $3,335 per year for an urban family of four.
· Require that all states receiving federal welfare contributions participate in the Aid to Families with Dependent Children—Unemployed Parents program (AFDC-UP) that permits assistance to families with both father and mother in the home, thus aiding the family while it is still intact.
· Bear a substantially greater portion of all welfare costs—at least 90 percent of total payments.
· Increase incentives for seeking employment and job training, but remove restrictions recently enacted by the Congress that would compel mothers of young children to work.
· Provide more adequate social services through neighborhood centers and family-planning programs.
· Remove the freeze placed by the 1967 welfare amendments on the percentage of children in a state that can be covered by federal assistance.
· Eliminate residence requirements.

As a long-range goal, the Commission recommends that the federal government seek to develop a national system of income supplementation based strictly on need with two broad and basic purposes:

· To provide, for those who can work or who do work, any necessary supplements in such a way as to develop incentives for fuller employment;
· To provide, for those who cannot work and for mothers who decide to remain with their children, a minimum standard of decent living, and to aid in the saving of children from the prison of poverty that has held their parents.

A broad system of supplementation would involve substantially greater federal expenditures than anything now contemplated. The cost will range widely depending on the standard of need accepted as the "basic allowance" to individuals and families, and on the rate at which additional income above this level is taxed. Yet if the deepening cycle of poverty and dependence on welfare can be broken, if the children of the poor can be given the opportunity to scale the wall that now separates them from the rest of society, the return on this investment will be great indeed.

Housing

After more than three decades of fragmented and grossly underfunded federal housing programs, nearly six million substandard housing units remain occupied in the United States.

The housing problem is particularly acute in the minority ghettos. Nearly two-thirds of all non-white families living in the central cities today live in neighborhoods marked with substandard housing and general urban blight. Two major factors are responsible.

First: Many ghetto residents simply cannot pay the rent necessary to support decent housing. In Detroit, for example, over 40 percent of the non-white occupied units in 1960 required rent of over 35 percent of the tenants' income.

Second: Discrimination prevents access to many non-slum areas, particularly the suburbs, where good housing exists. In addition, by creating a "back pressure" in the racial ghettos, it makes it possible for landlords to break up apartments for denser occupancy, and keeps prices and rents of deteriorated ghetto housing higher than they would be in a truly free market.

To date, federal programs have been able to do comparatively little to provide housing for the disadvantaged. In the 31-year history of subsidized federal housing, only about 800,-000 units have been constructed, with recent production averaging about 50,000 units a year. By comparison, over a period only three years longer, FHA insurance guarantees have made possible the construction of over ten million middle and upper-income units.

Two points are fundamental to the Commission's recommendations:

First: Federal housing programs must be given a new thrust aimed at overcoming the prevailing patterns of racial segregation. If this is not done, those programs will continue to concentrate the most impoverished and dependent segments of the population into the central-city ghettos where there is already a critical gap between the needs of the population and the public resources to deal with them.

Second: The private sector must be brought into the production and financing of low and moderate rental housing to supply the capabilities and capital necessary to meet the housing needs of the nation.

The Commission recommends that the federal government:

· Enact a comprehensive and enforceable federal open housing law to cover the sale or rental of all housing, including single family homes.

· Reorient federal housing programs to place more low and moderate income housing outside of ghetto areas.

· Bring within the reach of low and moderate income families within the next five years six million new and existing units of decent housing, beginning with 600,000 units in the next year.

To reach this goal we recommend:

· Expansion and modification of the rent supplement program to permit use of supplements for existing housing, thus greatly increasing the reach of the program.

· Expansion and modification of the below-market interest rate program to enlarge the interest subsidy to all sponsors and provide interest-free loans to nonprofit sponsors to cover pre-construction costs, and permit sale of projects to nonprofit corporations, cooperatives, or condominiums.

· Creation of an ownership supplement program similar to present rent supplements, to make home ownership possible for low-income families.

· Federal writedown of interest rates on loans to private builders constructing moderate-rent housing.

· Expansion of the public housing program, with emphasis on small units on scattered sites, and leasing and "turnkey" programs.

· Expansion of the Model Cities program.

· Expansion and reorientation of the urban renewal program to give priority to projects directly assisting low-income households to obtain adequate housing.

| NATIONAL ADVISORY COMMISSION ON RURAL POVERTY | THE PEOPLE LEFT BEHIND* |

THIS REPORT is about a problem which many in the United States do not realize exists. The problem is rural poverty. It affects some 14 million Americans. Rural poverty is so widespread, and so acute, as to be a national disgrace, and its consequences have swept into our cities, violently.

The urban riots during 1967 had their roots, in considerable part, in rural poverty. A high proportion of the people crowded into city slums today came there from rural slums. This fact alone makes clear how large a stake the people of this nation have in an attack on rural poverty.

The total number of rural poor would be even larger than 14 million had not so many of them moved to the city. They made the move because they wanted a job and a decent place to live. Some have found them. Many have not. Many merely exchanged life in a rural slum for life in an urban slum, at exorbitant cost to themselves, to the cities, and to rural America as well.

Even so, few migrants have returned to the rural areas they left. They have apparently concluded that bad as conditions are in an urban slum, they are worse in the rural slum they fled from. There is evidence in the pages of this report to support their conclusion.

* Summary from a September 1967 report by the President's National Advisory Committee on Rural Poverty.

This nation has been largely oblivious to these 14 million impoverished people left behind in rural America. Our programs for rural America are woefully out of date.

Some of our rural programs, especially farm and vocational agriculture programs, are relics from an earlier era. They were developed in a period during which the welfare of farm families was equated with the well-being of rural communities and of all rural people. This no longer is so.

They were developed without anticipating the vast changes in technology, and the consequences of this technology to rural people. Instead of combating low incomes of rural people, these programs have helped to create wealthy landowners while largely bypassing the rural poor.

Most rural programs still do not take the speed and consequences of technological change into account. We have not yet adjusted to the fact that in the brief period of 15 years, from 1950 to 1965, new machines and new methods increased farm output in the United States by 45 percent—and reduced farm employment by 45 percent. Nor is there adequate awareness that during the next 15 years the need for farm labor will decline by another 45 percent. Changes like these on the farm are paralleled on a broader front throughout rural America, affecting many activities other than farming and touching many more rural people than those on farms.

In contrast to the urban poor, the rural poor, notably the white, are not well organized, and have few spokesmen for bringing the nation's attention to their problems. The more vocal and better organized urban poor gain most of the benefits of current antipoverty programs.

Until the past few years, the nation's major social welfare and labor legislation largely bypassed rural Americans, especially farmers and farmworkers. Farm people were excluded from the Social Security Act until the mid-1950s. Farmers, farmworkers, and workers in agriculturally related occupations are still excluded from other major labor legislation, including the unemployment insurance programs, the Labor-Management Relations Act, the Fair Labor Standards Act, and most state workman's compensation acts.

Because we have been oblivious of the rural poor, we have

abetted both rural and urban poverty, for the two are closely linked through migration. The hour is late for taking a close look at rural poverty, gaining an understanding of its consequences, and developing programs for doing something about it. The commission is unanimous in the conviction that effective programs for solving the problems of rural poverty will contribute to the solution of urban poverty as well.

The facts of rural poverty are given in detail later in this report. They are summarized in the paragraphs that follow.

Rural poverty in the United States has no geographic boundaries. It is acute in the South, but it is present and serious in the East, the West, and the North. Rural poverty is not limited to Negroes. It permeates all races and ethnic groups. Nor is poverty limited to the farm. Our farm population has declined until it is only a small fraction of our total rural population. Most of the rural poor do not live on farms. They live in the open country, in rural villages, and in small towns. Moreover, contrary to a common misconception, whites outnumber nonwhites among the rural poor by a wide margin. It is true, however, that an extremely high proportion of Negroes in the rural South and Indians on reservations are destitute.

Hunger, even among children, does exist among the rural poor, as a group of physicians discovered recently in a visit to the rural South. They found Negro children not getting enough food to sustain life, and so disease-ridden as to be beyond cure. Malnutrition is even more widespread. The evidence appears in bad diets and in diseases which often are a product of bad diets.

Disease and premature death are startlingly high among the rural poor. Infant mortality, for instance, is far higher among the rural poor than among the least privileged group in urban areas. Chronic diseases also are common among both young and old. And medical and dental care is conspicuously absent.

Unemployment and underemployment are major problems in rural America. The rate of unemployment nationally is about 4 percent. The rate in rural areas averages about 18 percent. Among farmworkers, a recent study discovered that underemployment runs as high as 37 percent.

The rural poor have gone, and now go, to poor schools. One result is that more than 3 million rural adults are classified as illiterates. In both educational facilities and opportunities, the rural poor have been shortchanged.

Most of the rural poor live in atrocious houses. One in every 13 houses in rural America is officially classified as unfit to live in.

Many of the rural poor live in chronically depressed poverty-stricken rural communities. Most of the rural South is one vast poverty area. Indian reservations contain heavy concentrations of poverty. But there also are impoverished rural communities in the upper Great Lakes region, in New England, in Appalachia, in the Southwest, and in other sections.

The community in rural poverty areas has all but disappeared as an effective institution. In the past the rural community performed the services needed by farmers and other rural people. Technological progress brought sharp declines in the manpower needs of agriculture, forestry, fisheries, and mining. Other industries have not replaced the jobs lost, and they have supplied too few jobs for the young entries in the labor market. Larger towns and cities have taken over many of the economic and social functions of the villages and small towns.

The changes in rural America have rendered obsolete many of the political boundaries to villages and counties. Thus these units operate on too small a scale to be practicable. Their tax base has eroded as their more able-bodied wage earners left for jobs elsewhere. In consequence the public services in the typical poor rural community are grossly inadequate in number, magnitude, and quality. Local government is no longer able to cope with local needs.

As the communities ran downhill, they offered fewer and fewer opportunities for anyone to earn a living. The inadequately equipped young people left in search of better opportunities elsewhere. Those remaining behind have few resources with which to earn incomes adequate for a decent living and for revitalizing their communities.

For all practical purposes, then, most of the 14 million people in our poverty areas are outside our market economy. So far as they are concerned, the dramatic economic growth of the United States might as well never have happened. It has brought them few rewards. They are on the outside looking in, and they need help.

Congress and state legislatures from time to time have enacted many laws and appropriated large sums of money to aid the poverty-stricken and to help rural America. Very little of the legislation or the money has helped the rural poor. Major farm legislation directed at commercial farms has been successful in helping farmers adjust supply to demand, but it has not helped farmers whose production is very small. And because the major social welfare and labor legislation has discriminated against rural people, many of the rural poor—farmers and farmworkers particularly—have been denied unemployment insurance, denied the right of collective bargaining, and denied the protection of workman's compensation laws.

This commission questions the wisdom of massive public efforts to improve the lot of the poor in our central cities without comparable efforts to meet the needs of the poor in rural America. Unfortunately, as public programs improve the lot of the urban poor, without making similar improvements in conditions for the rural poor, they provide fresh incentive for the rural poor to migrate to the central cities. The only solution is a coordinated attack on both urban and rural poverty.

The commission has endeavored to chart a course to wipe out rural poverty. Emphasis has been placed on the problems of poor rural people, and problems of impoverished rural communities. Changes in existing programs and the development of new programs are considered. Action on the immediate needs of the rural poor is emphasized, as well as action to change the conditions which make them poor. Human development and the physical resources needed for this development are stressed. Improving the operation of the private economy in order to provide rural people with better opportunities for jobs and a decent living is emphasized.

It is the firm conviction of the commission that the complexity of the problems of rural poverty precludes the success of a single program or approach. Programs addressed to immediate needs will not erase the underlying conditions creating and perpetuating rural poverty. Programs addressed to these conditions will not immediately help the poor. The commission's recommendations complement and reinforce one another. In total, the recommendations will go far to solve the problems of rural poverty.

The commission is convinced that the abolition of rural poverty in the United States, perhaps for the first time in any nation, is completely feasible. The nation has the economic resources and the technical means for doing this. What it has lacked, thus far, has been the will. The commission rejects the view that poverty, in so rich a nation, is inevitable for any large group of its citizens.

Elsewhere in this report there appear the recommendations of the commission in detail. These recommendations call for action by all branches of government—local, state, and federal —as well as by private individuals and groups. The major thrust of the recommendations is discussed briefly in the paragraphs that follow.

1. The commission recommends that the United States adopt and put into effect immediately a national policy designed to give the residents of rural America equality of opportunity with all other citizens. This must include equal access to jobs, medical care, housing, education, welfare, and all other public services, without regard to race, religion, or place of residence.

2. The commission recommends, as a matter of urgency, that the national policy of full employment, inaugurated in 1946, be made effective. The need is even greater in rural areas than in urban areas. The commission urges that this need be given priority in legislation and appropriations. To the extent that private enterprise does not provide sufficient employment for all those willing and able to work, the commission believes it is the obligation of government to provide it.

3. The commission believes that the United States has the resources and the technical means to assure every person in the United States adequate food, shelter, clothing, medical care, and education and, accordingly, recommends action toward this end. Millions of rural residents today are denied the opportunity of earning a living. The commission believes it is the obligation of society and of government, to assure such people enough income to provide a decent living. In order to achieve this, basic changes are recommended in public assistance programs.

In some rural areas of the United States there is not only malnutrition but hunger. Existing public programs for food distribution to those in need have failed to meet the need. The commission recommends that the food stamp program be expanded nationwide and that eligibility be based upon per capita income. Food stamps should be given to the poorest of the poor without cost.

4. The commission recommends a thorough overhauling of our manpower policies and programs, particularly including public employment services, in order to deal effectively with rural unemployment and underemployment. The commission deplores the fact that the richest, most powerful nation in history compels millions of its citizens to engage in aimless wandering in search of jobs and places to live. The recommendations of the commission aim at a comprehensive and active manpower program which can be an effective weapon against poverty.

5. The commission recommends extensive changes in our rural education system, ranging from preschool programs to adult education. Rural schools must be brought up to par with urban schools. The educational system must reclaim youth and adults who drop out before obtaining sufficient education to cope with the complexities of today's world. An educational extension service is recommended to help teachers and schools meet the needs of all students.

6. The commission is deeply concerned at the evidence of disease and the lack of medical care in rural areas. The commission, therefore, recommends rapid expansion of health manpower—both professional and subprofessional—in rural areas, and the establishment of community health centers which can focus on the health needs of rural people.

7. The commission recommends development and expansion of family planning programs for the rural poor. Low-income families are burdened with relatively numerous children to feed, clothe, and house. They are prepared psychologically to accept family planning. As a matter of principle, they are entitled to facilities and services to help them plan the number and spacing of their children.

8. The commission recommends immediate action to provide housing in rural areas by public agencies and puts special

emphasis on a program providing rent supplements for the rural poor. The commission further recommends that a single unified housing agency be made responsible for housing programs in rural areas and that credit terms be made more responsive to need. The commission also urges a substantial increase in appropriations for Indian housing.

9. The commission believes that the overlapping patchwork of districts, organizations, plans, and programs for development impedes the economic development of lagging and poverty-stricken areas and regions. It, therefore, recommends the creation of multicounty districts, cutting across urban-rural boundaries, to cooperatively plan and coordinate programs for economic development. To finance development, the commission recommends federal grants, loans, and industrial development subsidies, as well as state and local tax reform.

10. The commission believes that without citizen responsibility, which includes the active involvement and participation of all, anti-poverty and economic development programs will flounder. Therefore, the commission recommends that increased attention be given to involving the poor in the affairs of the community, on both local and areawide levels. Specific suggestions are made for improving the effectiveness of the anti-poverty programs of the Office of Economic Opportunity and the Department of Agriculture.

11. The commission recommends that the Federal Government re-examine its commercial farm programs in order to make sure that adjustments in the supply of farm products are not made at the expense of the rural poor. Public programs are recommended to enlarge small farm operations and to retire submarginal land from commercial production, but with safeguards protecting the interests of low-income families living on submarginal land. The commission also recommends that the development of additional farmland with public funds cease until the nation's food and fiber needs require this development.

12. Without effective government at all levels, the recommendations in this report will not result in the eradication of rural poverty. The commission recommends changes in program development and administration to facilitate and encourage the effective involvement of local, state, and federal governments.

| MARTIN LUTHER KING, JR. | A NEW KIND OF POWER* |

BLACK POWER is now a part of the nomenclature of the national community. To some it is abhorrent, to others dynamic; to some it is repugnant, to others exhilarating; to some it is destructive, to others it is useful. Since Black Power means different things to different people and indeed, being essentially an emotional concept, can mean different things to the same person on differing occasions, it is impossible to attribute its ultimate meaning to any single individual or organization. One must look beyond personal styles, verbal flourishes, and the hysteria of the mass media to assess its values, its assets and liabilities, honestly.

First, it is necessary to understand that Black Power is a cry of disappointment. The Black Power slogan did not spring full grown from the head of some philosophical Zeus. It was born from the wounds of despair and disappointment. It is a cry of daily hurt and persistent pain. For centuries the Negro has been caught in the tentacles of white power. Many Negroes have given up faith in the white majority because "white power" with total control has left them empty handed. So in reality the call for Black Power is a reaction to the failure of white power.

It is no accident that the birth of this slogan in the civil rights movement took place in Mississippi—the state symbolizing the most blatant abuse of white power. In Mississippi the murder of civil rights workers is still a popular pastime. In that state more than forty Negroes and whites have either been lynched or murdered over the last three years and not a single man has been punished for these crimes. More than fifty Negro churches have been burned or bombed in Mississippi in the last two years,

* From *Where Do We Go from Here: Chaos or Community?*, abridged from pp. 32–66. Copyright © 1967 by Martin Luther King, Jr. Reprinted by permission of Harper & Row, Publishers.

yet the bombers still walk the streets surrounded by the halo of adoration. This is white power in its most brutal, cold-blooded, and vicious form.

Many of the young people proclaiming Black Power today were but yesterday the devotees of black-white cooperation and nonviolent direct action. With great sacrifice and dedication and a radiant faith in the future they labored courageously in the rural areas of the South; with idealism they accepted blows without retaliating; with dignity they allowed themselves to be plunged into filthy, stinking jail cells; with a majestic scorn for risk and danger they nonviolently confronted the Jim Clarks and the Bull Connors of the South, and exposed the disease of racism in the body politic. If they are America's angry children today this anger is not congenital. It is a response to the feeling that a real solution is hopelessly distant because of the inconsistencies, resistance, and faintheartedness of those in power. If Stokely Carmichael now says that nonviolence is irrelevant, it is because he, as a dedicated veteran of many battles, has seen with his own eyes the most brutal white violence against Negroes and white civil rights workers, and he has seen it go unpunished.

Their frustration is further fed by the fact that even when blacks and whites die together in the cause of justice, the death of the white person gets more attention and concern than the death of the black person. Stokely and his colleagues from SNCC were with us in Alabama when Jimmy Lee Jackson, a brave young Negro man, was killed and when James Reeb, a committed Unitarian white minister, was fatally clubbed to the ground. They remembered how President Johnson sent flowers to the gallant Mrs. Reeb, and in his eloquent "We Shall Overcome" speech paused to mention that one person, James Reeb, had already died in the struggle. Somehow the President forgot to mention Jimmy, who died first. The parents and sister of Jimmy received no flowers from the President. The students felt this keenly. Not that they felt that the death of James Reeb was less than tragic, but because they felt that the failure to mention Jimmy Jackson only reinforced the impression that to white America the life of a Negro is insignificant and meaningless.

There is also great disappointment with the federal govern-ment and its timidity in implementing the civil rights laws on its statute books. The gap between promise and fulfillment is distressingly wide. Millions of Negroes are frustrated and angered because extravagant promises made little more than a year ago are a mockery today. The old way of life—economic coercion, terrorism, murder, and inhuman contempt—have continued unabated. This gulf between the laws and their en-forcement is one of the basic reasons why Black Power advo-cates express contempt for the legislative process.

The disappointment mounts as they turn their eyes to the North. In the northern ghettos, unemployment, housing dis-crimination, and slum schools mock the Negro who tries to hope. There have been accomplishments and some material gain. But these beginnings have revealed how far we have yet to go. The economic plight of the masses of Negroes has worsened. The gap between the wages of the Negro worker and the white worker has widened. Slums are worse and Negroes attend more thoroughly segregated schools today than in 1954.

All of this represents disappointment lifted to astronomical proportions. It is disappointment with timid white moderates who feel that they can set the timetable for the Negro's free-dom. It is disappointment with a federal Administration that seems to be more concerned about winning an ill-considered war in Vietnam than about winning the war against poverty here at home. It is disappointment with white legislators who pass laws in behalf of Negro rights that they never intend to imple-ment. It is disappointment with the Christian church that appears to be more white than Christian, and with many white clergymen who prefer to remain silent behind the security of stained glass windows. It is disappointment with some Negro clergymen who are more concerned about the size of the wheel-base on their automobiles than about the quality of their service to a Negro community. It is disappointment with the Negro middle class that has sailed or struggled out of the muddy ponds into the relatively fresh flowing waters of the mainstream, and in the process have forgotten the stench of the back waters where their brothers are still drowning.

Second, Black Power, in its broad and positive meaning, is a call to black people to amass the political and economic strength to achieve their legitimate goals. No one can deny that the Negro is in dire need of this kind of legitimate power. Indeed one of the great problems that the Negro confronts is his powerlessness. From the old plantations of the South to the newer ghettos of the North, the Negro has been confined to a life of voicelessness and powerlessness. Stripped of the right to make decisions concerning his life and destiny, he has been subject to the authoritarian and sometimes whimsical decisions of the white power structure. The plantation and the ghetto were created by those who had power both to confine those who had no power and to perpetuate their powerlessness. The problem of transforming the ghetto is, therefore, a problem of power—a confrontation between the forces of power demanding change and the forces of power dedicated to preserving the status quo.

Power, properly understood, is the ability to achieve purpose. It is the strength required to bring about social, political, or economic changes. In this sense power is not only desirable but necessary in order to implement the demands of love and justice. One of the greatest problems of history is that the concepts of love and power are usually contrasted as polar opposites. Love is identified with a resignation of power and power with a denial of love. It was this misinterpretation that caused Nietzsche, the philosopher of the "will to power," to reject the Christian concept of love. It was this same misinterpretation which induced Christian theologians to reject Nietzsche's philosophy of the "will to power" in the name of the Christian idea of love. What is needed is a realization that power without love is reckless and abusive and love without power is sentimental and anemic. Power at its best is love implementing the demands of justice. Justice at its best is love correcting everything that stands against love.

There is nothing essentially wrong with power. The problem is that in America power is unequally distributed. This has led Negro Americans in the past to seek their goals through love and moral suasion devoid of power and white Americans to seek their goals through power devoid of love and conscience. It is leading a few extremists today to advocate for Negroes the same destructive and conscienceless power that they have justly abhorred in whites. It is precisely this collision of immoral power with powerless morality which constitutes the major crisis of our times.

In his struggle for racial justice, the Negro must seek to transform his condition of powerlessness into creative and positive power. One of the most obvious sources of this power is political. In *Why We Can't Wait*, published in 1964, I wrote at length of the need for Negroes to unite for political action in order to compel the majority to listen. I urged the development of political awareness and strength in the Negro community, the election of blacks to key positions, and the use of the bloc vote to liberalize the political climate and achieve our just aspirations for freedom and human dignity. To the extent that Black Power advocates these goals, it is a positive and legitimate call to action that we in the civil rights movement have sought to follow all along and which we must intensify in the future.

Black Power is also a call for the pooling of black economic resources to achieve economic security. While the ultimate answer to the Negroes' economic dilemma will be found in a massive federal program for all the poor along the lines of A. Philip Randolph's Freedom Budget,[1] a kind of Marshall Plan for the Disadvantaged, there is something that the Negro himself can do to throw off the shackles of poverty. Although the Negro is still at the bottom of the economic ladder, his collective annual income is upwards of thirty billion dollars. This gives him a considerable buying power that can make the difference between profit and loss in many businesses.

Finally, Black Power is a psychological call to manhood. For years the Negro has been taught that he is nobody, that his color is a sign of his biological depravity, that his being has been stamped with an indelible imprint of inferiority, that his whole history has been soiled with the filth of worthlessness. All too few people realize how slavery and racial segregation have scarred the soul and wounded the spirit of the black man. The whole dirty business of slavery was based on the premise that the Negro was a thing to be used, not a person to be respected.

[1] See pages 171–176.—Eds.

The job of arousing manhood within a people that have been taught for so many centuries that they are nobody is not easy. Even semantics have conspired to make that which is black seem ugly and degrading. In Roget's *Thesaurus* there are some 120 synonyms for "blackness" and at least sixty of them are offensive—such words as blot, soot, grime, devil, and foul. There are some 134 synonyms for "whiteness," and all are favorable, expressed in such words as purity, cleanliness, chastity, and innocence. A white lie is better than a black lie. The most degenerate member of a family is the "black sheep" not the "white sheep." Ossie Davis has suggested that maybe the English language should be "reconstructed" so that teachers will not be forced to teach the Negro child sixty ways to despise himself and thereby perpetuate his false sense of inferiority and the white child 134 ways to adore himself and thereby perpetuate his false sense of superiority.

The history books, which have almost completely ignored the contribution of the Negro in American history, have only served to intensify the Negroes' sense of worthlessness and to augment the anachronistic doctrine of white supremacy.

Even the Negroes' contribution to the music of America is sometimes overlooked in astonishing ways. Two years ago my oldest son and daughter entered an integrated school in Atlanta. A few months later my wife and I were invited to attend a program entitled "music that has made America great." As the evening unfolded, we listened to the folk songs and melodies of the various immigrant groups. We were certain that the program would end with the most original of all American music, the Negro spiritual. But we were mistaken. Instead, all of the students, including our children, ended the program by singing "Dixie."

As we rose to leave the hall, my wife and I looked at each other with a combination of indignation and amazement. All of the students, black and white, all of the parents present that night, and all of the faculty members had been victimized with just another expression of America's penchant for ignoring the Negro, making him invisible, and making his contributions insignificant. I wept within that night. I wept for my children and all black children who have been denied a knowledge of their heritage; I wept for all white children, who through daily miseducation, are taught that the Negro is an irrelevant entity in American society; I wept for all of the white parents and teachers who are forced to overlook the fact that the wealth of cultural and technological progress in America is a result of the commonwealth of inpouring contributions.

In all of the speaking that I have done in the United States before varied audiences, including some hostile whites, the only time that I have been booed was one night in a Chicago mass meeting by some young members of the Black Power movement. I went home that night with an ugly feeling. Selfishly I thought of my sufferings and sacrifices over the last twelve years. Why would they boo one so close to them? But as I lay awake thinking, I finally came to myself, and I could not for the life of me have less than patience and understanding for those young people. For twelve years I, and others like me, had held out radiant promises of progress. I had preached to them about my dream. I had lectured to them about the not too distant day when they would have freedom "all, here and now." I had urged them to have faith in America and in white society. Their hopes had soared. They were now booing because they felt that we were unable to deliver on our promises. They were booing because we had urged them to have faith in people who had too often proved to be unfaithful. They were now hostile because they were watching the dream that they had so readily accepted turn into a frustrating nightmare.

But no revolution can long be sustained by despair. This is the ultimate contradiction of the Black Power movement. It claims to be the most revolutionary wing of the social revolution taking place in the United States. Yet it rejects the one thing that keeps the fire of revolutions burning: the ever-present flame of hope. When hope dies, a revolution degenerates into an undiscriminating catchall for evanescent and futile gestures. The Negro cannot trust his destiny to a philosophy thrust up solely by despair, to a slogan that cannot be implemented into a program.

The Black Power movement of today, like the Garvey "Back to Africa" movement of the twenties, represents a dashing of hope, a conviction of the inability of the Negro to win, and a belief in the infinitude of the ghetto. While there is much grounding in past experience for all of these feelings, a revolution cannot succumb to any of them. Today's despair is a poor chisel to carve out tomorrow's justice.

Black Power is an implicit and often explicit belief in black separatism. Notice that I do not call it black racism. It is inaccurate to refer to Black Power as racism in reverse, as some have recently done. Racism is a doctrine of the congenital inferiority and worthlessness of a people. While a few angry proponents of Black Power have, in moments of bitterness, made wild statements that come close to this kind of racism, the major proponents of Black Power have never contended that the white man is innately worthless.

Yet behind Black Power's legitimate and necessary concern for group unity and black identity lies the belief that there can be a separate black road to power and fulfillment. Few ideas are more unrealistic. There is no salvation for the Negro through isolation.

One of the chief affirmations of Black Power is the call for the mobilization of political strength for black people. But we do not have to look far to see that effective political power for Negroes cannot come through separatism. Granted that there are cities and counties in the country where the Negro is in a majority, they are so few that concentration on them alone would still leave the vast majority of Negroes outside the mainstream of American political life.

Moreover, any program that elects all black candidates simply because they are black and rejects all white candidates simply because they are white is politically unsound and morally unjustifiable. It is true that in many areas of the South, Negroes still must elect Negroes in order to be effectively represented. SNCC staff members are eminently correct when they point out that in Lowndes County, Alabama, there are no white liberals or moderates and no possibility for cooperation between the races at the present time. But the Lowndes County experience cannot be made a measuring rod for the whole of America. The basic thing in determining the best candidate is not his color but his integrity.

Black Power alone is no more insurance against social injustice than white power. Negro politicians can be as opportunistic as their white counterparts if there is not an informed and determined constituency demanding social reform. What is most needed is a coalition of Negroes and liberal whites that will work to make both parties truly responsive to the needs of the poor. Black Power does not envision or desire such a program.

Just as the Negro cannot achieve political power in isolation, neither can he gain economic power through separatism. While there must be a continued emphasis on the need for blacks to pool their economic resources and withdraw economic support from discriminating firms, we must not be oblivious to the fact that the larger economic problems confronting the Negro community will only be solved by federal programs involving billions of dollars.

Neither can our resources supply quality integrated education. All of this requires billions of dollars which only an alliance of liberal-labor-civil rights forces can stimulate. In short, the Negroes' problem cannot be solved unless the whole of American society takes a new turn toward greater economic justice.

In a multi-racial society no group can make it alone. It is a myth to believe that the Irish, the Italians, and the Jews—the ethnic groups that Black Power advocates cite as justification for their views—rose to power through separatism. It is true that they stuck together. But their group unity was always enlarged by joining in alliances with other groups such as political machines and trade unions. To succeed in a pluralistic society, and an often hostile one at that, the Negro obviously needs organized strength, but that strength will only be effective when it is consolidated with constructive alliances from the majority group.

Undeniably there are white elements that cannot be trusted, and no militant movement can afford to relax its vigilance against half-hearted associates or conscious betrayers. Every alliance must be considered on its own merits. Negroes may embrace some and walk out on others where their interests are imperiled. Occasional betrayals, however, do not justify the rejection of the principle of Negro-white alliance.

The history of the movement reveals that Negro-white alliances have played a powerfully constructive role, especially in recent years. While Negro initiative, courage, and imagination precipitated the Birmingham and Selma confrontations and revealed the harrowing injustice of segregated life, the organized strength of Negroes alone would have been insufficient to move Congress and the Administration without the weight of the aroused conscience of white America. In the period ahead, Negroes will continue to need this support. Ten percent of the population cannot by tensions alone induce 90 percent to change a way of life.

The ability of Negroes to enter alliances is a mark of their growing strength, not of their weakness. In entering an alliance, the Negro is not relying on white leadership or ideology, he is taking his place as an equal partner in a common endeavor. His organized strength and his new independence pave the way for alliances. Far from losing independence in an alliance, he is using it for constructive and multiplied gains.

In the final analysis the weakness of Black Power is its failure to see that the black man needs the white man and the white man needs the black man. However much we may try to romanticize the slogan, there is no separate black path to power and fulfillment that does not intersect white roots, and there is no separate white path to power and fulfillment, short of social disaster, that does not share that power with black aspirations for freedom and human dignity. We are tied together in a single garment of destiny. The language, the cultural patterns, the music, the material prosperity, and even the food of America are an amalgam of black and white.

America must be a nation in which its multiracial people are partners in power. This is the essence of democracy toward which all Negro struggles have been directed.

Probably the most destructive feature of Black Power is its unconscious and often conscious call for retaliatory violence. Many well-meaning persons within the movement rationalize that Black Power does not really mean black violence; that those who shout the slogan do not really mean it that way; that the violent connotations are solely the distortions of a vicious press. That the press has fueled the fire is true. But as one who has worked and talked intimately with devotees of

Black Power, I must admit that the slogan is mainly used by persons who have lost faith in the method and philosophy of nonviolence.

One of the main questions that the Negro must confront in his pursuit of freedom is that of effectiveness. What is the most effective way to achieve the desired goal? If a method is not effective, no matter how much steam it releases, it is an expression of weakness, not of strength. Now the plain, inexorable fact is that any attempt of the American Negro to overthrow his oppressor with violence will not work. We do not need President Johnson to tell us this by reminding Negro rioters that they are outnumbered ten to one.

It is not overlooking the limitations of nonviolence and the distance we have yet to go to point out the remarkable record of achievements that have already come through nonviolent action. The 1960 sit-ins desegregated lunch counters in more than 150 cities within a year. The 1961 freedom rides put an end to segregation in interstate travel. The 1956 bus boycott in Montgomery, Alabama, ended segregation on the buses not only of that city but in practically every city of the South. The 1963 Birmingham movement and the climactic March on Washington won passage of the most powerful civil rights law in a century. The 1965 Selma movement brought enactment of the Voting Rights Law. Our nonviolent marches in Chicago last summer brought about a housing agreement which, if implemented, will be the strongest step toward open housing of any city in the nation. Most significant is the fact that this progress occurred with a minimum human sacrifice and loss of life. Fewer people have been killed in ten years of nonviolent demonstrations across the South than were killed in one night of rioting in Watts.

Are we seeking power for power's sake? Or are we seeking to make the world and our nation better places to live? If we seek the latter, violence can never provide the answer. The ultimate weakness of violence is that it is a descending spiral, begetting the very thing it seeks to destroy. Instead of diminishing evil, it multiplies it. Through violence you may murder the liar, but you cannot murder the lie, nor establish the truth. Through violence you may murder the hater, but you do not murder hate. In fact, violence merely increases hate. So it goes. Returning violence for violence multiplies violence, adding deeper darkness to a night already devoid of stars. Darkness cannot drive out darkness: only light can do that. Hate cannot drive out hate: only love can do that.

The beauty of nonviolence is that in its own way and in its own time it seeks to break the chain reaction of evil. With a majestic sense of spiritual power, it seeks to elevate truth, beauty, and goodness to the throne. Therefore, I will continue to follow this method because I think it is the most practically sound and morally excellent way for the Negro to achieve freedom.

One of the greatest paradoxes of the Black Power movement is that it talks unceasingly about not imitating the values of white society, but in advocating violence it is imitating the worst, the most brutal, and the most uncivilized value of American life. American Negroes have not been mass murderers. They have not murdered children in Sunday School, nor have they hung white men on trees bearing strange fruit. They have not been hooded perpetrators of violence, lynching human beings at will and drowning them at whim. I, for one, would not like to see the Negro imitate this element in American life.

Humanity is waiting for something other than blind imitation of the past. If we want to truly advance a step further, if we want to turn over a new leaf and really set a new man afoot, we must begin to turn mankind away from the long and desolate night of violence. May it not be that the new man the world needs is the nonviolent man? Longfellow said, "In this world a man must either be an anvil or a hammer." We must be hammers shaping a new society rather than anvils molded by the old. This will make us not only new men, but will give us a new kind of power. It will not be Lord Acton's image of power that tends to corrupt or absolute power that corrupts absolutely. It will be power infused with love and justice that will change dark yesterdays into bright tomorrows, and lift us from the fatigue of despair to the buoyancy of hope. A dark, desperate, confused, and sin-sick world waits for this new kind of man and this new kind of power.

| BERNARD E. LOSHBOUGH | SOCIAL ACTION PROGRAMS IN URBAN RENEWAL* |

IN LAYING THE GROUNDWORK for this discussion of "Social Action Programs in Urban Renewal," I will state immediately my conviction, based on ACTION-Housing's experience in Pittsburgh, that a social action program needs to engage both the resources of the city and the energetic participation of the neighborhood people. Without both elements, a social action program cannot be effective.

People need to understand and desire renewal and development of their neighborhood before the undertaking of large programs. This is a businesslike approach to problems. The first step in engaging participation and developing understanding is the drawing up of a balance sheet of community assets and liabilities, a balance sheet to be made by the neighborhood people concerned, with professional guidance. Short-range goals must be established, as well as long-range goals reaching many years ahead.

Then comes the formulation of a detailed physical plan, hammered out building by building and area by area in partnership with the Urban Redevelopment Authority, City Planning Department, Board of Public Education, Public Health, local businessmen, and residents. It must fit into comprehensive planning for the overall metropolis.

Concurrently, it is necessary to develop an overall, workable social plan, taking into account the economic status and basic needs of the people, and placing particular emphasis upon education in the broadest sense, opening up and training for employment opportunities, and widening of cultural horizons.

Today, social action programs can be soundly and realistically based. Money and tools for detailed physical planning are

* From *Poverty in America*, edited by Margaret S. Gordon, Chandler Publishing Company, San Francisco. Copyright © 1965 by Chandler Publishing Company. Reprinted by permission.

available through governmental urban renewal. For the first time, money and tools for wide-scale social planning can be attained through the Economic Opportunity Act.

Today's citizens are faced with a host of confusing urban problems, with little faith in their ability as individuals to solve them. Through social action, urban renewal and war on poverty programs, the citizens, who are the consumers of public and private services, can find the allies and resources to meet the problems. In the process, they can be armed with the sophistication and the knowledge of the proper channels through which to utilize the public and private resources available. Their first need is for information and guidance, followed by joint action with their fellow citizens.

This intensive participation of all neighborhood people, including the poverty-stricken, is basic to the success of any social action program. People themselves must take part in planning, decision-making, and implementation of programs for their own betterment, or we may end up with modern, antiseptic cities and alienated people.

This participation, with co-related aid from education, government, foundations, private enterprise, social agencies and other institutions, is what Pittsburgh's ACTION-Housing has been striving to bring about since 1959 through a community development process. This process is called Neighborhood Urban Extension. It is one of a number of approaches to social action that have emerged in the United States and have been and are being tested under operating conditions.

Through the "Gray Areas Program," the Ford Foundation has given financial assistance to experiments in a number of cities, including Boston, New Haven, Washington, D.C., Philadelphia, and Oakland, California; and also in one state, North Carolina, where the concern includes rural problems. Although it provides grant funds to these programs, the Ford Foundation does not enter into selection of staff, administration, or methodology. This autonomy gives operating responsibility to the grantee, where it should be, and allows for testing of various methods in various cities.

The approach is one of systems analysis and "social invention," in the words of the foundation's Director of Public Affairs, Dr. Paul Ylvisaker. It places "the foundation's first bet on the city's school system, and more on school outlook methods than on buildings; on employment systems; administration of justice; and a growing list of similarly critical production processes which are currently bottlenecks in the process of citizen building."

The courage and foresight of the foundation in funneling $15 million into these projects over several years has been of great significance to urban development in the United States. It has jolted public indifference to urban problems, and, I would venture to speculate, greatly accelerated the formulation and passage of the Economic Opportunity Act.

These Gray Area projects are operated by a new kind of urban organization, a melding of the public and private sectors, called "halfway houses," on whose boards sit public officials, high-level representatives of commerce and industry, and other civic leaders. In these cities local philanthropy also has been active.

Careful research and professional planning are done by staff specialists, and imaginative efforts are undertaken to modernize school systems, streamline employment services, and rejuvenate other urban resources. In most project areas, particularly in Boston and New Haven, this social development program goes hand-in-hand with massive urban renewal, and in most of the communities there have been some impressive changes in urban institutions and creation of effective new services. However, the governing philosophy is usually to work with and strengthen existing agencies, rather than to replace them.

These Gray Area projects, which usually encourage the formation, cooperation and support of citizen groups, are making creative and substantive contributions to urban renewal and development. The projects have concentrated on changing and improving the concept and performance of executive agencies—public and private—which already had public mandates and acceptance; for example, mayors, governors, school boards, and the like.

Neighborhood Urban Extension

Pittsburgh has ACTION-Housing's Neighborhood Urban Extension approach through which, I believe, we are finding a way to enlist both people and resources in effective programs of social action.

Neighborhood Urban Extension derives much of its philosophy and methodology from agricultural extension techniques developed more than fifty years ago in the United States under the direction of M. L. Wilson.[1]

ACTION-Housing defines this approach as follows:

Neighborhood Urban Extension is a planing-education-action process for vitalizing and revitalizing urban areas through extension of the resources of the metropolis to the people of neighborhoods who are alerted and assisted to utilize these resources in programs to help themselves achieve a better living environment.[2]

My own four years of work in the community development programs of rural India convinced me of the need for involvement of people in planning social-action programs for urban America. Planning for neighborhood urban extension in Pittsburgh began back in 1959. It included short-term action-research projects and conferences, with citizens, as well as specialists and officials, many from the Ford Foundation, participating from the beginning.

Numerous conferences and meetings were held with local officials, national and international specialists in community development, members of citizens' councils, settlement house officials, officials of the Pennsylvania State Agricultural Extension Service, and other educators from major universities throughout the country.

Eleven action-research projects of six weeks' duration included homemaking, parent-school relations, neighborhood business, home modernization, church-community relations, and a neighborhood youth corps, and were carried out with citizens in a number of neighborhoods in 1962. Programs in other cities were studied. In one declining old neighborhood in Pittsburgh, where neighborhood leaders had been asking ACTION-Housing for assistance, a comprehensive pilot program was carried out for three years.

[1] M. L. Wilson, retired Administrator of Agricultural Extension and former Assistant Secretary, U.S. Department of Agriculture, Washington, D.C.

[2] Plan of Operations, Neighborhood Urban Extension, Pittsburgh, March 1963.

Based on this preparation, a full-scale, five-year demonstration was begun in 1963 in three large Pittsburgh neighborhoods. The Ford Foundation has granted a total of $475,000 for the five-year demonstration in the three neighborhoods, an amount more than matched by grants from Pittsburgh foundations and corporations and from the neighborhood people themselves, making a total of more than $1 million.

ACTION-Housing, as an across-the-board civic organization with representation of powerful interests and considerable city and county backing, regardless of political affiliation, mobilizes the resources of the city so that they become available to neighborhood people. Citizen groups in the neighborhood determine their own needs, do their own planning, establish relations with the resources that can meet their needs, and get them extended into the neighborhood, where they are coordinated and utilized. Citizens are assisted to organize, plan, and act by neighborhood extension workers supplied by ACTION-Housing and other public and private agencies' staffs, with subject-matter specialists.

The relationship between ACTION-Housing and the citizen group in each neighborhood is delineated by a signed agreement which specifies mutual goals, and the responsibilities and rights of each party. The written agreement provides for joint decisions on planning and programming, and for joint financing of the program. Both parties enter the relationship freely and voluntarily. The heart of the relationship is the written agreement.

Before any worker is hired and assigned to a neighborhood, he is interviewed by citizen leaders. If they have valid objections, he is not hired. The final decision, however, rests with the Executive Director of ACTION-Housing.

This demonstration is now in its fifth year in two of the three neighborhoods, and in its eighth in the other. Many hundreds of citizens participate diligently in planning, decision-making, and action in each of the three neighborhoods.

These citizen councils act with great independence, having regular and direct negotiations with department heads, the mayor's office, City Council, and other officials. Their method is one of harmonious cooperation when possible, but militant action when absolutely necessary. This was the case last summer when, after years of broken promises from Pennsylvania's Highways Department concerning the building of a new bridge, and many fruitless negotiations, housewives and men of one neighborhood blockaded the old bridge for weeks and forced the state to act. The bridge is now being built.

Similarly, following repeated charges of laxity in law enforcement made by a neighborhood urban extension council, the mayor of our city has asked the International Association of Chiefs of Police to undertake a "comprehensive study into all phases of Police Bureau administration" in Pittsburgh.

Militant action by these Pittsburgh citizens' councils is a method to be used on occasion, rather than a permanent operating philosophy. The Neighborhood Urban Extension approach is one of "consensus" rather than one of pre-determined and inevitable conflict.

In planning, decision-making and prompt implementation, Neighborhood Urban Extension works to create such a consensus of all the neighborhood people, including the hard-core poverty-stricken, government, universities and public and private school systems, commerce and industry, churches, social agencies, and the other major urban resources.

At a Ford Foundation conference I attended in December, 1964, Jack Conway, who later became Deputy Director of the Office of Economic Opportunity, stated that there are three basic strengths for a community action program—

1. Strong public commitment,

2. Involvement of the private community, including business, labor and civil rights groups, and

3. Involvement of the poor themselves.

He predicted, "Without participation of the poor this program will not be a success."

ACTION-Housing's experience bears out another contention that is coming to be widely recognized. This is that social and economic issues cannot be separated. The nurturing of social responsibilities goes hand-in-hand with the development of a sound economy.

In times past, slums in the United States, made up largely of successive waves of millions of immigrants, were not the nearly hopeless traps they have become in recent years. Poverty, hunger, discrimination, and intolerable conditions were prevalent, certainly. Although the aged, for the most part, accepted their lot, they worked and prayed for their children. For the ambitious, energetic youth, there usually was opportunity to set forth and find employment and decent housing elsewhere than in the slums—in a country that was building and expanding, with some pauses, in every direction. Many of these sons and daughters of immigrants have become the professional, political, and business leaders of modern times.

In recent years, racial discrimination and radical technological changes have fundamentally worsened the situation in the blighted, gray areas and slums of our inner cities. Today, the future of the untrained, deprived white dropout seems bleak enough, but if such a youth's skin also happens to be black, there may seem to be no way out.

As a large proportion of middle and moderate income families have rushed out to suburbia, large areas of our inner cities have become festering reservations of the unskilled and helpless. The functionally illiterate, the apathetic aged, the displaced victims of a rapidly industrializing society, racketeers, dope pushers, and delinquents, are crowded into an environment of inadequate, deteriorating housing in neighborhoods deficient in educational, social and recreational facilities.

This describes, in general, two of the three large Pittsburgh neighborhoods in which ACTION-Housing's Neighborhood Urban Extension process is being demonstrated. In one neighborhood, incidentally, the population is 70 percent Negro, many of whom are citizens with highly developed educational and professional qualifications as well as adequate means. But others have all the problems that emerge from neglect, deprivation and poverty.

Pittsburgh is almost across the continent from California. Few persons here can be expected to know intimately the neighborhoods concerned and their special circumstances and problems. It, therefore, would be inappropriate and time-wasting for me to attempt to itemize in detail the activities of the neighborhood extension councils over the past years. Instead, I will summarize their major accomplishments, with reference to the difficulties faced, and then try to illustrate with a few brief examples what these social action programs have meant to all the participants, particularly to the neighborhood people themselves.

Accomplishments

All three neighborhoods are well along in comprehensive physical and social planning. In one, the people themselves, with the support of local industry, hired their own professional planner, and after three years of seeking agreements and threshing out details in cooperation with the City Planning Department, the plan was approved by Pittsburgh's City Council and is now being implemented. It calls for the razing of some 2,000 houses, all this decided by the residents and owners and others concerned. It becomes a part of the overall Pittsburgh Community Renewal Program being developed by the city. It includes a $3-million, 96-acre, 27-block conservation project being worked out by the Urban Redevelopment Authority, with the aid of federal and city financing—the first such urban renewal project in the city putting major emphasis upon modernization rather than clearance.

In the same neighborhood, to implement this overall physical plan, the Citizens Renewal Council has worked for months, with the cooperation of the City Planning Department, to obtain badly needed zoning changes. Last month, Pittsburgh's City Council approved these drastic zoning changes, which had been the subject of long controversy and struggle. In certain key areas, where conflict might later have arisen, these changes, in effect, assure that the general physical plan for the neighborhood, developed by a consensus of the neighborhood and city planning, will be adhered to. In these areas any new building or rebuilding must conform to the plan.

Each neighborhood has had and is conducting massive housing code enforcement campaigns, obtaining cooperation from the county Health Department, and a high percentage of voluntary compliance. The citizens' councils have made appearances before the City Council against slum landlord practices. Although much remains to be done, many abandoned and dilapidated houses have been razed, and there has been some alleviation of overcrowded tenement housing.

Committees of the councils have been instrumental, with substantial cooperation from local government, in obtaining improved and broadened public services, notably in the areas of police and fire protection, removal of abandoned automobiles, better lighting, repair and cleaning of streets, more attention to sewage problems. Contracts were signed recently by the University of Pittsburgh's Institute of Local Government, ACTION-Housing, and a neighborhood, for a ten-month program which should produce an overall plan for model public services for the community. This contract has the approval of the mayor's office.

Pittsburgh's major universities, the Board of Public Education and the parochial school system have been represented from the beginning by leading educators consulting on the overall program, and have participated, usually under contract, in aiding in the carrying out of many of its important phases. There are such programs as the following:

1. Tutorial courses in remedial reading and motivation for elementary school children, staffed by hundreds of volunteer high school and college students, and now on a year-round basis in several public and parochial schools.

2. Courses in merchandising and marketing for neighborhood merchants.

3. In-the-home day care for preschool children of working mothers.

4. Home economics courses for housewives.

5. Research projects in evaluation and the role of the churches in urban renewal.

6. Extension courses leading to diplomas for high school drop-outs.

and a number of others.

The councils have worked with the Board of Public Education in determining sites for new school buildings, as well as obtaining temporary demountable school classrooms to meet emergency situations.

For the past several years, the councils and their employment committees have pioneered in retraining and placement of the unemployed. In two of the neighborhoods, employment centers, staffed by professionals and aided by the federal government and the state Bureau of Employment Security, have been established in convenient locations. Through volunteer counselors, neighborhood people who know the problems, more than 1,500 of the unemployed have registered and have received counseling. Some have found jobs on their own. Approximately 200 actually have been placed in jobs, and hundreds more are finishing or are entering upon retraining courses in such fields as hospital aides and dieticians, research technicians, and machine tool workers.

However, training for employment is often an uphill job. Among its other training programs, ACTION-Housing is now in its eighth month of carrying out a Special Group Manpower Demonstration Project under contract with the Office of Manpower, Automation and Training of the United States Department of Labor. This demonstration project proposes to test the practicality of training young men, grade school graduates between the ages of 17 and 22, for placement in jobs as research aides and service station mechanic-attendant-dealers. As a further purpose, it tests the effectiveness of the neighborhood-based employment centers and volunteer counselors.

These men are residents of two of the declining Pittsburgh neighborhoods, mostly hard-core unemployed, half of whom are married and half single, few with more than an eighth grade education, many with racial frustrations, heavy marital obligations, police records—though often for minor infractions—and little previous job experience.

In this special group, the preliminary findings have been that many of the young men are hostile to school authority, unpunctual, even afraid to work. Often they are unable to adjust to classroom teaching methods and drop out. Some just don't know what they want to do; some just become belligerent at being told what to do; some indicate a fear of going through the training, working hard to finish, then finding themselves still on the jobless rolls. Some dropped out, however, because they found other jobs, in a climate where unemployment has declined in Pittsburgh, though this may be a temporary situation.

There seems to be a need for intensive changing of attitudes, perhaps through pre-training work in the neighborhoods. The volunteer counselors are proving their worth, particularly in recruiting and in stimulating trainees to attend the courses. Some trainees have completed their courses and have been placed. One young man wrote to his neighborhood volunteer counselor:

> I would like to extend a sincere thanks for my training and employment. It's a rewarding thought to know such an organization as yours exists, that will turn despair into hope.

This summation, which recounts only the high spots of the Neighborhood Urban Extension demonstration, may afford some indication of its scope.

As Pittsburgh's Mayor Joseph M. Barr has said:

> I am not reluctant to acknowledge that Pittsburgh's community action program, which was one of the first funded under the anti-poverty program and which federal officials have indicated is sound in concept, borrowed heavily from the Ford-sponsored urban extension program run by ACTION-Housing in this city.

However, for deeper insights into the meaning and value of this comprehensive social action program, it may serve well to cite a few examples of participation, such as:

> —The experience of one man who had worked for twenty-three years to end an overflowing sewage problem which had damaged his house and those of his neighbors. When a block club was organized, one of hundreds which are active, the whole matter was satisfactorily resolved, and new sewer lines put in, in a matter of months. Since the offending sewer lines were on private property, individual families had to be persuaded to invest $600 each to repair the sewer and end the nuisance.
> —The white realtor, head of the planning committee in a predominantly Negro neighborhood, who invested his own money to buy up two rows of dilapidated houses, landscaped and placed a courtyard between them, rewired, installed new doors, windows, plumbing and kitchen facilities, repainted, and now rents these two-bedroom modernized houses at rentals between $65 and $75 per month. It is not unusual in Pittsburgh to pay $90 per month rent for slum dwellings of the same size.
> —The personnel director of a large steel company and the head of the local steelworkers union who worked together supplying space and training for the volunteer counselors who

have been instrumental in placing of unemployed in retraining and jobs.

—The neighborhood volunteer counselor who not only aided a number of people in the evenings on his own time, but who made it a point to call at the house of one notoriously absent trainee every morning to see that he got off to class.

—The volunteer college student tutor who told of her three slow-learner elementary school pupils phoning her and coming to her house at odd hours for story reading, and her remark that "these children don't need a teacher; they need a friend."

—The neighborhood owner who was inspired to modernize his house and who told of how his nearby neighbors all followed suit.

—The fifteen young women, all without previous training or work skills, who braved Pittsburgh's worst snowstorm of last winter to attend the opening class in machine shop skills, held many miles from their homes. Incidentally, all but two of these girls finished the course. The two drop-outs found jobs in the meantime. However, these girls, all Negro, have had difficulty in finding jobs in the field in which they were trained.

There is evidence that, with proper organization and guidance, social action programs in which the people themselves participate can do much to bring about the revitalizing of the declining neighborhoods of the inner city, if they utilize and coordinate all the resources of the community, particularly education. However, the key to effectiveness is the local leadership and active participation of the people themselves, and their desire for a better way of life.

In his special message to Congress of February 9, 1965, President Johnson said:

I have recommended a community extension program which will bring the resources of the university to focus on problems of the community just as they have long been concerned with rural areas. Among other things this program will help provide training and technical assistance to aid in making our communities more attractive and vital.

In the three Pittsburgh neighborhoods, ACTION-Housing has, in effect, been acting as the extension arm of our universities in some phases of urban renewal and development, notably in social action programs. With the support of private enterprise, public and private agencies, and a broad panel of civic leaders, it has been engaged in pioneering its own war on poverty since 1959. It has been most active more recently in setting up programs, under contract, with the Office of Manpower, Automation and Training, and carries out contracts with the Mayor's Committee on Human Resources, Inc., which has received a major grant to carry out Pittsburgh's Community Action Program under the Economic Opportunity Act.

No city has exactly the same problem, but it is hoped that ACTION-Housing's experience in the evolving of the Neighborhood Urban Extension process will be useful to other cities throughout the nation in formulating and developing programs of social action in urban renewal and development. It is not only the poverty-stricken and the people of the gray areas, but all the citizens of our urban areas who will benefit from effective social action programs.

In conclusion, I am reminded of the remark made by the president of one of Pittsburgh's largest corporations, with plants all over the world, who inquired about the progress of Neighborhood Urban Extension. When told, he made this pronouncement: "If such programs as these can't succeed, our economy—indeed our entire society—is in deep trouble."

FRANK	POVERTY AND
RIESSMAN	
and ARTHUR	NEW CAREERS FOR
PEARL	NONPROFESSIONALS*

THERE SHOULD BE NO CONFUSION on one point. *Poverty will not be easy to eradicate.* Poverty is not a superficial blemish on an otherwise healthy structure. It is not a passing phase of a society in flux. The causes of poverty are deep-seated. Short-term stop-gap measures will not bring about a permanent solution to the problem. The need to reorganize and revitalize many of

* From *New Careers for the Poor* by Frank Riessman and Arthur Pearl. Copyright © by The Free Press, a division of The Macmillan Company, 1965. Reprinted by permission.

the structures and institutions central to society is the alternative to relegating large numbers of citizens to a spectator class— a permanent, stable "nonworking" class, whose children and grandchildren will also be unable to perform meaningful functions in our society. The prospect of many millions of Americans in such a nonproductive situation is not a science-fiction terror. The danger is real and upon us.

This presentation will include a description of the problem, an analysis of its causes and effects, an evaluation of suggested remedies, and a proposal for redress of the condition.

The complex of goals of the new career proposal includes the following:

1. A sufficient number of jobs for all persons without work.

2. The jobs to be so defined and distributed that placements exist for the unskilled and uneducated.

3. The jobs to be permanent and provide opportunity for lifelong careers.

4. An opportunity for the motivated and talented poor to advance from low-skill entry jobs to any station available to the more favored members of society.

5. The work to contribute to the well-being of society.

To devise a program which will provide, in sufficient numbers, socially useful, compensated positions and which will also furnish equal chances for upward mobility, is no small task. If the poor and the currently unemployable are going to be brought into productive society there must be some determination of the capabilities of this group. What can the poor do? How can useful functions be developed that will meet the limitations of the population? What must be done to educate the uneducated in the labor force? What must be done to prevent future uneducated generations from developing? What responsibilities for providing the necessary jobs should be delegated to private industry? And, what is the public sector's responsibility? These are the basic questions confronting us. . . .

A Glance into the Future

The areas of health, education, and other services intended to help or uplift persons offer the greatest promise for employ-

MAN AGAINST POVERTY

ment opportunities in the future. Through extrapolation of populations, it is projected that between the years 1960 and 1975 there will be a 65 percent increase in professional, technical, or kindred worker occupations.[1] During this interval the elementary school population will increase by fifteen percent. There will be in excess of 50 percent more youth of secondary school age, and at least a 70 percent increase in youth of college-attending age.[2]

The increase in numbers of persons of school age cannot by itself be used as the sole gauge for estimating teacher need. Not only will students increase in number, but there will be a tendency for students to stay in school longer. Even without campaigns and public concern, the dropout rate in this country has been declining steadily. Many more youth complete high school now than was the case thirty years ago. A constantly increasing proportion of high school graduates go on to college. A higher percentage of those who enter college achieve graduation, and a higher percentage of those who complete college go on to attain higher degrees.

Between 1960 and 1970, 7.5 million youth will terminate an educational process without attaining a high school education, only if no remedial steps are instituted in this decade.[3] If youth could be attracted to education, and, most importantly, if education could be realistically perceived by youth to have value, many more students would be retained in high school than is currently estimated. The increased enrollment resulting from more effective programming would further increase demand for teaching personnel. Most projections of demand for teachers not only rely on a substantial loss of youth before high school graduation, but also assume that the teacher–pupil ratio will remain fairly constant.

The estimated pupil–teacher ratio for elementary, secondary, public and private schools combined for 1960 was 24.7 to 1.

[1] U.S. Labor Department, *Manpower Report of the President and a Report on Manpower, Requirements, Resources, Utilization and Training,* U.S. Government Printing Office, Washington 25, D.C.: 1963, p. 100.
[2] Source: U.S. Department of Commerce, Bureau of the Census.
[3] Daniel Schreiber, ed., *The School Dropout,* National Education Association, Washington, D.C.: 1964, p. 2.

This rate is projected to decline to 24.3 to 1 by the middle of the decade and then remain stationary.[4]

Neither the assumed drop-out rate nor the assumed class size can be accepted without challenge. While no recommendation is made here that persons should be hired as teachers because our society can find nothing else for them to do, it is strongly urged that many more persons could play productive roles in the educational systems of the country than are currently being utilized. It is lamentable that research findings which give a factual base for the determination of optimal (or even tolerable) loads are almost totally lacking. To accurately appraise the maximum educational return for tax dollar investment it would be necessary to experimentally manipulate and compare outcomes in a variety of situations and contexts. Assessment would have to be made for teachers with differing skills and attributes, for youth of different ages, and for youth from diverse social backgrounds in schools and classrooms with different intellectual and emotional climates. There would have to be evaluation of the impact that the kind and level of course content had upon optimal classroom population, and also the influence of different techniques used to present material. In the absence of definite findings, any assumption that pupil-teacher ratio is relatively fixed is unnecessary and unwise.

The proposal to substantially increase the numbers of persons with teaching responsibilities carries with it a call for rigorous evaluation. If such an investment should not result in significantly improved educational outcomes for any substantial segment of the population, and if careful study of the process of utilization of "new careers" in teaching does not reveal faulty execution, then deployment of available manpower in such channels should be discontinued in favor of investments where "pay-off" could be demonstrated.

Central to this presentation is a very simple thesis—for the present and the foreseeable future our society can and should afford many improvements and additions to the services offered its citizens. As long as there are people without work and work which, most agree, should be done, then the role of a rational

---

[4] *Manpower Report of the President, op. cit.,* p. 126.

society is to provide the machinery and the procedures which make possible a connection between worker resource and manpower requirements. Improving education is one generally recognized need. The symptoms are clear. High incidence of school failure, premature school leaving, inability to generalize obtained education to work or life experience, are all obvious indices that what we possess is not the best of all education worlds. As will be elaborated later, advocating the addition of indigenous low-income people to the education system has both experimental and theoretical justification. Such a proposal is intended to produce a better educational system as well as affording employment to millions of persons.

Education is not the only area where expansion of work opportunities can be anticipated. In the next decade it is expected that more managers, officials, proprietors, clerks, sales persons, craftsmen, foremen, and service workers will be needed. Only for the unskilled laborer in the city or on the farm are the prospects poor for increased employment opportunity.[5] Those developing job opportunities which do not require substantial change in job definition are treated but lightly in this book. There have been procedures established which allow for the entrance of the disadvantaged into these available job openings. The point being emphasized, however, is that the available opportunities are too limited. There are not enough jobs being developed to accommodate the numbers who need work. There is no assurance that the work is permanent, and there is often no path to a better station from the entry job.

Another area where potential for employment is great is in the broad field of health services. Almost every aspect of health service could be enlarged and improved. One segment of the population whose health needs are likely to require special attention are the elderly.

Between 1960 and 1975 the population over the age of sixty-five will increase by almost one-third. There will not only be more persons of retirement age, but they will live longer, and they will be less reluctant to call for health services. The number of persons needed, in a variety of roles, to attend to the problems of the aging, even under current definition, are already

[5] *Ibid.,* p. 100.

beyond the call of available resources. With increased demands for service, the solution can come only from increasing the numbers of persons involved in health work. Therefore, in this field, as in education, there is perceived to be a major opportunity for career development.

The New Career Concept

The new career concept has as a point of departure the creation of jobs normally allotted to highly-trained professionals or technicians, but which could be performed by the unskilled, inexperienced, and relatively untrained worker; or, the development of activities not currently performed by anyone, but for which there is a readily acknowledged need and which can also be satisfactorily accomplished by the unskilled worker.

Detailed descriptions of both reconstituted job endeavors and creation of new activities are to be found in later chapters.[6] In both instances there is a common need for careful scrutiny of the job function for the purpose of defining duties which are structured at the level of the jobless.

Providing jobs which the poor can perform is only a first step along the path to a new career. The job must be made permanent and must be incorporated into the matrix of the industry or agency. If the position, for example, is in government, there must be legitimation of the activity by civil service certification and incorporation of the function into the agency table of organization. In the private sector, created positions must, by similar procedures, become securely fused into the organic operation.

Persons filling entry positions must have latitude for limited advancement without being required to undergo extensive additional training. This type of opportunity is generally available to governmental and private agency personnel assigned to clerical or nonprofessional services. Advancement within the "same line" provides an inducement to "life career" for the least capable and gifted. For the many who aspire to more, and are capable of it, such a narrow range of possible achievement would hardly suffice.

[6] See Reissman and Pearl, *New Change for the Poor.*—Eds.

The chance for truly substantial advancement in job station is crucial to the new career concept. If significant rise to higher stations is to be a genuine possibility for the entering unskilled worker, then jobs which will require knowledge, experience and skill, and present more challenge than the entry positions, must be created. These jobs would have to be intermediate between the unskilled beginning duty and the terminal professional status. To be eligible for an intermediate position a worker would be required to perform notably at the less advanced position and participate in a training program offered partially on the job and partially in a sequence of college courses (or receive training which could be allowed college credit).

Establishing a continuum ranging from nonskilled entry positions, extending through intermediate sub-professional functions, and terminating in full professional status, changes the nature of the upward mobility in our society. No longer would professional status be attained *only* by first completing between five and eight years of college. The requiring of this training *prior* to entrance into a field of endeavor effectively eliminates almost all of the poor from eligibility. A sequence beginning with the unskilled aide and proceeding through an assistant (two years of college equivalence plus experience); an associate (four years of college equivalence plus experience); and terminating in an accreditation as professional is manageable and opens areas to which the poor can now hardly hope to aspire.

If such a program were accepted in the field of medicine, it would be possible for a person to enter the field as a hospital aide (menial worker, only); graduate to a medical assistant (engage in slightly more responsible work); move upward to a medical associate (engage in a more demanding relationship with patients under direct supervision of doctors); continue up a sequence of increasing challenge and responsibility until ultimately the status of medical doctor was reached.

The unique quality of the new career proposal might be best emphasized by consideration of the present inability of a registered nurse to obtain credit for training and skill toward becoming a medical doctor. It is proposed that ultimately such a course would be available. The nurse-to-doctor sequence, while probably more fraught with difficulty than most, would indicate the nature of resistance to be encountered and overcome before the new career concept can become a reality.

Probably only a small percentage of the persons who would enter a new career sequence as nonskilled aides would emerge as full-fledged professionals. Each advance based on merit would constitute a screening process which only the most sensitive, motivated, and capable would ford, but while all might not achieve the highest rung, the *opportunity* for attainment of a higher station would be available to all.

It is not recommended that there be only this arduous and circuitous route to professional status. The traditional path to the M.D., the Ph.D., the education or social work degree would be always an available alternative. However, there would be advantages to the aspiring professional in the development of a sequence of "landings" designed for subprofessionals. At the present time, if a student fails to attain full professional status there is no defined role for him. A person might invest almost a decade in education, only to be informed that he is not to be allowed to become a professional. There is no designated function for the "almost" doctor, lawyer, teacher, social worker, or psychologist. If a sequence of positions had been established, the person unable to attain full status might be eligible for an intermediate position.

Defining the Entry Jobs

For *full* implementation of the new career concept there must be large-scale study of the activities performed by professionals in the fields mentioned above (and others) to delineate specific duties and functions which the unskilled can perform. Such studies must define precisely the relative challenge, complexity, and time expended on each function. The number of jobs required at each level and the number of levels necessary for a complete sequence can be *initially* estimated from the results obtained from such a study. Continued study would be needed for revision of job needs and duties arising from changing situations and technological development.

Inauguration of the new career concept should not, however, await the conclusions of an extensive job study. There is need for immediate test of the concept by demonstration and experimentation in a diversity of settings, with a broad range of persons, and in the performance of a variety of tasks.

There is sufficient experience for initial experimentation. An educated reckoning of job activities which the unskilled can perform can be continually refined after experimentation. Research, while needed, cannot be an excuse for inactivity. It is only through activity that data can be obtained for use in evaluation and further development.

On the other hand, the exigencies of the moment cannot justify unthinking exuberance. *Any* activity is not necessarily good activity. The plight of the poor is tragic and action is needed, but the action which is needed is long-term commitment to an ultimate solution, not a transient concern with superficialities.

The trouble with crash programs is that often they do just that. Poverty seems so ridiculously out of place in an affluent society, and so readily susceptible to remediation that enthusiasm and concern alone appear sufficient to produce change. The answer to poverty may seem to be found in a single word— "money." This is too sanguine a view. If care is not taken, money designed to aid the poor can be channeled in many useless directions. In the haste to meet the emergency, jobs which might, with careful preparation, be tailored for the poor could be filled by those in less dire need—e.g., middle-class housewives, students, or retired persons—or they might become second jobs for persons already employed.[7] A strategy which might satisfy both short-term concern for the jobless and long-range interest in ultimate solutions might combine both types of programs. Investment in short-run or symptom-solution programs would be reduced as long-range programs, attacking the significant causes of poverty, gain a foundation of knowledge and experience.

Will the Best New Careerist Please Stand Up

Selecting persons to enter new career sequences presents a formidable problem. The sequences are projected in areas of

---

[7] There is no attempt being made [here] to arrange for employment of the poor at the expense of more affluent groups. The point being stressed is that persons with means and education have job opportunities available to them; this simply is not the case for the uneducated poor.

considerable sensitivity and persons will be requested to play significant roles in education, in the socialization of children, and in the care and treatment of the sick. These are not positions which can be filled in a cavalier fashion. However, it should be clearly appreciated that if traditional measures are used to screen prospective workers, those who most need employment will in all probability be excluded.

If applicants are to be denied opportunity for employment in new career sequences on the basis of measured intelligence or aptitude, or delinquency record, or lack of school attainment, then the current jobless will, in disproportionately large numbers, remain jobless. There is a compelling reason to reject screening procedures which are based on test scores or prior records. These indices may reflect only the effect of an impoverished existence and would therefore not predict capabilities in a new context. Alien and defeated, the poor have had little incentive to excel in conventional academic activity.

One of the objectives of experimental demonstration with new career programs should be determination of attributes of persons best suited to perform new roles. In the absence of criteria which have been subjected to rigorous validation, the fewer the prejudgments of potential ability the better.

Selecting new career candidates without discrimination is not as reckless a procedure as it might appear at first blush. All candidates would be subjected to short-term intensive training which would constitute a preliminary screen. To be eligible for placement, trainees would have to demonstrate an ability to perform the job and give some evidence of motivation and personal stability.

The new career assignment itself provides the greatest protection against abuse. In his initial assignment the new careerist is in a position of minimal sensitivity and responsibility. He is closely supervised by highly-trained professionals. He can attain more responsibility only by demonstrating capability. He is to be judged not on past record or tenuously related tests, but on actual performance.

Despite precautions and protections, there will be some risk in permitting persons with dubious backgrounds to perform in new career positions but it must also be recognized that there is risk in denying such persons an opportunity to participate in the program. The most obvious consequence will be that the program will fail to come to grips with one of the prime reasons for its existence. The result would be perpetuation of dynastic dependence—a vicious phenomenon of welfare recipient begetting welfare recipient.

Denial of opportunity to play a meaningful role in society may not only result in passive noncontribution, but could also trigger off violent reactions among the alienated and rejected. One likely course of action of any group denied access to status, dignity, and self-esteem by activity within the system would be the development of codes and behaviors affording status and leadership and an acceptable self-image. The recent violent outbursts by groups of slum youth in many cities in the country, resulting in wanton destruction of property and injury to persons, seem to have come about precisely because of the frustration of enforced exclusion from functioning society.[8]

Not all the risks would, however, take the form of affronts to society. Harm might come from failure to realize the specific talents of those persons who are excluded from jobs without trial. It may be precisely those persons who have exhibited leadership capacity in delinquent gangs who possess attributes to make unique contributions in new career roles.

A profound change must be made to occur in programs designed for slum youth. Schools must be revitalized, rehabilitation programs tailored to the needs of the community, health services altered—all of which will require enthusiastic workers, workers who can inspire the residents, and can offer trust and support, thus serving as ego models. It may well be that the very person who today is most troublesome to society can tomorrow become its most valuable contributor.

The Economic Opportunity Act of 1964 calls for the development of community action programs for the poor, with the

---

[8] Although varying in specific details and emphasis, many social scientists explain organized juvenile delinquency as the result of denial of equal access to the benefits of society. See, for example:

Richard A. Cloward and Lloyd E. Ohlin, *Opportunity and Delinquency: A Theory of Delinquent Gangs,* The Free Press, Glencoe, Ill., 1960.

Albert K. Cohen, *Delinquent Boys: The Culture of the Gang,* The Free Press, Glencoe, Ill., 1955.

Louis Yablonsky, *The Violent Gang,* The Macmillan Co., New York, 1962.

poor, and by the poor. If appropriately implemented, this requires involvement and self-determination by the poor and can
provide the basis for millions of nonprofessional and subprofessional jobs and new careers. The main danger lies in the
possibility that the jobs created by the local communities receiving grants under the act will not be integrated into the system
but will remain as appendages. In other words, the local groups
may gladly accept funds to hire the poor in nonprofessional
positions that will last as long as the funds are forthcoming.
But these local groups will probably be unwilling to change
their tables of organization to fully incorporate nonprofessional
career lines, unless the administrators of the act make this an
indispensable prerequisite for receiving federal support. Thus
the antipoverty warriors can be among the most crucial allies
of the new careers movement, if the act is utilized as an impetus for changing the employment system.

This book is predicated on the assumption that there will
be a continuing increase in the need for human services in the
health, welfare, and education fields, and that the jobs created
will not easily be automated out of existence. We envision
millions of new nonprofessional jobs and careers in the helping
professions, largely in the public sector.

Any proposal has minimum and maximum possibilities. The
new careers concept has three major objectives, the achievement of which should be possible, to varying degrees, depending upon whether the new jobs are simply appended to the
system on a temporary basis, or whether they are incorporated
and become an integral part of the system. The three aims are:

1. Development of large numbers of new nonprofessional
careers for the poor, including the opportunity for advancement
into subprofessional and professional positions. In order to
achieve this objective it is necessary to reject the irrational job
definitions that have characterized our credential-centered society. Moreover, the relationship of work and education has
to be recast so that the two become more concomitant and
overlapping, thus enabling disadvantaged youths and adults
to enter rapidly into the mainstream of American work life.
The first objective, then, is offered as one very important dimension in the war on poverty; but, of course, it is recognized

that it is only one dimension, and that various aspects of the alternative anti-poverty strategies must be integrated in a total approach to the problem.

2. Greatly improved service for the poor by taking service from the poor—hiring the nonprofessional. . . . The helper principle holds that one very important way in which people are helped is through helping others. The [author's] entire book suggests that the poor be employed as nonprofessionals in the helping professions, and that in the process of serving others they will be helping to rehabilitate themselves. This can be done on a grand scale because of the great need for services as well as the need for improving the quality of services.

3. A major change in the helping professions themselves through a reorganization of the professional's role in the direction of increased supervision, consultation, teaching, programming, and planning. The achievement of this objective would allow the professional much greater flexibility and range. He could be more fully a professional, less engaged in nonprofessional tasks, and could be far more creative as his energies are released in the new role functions. Finally, his new connections with the poor, resulting from the increased service for the poor and from the poor, can reduce the tremendous interclass distance which has hampered the development of both the disadvantaged and the professional. The new careers movement can begin to provide the basis for the much needed unity of the professional and the poor.

| RICHARD A. CLOWARD and FRANCES FOX PIVEN | A STRATEGY TO END POVERTY* |

HOW CAN THE POOR be organized to press for relief from poverty? How can a broad-based movement be developed and the current disarray of activist forces be halted? These questions

* From *The Nation*, May 2, 1966.

confront, and confound, activists today. It is our purpose to advance a strategy which affords the basis for a convergence of civil rights organizations, militant anti-poverty groups and the poor. If this strategy were implemented, a political crisis would result that could lead to legislation for a guaranteed annual income and thus an end to poverty.

The strategy is based on the fact that a vast discrepancy exists between the benefits to which people are entitled under public welfare programs and the sums which they actually receive. This gulf is not recognized in a society that is wholly and self-righteously oriented toward getting people *off* the welfare rolls. It is widely known, for example, that nearly 8 million persons (half of them white) now subsist on welfare, but it is not generally known that for every person on the rolls at least one more probably meets existing criteria of eligibility but is not obtaining assistance.

The discrepancy is not an accident stemming from bureaucratic inefficiency; rather, it is an integral feature of the welfare system which, if challenged, would precipitate a profound financial and political crisis. The force for that challenge, and the strategy we propose, is a massive drive to recruit the poor *onto* the welfare rolls.

The distribution of public assistance has been a local and state responsibility, and that accounts in large part for the abysmal character of welfare practices. Despite the growing involvement of federal agencies in supervisory and reimbursement arrangements, state and local community forces are still decisive. The poor are most visible and proximate in the local community; antagonism toward them (and toward the agencies which are implicated with them) has always, therefore, been more intense locally than at the federal level. In recent years, local communities have increasingly felt class and ethnic friction generated by competition for neighborhoods, schools, jobs and political power. Public welfare systems are under the constant stress of conflict and opposition, made only sharper by the rising costs to localities of public aid. And, to accommodate this pressure, welfare practice everywhere has become more restrictive than welfare statute; much of the time it verges on lawlessness. Thus, public welfare systems try to keep their budgets down and their rolls low by failing to inform people of the rights available to them; by intimidating and shaming them to the degree that they are reluctant either to apply or to press claims, and by arbitrarily denying benefits to those who are eligible.

A series of welfare drives in large cities would, we believe, impel action on a new federal program to distribute income, eliminating the present public welfare system and alleviating the abject poverty which it perpetrates. Widespread campaigns to register the eligible poor for welfare aid, and to help existing recipients obtain their full benefits, would produce bureaucratic disruption in welfare agencies and fiscal disruption in local and state governments. These disruptions would generate severe political strains, and deepen existing divisions among elements in the big-city Democratic coalition: the remaining white middle class, the white working-class ethnic groups and the growing minority poor. To avoid a further weakening of that historic coalition, a national Democratic Administration would be constrained to advance a federal solution to poverty that would override local welfare failures, local class and racial conflicts and local revenue dilemmas. By the internal disruption of local bureaucratic practices, by the furor over public welfare poverty, and by the collapse of current financing arrangements, powerful forces can be generated for major economic reforms at the national level.

The ultimate objective of this strategy—to wipe out poverty by establishing a guaranteed annual income—will be questioned by some. Because the ideal of individual social and economic mobility has deep roots, even activists seem reluctant to call for national programs to eliminate poverty by the outright redistribution of income. Instead, programs are demanded to enable people to become economically competitive. But such programs are of no use to millions of today's poor. For example, one-third of the 35 million poor Americans are in families headed by females; these heads of family cannot be aided appreciably by job retraining, higher minimum wages, accelerated rates of economic growth, or employment in public works projects. Nor can the 5 million aged who are poor, nor those whose poverty results from the ill health of the wage earner. Programs to enhance individual mobility will chiefly benefit the very young, if not the as yet unborn. Individual mobility is no answer to the question of how to abolish the massive problem of poverty now.

It has never been the full answer. If many people in the past have found their way up from poverty by the path of individual mobility, many others have taken a different route. Organized labor stands out as a major example. Although many American workers never yielded their dreams of individual achievement, they accepted and practiced the principle that each can benefit only as the status of workers as a whole is elevated. They bargained for collective mobility, not for individual mobility; to promote their fortunes in the aggregate, not to promote the prospects of one worker over another. And if each finally found himself in the same relative economic relationship to his fellows as when he began, it was nevertheless clear that all were infinitely better off. That fact has sustained the labor movement in the face of a counter pull from the ideal of individual achievement.

But many of the contemporary poor will not rise from poverty by organizing to bargain collectively. They either are not in the labor force or are in such marginal and dispersed occupations (e.g., domestic servants) that it is extremely difficult to organize them. Compared with other groups, then, many of today's poor cannot secure a redistribution of income by organizing within the institution of private enterprise. A federal program of income redistribution has become necessary to elevate the poor en masse from poverty.

Several ways have been proposed for redistributing income through the federal government. It is not our purpose here to assess the relative merits of these plans, which are still undergoing debate and clarification. Whatever mechanism is eventually adopted, however, it must include certain features if it is not merely to perpetuate in a new guise the present evils of the public welfare system.

First, adequate levels of income must be assured. (Public welfare levels are astonishingly low; indeed, states typically define a "minimum" standard of living and then grant only a percentage of it, so that families are held well below what the government itself officially defines as the poverty level.) Furthermore, income should be distributed without requiring that recipients first divest themselves of their assets, as public welfare now does, thereby pauperizing families as a condition of sustenance.

Second, the right to income must be guaranteed, or the oppression of the welfare poor will not be eliminated. Because benefits are conditional under the present public welfare system, submission to arbitrary governmental power is regularly made the price of sustenance. People have been coerced into attending literacy classes or participating in medical or vocational rehabilitation regimes, on pain of having their benefits terminated. Men are forced into labor on virtually any terms lest they forfeit their welfare aid. One can prize literacy, health and work, while still vigorously opposing the right of government to compel compliance with these values.

Conditional benefits thus result in violations of civil liberties throughout the nation, and in a pervasive oppression of the poor. And these violations are not less real because the impulse leading to them is altruistic and the agency is professional. If new systems of income distribution continue to permit the professional bureaucracies to choose when to give and when to withhold financial relief, the poor will once again be surrendered to an arrangement in which their rights are diminished in the name of overcoming their vices. Those who lead an attack on the welfare system must therefore be alert to the pitfalls of inadequate but placating reforms which give the appearance of victory to what is in truth defeat.

How much economic force can be mobilized by this strategy? This question is not easy to answer because few studies have been conducted of people who are *not* receiving public assistance even though they may be eligible. For the purposes of this presentation, a few facts about New York City may be suggestive. Since practices elsewhere are generally acknowledged to be even more restrictive, the estimates of unused benefits which follow probably yield a conservative estimate of the potential force of the strategy set forth in this article.

Basic assistance for food and rent: The most striking characteristic of public welfare practice is that a great many people who appear to be eligible for assistance are not on the welfare rolls. The average monthly total of New York City residents receiving assistance in 1959 was 325,771, but according to the 1960 census, 716,000 persons (unrelated or in families) appeared to be subsisting on incomes at or below the prevailing welfare eligibility levels (e.g., $2,070 for a family of four). In that same year, 539,000 people subsisted on incomes *less than 80 percent* of the welfare minimums, and 200,000 lived alone or in families on incomes reported to be *less than half* of eligibility levels. Thus it appears that for every person on welfare in 1959, at least one more was eligible.

The results of two surveys of selected areas in Manhattan support the contention that many people subsist on incomes below welfare eligibility levels. One of these, conducted by Greenleigh Associates in 1964 in an urban-renewal area on New York's upper West Side, found 9 percent of those *not* on the rolls were in such acute need that they appeared to qualify for *emergency* assistance. The study showed, further, that a substantial number of families that were not in a "critical" condition would probably have qualified for supplemental assistance.

The other survey, conducted in 1961 by Mobilization for Youth, had similar findings. The area from which its sample was drawn, sixty-seven square blocks on the Lower East Side, is a poor one, but by no means the poorest in New York City. Yet 13 percent of the total sample who were not on the welfare rolls reported incomes falling below the prevailing welfare schedules for food and rent.

There is no reason to suppose that the discrepancy between those eligible for and those receiving assistance has narrowed much in the past few years. The welfare rolls have gone up, to be sure, but so have eligibility levels. Since the economic circumstances of impoverished groups in New York have not improved appreciably in the past few years, each such rise increases the number of people who are potentially eligible for some degree of assistance.

Even if one allows for the possibility that family-income figures are grossly underestimated by the census, the financial implications of the proposed strategy are still very great. In 1965, the monthly average of persons receiving cash assistance in New York was 490,000, at a total cost of $440 million; the rolls have now [1966] risen above 500,000, so that costs will exceed $500 million in 1966. An increase in the rolls of a mere 20 percent would cost an already overburdened municipality some $100 million.

Special grants: Public assistance recipients in New York are also entitled to receive "nonrecurring" grants for clothing, household equipment and furniture—including washing machines, refrigerators, beds and bedding, tables and chairs. It hardly needs to be noted that most impoverished families have grossly inadequate clothing and household furnishings. The Greenleigh study, for example, found that 52 percent of the families on public assistance lacked anything approaching adequate furniture. This condition results because almost nothing is spent on special grants in New York. In October 1965, a typical month, the Department of Welfare spent only $2.50 per recipient for heavy clothing and $1.30 for household furnishings. Taken together, grants of this kind amounted in 1965 to a mere $40 per person, or a total of $20 million for the entire year. Considering the real needs of families, the successful demand for full entitlements could multiply these expenditures tenfold or more—and that would involve the disbursement of many millions of dollars indeed.

One must be cautious in making generalizations about the prospects for this strategy in any jurisdiction unless the structure of welfare practices has been examined in some detail. We can, however, cite other studies conducted in other places to show that New York practices are not atypical. In Detroit, for example, Greenleigh Associates studied a large sample of households in a low-income district in 1965. Twenty percent were already receiving assistance, but 35 percent more were judged to need it. Although the authors made no strict determination of the eligibility of these families under the laws of Michigan, they believed that "larger numbers of persons were eligible than receiving." A good many of these families did not know that public assistance was available; others thought they would be deemed ineligible; not a few were ashamed or afraid to ask.

Similar deprivations have been shown in nationwide studies. In 1963, the federal government carried out a survey based on a national sample of 5,500 families whose benefits under Aid to Dependent Children had been terminated. Thirty-four percent of these cases were *officially in need of income at the point of closing:* this was true of 30 percent of the white and 44 percent of the Negro cases. The chief basis for termination given in local department records was "other reasons" (i.e., other than improvement in financial condition, which would make dependence on welfare unnecessary). Upon closer examination, these "other reasons" turned out to be "unsuitable home" (i.e., the presence of illegitimate children), "failure to comply with departmental regulations" or "refusal to take legal action against a putative father." (Negroes were especially singled out for punitive action on the ground that children were not being maintained in "suitable homes.") The amounts of money that people are deprived of by these injustices are very great.

In order to generate a crisis, the poor must obtain benefits which they have forfeited. Until now, they have been inhibited from asserting claims by self-protective devices within the welfare system: its capacity to limit information, to intimidate applicants, to demoralize recipients, and arbitrarily to deny lawful claims.

Ignorance of welfare rights can be attacked through a massive educational campaign. Brochures describing benefits in simple, clear language, and urging people to seek their full entitlements, should be distributed door to door in tenements and public housing projects, and deposited in stores, schools, churches and civic centers. Advertisements should be placed in newspapers; spot announcements should be made on radio. Leaders of social, religious, fraternal and political groups in the slums should also be enlisted to recruit the eligible to the rolls. The fact that the campaign is intended to inform people of their legal rights under a government program, that it is a civic-education drive, will lend it legitimacy.

But information alone will not suffice. Organizers will have to become advocates in order to deal effectively with improper rejections and terminations. The advocate's task is to appraise the circumstances of each case, to argue its merits before welfare, to threaten legal action if satisfaction is not given. In some cases, it will be necessary to contest decisions by requesting a "fair hearing" before the appropriate state supervisory agency; it may occasionally be necessary to sue for redress in the courts. Hearings and court actions will require lawyers, many of whom, in cities like New York, can be recruited on a voluntary basis, especially under the banner of a movement to end poverty by a strategy of asserting legal rights. However, most cases will not require an expert knowledge of law, but only of welfare regulations; the rules can be learned by laymen, including welfare recipients themselves (who can help to man "information and advocacy" centers). To aid workers in these centers, handbooks should be prepared describing welfare rights and the tactics to employ in claiming them.

Advocacy must be supplemented by organized demonstrations to create a climate of militancy that will overcome the invidious and immobilizing attitudes which many potential recipients hold toward being "on walfare." In such a climate, many more poor people are likely to become their own advocates and will not need to rely on aid from organizers.

As the crisis develops, it will be important to use the mass media to inform the broader liberal community about the inefficiencies and injustices of welfare. For example, the system will not be able to process many new applicants because of cumbersome and often unconstitutional investigatory procedures (which cost twenty cents for every dollar disbursed). As delays mount, so should the public demand that a simplified affidavit supplant these procedures, so that the poor may certify to their condition. If the system reacts by making the proof of eligibility more difficult, the demand should be made that the Department of Health, Education and Welfare dispatch "eligibility registrars" to enforce federal statutes governing local programs. And throughout the crisis, the mass media should be used to advance arguments for a new federal income distribution program.[1]

Although new resources in organizers and funds would have

---

[1] In public statements, it would be important to distinguish between the income-distributing function of public welfare, which should be replaced by new federal measures, and many other welfare functions, such as foster care and adoption services for children, which are not at issue in this strategy.

to be developed to mount this campaign, a variety of conventional agencies in the large cities could also be drawn upon for help. The idea of "welfare rights" has begun to attract attention in many liberal circles. A number of organizations, partly under the aegis of the "war against poverty," are developing information and advocacy services for low-income people [see "Poverty, Injustice and the Welfare State" by Richard A. Cloward and Richard M. Elman, *The Nation*, issues of February 28 and March 7, 1966]. It is not likely that these organizations will directly participate in the present strategy, for obvious political reasons. But whether they participate or not, they constitute a growing network of resources to which people can be referred for help in establishing and maintaining entitlements. In the final analysis, it does not matter who helps people to get on the rolls or to get additional entitlements, so long as the job is done.

Since this plan deals with problems of great immediacy in the lives of the poor, it should motivate some of them to involve themselves in regular organizational activities. Welfare recipients, chiefly ADC[2] mothers, are already forming federations, committees and councils in cities across the nation; in Boston, New York, Newark, Cleveland, Chicago, Detroit and Los Angeles, to mention a few. Such groups typically focus on obtaining full entitlements for existing recipients rather than on recruiting new recipients, and they do not yet comprise a national movement. But their very existence attests to a growing readiness among ghetto residents to act against public welfare.

To generate an expressly political movement, cadres of aggressive organizers would have to come from the civil rights movement and the churches, from militant low-income organizations like those formed by the Industrial Areas Foundation (that is, by Saul Alinsky),[3] and from other groups on the Left. These activists should be quick to see the difference between programs to redress individual grievances and a large-scale social-action campaign for national policy reform.

[2] Aid to Dependent Children.—Eds.
[3] Alinsky has been most successful in the Woodlawn and Back of the Yards areas of Chicago, where his Industrial Areas Foundation has organized the poor to do their own planning and to use protest methods, almost to the point of violence, to obtain what they need from City Hall.—Eds.

Movements that depend on involving masses of poor people have generally failed in America. Why would the proposed strategy to engage the poor succeed?

First, this plan promises immediate economic benefits. This is a point of some importance because, whereas America's poor have not been moved in any number by radical political ideologies, they have sometimes been moved by their economic interests. Since radical movements in America have rarely been able to provide visible economic incentives, they have usually failed to secure mass participation of any kind. The conservative "business unionism" of organized labor is explained by this fact, for membership enlarged only as unionism paid off in material benefits. Union leaders have understood that their strength derives almost entirely from their capacity to provide economic rewards to members. Although leaders have increasingly acted in political spheres, their influence has been directed chiefly to matters of governmental policy affecting the well-being of organized workers. The same point is made by the experience of rent strikes in Northern cities. Their organizers were often motivated by radical ideologies, but tenants have been attracted by the promise that housing improvements would quickly be made if they withheld their rent.

Second, for this strategy to succeed, one need not ask more of most of the poor than that they claim lawful benefits. Thus the plan has the extraordinary capability of yielding mass influence *without* mass participation, at least as the term "participation" is ordinarily understood. Mass influence in this case stems from the consumption of benefits and does not require that large groups of people be involved in regular organizational roles.

Moreover, this kind of mass influence is cumulative because benefits are continuous. Once eligibility for basic food and rent grants is established, the drain on local resources persists indefinitely. Other movements have failed precisely because they could not produce continuous and cumulative influence. In the Northern rent strikes, for example, tenant participation depended largely on immediate grievances; as soon as landlords made the most minimal repairs, participation fell away and with it the impact of the movement. Efforts to revive tenant participation by organizing demonstrations around broader housing issues (e.g., the expansion of public housing) did not succeed because the incentives were not immediate.

Third, the prospects for mass influence are enhanced because this plan provides a practical basis for coalition between poor whites and poor Negroes. Advocates of low-income movements have not been able to suggest how poor whites and poor Negroes can be united in an expressly lower-class movement. Despite pleas of some Negro leaders for joint action on programs requiring integration, poor whites have steadfastly resisted making common cause with poor Negroes. By contrast, the benefits of the present plan are as great for whites as for Negroes. In the big cities, at least, it does not seem likely that poor whites, whatever their prejudices against either Negroes or public welfare, will refuse to participate when Negroes aggressively claim benefits that are unlawfully denied to them as well. One salutary consequence of public information campaigns to acquaint Negroes with their rights is that many whites will be made aware of theirs. Even if whites prefer to work through their own organizations and leaders, the consequences will be equivalent to joining with Negroes. For if the object is to focus attention on the need for new economic measures by producing a crisis over the dole, anyone who insists upon extracting maximum benefits from public welfare is in effect part of a coalition and is contributing to the cause.

The ultimate aim of this strategy is a new program for direct income distribution. What reason is there to expect that the federal government will enact such legislation in response to a crisis in the welfare system?

We ordinarily think of major legislation as taking form only through established electoral processes. We tend to overlook the force of crisis in precipitating legislative reform, partly because we lack a theoretical framework by which to understand the impact of major disruptions.

By crisis, we mean a *publicly visible* disruption in some institutional sphere. Crisis can occur spontaneously (e.g., riots) or as the intended result of tactics of demonstration and protest which either generate institutional disruption or bring unrecognized disruption to public attention. Public trouble is a political liability; it calls for action by political leaders to stabilize the situation. Because crisis usually creates or exposes conflict, it threatens to produce cleavages in a political consensus which politicians will ordinarily act to avert.

Although crisis impels political action, it does not itself determine the selection of specific solutions. Political leaders will try to respond with proposals which work to their advantage in the electoral process. Unless group cleavages form around issues and demands, the politician has great latitude and tends to proffer only the minimum action required to quell disturbances without risking existing electoral support. Spontaneous disruptions, such as riots, rarely produce leaders who articulate demands; thus no terms are imposed, and political leaders are permitted to respond in ways that merely restore a semblance of stability without offending other groups in a coalition.

When, however, a crisis is defined by its participants—or by other activated groups—as a matter of clear issues and preferred solutions, terms are imposed on the politicians' bid for their support. Whether political leaders then design solutions to reflect these terms depends on a twofold calculation: first, the impact of the crisis and the issues it raises on existing alignments and, second, the gains or losses in support to be expected as a result of a proposed resolution.

As to the impact on existing alignments, issues exposed by a crisis may activate new groups, thus altering the balance of support and opposition on the issues; or it may polarize group sentiments, altering the terms which must be offered to insure the support of given constituent groups. In framing resolutions, politicians are more responsive to group shifts and are more likely to accommodate to the terms imposed when electoral coalitions threatened by crisis are already uncertain or weakening. In other words, the politician responds to group demands, not only by calculating the magnitude of electoral gains and losses, but by assessing the impact of the resolution on the stability of existing or potential coalitions. Political leaders are especially responsive to group shifts when the terms of settlement can be framed so as to shore up an existing coalition, or as a basis for the development of new and more stable alignments, *without* jeopardizing existing support. Then, indeed, the calculation of net gain is most secure.

The legislative reforms of the Depression years, for example, were impelled not so much by organized interests exercised through regular electoral processes as by widespread economic crisis. That crisis precipitated the disruption of the regionally based coalitions underlying the old national parties. During the realignments of 1932, a new Democratic coalition was formed, based heavily on urban working-class groups. Once in power, the national Democratic leadership proposed and implemented the economic reforms of the New Deal. Although these measures were a response to the imperative of economic crisis, the types of measures enacted were designed to secure and stabilize the new Democratic coalition.

The civil rights movement, to take a recent case, also reveals the relationship of crisis and electoral conditions in producing legislative reform. The crisis in the South took place in the context of a weakening North-South Democratic coalition. The strains in that coalition were first evident in the Dixiecrat desertion of 1948, and continued through the Eisenhower years as the Republicans gained ground in the Southern states. Democratic Party leaders at first tried to hold the dissident South by warding off the demands of enlarging Negro constituencies in Northern cities. Thus for two decades the national Democratic Party campaigned on strongly worded civil rights planks but enacted only token measures. The civil rights movement forced the Democrats' hand: a crumbling Southern partnership was forfeited, and major civil rights legislation was put forward, designed to insure the support of Northern Negroes and liberal elements in the Democratic coalition. That coalition emerged strong from the 1964 election, easily able to overcome the loss of Southern states to Goldwater. At the same time, the enacted legislation, particularly the Voting Rights Act, laid the ground for a new Southern Democratic coalition of moderate whites and the hitherto untapped reservoir of Southern Negro voters.

The electoral context which made crisis effective in the South is also to be found in the big cities of the nation today. Deep tensions have developed among groups comprising the political coalitions of the large cities—the historic stronghold of the

Democratic Party. As a consequence, urban politicians no longer turn in the vote to national Democratic candidates with unfailing regularity. The marked defections revealed in the elections of the 1950s and which continued until the Johnson landslide of 1964 are a matter of great concern to the national party. Precisely because of this concern, a strategy to exacerbate still further the strains in the urban coalition can be expected to evoke a response from national leaders.

The weakening of the urban coalition is a result of many basic changes in the relationship of local party leadership to its constituents. First, the political machine, the distinctive and traditional mechanism for forging alliances among competing groups in the city, is now virtually defunct in most cities. Successive waves of municipal reform have deprived political leaders of control over the public resources—jobs, contracts, services and favors—which machine politicians formerly dispensed to voters in return for electoral support. Conflicts among elements in the urban Democratic coalition, once held together politically because each secured a share of these benefits, cannot now be so readily contained. And as the means of placating competing groups have diminished, tensions along ethnic and class lines have multiplied. These tensions are being intensified by the encroachments of an enlarging ghetto population on jobs, schools and residential areas. Big-city mayors are thus caught between antagonistic working-class ethnic groups, the remaining middle class, and the rapidly enlarging minority poor.

Second, there are discontinuities in the relationship between the urban party apparatus and its ghetto constituents which have so far remained unexposed but which a welfare crisis would force into view. The ghetto vote has been growing rapidly and has so far returned overwhelming Democratic majorities. Nevertheless, this voting bloc is not fully integrated in the party apparatus, either through the representation of its leaders or the accommodation of its interests.

While the urban political apparatus includes members of new minority groups, these groups are by no means represented according to their increasing proportions in the population. More important, elected representation alone is not an adequate mechanism for the expression of group interests. Influence in urban politics is won not only at the polls but through the sustained activity of organized interests—such as labor unions, home-owner associations and business groups. These groups keep watch over the complex operations of municipal agencies, recognizing issues and regularly asserting their point of view through meetings with public officials, appearances at public hearings and the like, and by exploiting a whole array of channels of influence on government. Minority constituencies—at least the large proportion of them that are poor—are not regular participants in the various institutional spheres where organized interest groups typically develop. Thus the interests of the mass of minority poor are not protected by associations which make their own or other political leaders responsive by continuously calling them to account. Urban party organizations have become, in consequence, more an avenue for the personal advancement of minority political leaders than a channel for the expression of minority-group interests. And the big-city mayors, struggling to preserve an uneasy urban consensus, have thus been granted the slack to evade the conflict-generating interests of the ghetto. A crisis in public welfare would expose the tensions latent in this attenuated relationship between the ghetto vote and the urban party leadership, for it would thrust forward ghetto demands and back them with the threat of defections by voters who have so far remained both loyal and quiescent.

In the face of such a crisis, urban political leaders may well be paralyzed by a party apparatus which ties them to older constituent groups, even while the ranks of these groups are diminishing. The national Democratic leadership, however, is alert to the importance of the urban Negro vote, especially in national contests where the loyalty of other urban groups is weakening. Indeed, many of the legislative reforms of the Great Society can be understood as efforts, however feeble, to reinforce the allegiance of growing ghetto constituencies to the national Democratic Administration. In the thirties, Democrats began to put forward measures to circumvent the states in order to reach the big-city elements in the New Deal coalition; now it is becoming expedient to put forward measures to circumvent the weakened big-city mayors in order to reach the new minority poor.

Recent federal reforms have been impelled in part by widespread unrest in the ghetto, and instances of more aggressive Negro demands. But despite these signs that the ghetto vote may become less reliable in the future, there has been as yet no serious threat of massive defection. The national party has therefore not put much pressure on its urban branches to accommodate the minority poor. The resulting reforms have consequently been quite modest (e.g., the war against poverty, with its emphasis on the "involvement of the poor," is an effort to make the urban party apparatus somewhat more accommodating).

A welfare crisis would, of course, produce dramatic local political crisis, disrupting and exposing rifts among urban groups. Conservative Republicans are always ready to declaim the evils of public welfare, and they would probably be the first to raise a hue and cry. But deeper and politically more telling conflicts would take place within the Democratic coalition. Whites—both working-class ethnic groups and many in the middle class— would be aroused against the ghetto poor, while liberal groups, which until recently have been comforted by the notion that the poor are few and, in any event, receiving the beneficent assistance of public welfare, would probably support the movement. Group conflict, spelling political crisis for the local party apparatus, would thus become acute as welfare rolls mounted and the strains on local budgets became more severe. In New York City, where the mayor is now facing desperate revenue shortages, welfare expenditures are already second only to those for public education.

It should also be noted that welfare costs are generally shared by local, state and federal governments, so that the crisis in the cities would intensify the struggle over revenues that is chronic in relations between cities and states. If the past is any predictor of the future, cities will fail to procure relief from this crisis by persuading states to increase their proportionate share of urban welfare costs, for state legislatures have been notoriously unsympathetic to the revenue needs of the city (especially where public welfare and minority groups are concerned).

If this strategy for crisis would intensify group cleavages, a federal income solution would not further exacerbate them. The demands put forward during recent civil rights drives in the Northern cities aroused the opposition of huge majorities. Indeed, such fierce resistance was evoked (e.g., school boycotts followed by counter-boycotts), that accessions by political leaders would have provoked greater political turmoil than the protests themselves, for profound class and ethnic interests are at stake in the employment, educational and residential institutions of our society. By contrast, legislative measures to provide direct income to the poor would permit national Democratic leaders to cultivate ghetto constituencies without unduly antagonizing other urban groups, as is the case when the battle lines are drawn over schools, housing or jobs. Furthermore, a federal income program would not only redeem local governments from the immediate crisis but would permanently relieve them of the financially and politically onerous burdens of public welfare[4]—a function which generates support from none and hostility from many, not least of all welfare recipients.

We suggest, in short, that if pervasive institutional reforms are not yet possible, requiring as they do expanded Negro political power and the development of new political alliances, crisis tactics can nevertheless be employed to secure particular reforms in the short run by exploiting weaknesses in current political alignments. Because the urban coalition stands weakened by group conflict today, disruption and threats of disaffection will count powerfully, provided that national leaders can respond with solutions which retain the support of ghetto constituencies while avoiding new group antagonisms and bolstering the urban party apparatus. These are the conditions, then, for an effective crisis strategy in the cities to secure an end to poverty.

No strategy, however confident its advocates may be, is foolproof. But if unforeseen contingencies thwart this plan to bring about new federal legislation in the field of poverty, it should also be noted that there would be gains even in defeat. For one thing, the plight of many poor people would be somewhat eased in the course of an assault upon public welfare. Existing recipients would come to know their rights and how to defend

---

[4] It should also be noted that the federal government, unlike local jurisdictions, has taxing powers which yield substantially increased revenues as an automatic by-product of increases in national income.

them, thus acquiring dignity where none now exists; and millions of dollars in withheld welfare benefits would become available to potential recipients now—not several generations from now. Such an attack should also be welcome to those currently concerned with programs designed to equip the young to rise out of poverty (e.g., Head Start), for surely children learn more readily when the oppressive burden of financial insecurity is lifted from the shoulders of their parents. And those seeking new ways to engage the Negro politically should remember that public resources have always been the fuel for low-income urban political organization. If organizers can deliver millions of dollars in cash benefits to the ghetto masses, it seems reasonable to expect that the masses will deliver their loyalties to their benefactors. At least, they have always done so in the past.

COMMUNITY OPERATED SCHOOLS

A Way Out?

ROGER R. WOOCK

FOR THE PAST DECADE educators and the general public have become increasingly aware that urban schools have been failing to educate poor Negro and Spanish-speaking youngsters. The titles of Nat Hentoff's *Our Children Are Dying*[1] and, more recently, Jonathan Kozol's *Death at an Early Age*,[2] may seem extreme, yet failure to learn the basic skills of reading, writing and arithmetic means death in our highly linguistic and competitive society. The violence in America's large cities during the summers of 1965, 1966, and 1967 involved large numbers of young men who were or had recently been school drop-outs.[3]

[1] Viking Press, New York, 1966.
[2] Houghton-Mifflin, Boston, 1967.
[3] See Robert Conot's *Rivers of Blood, Years of Darkness,* Bantam, New York, 1967, for a good background study of the leaders in the 1965 Watts riot.

They received an education in frustration and despair that very effectively prepared them to participate in these riots.

To be aware that a special and desperate kind of educational crisis exists among our urban poor is not to say that the rest of American education is very good. But the extent of the educational inadequacy of poor nonwhite children is becoming a matter of wide public concern and is easily documented. On November 2, 1967, the New York City Board of Education, for the second year, published the reading scores by school for the New York City system.[4] It is a picture of failure related directly to social class and ethnic background.

Given the growing awareness of this educational deficiency, it is understandable that educators are searching frantically for remedies. Their main effort thus far is probably best identified as "compensatory education." The implications of this phrase are clear. One compensates for "cultural deprivation," for "stimulus deprivation," or for "social disadvantage." It is certainly true that the homes and the neighborhoods of poor youngsters are affected by their poverty, as are all aspects of their lives. Also, no one could deny that out-of-school experience does affect academic performance, although exactly how and to what extent is far from clear. It seems reasonable then, to most educators, to add "enrichment" programs and special "remedial" instruction in order to bring the performance of poor nonwhite youngsters up to that of middle-class white youngsters.

Columnist Joseph Alsop argues that compensatory education will dramatically improve nonwhite performance in our urban schools and lead to desegregation since, he believes, white opposition to Negro socio-economic aspirations is based on the poor school achievement of Negro youngsters. Most school men would agree, but would also support the compensatory programs because they are less disruptive within the schools than other approaches. Remedial reading and cultural enrichment can be added to existing school curricula without changing relationships within the school system, between the school and the community, and without moving youngsters across district lines. Although school men would indeed like to see nonwhite youngsters learning at the same rate and at the same level as

[4] See the *New York Times,* November 2, 1967.

white youngsters, it must be pointed out that they are not willing to entertain any radical suggestions for school reorganization to accomplish this end. The supporters of compensatory education range across the political spectrum. They include conservatives like Alsop and liberals like Negro social psychologist Kenneth Clark. Although Clark rejects the concept of "cultural deprivation," he apparently believes that nonwhite youngsters can be educated in segregated schools without very radically altering the structure of the school system or the power relationships between the school and the community.[5]

In spite of wide support and several billion dollars spent on a great variety of compensatory programs, the results in educational terms are practically negligible.

Higher Horizons in New York City was one of the most publicized and, during its life, most highly praised of the compensatory education programs. It featured four different approaches designed to increase learning. First of all, teachers were trained and encouraged to improve the student's level of aspiration. Second, counseling and guidance services were extended and increased. Third, an effort was made to broaden the cultural background of the youngsters by visits to museums, libraries, concert halls, etc. And finally, special remedial teachers were provided to upgrade reading, writing and arithmetic skills. In 1964, five years after its inception, the Higher Horizons program was evaluated by the New York City Board of Education. No significant difference in performance was found between students who participated in Higher Horizons and similar students in schools without the program. There was *no difference* in academic achievement.[6]

Another much heralded effort at compensatory education was the Banneker Project. The Banneker district is an almost

[5] See Kenneth B. Clark's chapter, "Ghetto Schools: Separate and Unequal," in *Dark Ghetto,* Random House, New York, 1965, in which he argues that the main thing needed is a change in attitude and expectation on the part of teachers and school administrators in nonwhite schools.

[6] Wrightstone, Forlano, Frankel, Lewis, Turner, and Bolger, "Evaluation of Higher Horizons Programs for Underprivileged Children," New York City Board of Education, 1964. See also discussion in *Racial Isolation in the Public Schools,* A Report of the United States Commission on Civil Rights, 1967, pp. 122–26.

100 percent Negro area in the center of St. Louis, Missouri, with a very low average family income. Unlike Higher Horizons and programs in most other cities, this project did not involve the expenditure of much additional money. The principle objective of this program, initiated in 1957, was to improve student achievement by raising the expectation of teachers, the motivation of students, and the aspiration of parents. Teacher meetings and conferences with parents and community groups were increased. A sense of competition was instilled among the Banneker schools. Reading scores and grades, for example, were made public and comparisons were drawn between the schools in the district. Dr. Samuel Shepard, the program's director and school superintendent of the district, reported after three years that reading levels had increased significantly and were on the average only about one-half year below the national norms. However, in the subsequent years this gain in reading scores was not maintained. By 1965–66 none of the Banneker schools were above grade level. In this way, they were comparable to other nearly all Negro schools.[7]

The More Effective Schools program in New York City is more difficult to judge at this time since it has been in operation only since 1964. MES was initiated in ten elementary schools and expanded to eleven more schools in 1965–66. The program includes smaller class size, extra teachers, guidance personnel, psychological services and administrative personnel. An evaluation completed by New York's Center for Urban Education in September of 1967 indicated that MES had improved the climate and morale in the schools but there was little comparable improvement in reading scores.[8] From the fourth

[7] *Ibid., Racial Isolation in the Public Schools,* pp. 120–22. This temporary improvement found in the Banneker district characterizes many compensatory programs. It is generally believed that this improvement is due to the "Hawthorne Effect." This phenomenon, taking its name from the Hawthorne Electric Plant where it was first discovered, relates change in human experimental situations to the subject's response to the experimental situation itself and the associated attention rather than to the particular variable manipulated. When the publicity and the novelty surrounding programs such as Higher Horizons and the Banneker Project fade, the learning improvement fades also.

[8] David Fox, "Evaluation of New York City Title I, Educational Projects 1966–1967, Expansion of the More Effective Schools Program," Center for Urban Education, 1967.

grade on, no nonwhite school in the MES program is reading at grade level. And even in MES schools the cumulative deficit phenomenon is seen.[9]

There seems no doubt that the report of the United States Commission on Civil Rights, *Racial Isolation in the Public Schools*,[10] is correct in its thesis that compensatory programs in predominantly nonwhite schools have just not provided sustained success in raising the achievement levels of nonwhite youngsters. The future of compensatory education at this point seems rather bleak. There are no new radical proposals on the horizon. Yet the federal government and school systems themselves are providing more funds for programs which simply are not working. Indeed it seems that as more evidence of failure accumulates, more money becomes available.

The sense of desperation in educators' attempts to increase learning through these programs is possibly related to the controversial alternative of desegregating our city schools. Desegregation, as viewed by many educators, would involve the schools directly in political conflict with community groups, and would result in changed power relationships both within the city school systems and possibly between urban and suburban communities.

The argument supporting desegregation as the answer to the school failure of nonwhite youngsters is basically psychological, as was the Supreme Court's historic 1954 decision in *Brown* vs. *Board of Education*. This position argues that the fact of forced separation—that minority group youngsters are kept in separate schools and not allowed to interact with majority youngsters—in itself produces inferior learning. Recent evidence on this critical relationship can be found in the Office of Education report titled, *Equality of Educational Opportunity*.[11] This study indicates that when nonwhite youngsters at all levels

[9] "Cumulative deficit" refers to the fact that as Negro and white children progress through school, Negroes fall farther and farther behind. What may be a reading difference of six months in the second grade is likely to become two years and six months by the seventh grade.

[10] *Racial Isolation in the Public Schools*, op. cit., pp. 73–115.

[11] *Equality of Educational Opportunity, Summary Report*, U.S. Department of Health, Education and Welfare, Office of Education, 1966, pp. 28–31.

are in the minority in predominantly white schools, they do tend to perform better and achieve more academically than when they are in segregated nonwhite schools. Questions can be raised, however, about the socio-economic background of the integrated nonwhite youngsters. Are they, for example, sons and daughters of middle-class professionals living in suburban communities or are they poor nonwhites who have been bused into middle-class neighborhoods? The Office of Education report unfortunately does not answer these questions.

Perhaps a stronger case can be made from the report on school desegregation in White Plains, New York (a suburban community of 60,000 in Westchester County, just north of New York City). It has been reported by the school board that there is significantly increased learning for nonwhite children after desegregation. There is, in addition, a slight increase in learning for white children in the integrated schools.[12]

One would be safe, then, in answering with a tentative "yes" the question of whether school desegregation can raise achievement levels for nonwhite youngsters. A more significant question, however, is, how widespread is school desegregation and how likely is it to become the important method of increasing learning among nonwhite students? The Supreme Court decision in 1954 ordered the desegregation of schools "with all deliberate speed." The last best estimate is that in the nation as a whole, the great majority of nonwhite youngsters attend segregated schools. In the South the figure approaches 90 percent.[13] In spite of the Supreme Court decision and agitation by civil rights leaders, *more* Negro youngsters and *more* white youngsters are attending segregated schools in our large cities in 1967 than was the case a decade ago.[14] Out of educators' attempts to reverse this trend have come the following proposals.

1. The Open Enrollment Plan in New York City—which called for the voluntary transfer of youngsters from crowded, usually poor Negro and Puerto Rican schools to less crowded, usually white middle-class schools—has been a resounding failure as a solution to segregation. About all that was accomplished

[12] As reported in the *New York Times*, October 16, 1967.
[13] *Racial Isolation in the Public Schools, op. cit.*, pp. 1–7.
[14] *Ibid.*, pp. 8–15.

was the siphoning off of a few thousand nonwhite youngsters from the most upwardly mobile families living in ghetto communities.

2. Rezoned attendance districts and carefully planned new construction of schools have had, and can have, only marginal effects in large cities. It is hard to imagine how any rezoning or new building plan could put a Negro youngster living at 127th Street and Lenox Avenue (the center of Harlem) into a desegregated school.

3. Moving youngsters from one school district to another, or "busing," has to no one's surprise met with considerable opposition. White parents in lower-middle- and middle-class neighborhoods object to their youngsters' being "bused" to predominantly Negro schools and to Negroes being bused to white schools. Because of organized opposition by white communities, most big city boards of education have been unwilling to press for the mass movement of children across "neighborhood" lines. There is also, it must be admitted, no clear evidence that all or even most nonwhite parents are in favor of it, although many are willing to go along with "busing" if the result is better education for their youngsters.

4. The construction of vast educational complexes in central urban locations has been proposed, to serve youngsters from both the inner city ghettos and middle-class neighborhoods. When one considers the difficulty that any board of education has in obtaining financial support, even with growing federal assistance, one must ask if it is a political possibility that the city residents would, or indeed could, increase their educational expenditures by the fantastic amount required to build educational complexes. Unless there is a tremendous flow of federal aid, in the range of several billion dollars for each of our major cities, the educational-complex idea seems unrealistic.

5. Robert Havighurst's Metropolitan School Concept is probably the most rational and far-reaching proposal for dealing with school desegregation and other important educational problems as well.[15] Havighurst proposes a school area that would include both the city and its surrounding suburbs. Tax

[15] Robert J. Havighurst, "Metropolitan Development and the Educational System," *School Review*, 1961, pp. 251–69.

money would be raised generally from this metropolitan area for the support of public education. This would permit areawide planning, construction and the transportation of youngsters, not only across attendance areas within the city but from city to suburb and vice versa. As exciting as this plan is, the probabilities of its being implemented in the near future seem far from good. Beginning in October 1967, the State Republican Party of New Jersey began to call for the resignation of Dr. Carl Marberger, State Commissioner of Education, for suggesting publicly that New Jersey's school children might have to be "bused" across city lines to effect school desegregation. Democratic Governor Richard Hughes hastily assured the public that as long as he is governor there would be no "busing" of youngsters across city lines. The massive Republican election victory in the New Jersey State Legislature and Senate in November 1967 has been attributed in part to Dr. Marberger's statement. Is it realistic to expect that suburbanites, who have escaped what they view as the evils of the city, will shoulder part of the financial burdens required to reduce those evils and send their children to school once again with the "disadvantaged?"

Though school desegregation may well be an important ingredient in increasing school performance for nonwhite youngsters, the political and economic facts make it unlikely that either the massive construction or political reorganization necessary to really bring about desegregation is going to be implemented in the next twenty, thirty, or even forty years.

The educational and social plight of nonwhites will not wait forty years. Both parents and activist leaders in the ghetto communities are demanding improved learning for their youngsters now! If compensatory education programs don't work and school desegregation is impossible to achieve, is there any hope of fulfilling these demands?

The one positive development on the urban scene in the past five years is the increasing demand for local community power in the operation and control of nonwhite schools. Community leaders who are advocates of Black Power and those who reject that concept are *both* becoming vocal, and insistent that they should be involved in the operation of public schools in their neighborhoods. The citywide board of education, burdened with its traditional bureaucratic structure, has failed and, they argue, it would be impossible for anyone to do worse. An objective scanning of the reading scores in nonwhite schools in New York City tends to support this argument. These leaders believe that they and educators working directly for the community can do much better, particularly through instilling in nonwhite youngsters a racial and ethnic pride in their own background, their culture, and the history of their people. They believe further that this pride will offset the psychological damage generally associated with school segregation.

Dan Dodson has pointed out that the historical experience of segregation has led to a sense of powerlessness among Negroes which can result in apathy and resignation about schooling.[16] The advocates of community-controlled schools would argue that by taking power in their schools, they can greatly reduce this apathy in their children. Schools which are predominantly nonwhite, they believe, when operated, controlled, and directed by largely nonwhite professionals and community residents, will produce youngsters whose self-concepts are as positive as those of white youngsters. These spokesmen are, of course, demanding real power in the operation of public schools, not "community participation" in the traditional sense of that word. They are not interested in turning people out for parent association meetings in which the virtues of the school can be described or in urging parents to get tough with their youngsters so they will be more docile in school. They demand decision-making power in hiring, planning curriculum, and spending money.

Educators unfortunately tend to view these demands for power either with utter abhorrence for nonprofessional and poorly schooled people who presume to tell them how to operate schools, or with the firm conviction that community residents will fail in attempts to direct the education of their own youngsters. Neither of these reactions is intelligent or helpful. If teachers and school administrators are indeed public servants, as they claim to be, it seems not illogical or unreasonable to

[16] Dan Dodson, "Education and the Powerless," in Passow, Goldberg, and Tanenbaum, editors, *Education of the Disadvantaged,* Holt, Rinehart & Winston, New York, 1967, pp. 62–73.

expect them to be responsible to local school boards and committees rather than to one citywide school board and bureaucratic structure.

There are several questions that may reasonably be put to the leaders of the local-control movement. Can they really develop the broad community interest and concern needed to operate their own schools? Will local school boards be able to find competent teachers and administrators to perform the educational tasks required? Will, as some community leaders insist, these teachers and school administrators be nonwhite? If so, where will they come from? If they are not to be all nonwhite, then what inducements will be offered to bring capable white teachers into primarily nonwhite schools? Advocates of community-operated schools have yet to indicate what educational changes they will make. Will the curriculum be different? Will new subject matter be introduced? Will new teaching methods be used? Or is the expected improvement in learning to come about simply through the changed attitudes and expectations of educators?

In New York City the chances of some type of local educational control developing seem reasonably good. Already there are militant local school committees in all ghetto neighborhoods. The Ford Foundation has provided $51,000 for a community planning board in East Harlem. The most ambitious plan for community power is the one presented to the Mayor of New York by his special panel on school decentralization, headed by McGeorge Bundy, president of the Ford Foundation. The plan calls for the radical reorganization of New York City into thirty to sixty largely independent community school districts, each having from about 12,000 to 40,000 students. The local boards, with the majority of their members elected within each of the new districts, would have the power to appoint the community school superintendent as well as the faculty, determine curriculum policy, formulate budgets, and determine expenditures.[17]

In spite of opposition to the Bundy report from the board of education, the school administrators and the New York City teachers' union, it seems quite likely that some kind of

[17] See the *New York Times,* November 8, 1967.

substantial decentralization will take place. Not one of these three groups has any new or radical proposals, and all three are highly suspect in the eyes of the nonwhite community. The present course is too obviously disastrous to continue.

The final question about the local community role in school affairs is a moral one. Do nonwhite Americans have a right to increased control over their own lives? If they do, then they must surely have greater power in making educational decisions which vitally affect the lives of their children. Dan Dodson speaks movingly about schools in which minority groups have taken power:

> Every classroom should be a laboratory in how to take power, how to shield the group from power which is abused, how to work through shared relationships.
>
> You asked about curriculum. Curriculum is the composite of the confrontations which the school provides the youth in his search for selfhood.
>
> The great documents of history have been produced by those who were outside the power order . . . They have not come from those in the power stream who were defending their entrenched positions. Teachers who are handmaidens of the power order should not sell these children of the ghetto short. Out of their protestations is coming the fulfillment of the greatest faith we have—that all men love freedom and that all men have the capacity to participate worthily in the collective direction of their own destiny.[18]

[18] Dodson, *op. cit.*, p. 72.

PART THREE

POVERTY IN THE WORLD

A. THE PROBLEMS

INTRODUCTION

THE UNITED STATES is in many ways unlike the rest of the world. What is good for us, what helps to solve our problems, may not be particularly useful for the greater part of mankind. In looking at poverty outside of the United States we have chosen to focus on what are called "underdeveloped" or "developing" nations, where it is the rule rather than the exception. We are clearly aware that poverty exists in Manchester, Barcelona, Naples, and Warsaw, but these pockets in the developed world are less critical than the massive poverty of Asia, Africa and Latin America. In the underdeveloped world, the extent and pervasiveness of poverty makes it more difficult to comprehend and thus to reduce and eventually eliminate.

Oscar Lewis, an anthropologist, offers a theory of the "culture of poverty," and relates it to rapidly changing societies. In contradiction to Frantz Fanon, he finds little revolutionary ferment among the very poor in the areas he has studied. Robert Heilbroner outlines, in terms of economic resources and productive capacity, the grim picture of two-thirds of the world. Charles Abrams looks at housing conditions in urban areas of the underdeveloped world and finds them creating acute economic and social problems. Imperialism has played a crucial role in developing present conditions in Africa, Asia and Latin America. Conor Cruise O'Brien views imperialism in its contemporary forms.

Violence and revolution play an increasingly important role in determining the fate of the world's poor. Frantz Fanon's thoughtful analysis from the perspective of the former colonial peoples suggests that this violence and revolution will continue and increase in scope. Latin America is an underdeveloped area of particular concern to the United States. Edmundo Flores offers a singularly pessimistic view of our present attempt— the Alliance for Progress—to help this region help itself. He concludes flatly that it is a dismal failure.

| OSCAR | THE CULTURE |
| LEWIS | OF POVERTY* |

BECAUSE the research design of this study was concerned with testing the concept of a culture of poverty in different national contexts and because this concept is helpful in understanding the Ríos family, I shall briefly summarize some of its dimensions here.

Although a great deal has been written about poverty and the poor, the concept of a culture of poverty is relatively new. I first suggested it in 1959 in my book *Five Families: Mexican Case Studies in the Culture of Poverty*. The phrase is a catchy one and has become widely used and misused.[1] Michael Harrington used it extensively in his book *The Other America* (1961), which played an important role in sparking the national anti-poverty program in the United States. However, he used it in a somewhat broader and less technical sense than I had intended. I shall try to define it more precisely as a conceptual model, with special emphasis upon the distinction between poverty and the culture of poverty. The absence of

* From *La Vida* by Oscar Lewis. © Copyright 1965, 1966 by Oscar Lewis. Reprinted by permission of Random House, Inc.
[1] There has been relatively little discussion of the culture of poverty concept in the professional journals, however. Two articles deal with the problem in some detail: Elizabeth Herzog, "Some Assumptions About the Poor," in *The Social Service Review*, December 1963, pp. 389–402; Lloyd Ohlin, "Inherited Poverty," Organization for Economic Cooperation and Development (no date), Paris.

intensive anthropological studies of poor families from a wide variety of national and cultural contexts and especially from the socialist countries, is a serious handicap in formulating valid cross-cultural regularities. The model presented here is therefore provisional and subject to modification as new studies become available.

Throughout recorded history, in literature, in proverbs and in popular sayings, we find two opposite evaluations of the nature of the poor. Some characterize the poor as blessed, virtuous, upright, serene, independent, honest, kind and happy. Others characterize them as evil, mean, violent, sordid and criminal. These contradictory and confusing evaluations are also reflected in the in-fighting that is going on in the current war against poverty. Some stress the great potential of the poor for self-help, leadership and community organization, while others point to the sometimes irreversible, destructive effect of poverty upon individual character, and therefore emphasize the need for guidance and control to remain in the hands of the middle class, which presumably has better mental health.

These opposing views reflect a political power struggle between competing groups. However, some of the confusion results from the failure to distinguish between poverty *per se* and the culture of poverty and the tendency to focus upon the individual personality rather than upon the group—that is, the family and the slum community.

As an anthropologist I have tried to understand poverty and its associated traits as a culture or, more accurately, as a subculture[2] with its own structure and rationale, as a way of life which is passed down from generation to generation along family lines. This view directs attention to the fact that the culture of poverty in modern nations is not only a matter of economic deprivation, of disorganization or of the absence of something. It is also something positive and provides some rewards without which the poor could hardly carry on.

Elsewhere I have suggested that the culture of poverty transcends regional, rural–urban and national differences and shows remarkable similarities in family structure, interpersonal rela-

---

[2] While the term "subculture of poverty" is technically more accurate, I have used "culture of poverty" as a shorter form.

tions, time orientation, value systems and spending patterns. These cross-national similarities are examples of independent invention and convergence. They are common adaptations to common problems.

The culture of poverty can come into being in a variety of historical contexts. However, it tends to grow and flourish in societies with the following set of conditions: (1) a cash economy, wage labor and production for profit; (2) a persistently high rate of unemployment and underemployment for unskilled labor; (3) low wages; (4) the failure to provide social, political and economic organization, either on a voluntary basis or by government imposition, for the low-income population; (5) the existence of a bilateral kinship system rather than a unilateral one;[3] and finally, (6) the existence of a set of values in the dominant class which stresses the accumulation of wealth and property, the possibility of upward mobility and thrift, and explains low economic status as the result of personal inadequacy or inferiority.

The way of life which develops among some of the poor

[3] In a unilineal kinship system, descent is reckoned either through males or through females. When traced exclusively through males it is called patrilineal or agnatic descent; when reckoned exclusively through females it is called matrilineal or uterine descent. In a bilateral or cognatic system, descent is traced through males and females without emphasis on either line.

In a unilineal system, the lineage consists of all the descendants of one ancestor. In a patrilineal system, the lineage is composed of all the descendants through males of one male ancestor. A matrilineage consists of all the descendants through females of one female ancestor. The lineage may thus contain a very large number of generations. If bilateral descent is reckoned, however, the number of generations that can be included in a social unit is limited, since the number of ancestors doubles every generation.

Unilineal descent groups ("lineages" or "clans") are corporate groups in the sense that the lineage or clan may act as a collectivity: it can take blood vengeance against another descent group, it can hold property, etc. However, the bilateral kin group (the "kindred") can rarely act as a collectivity because it is not a "group" except from the point of view of a particular individual, and, furthermore, has no continuity over time.

In a unilineal system, an individual is assigned to a group by virtue of his birth. In contrast, a person born into a bilateral system usually has a choice of relatives whom he chooses to recognize as "kin" and with whom he wants to associate. This generally leads to a greater diffuseness and fragmentation of ties with relatives over time.

under these conditions is the culture of poverty. It can best be studied in urban or rural slums and can be described in terms of some seventy interrelated social, economic and psychological traits.[4] However, the number of traits and the relationships between them may vary from society to society and from family to family. For example, in a highly literate society, illiteracy may be more diagnostic of the culture of poverty than in a society where illiteracy is widespread and where even the well-to-do may be illiterate, as in some Mexican peasant villages before the revolution.

The culture of poverty is both an adaptation and a reaction of the poor to their marginal position in a class-stratified, highly individuated, capitalistic society. It represents an effort to cope with feelings of hopelessness and despair which develop from the realization of the improbability of achieving success in terms of the values and goals of the larger society. Indeed, many of the traits of the culture of poverty can be viewed as attempts at local solutions for problems not met by existing institutions and agencies because the people are not eligible for them, cannot afford them, or are ignorant or suspicious of them. For example, unable to obtain credit from banks, they are thrown upon their own resources and organize informal credit devices without interest.

The culture of poverty, however, is not only an adaptation to a set of objective conditions of the larger society. Once it comes into existence it tends to perpetuate itself from generation to generation because of its effect on the children. By the time slum children are age six or seven they have usually absorbed the basic values and attitudes of their subculture and are not psychologically geared to take full advantage of changing conditions or increased opportunities which may occur in their lifetime.

Most frequently the culture of poverty develops when a stratified social and economic system is breaking down or is being replaced by another, as in the case of the transition from feudalism to capitalism or during periods of rapid technological

---

[4] "The Culture of Poverty," in John J. TePaske and S. N. Fischer, eds., *Explosive Forces in Latin America,* Ohio State University Press, Columbus, Ohio, 1964, pp. 149–73.

change. Often it results from imperial conquest in which the native social and economic structure is smashed and the natives are maintained in a servile colonial status, sometimes for many generations. It can also occur in the process of detribalization, such as that now going on in Africa.

The most likely candidates for the culture of poverty are the people who come from the lower strata of a rapidly changing society and are already partially alienated from it. Thus landless rural workers who migrate to the cities can be expected to develop a culture of poverty much more readily than migrants from stable peasant villages with a well-organized traditional culture. In this connection there is a striking contrast between Latin America, where the rural population long ago made the transition from a tribal to a peasant society, and Africa, which is still close to its tribal heritage. The more corporate nature of many of the African tribal societies, in contrast to Latin American rural communities, and the persistence of village ties tend to inhibit or delay the formation of a full-blown culture of poverty in many of the African towns and cities. The special conditions of apartheid in South Africa, where the migrants are segregated into separate "locations" and do not enjoy freedom of movement, create special problems. Here the institutionalization of repression and discrimination tend to develop a greater sense of identity and group consciousness.

The culture of poverty can be studied from various points of view: the relationship between the subculture and the larger society; the nature of the slum community; the nature of the family; and the attitudes, values and character structure of the individual.

1. The lack of effective participation and integration of the poor in the major institutions of the larger society is one of the crucial characteristics of the culture of poverty. This is a complex matter and results from a variety of factors which may include lack of economic resources, segregation and discrimination, fear, suspicion or apathy, and the development of local solutions for problems. However, "participation" in some of the institutions of the larger society—for example, in the jails, the army and the public relief system—does not *per se* eliminate

the traits of the culture of poverty. In the case of a relief system which barely keeps people alive, both the basic poverty and the sense of hopelessness are perpetuated rather than eliminated.

Low wages, chronic unemployment and underemployment lead to low income, lack of property ownership, absence of savings, absence of food reserves in the home, and a chronic shortage of cash. These conditions reduce the possibility of effective participation in the larger economic system. And as a response to these conditions we find in the culture of poverty a high incidence of pawning of personal goods, borrowing from local moneylenders at usurious rates of interest, spontaneous informal credit devices organized by neighbors, the use of second-hand clothing and furniture, and the pattern of frequent buying of small quantities of food many times a day as the need arises.

People with a culture of poverty produce very little wealth and receive very little in return. They have a low level of literacy and education, usually do not belong to labor unions, are not members of political parties, generally do not participate in the national welfare agencies, and make very little use of banks, hospitals, department stores, museums or art galleries. They have a critical attitude toward some of the basic institutions of the dominant classes, hatred of the police, mistrust of government and those in high position, and a cynicism which extends even to the church. This gives the culture of poverty a high potential for protest and for being used in political movements aimed against the existing social order.

People with a culture of poverty are aware of middle-class values, talk about them and even claim some of them as their own, but on the whole they do not live by them. Thus it is important to distinguish between what they say and what they do. For example, many will tell you that marriage by law, by the church, or by both, is the ideal form of marriage, but few will marry. To men who have no steady jobs or other sources of income, who do not own property and have no wealth to pass on to their children, who are present-time oriented and who want to avoid the expense and legal difficulties involved in formal marriage and divorce, free unions or consensual marriage makes a lot of sense. Women will often turn down offers of marriage because they feel it ties them down to men who are immature, punishing and generally unreliable. Women feel that consensual union gives them a better break; it gives them some of the freedom and flexibility that men have. By not giving the fathers of their children legal status as husbands, the women have a stronger claim on their children if they decide to leave their men. It also gives women exclusive rights to a house or any other property they may own.

2. When we look at the culture of poverty on the local community level, we find poor housing conditions, crowding, gregariousness, but above all a minimum of organization beyond the level of the nuclear and extended family. Occasionally there are informal, temporary groupings or voluntary associations within slums. The existence of neighborhood gangs which cut across slum settlements represents a considerable advance beyond the zero point of the continuum that I have in mind. Indeed, it is the low level of organization which gives the culture of poverty its marginal and anachronistic quality in our highly complex, specialized, organized society. Most primitive peoples have achieved a higher level of socio-cultural organization than our modern urban slum dwellers.

In spite of the generally low level of organization, there may be a sense of community and *esprit de corps* in urban slums and in slum neighborhoods. This can vary within a single city, or from region to region or country to country. The major factors influencing this variation are the size of the slum, its location and physical characteristics, length of residence, incidence of home and land ownership (versus squatter rights), rentals, ethnicity, kinship ties, and freedom or lack of freedom of movement. When slums are separated from the surrounding area by enclosing walls or other physical barriers, when rents are low and fixed and stability of residence is great (twenty or thirty years), when the population constitutes a distinct ethnic, racial or language group, is bound by ties of kinship or *compadrazgo,* and when there are some internal voluntary associations, then the sense of local community approaches that of a village community. In many cases this combination of favorable conditions does not exist. However, even where internal organization and *esprit de corps* is at a bare minimum and people move around a great deal, a sense of territoriality develops which sets off the slum neighborhoods from the rest of the city. In Mexico City and San Juan this sense of territoriality results from the unavailability of low-income housing outside the slum areas. In South Africa the sense of territoriality grows out of the segregation enforced by the government, which confines the rural migrants to specific locations.

3. On the family level the major traits of the culture of poverty are the absence of childhood as a specially prolonged and protected stage in the life cycle, early initiation into sex, free unions or consensual marriages, a relatively high incidence of the abandonment of wives and children, a trend toward female- or mother-centered families and consequently a much greater knowledge of maternal relatives, a strong predisposition to authoritarianism, lack of privacy, verbal emphasis upon family solidarity which is only rarely achieved because of sibling rivalry, and competition for limited goods and maternal affection.

4. On the level of the individual the major characteristics are a strong feeling of marginality, of helplessness, of dependence and of inferiority. I found this to be true of slum dwellers in Mexico City and San Juan among families who do not constitute a distinct ethnic or racial group and who do not suffer from racial discrimination. In the United States, of course, the culture of poverty of the Negroes has the additional disadvantage of racial discrimination, but as I have already suggested, this additional disadvantage contains a great potential for revolutionary protest and organization which seems to be absent in the slums of Mexico City or among the poor whites in the South.

Other traits include a high incidence of maternal deprivation, of orality, of weak ego structure, confusion of sexual identification, a lack of impulse control, a strong present-time orientation with relatively little ability to defer gratification and to plan for the future, a sense of resignation and fatalism, a widespread belief in male superiority, and a high tolerance for psychological pathology of all sorts.

People with a culture of poverty are provincial and locally oriented and have very little sense of history. They know only their own troubles, their own local conditions, their own neighborhood, their own way of life. Usually they do not have the knowledge, the vision or the ideology to see the similarities between their problems and those of their counterparts elsewhere in the world. They are not class-conscious, although they are very sensitive indeed to status distinctions.

When the poor become class-conscious or active members of trade-union organizations, or when they adopt an internationalist outlook on the world, they are no longer part of the culture of poverty, although they may still be desperately poor. Any movement, be it religious, pacifist or revolutionary, which organizes and gives hope to the poor and effectively promotes solidarity and a sense of identification with larger groups, destroys the psychological and social core of the culture of poverty. In this connection, I suspect that the civil rights movement among the Negroes in the United States has done more to improve their self-image and self-respect than have their economic advances, although, without doubt, the two are mutually reinforcing.

The distinction between poverty and the culture of poverty is basic to the model described here. There are degrees of poverty and many kinds of poor people. The culture of poverty refers to one way of life shared by poor people in given historical and social contexts. The economic traits which I have listed for the culture of poverty are necessary but not sufficient to define the phenomena I have in mind. There are a number of historical examples of very poor segments of the population which do not have a way of life that I would describe as a subculture of poverty. Here I should like to give four examples:

1. Many of the primitive or preliterate peoples studied by anthropologists suffer from dire poverty which is the result of poor technology and/or poor natural resources, or of both, but they do not have the traits of the subculture of poverty. Indeed, they do not constitute a subculture because their societies are not highly stratified. In spite of their poverty they have a relatively integrated, satisfying and self-sufficient culture. Even the simplest food-gathering and hunting tribes have a considerable amount

of organization, bands and band chiefs, tribal councils and local self-government—traits which are not found in the culture of poverty.

2. In India the lower castes (the Chamars, the leather workers, and the Bhangis, the sweepers) may be desperately poor, both in the villages and in the cities, but most of them are integrated into the larger society and have their own *panchayat*[5] organizations which cut across village lines and give them a considerable amount of power.[6] In addition to the caste system, which gives individuals a sense of identity and belonging, there is still another factor, the clan system. Wherever there are unilateral kinship systems or clans one would not expect to find the culture of poverty, because a clan system gives people a sense of belonging to a corporate body with a history and a life of its own, thereby providing a sense of continuity, a sense of a past and of a future.

3. The Jews of Eastern Europe were very poor, but they did not have many of the traits of the culture of poverty because of their tradition of literacy, the great value placed upon learning, the organization of the community around the rabbi, the proliferation of local voluntary associations, and their religion which taught that they were the chosen people.

4. My fourth example is speculative and relates to socialism. On the basis of my limited experience in one socialist country—Cuba—and on the basis of my reading, I am inclined to believe that the culture of poverty does not exist in the socialist countries. I first went to Cuba in 1947 as a visiting professor for the State Department. At that time I began a study of a sugar plantation in Melena del Sur and of a slum in Havana. After the Castro Revolution I made my second trip to Cuba as a correspondent for a major magazine, and I revisited the same slum and some of the same families. The physical aspect

---

[5] A formal organization designed to provide caste leadership.

[6] It may be that in the slums of Calcutta and Bombay an incipient culture of poverty is developing. It would be highly desirable to do family studies there as a crucial test of the culture-of-poverty hypothesis.

of the slum had changed very little, except for a beautiful new nursery school. It was clear that the people were still desperately poor, but I found much less of the despair, apathy and hopelessness which are so diagnostic of urban slums in the culture of poverty. They expressed great confidence in their leaders and hope for a better life in the future. The slum itself was now highly organized, with block committees, educational committees, party committees. The people had a new sense of power and importance. They were armed and were given a doctrine which glorified the lower class as the hope of humanity. (I was told by one Cuban official that they had practically eliminated delinquency by giving arms to the delinquents!)

It is my impression that the Castro regime—unlike Marx and Engels—did not write off the so-called lumpen proletariat as an inherently reactionary and anti-revolutionary force, but rather saw its revolutionary potential and tried to utilize it. In this connection, Frantz Fanon makes a similar evaluation of the role of the lumpen proletariat based upon his experience in the Algerian struggle for independence. In his recently published book[7] he wrote:

> It is within this mass of humanity, this people of the shanty towns, at the core of the lumpen proletariat, that the rebellion will find its urban spearhead. For the lumpen proletariat, that horde of starving men, uprooted from their tribe and from their clan, constitutes one of the most spontaneous and most radically revolutionary forces of a colonized people.

My own studies of the urban poor in the slums of San Juan do not support the generalizations of Fanon. I have found very little revolutionary spirit or radical ideology among low-income Puerto Ricans. On the contrary, most of the families I studied were quite conservative politically and about half of them were in favor of the Republican Statehood Party. It seems to me that the revolutionary potential of people with a culture of poverty will vary considerably according to the national context and the

7 Frantz Fanon, *The Wretched of the Earth,* Grove Press, New York, 1965, p. 103.

particular historical circumstances. In a country like Algeria which was fighting for its independence, the lumpen proletariat was drawn into the struggle and became a vital force. However, in countries like Puerto Rico, in which the movement for independence has very little mass support, and in countries like Mexico which achieved their independence a long time ago and are now in their post-revolutionary period, the lumpen proletariat is not a leading source of rebellion or of revolutionary spirit.

In effect, we find that in primitive societies and in caste societies, the culture of poverty does not develop. In socialist, fascist and in highly developed capitalist societies with a welfare state, the culture of poverty tends to decline. I suspect that the culture of poverty flourishes in, and is generic to, the early free-enterprise stage of capitalism and that it is also endemic in colonialism.

It is important to distinguish between different profiles in the subculture of poverty depending upon the national context in which these subcultures are found. If we think of the culture of poverty primarily in terms of the factor of integration in the larger society and a sense of identification with the great tradition of that society, or with a new emerging revolutionary tradition, then we will not be surprised that some slum dwellers with a lower per capita income may have moved farther away from the core characteristics of the culture of poverty than others with a higher per capita income. For example, Puerto Rico has a much higher per capita income than Mexico, yet Mexicans have a deeper sense of identity.

I have listed fatalism and a low level of aspiration as one of the key traits for the subculture of poverty. Here too, however, the national context makes a big difference. Certainly the level of aspiration of even the poorest sector of the population in a country like the United States with its traditional ideology of upward mobility and democracy is much higher than in more backward countries like Ecuador and Peru, where both the ideology and the actual possibilities of upward mobility are extremely limited and where authoritarian values still persist in both the urban and rural milieus.

Because of the advanced technology, high level of literacy,

the development of mass media and the relatively high aspiration level of all sectors of the population, especially when compared with underdeveloped nations, I believe that although there is still a great deal of poverty in the United States (estimates range from 30 to 50 million people), there is relatively little of what I would call the culture of poverty. My rough guess would be that only about 20 percent of the population below the poverty line (between 6 and 10 million people) in the United States have characteristics which would justify classifying their way of life as that of a culture of poverty. Probably the largest sector within this group would consist of very low-income Negroes, Mexicans, Puerto Ricans, American Indians and Southern poor whites. The relatively small number of people in the United States with a culture of poverty is a positive factor because it is much more difficult to eliminate the culture of poverty than to eliminate poverty *per se*.

Middle-class people, and this would certainly include most social scientists, tend to concentrate on the negative aspects of the culture of poverty. They tend to associate negative valences to such traits as present-time orientation and concrete versus abstract orientation. I do not intend to idealize or romanticize the culture of poverty. As someone has said, "It is easier to praise poverty than to live in it"; yet some of the positive aspects which may flow from these traits must not be overlooked. Living in the present may develop a capacity for spontaneity and adventure, for the enjoyment of the sensual, the indulgence of impulse, which is often blunted in the middle-class, future-oriented man. Perhaps it is this reality of the moment which the existentialist writers are so desperately trying to recapture but which the culture of poverty experiences as natural, everyday phenomena. The frequent use of violence certainly provides a ready outlet for hostility so that people in the culture of poverty suffer less from repression than does the middle class.

In the traditional view, anthropologists have said that culture provides human beings with a design for living, with a ready-made set of solutions for human problems so that individuals don't have to begin all over again each generation. That is, the core of culture is its positive adaptive function. I, too, have called attention to some of the adaptive mechanisms in the culture of poverty—for example, the low aspiration level helps to reduce frustration, the legitimization of short-range hedonism makes possible spontaneity and enjoyment. However, on the whole it seems to me that it is a relatively thin culture. There is a great deal of pathos, suffering and emptiness among those who live in the culture of poverty. It does not provide much support or long-range satisfaction and its encouragement of mistrust tends to magnify helplessness and isolation. Indeed, the poverty of culture is one of the crucial aspects of the culture of poverty.

The concept of the culture of poverty provides a high level of generalization which, hopefully, will unify and explain a number of phenomena viewed as distinctive characteristics of racial, national or regional groups. For example, matrifocality, a high incidence of consensual unions and a high percentage of households headed by women, which have been thought to be distinctive of Caribbean family organization or of Negro family life in the U.S.A., turn out to be traits of the culture of poverty and are found among diverse peoples in many parts of the world and among peoples who have had no history of slavery.

The concept of a cross-societal subculture of poverty enables us to see that many of the problems we think of as distinctively our own or distinctively Negro problems (or that of any other special racial or ethnic group), also exist in countries where there are no distinct ethnic minority groups. This suggests that the elimination of physical poverty *per se* may not be enough to eliminate the culture of poverty which is a whole way of life.

What is the future of the culture of poverty? In considering this question, one must distinguish between those countries in which it represents a relatively small segment of the population and those in which it constitutes a very large one. Obviously the solutions will differ in these two situations. In the United States, the major solution proposed by planners and social workers in dealing with multiple-problem families and the so-called hard core of poverty has been to attempt slowly to raise their level of living and to incorporate them into the middle class. Wherever possible, there has been some reliance upon psychiatric treatment.

In the underdeveloped countries, however, where great masses of people live in the culture of poverty, a social-work solution does not seem feasible. Because of the magnitude of the problem, psychiatrists can hardly begin to cope with it. They have all they can do to care for their own growing middle class. In these countries the people with a culture of poverty may seek a more revolutionary solution. By creating basic structural changes in society, by redistributing wealth, by organizing the poor and giving them a sense of belonging, of power and of leadership, revolutions frequently succeed in abolishing some of the basic characteristics of the culture of poverty even when they do not succeed in abolishing poverty itself.

<table>
<tr><td>**ROBERT L.**
HEILBRONER</td><td>**THE TABLEAU**

OF UNDER-

DEVELOPMENT*</td></tr>
</table>

To BEGIN to understand economic development we must have a picture of the problem with which it contends. We must conjure up in our mind's eye what underdevelopment means for the two billion human beings for whom it is not a statistic but a living experience of daily life. Unless we can see the Great Ascent from the vantage point of those who must make the climb, we cannot hope to understand the difficulties of the march.

It is not easy to make this mental jump. But let us attempt it by imagining how a typical American family, living in a small suburban house on an income of six or seven thousand dollars,[1] could be transformed into an equally typical family of the underdeveloped world.

We begin by invading the house of our imaginary American family to strip it of its furniture. Everything goes: beds, chairs, tables, television set, lamps. We will leave the family with a

* From *The Great Ascent* by Robert L. Heilbroner. Copyright © 1963 by Robert L. Heilbroner. Reprinted by permission of Harper & Row, Publishers.
[1] Median family income for 1967 is $6,600.—Eds.

few old blankets, a kitchen table, a wooden chair. Along with the bureaus go the clothes. Each member of the family may keep in his "wardrobe" his oldest suit or dress, a shirt or blouse. We will permit a pair of shoes to the head of the family, but none for the wife or children.

We move into the kitchen. The appliances have already been taken out, so we turn to the cupboards and larder. The box of matches may stay, a small bag of flour, some sugar and salt. A few moldy potatoes, already in the garbage can, must be hastily rescued, for they will provide much of tonight's meal. We will leave a handful of onions, and a dish of dried beans. All the rest we take away: the meat, the fresh vegetables, the canned goods, the crackers, the candy.

Now we have stripped the house: the bathroom has been dismantled, the running water shut off, the electric wires taken out. Next we take away the house. The family can move to the toolshed. It is crowded, but much better than the situation in Hong Kong, where (a United Nations report tells us) "it is not uncommon for a family of four or more to live in a bed-space, that is, on a bunk bed and the spaces it occupies—sometimes in two or three tiers—their only privacy provided by curtains."[2]

But we have only begun. All the other houses in the neighborhood have also been removed; our suburb has become a shantytown. Still, our family is fortunate to have a shelter; 250,-000 people in Calcutta have none at all and simply live in the streets. Our family is now about on a par with the city of Cali in Colombia, where, an official of the World Bank writes, "on one hillside alone, the slum population is estimated at 40,000—without water, sanitation, or electric light. And not all the poor of Cali are as fortunate as that. Others have built their shacks near the city on land which lies beneath the flood mark. To these people the immediate environment is the open sewer of the city, a sewer which flows through their huts when the river rises."[3]

And still we have not reduced our American family to the

---

[2] *Social Aspects of Urban Development,* Committee on Information from Non-Self-Governing Territories, March 10, 1961, p. 129.

[3] "The Cauca Valley," unpublished World Bank memo by George Young. (With the kind permission of the author.)

level at which life is lived in the greatest part of the globe. Communication must go next. No more newspapers, magazines, books—not that they are missed, since we must take away our family's literacy as well. Instead, in our shantytown we will allow one radio. In India the national average of radio ownership is one per 250 people, but since the majority of radios is owned by city dwellers, our allowance is fairly generous.

Now government services must go. No more postman, no more fireman. There is a school, but it is three miles away and consists of two classrooms. They are not too overcrowded since only half the children in the neighborhood go to school. There are, of course, no hospitals or doctors nearby. The nearest clinic is ten miles away and is tended by a midwife. It can be reached by bicycle, provided that the family has a bicycle, which is unlikely. Or one can go by bus—not always inside, but there is usually room on top.

Finally, money. We will allow our family a cash hoard of five dollars. This will prevent our breadwinner from experiencing the tragedy of an Iranian peasant who went blind because he could not raise the $3.94 which he mistakenly thought he needed to secure admission to a hospital where he could have been cured.[4]

Meanwhile the head of our family must earn his keep. As a peasant cultivator with three acres to tend, he may raise the equivalent of $100 to $300 worth of crops a year. If he is a tenant farmer, which is more than likely, a third or so of his crop will go to his landlord, and probably another 10 percent to the local moneylender. But there will be enough to eat. Or almost enough. The human body requires an input of at least 2,000 calories to replenish the energy consumed by its living cells. If our displaced American fares no better than an Indian peasant, he will average a replenishment of no more than 1,700–1,900 calories. His body, like any insufficiently fueled machine, will run down. That is one reason why life expectancy at birth in India today averages less than forty years.

But the children may help. If they are fortunate, they may find work and thus earn some cash to supplement the family's income. For example, they may be employed as are children

---

[4] *New York Times Magazine,* April 30, 1961.

in Hyderabad, Pakistan, sealing the ends of bangles over a small kerosene flame, a simple task which can be done at home. To be sure, the pay is small: eight annas—about ten cents—for sealing bangles. That is, eight annas per *gross* of bangles. And if they cannot find work? Well, they can scavenge, as do the children in Iran who in times of hunger search for the undigested oats in the droppings of horses.

And so we have brought our typical American family down to the very bottom of the human scale. It is, however, a bottom in which we can find, give or take a hundred million souls, at least a billion people.[5] Of the remaining billion in the backward areas, most are slightly better off, but not much so; a few are comfortable; a handful rich.

Of course, this is only an impression of life in the underdeveloped lands. It is not life itself. There is still lacking the things that underdevelopment gives as well as those it takes away: the urinous smell of poverty, the display of disease, the flies, the open sewers. And there is lacking, too, a softening sense of familiarity. Even in a charnel house life has its passions and pleasures. A tableau, shocking to American eyes, is less shocking to eyes that have never known any other. But it gives one a general idea. It begins to add pictures of reality to the statistics by which underdevelopment is ordinarily measured. When we are told that half the world's population enjoys a standard of living of "less than $100 a year," this is what the figures mean.

The Map of Underdevelopment

What we have gained thus far is largely a tourist's view of underdevelopment, indeed perhaps a tourist's stereotype. The very sharpness with which the grinding poverty strikes us is itself

[5] Such an estimate is, of necessity, highly conjectural. It takes in only 300 million of India's population and 50 million of Pakistan's, a charitable figure. It includes 50 million Arabs and 100 million Africans, a large underestimate. From South and Central America's poverty it adds in but another 50 millions. The remainder of the billion can be made up from mainland China alone. And we have kept as a statistical reserve the Afghans, Burmese, Indonesians, Koreans, Vietnamese—nearly 200 million in all, among whom is to be found some of the worst poverty on the face of the globe.

testimony that we are still looking at the scene with American eyes—that we are seeing it from a vantage point different from that of the underdeveloped lands themselves. Hence if we are to shake off the sense of an alien scrutiny, we must begin to enter within the framework of underdevelopment itself. Obviously, we cannot acquire the feeling of life in these areas as if it were our life. But we can begin to pierce the surface of things by looking for the causes of this ubiquitous poverty. What lies behind the squalor and want which, with only local variations, provide the great central theme of the underdeveloped lands?

It will help us to acquire an understanding of their common plight if we [were to] spread out a map of underdevelopment and examine it. Such a map, to be completely accurate, would have over one hundred nations and perhaps fifty territories marked on it. The list runs the alphabetical gamut from Afghanistan to Zanzibar.[6] Nonetheless even a general overview reveals a number of significant facts.

Perhaps what strikes us first, when we look at the map, is the diversity which characterizes the underdeveloped nations. In size and shape, in terrain and ecology, in political development and history there seems to be no common denominator to their condition. At least two underdeveloped nations—Brazil and China—are bigger than the United States; while three others —El Salvador, Lebanon, and Albania—would not together fill up West Virginia. Some are almost empty: Libya, with an area half the size of India, has a population smaller than the Bronx; others are fantastically crowded: Java, roughly the size of Alabama, has a population equal to one-third of the United States. Some, like China, are Communist; some, like India, are "socialist"; some are capitalist; and some, like Saudi Arabia, have been described as "rushing madly from the eleventh century into the twelfth."

But if the first impression is one of diversity, when we look

6 The classification of underdeveloped countries is at best somewhat arbitrary and the income divisions uncertain. We do not, for instance, count Russia as a backward nation, even though its per capita income might classify it as such. Were we to include its more backward regions, many of which lie to the east and south, the beltlike impression of the map would be further intensified.

again at the map, an obvious but important common characteristic strikes us. It is that underdevelopment is largely concentrated in the eastern and southern continents: Africa
(including the Near East), the land mass and archipelagoes of
Asia, and the great pear-shaped expanse of South America
with its Central American stem. This does not mean there is no
underdevelopment elsewhere. Europe has severely underdeveloped areas in Spain and Portugal, in Yugoslavia, southern Italy,
Greece, and the Black Sea countries. Oceania has its primitive
islands. Greenland has a per-capita income of $100. Parts of
Canada, even a few pockets of the United States, can be called
underdeveloped.

There is no doubt, however, that the great core of the problem lies in the land areas of the East and South. For Latin
America as a whole the per-capita income is between $300 and
$400; for Asia entire it is between $50 and $100; for Africa
and the Middle East perhaps less.

Is there a reason for this geographic massing of under-devel-
opment? One possible explanation occurs to us immediately.
It springs from the fact that most of the poorer nations are
wholly or partly in the tropics. Can their poverty be traced to
this simple cause?

It is curious that this question, which seems so open to em-
pirical investigation, is in fact far from simple to analyze. Not
many years ago the prima-facie "evidence" made the climatic
theory of underdevelopment virtually the prevalent explanation
of economic backwardness. To some, the lush vegetation suggested that agriculture was virtually effortless and that the
stimulus of a more grudging nature was therefore lacking. By
others the heat was blamed for the chronic "laziness" of the
natives. Or, again, the moist, disease-bearing terrain was thought
to be inimical to sustained effort.[7]

Today we are somewhat more chary of ascribing underdevelopment to the influence of climate alone. To be sure, there

[7] A less widely advertised theory (although still held in certain quarters) has attributed underdevelopment to the "childlike" mentality of
the nonwhite races. The extraordinary strides made by Japan and the
enormous (if tragic) effort mounted by China should effectively con-
trovert the view that mass poverty has an anthropological rather than a
social base.

are parts of the world where the heat is simply debilitating: not many years ago in Azizia in Tripolitania a temperature of 132° was recorded in the shade. But such locales are the exception rather than the rule. Most of the tropics are not *that* hot, and even when the heat is fierce, it is frequently concentrated during certain hours of the day or months of the year. In addition, some tropical locales have shown vigorous economic growth, such as the Queensland region of Australia, or for that matter Washington, D.C., where summer service has traditionally been classified by the British Foreign Office as a "tropical" assignment.

This is not to brush aside the serious adverse effects of tropical heat (and of the disease-bearing attributes of humid and warm terrain). What is difficult is to separate out the sheerly climatic from the cultural factors, or to demonstrate with certainty the degree to which climate has produced non-developmental cultures.

As Dr. Benjamin Higgins, an authority on economic development, has written:

> The attitude toward work, leisure, and income in Australia seems much the same from subtropical Darwin, where summer heat is more intense than in most equatorial countries, to chilly Hobart, with its ten-month-long winter and cool summers. Nor is there any significant difference in attitudes or productivity between Indonesians living at sea level and those living in the invigorating climate 4,000 feet up in the mountains.[8]

And to reinforce the difficulty of ascribing backwardness to climate alone, let us remember that not all underdeveloped countries are tropical. Korea has all the rigors of a temperate climate, as do much of Peru, Bolivia, highlands Africa, or northern China.

A more sophisticated investigation into the relationship between climate and economic backwardness might concern itself with rainfall. Much of the problem of the African continent revolves around its inability to secure for itself an adequate share of the precipitation which annually falls on the earth's sur-

[8] *Economic Development,* W. W. Norton, New York, 1959, pp. 266–67.

face. Along the great northern strip of African coast, the Arab peoples have for centuries contended with a rainfall that is sporadic and insufficient, while large areas of tropical Africa alternately wash away under torrential downpours or parch under none. Asia too has had to adjust to an unfavorable distribution of annual rainfall: the great monsoons provide the critical source of water for all of South Asian agriculture and when the monsoons are late, the crops die in the fields.

Yet South America as a whole has no such problem. Nor did northern Africa always present a desert appearance. Better tilled, irrigated, and tended, it was the granary of the ancient Roman Empire. Hence, as with climate, the pattern of rainfall provides at best only a partial explanation for underdevelopment. In a few areas of the world, these two factors can be charged with presenting an environment too arduous to permit the accumulation of a surplus on which a more materially advanced civilization might be built. (The same is true, of course, of the extreme frigid zones.) Yet a global view of underdevelopment—a view which embraces the great plains of Mongolia as well as the jungles of Malaya—would be hard-pressed to attribute economic backwardness to these factors alone.

What is certain, of course, is that adverse climate and insufficient rainfall pose obstacles for which unusually large economic efforts will be needed. But given this effort—given air-conditioning, water storage, irrigation on a large enough scale—the deficiencies of nature can be repaired, as witness the economic progress of both Australia and Israel. The tropics and the deserts will always have to reckon with and adapt to their geographic liabilities, but there is no reason why many of these regions cannot, on that account alone, eventually join the ranks of the more prosperous nations of the world.

If climate and rainfall give us only a partial insight into the causes for underdevelopment, the geographic approach to the problem at least suggests a second important factor to which we must pay heed: the availability of resources. Surely the presence of good soil or healthy forests or useful mineral deposits must be propitious for economic progress, and conversely we would expect that the poorer countries of the world were those which, by an accident of geography, were deprived of these benefits.

Unquestionably the availability of resources plays a role in the general map of underdevelopment. The author of a recent survey of Africa writes: "If there is one physical generalization for which a strong case can be made in tropical Africa, it is that good soils are the exception. Most of the soils are no better than the poorest mid-latitude soils; some are poorer, and all are more easily impoverished than enriched."[9]

Much of Africa is held back by its poor soil. The north, of course, suffers from totally infertile sand, and the tropical regions from earths that compact to the hardness of concrete or that tear away in the violent rainstorms: in Agulu, Nigeria, there is a gully one mile square and five hundred feet deep which has expanded its area fourfold in only six years.

It is not only Africa which suffers from this basic handicap. A great deal of the rain-forest soil of the South American continent is also much less suitable for raising crops than its luxuriant forest cover would suggest. Across large areas of Asia, as well, the soil is also wanting: vast tracts of India are arid, while in China the land has long since been deforested and much of it overworked.

Not only an absence of good soil, but an absence of resources of other kinds can be found to hamper most areas of the under-developed world. Navigable rivers, promising hydroelectric sites, accessible deposits of coal and iron, of manganese, tin, bauxite, and the thousand and one raw materials of modern industry are more often than not lacking from the balance sheets of many, perhaps most, of the nations at the lower end of the world's income scale.

And yet, just as climatic conditions proved at best only a partial explanation of backwardness, so we can attribute to a lack of physical resources only a subsidiary role in causing underdevelopment. For one thing, some of the poorer countries are actually rich in resources. Indonesia, for example, is blessed with a fertile volcanic soil and has much underground wealth. South America has vast arable lands and great mineral

[9] George Kimble, *Tropical Africa,* The Twentieth Century Fund, New York, 1960, I, p. 73.

potentials; Africa boasts huge reserves of subsoil treasure. And in many other nations what best describes the situation is not so much that resources are lacking, as that their presence is simply unknown. Typical is the case of Libya, which, until a few years ago, could have been written off as a nation almost bereft of any of the gifts of nature. Today Libya is known to be the site of tremendous oil deposits. In nearly every underdeveloped nation, a scientific inventory of available wealth has never been undertaken for lack of both skills and money: they are "poor" in resources because no one has yet systematically looked for them.

Equally important is that known *potential* resources exist in many areas, provided that economic development will bring them into being. A dam across the Niger River can create thousands of new acres of arable land for Nigeria. A dam across the Awash River in Ethiopia can make that valley one of the richest in all Africa. The irrigation of desert land around the Mediterranean can restore the ancient granary of Rome. The scientific treatment of soils in India or Pakistan has already begun to bring back to life land which was dead.

Without doubt the uneven allocation of the gifts of nature will make development much more onerous and expensive in some areas than in others. It will certainly influence the direction which development will take: encouraging animal husbandry here and rice culture there, making coal the most economic source of power in one area, oil in another, atomic power in a third. The pace and pattern of change must inevitably reflect the variety of natural habitats in which it must take place. But viewing the problem as a whole, there is no reason to consign the great bulk of the underdeveloped world to permanent poverty because of a tragic and uncorrectable decree of nature.

A brief glance at resources and climate has not unlocked the riddle of underdevelopment. If it offers cogent reasons why some areas have remained backward, it cannot answer the question for others. China, for example, is not a victim of geographic discrimination. Neither is much of South America. Neither are at least large areas of Africa. Rather, a review of the anomalous and not clearly understood relationship between

nature and underdevelopment calls our attention to the *historic*
—that is, the social and cultural—reasons for economic backwardness. Speaking in the large, economic underdevelopment
is not so much a reflection of nature as of human attitudes and
institutions.

The point is important, for it calls our attention to the fact
that development is not in any sense a "natural" process. It
is, on the contrary, a process which has been realized only in a
small portion of the world where cultural and political history
have combined to bring about an extraordinary and atypical
encouragement to certain types of economic behavior. The roots
of economic growth in the West reach very deep into the origins
of the Western outlook and the permutations of Western social
and political history.[10] Economic development in the West was
the final link in a long chain, many links of which are missing in
the Eastern and Southern background.

. . . Our preliminary survey of the physical map of underdevelopment, although it does not lead us to the ultimate reason
for stagnation, does at least serve to point up an important
aspect of the problem. This is the wide diversity of conditions
with which economic development must contend. Variations in
climate and resources—compounded by variations in local
customs and institutions—make of the actual work of development a many-faceted rather than a universally similar task.
Bolivia, for example, must cope with the problems of high-
altitude plateaus, Brazil with those of sea-level jungles. In Hong
Kong the basic aspect of underdevelopment is urban; in Afghanistan it is rural. In India a major problem is the cow, for here
lives a third of the world's cattle population eating up man's
subsistence and immune from effective economic utilization
because of religious custom; in Ghana it is swollen shoot disease, which threatens the cocoa plant on which Ghana must
depend for its major export earnings.

Thus from country to country the face of underdevelopment
changes. Starting from a common poverty, sharing . . . common
bonds of backwardness, each must nonetheless find its unique

[10] For a suggestive discussion of some of the behavioral "causes" of
development, see David McClelland, *The Achieving Society,* Van
Nostrand, Princeton, N.J., 1961.

avenue of development and cope with its unique disadvantages. As Paul Hoffman, Director of the United Nations Special Fund, has summarized it succinctly: "A hundred nations, a hundred problems."

| CHARLES ABRAMS | LAND AND HOUSING* |

EVER SINCE the dawn of civilization, man's effort to keep alive has been involved with the land. He has looked to the land for his food and clothing, and for the space to cook, wash, spend his leisure time, and sleep. Land has played an important part in the building of his house too, for from it he has extracted the mud, stones, wood, grass, or bamboo that he could put together with his own hands. The enclosure he managed to erect met his simple needs, i.e., a place for mating, a repository for his few possessions, and a protection against weather. He had access to the field and to sunshine, proximity to work and family, and the relatively ample space in which to move about.

As masses of people head cityward today, they find the land staked out into small lots, to be bought or rented. Even if they can buy the land, they no longer can build homes with their own tools and talents. Nor have they the time to build. In many instances their meager diet provides them with too little energy after their daily exertions and their long, tiring journeys from work.[1] Materials must now be bought from manufacturers or

* From *Man's Struggle for Shelter in an Urbanizing World* by Charles Abrams by permission of The M.I.T. Press, Cambridge, Massachusetts. Copyright © 1964 by Charles Abrams.

[1] In India, for example, the calorie intake in the mid-1950s was 1,700, while the estimated requirements were 2,250; in the Philippines, 1,960 as against 2,230; and in French North Africa, 1,920 as against 2,430. Douglas H. K. Lee, *Climate and Economic Development in the Tropics,* Harper, New York, 1957.

middlemen. Moreover, laws prescribe how and where people can build. To buy or rent a home, there must be a constant flow of money from a steady job. In short, the house has become a commodity, like bread. The individual no longer initiates or controls its production and, worse still, is seldom able to buy or rent what he needs.[2]

The problem has been complicated, moreover, by the fact that people have been pouring into the cities much faster than the emerging industries can absorb them. Between 1960 and 1970, 200 million people are expected to move into the cities of Asia, Africa, and Latin America.[3] The ever-growing horde descending upon the cities has intensified and will continue to intensify the demand for housing, and it has heightened the competition for wages to pay for homes. The migrant generally arrives without income or skills and often continues to live on a marginal level for most of his stay. As a result, street sleeping, slums, overcrowding, and squatting have produced a new human predicament in the burgeoning cities.

A street sleeper is a mobile squatter without a house. If the climate and the authorities are clement, the street sleeper continues bedding down in the streets until he can find a better cover and the means to pay for it. Others accept the pavement as their established abode.

While there was considerable street sleeping in Europe in the early stages of industrialization, it has been eliminated there

[2] From rough data, the estimate has been made that only about 10 to 30 percent of urban households in Asia had incomes of the $50 to $70 per month required in the mid-1950s to support a house costing $1,000, the rental or purchase cost of which would be about $10 a month. See United Nations Economic and Social Council, *Financing of Housing and Community Improvement Programmes,* New York, March 7, 1955, pp. 17, 18.

[3] Estimates of housing needs are precarious. Descriptions of housing conditions in Asiatic cities may be more informative than statistical estimates, which, even where accurate, obsolesce in a few months. One estimate in 1951 was that from 100 to 150 million rural and urban families in Asia lived in overcrowded, insanitary, and substandard shelter. See United Nations Report of Mission of Experts, *Low Cost Housing in South and South-East Asia,* New York, March 12, 1951, p. 3. Another estimate is that in Asia, Africa, and Latin America, half the population either is homeless or lives under unsafe or grossly overcrowded housing conditions. See United Nations Meeting of Experts, February 7–21, 1962, Working Paper 4, *The Role of Housing and Urban Development in National Development Programs,* New York, 1962, pp. 9, 10.

except for derelicts and vagrants. But in Calcutta, some 600,000 people sleep in the streets. Census figures for Bombay made public in 1963 showed that 1 in every 66 persons was homeless, while another 77,000 people lived under stairways, in cattle sheds, on landings, or in similar spaces.[4] Though many workers in the cities can afford to pay for minimum shelter, the means for producing it have not yet been developed. Some people have therefore put up bamboo and burlap lean-tos on the cement walks, where the women cook over smoky fire pots using cow dung as fuel. Ten or more people in India share these tiny bustees. In Hong Kong, it has not been unusual for street cleaners to find forsaken carcasses, which they remove on their morning rounds.[5]

In Lagos, Nigeria, a street sleeper will watch a shop at night and keep away other street sleepers in return for the nightly use of a threshold. A few thousand homeless will seek a spot on the piers in the rat-ridden lagoon or scout around for an unguarded space on which to lay a straw mat.

Street sleeping permits no family life, no privacy, no relief from heat, no escape from cold or rain, and no decent means for disposing of human waste. It is the way of the stray animal, the lowest form of urban life.

More commonly workers have swarmed into city slums. The word "slum" is a catchall for poor housing of every kind as well as a label for the environment. The same word denotes a Chicago mansion turned into furnished rooms and a cardboard carton sheltering a human being in Lima.

Because of its inclusiveness, the word too often obscures the vast differences between one type of slum and another. Slums may be either rented or owner-occupied, either legal or illegal. They include cabins, shanties, dens, dugouts, sheds, stalls, and other manifestations of poverty. Some are single-family shelters

[4] Thomas F. Brady, "India's 'Big Town,'" *New York Times,* November 2, 1963. According to the *Manchester Guardian,* December 13, 1963, there were about 1,700 adults and 50 children sleeping in the streets of London in 1904, compared with 129 adults on one cold November night in 1963 and 120 on another night in the same year.

[5] Harold Ingrams, *Hong Kong,* Her Majesty's Stationery Offices, London, 1952, p. 81. When I was in Hong Kong in 1963, J. F. Fraser, director of housing in the colony, told me that after the massive housing program and the curtailment of illegal immigration, this manifestation of suffering and homelessness is no longer as frequent as before.

converted into several smaller compartments; some are one-story and others six-story tenements. Although most slums are in the industrial cities, many are found in mining towns and farm areas. Others line the back alleys of mansions.

Some slums are new and some the abandoned houses of those who have moved up in the economic scale. The new slum is built because it has a use at the price, while the old slum survives because there is nothing cheaper and more serviceable to replace it. The new huts built of scavenged scrap by in-migrants to Asian or South American cities are often worse than the old ones.

Slums flourish in many environments. They emerge from marshes, hillsides, or war ruins in the Philippines; they are built within old forts or on swamps in Puerto Rico and India; and they line the hills in Latin America. Punctuating the cemeteries and the side roads near new apartment houses in Karachi, slums also appear as holes in ancient caves near Rawalpindi and in southern Spain. They abound in the Casbah of Tunis and in the resort centers of Havana and the West Indies; they are the thousands of dark single rooms of Ahmedabad, Cawnpore, and Nagpur.

Slum life is not always the symbol of retrogression. It may in fact be the first advance from homelessness into shelter, or the way station on the road from abject poverty to hope. The slum exists because no nation is able to produce adequate housing at a cost that workers can afford. It is the shelter that the industrial age provides for its rank and file. Housing has remained the Cinderella of the Industrial Revolution, and the slum the humble cover to which she has been indefinitely assigned.

One of the most troublesome aspects of slum life continues to be the simple disposal of human excrement, which may be discharged into a ditch shared by dozens of families or left to decompose between shacks. Skyscrapers may shoot up side by side with colonies of slum dwellers whose only latrine is a rarely cleaned trench shared sometimes by hundreds of families. In the age of the atom, the disposal of human feces remains one of the stubbornly persistent problems of urban man.

Absence of a system for removing excrement from living areas continually exposes the healthy to the contaminated wastes of the ill and the disease carrier. In the crowded urban communities that have mushroomed in recent years, such pollution is accepted as part of the way of life. For example, in Lagos, Nigeria, out of 4,759 schoolchildren whose stools were examined, 85 percent were infected with parasites, roundworm and hookworm being the most common forms. Dysentery and diarrhea accounted for 10.1 percent of all deaths in 1960. In the same year, 54.5 percent of all the deaths in Nigeria's capital city occurred among children under five years of age. Although pail collection is common in undeveloped areas, it is far from being the most sanitary form of waste disposal. Yet in many areas even this primitive service is absent or haphazard; often night soil is allowed to accumulate for weeks or months before it is removed. Sometimes it is left to decompose.

The afflictions of slum living are intensified by crowding and lack of privacy. If there were an adequate supply of urban slums for everyone who needed shelter, their baneful effects might be confined to squalor, darkness, and decrepitude. But the general shortage of slums means that those that exist are also packed with people. "Crowding" in these instances means that the houses are crowded onto almost all available space; it also refers to crowding within the house itself. For example, the number of people per room in Guatemala averages more than three, compared with a little less than one person per room in Australia, the United States, the United Kingdom, and Switzerland.[6]

Lack of privacy, exposure to contagion, and social disintegration are only a few of the by-products of a life with almost no room to breathe, ail, or die. In the single-room tenements of Bombay, occupancy in 1948 already ranged from six to nine persons per room with an overall average of seven, while crowding ten persons into a space 10 by 15 feet was common.[7] Average floor space per person was about 27 square feet. In such tenements, one occupant could not see another in the dark passages or rooms. Sickly complexions, emaciated bodies, and the drawn faces of the children tell their tale.

[6] United Nations, *Technical Assistance Newsletter,* v. II, no. 2, New York, May 1961.
[7] National Planning Commission of India, *National Housing,* Vora & Co., Bombay, February 1948.

In Panama, where shelters bulge at the seams with as many as twenty individuals living in a room 15 by 15 feet, sleeping is done in relays. In Kingston, Jamaica, nine persons occupy tiny huts 6 by 10 feet. In Accra, Ghana, occupancy per single house in 1960 was 19.3 persons; the occupancy was even higher in Kumasi. In Lagos, Nigeria, which has three migrants to every natural birth, as many as eighty people share a small house on a site scheduled for clearance, and even in the fringe areas, sixteen to twenty persons per house is not unusual.

In-migration into some cities of the Far East has created living conditions without any vestige of privacy or room for motion. In Hong Kong, five or six human beings share cubicles measuring 40 square feet. Density is as high as two thousand persons per acre in one-story hutments in which there is no water, sanitation, or organized system of refuse disposal. Fowl or pigs share some of the huts or the tiny open spaces around them.

In a single shophouse in Singapore, I saw families of six to eight people facing life in airless, windowless rooms 7 by 10 feet, with as many as five children sleeping on the roach-ridden floor beneath the bed. About a third of the occupants in the average shophouse have no window at all; the rest have either one window (which is usually shuttered) or only access to a light shaft. Frequently the occupant uses his rented space not only for sleeping but as a "farm" for growing bean sprouts or as a shop. The illness of a child or a parent means that the whole family must share the discomforts, if not the disease as well. Yet this is the way of life for tens of thousands of people in Singapore and elsewhere.[8]

Both Hong Kong and Singapore have undertaken extensive rehousing programs, but the demand for space is so intense and the size of the average household so large that it is not unusual to see five and sometimes as many as ten people sharing one of the new rooms. In Singapore, of 10,125 applications to the Housing and Redevelopment Board, the family size of nearly half was listed as seven persons or more. Many of these families would be assigned single rooms. In Hong Kong's new housing

[8] Charles Abrams, Susumu Kobe, and Otto Koenigsberger, *Report for the Government of Singapore,* prepared by an Expert Mission appointed under the United Nations Technical Assistance Programme (min., Singapore, August 1963).

projects, I saw families of ten sharing a single room for their shelter, and often it was also the workshop from which they were trying to eke out a living.

It is virtually impossible, particularly in tropical areas, to keep water clean when it must be carried long distances and retained for hours or days in exposed tubs or cans. Often the water is contaminated at the source. In one slum area I inspected in Kingston, Jamaica, a single tap serves seven hundred persons; in another, occupied by eight thousand people, there was no water at all.

The housing situation is no better in many villages. In fourteen villages of Upper and Lower Egypt, for example, 27.5 percent of the shelters have no roofs at all. These settlements are usually clusters of cramped, drafty, dark mud huts crowded together to avoid encroaching on the farmland.[9] Conditions such as these, coupled with average peasant income of $11.50 a year per person, accelerate the move to the cities, where the housing conditions are most often worse.

The magnitude of the problem in the underdeveloped world may be gleaned from the fact that more than a billion people in Africa, Asia, and Latin America, or roughly half the population of these continents, are homeless or live in housing that is described by the United Nations as a menace to health and an affront to human dignity.[10] Worse still, in almost all the developing areas, housing conditions are steadily deteriorating. Many families pay so much for the privilege of bedding down on a floor or other space that little is left for the bare essentials of life. And as the surge to the cities goes on, the competition for space will become keener, rents will rise further, squatting and overcrowding will increase, and the effort to carry on some semblance of family life will become less and less hopeful.

Some Social By-Products

In the more developed areas, whose slums might be viewed in Asia as châteaux, overcrowded slums have been found to

[9] Hassan Fathy, "Rural Self-Help Housing," *International Labor Review,* January 1962.

[10] United Nations, *The United Nations Development Decade,* Proposals for Action, Report of the Secretary-General, New York, 1962.

yield a high juvenile delinquency rate; high rates of family dependence on public assistance; high proportions of illiteracy; high proportions of employed women; more unemployment, poverty, and divorce; more nonsupport cases and alcoholism; a high incidence of mental disorders and mental deficiency; low marriage rates; a low average educational level; and high residential mobility.

It would be a mistake, however, to view the slum's impact as the same everywhere, or to see poor housing as the only cause of social abnormality. Although bad housing contributes to juvenile delinquency and crime, its influence may in some cases be mitigated by compensating elements, such as strong parental influences, constructive discipline in the school or community, good associations, and counteracting ethical values. Environment is more than physical environment; it is a combination of physical, social, and personal factors that influence parents and children. Yet the change in a normal boy from rural Puerto Rico when he moves into a slum in New York City is often appalling—despite New York's well-organized educational and social services.

Many aspects of the shelter problem need further study. Though much has been written on slum life in Europe and the United States, less is known about slums in the underdeveloped countries. We understand even less about the effects of overcrowding and of poor housing on the emotions. What, for example, is the child's response to sexual intimacy between adults in a jammed household?

Little is known also of the destruction of human dignity when the home and community in which the family once had a place no longer exist. In the tribal communities or in those in which housing was built as part of a compound, the job of keeping the common grounds clean was often assigned to particular members. In the shift to crowded cities, this responsibility has either been passed on to governments that are unable to cope with it, or has been left to the people themselves. In Africa, for example, the collective accountability of tribal life is being replaced by individuation, self-interest, and self-preservation. The Indian village, which for all its hardships offered community life and access to the open field, has no compensatory alterna-

tive in the herding and the disunity of the new urban agglomera-
tions. The working father is no longer near home, and the
working mother hurries toward the factory or the crowded
marketplace to help pay the landlord. The child, seeing its
parents only at evening, quickens to outside forces more readily
than ever before. The females left behind in the villages find
the opportunities for marriage diminishing as the young males
emigrate.

From the earliest days of civilization, man had been able to
create a home with his own hands. Now, for the first time, this
is no longer within his competence. The hovels he lives in are
worse than those he built when he emerged from the cave.
Indeed, the caves still in use are often sounder shelters with
better roofs and more privacy than the slums of some Asian
cities.

A large group of houses can make a "neighborhood" if the
people who live there bring to it the elements of intimate association and a unity of interest. The neighborhood is a place
where children meet and influence each other and where the
residents have a feeling of belonging. But often the big city is
merely the aggregate of heterogeneous clusters of hovels, plus
shops, factories, streets, and public services. This mass of
makeshifts in the teeming cities has provided no substitute for
the village institutions that bestow relative equality of status,
humble as it may be. The new city formations are saturated,
impersonal, tentative, and without the mellowed traditions or
folkways of the older way of life. Restraints and sanctions are
absent, and the lack of living space undermines family discipline
by driving the child into the streets.

The inhuman densities inside the shelter might be relieved by
adequate space outside, but too often the only outside space is
a narrow, rutted path that must provide room for movement of
people, the carrying off of waste and rain water, cooking,
peddling one's wares, and sometimes space for draft animals as
well. Where streets are paved and wide enough, however, the
street has assumed some of the functions that the home unit
lacks. In Asia, the street is often the mass dining room for the
family and the place where one gets his oxygen amid the mis-

cellaneous odors of culinary activity. It is the market, the display room for wares, the social meeting place and the recreational outlet, the source of livelihood for the peddler, the rickshaw or trishaw man, as well as the theater of action in which every child, visitor, tradesman, and hawker among the thousands converging on the street are the players. The street is often convulsive, yet exciting. To share it with the automobile is hard. It is inefficient for its many new tasks, but still vital; it is exasperating, but a way of life—a slumscape of the turbulent cities. Here and in their cubicles, the family demonstrates that remarkable genius of the human species which has been responsible for survival through its centuries of trial.

The growing city, with all its faults, is the crucible in which man's destiny will be determined. The slum may be with us always, and for many people it may be the only escape from famine and stagnation, the temporary anchorage of struggling mankind slowly moving toward something better. But the prospect of something better should be there, however remote.

From earliest history, the city has been linked with man's freedoms[11]—a refuge in the days of Cain and Joshua, the hub of a vigorous political life in Greece, the impetus to law in Rome. When man's mind roamed free in Utopian dreams, it was the city that was so often closest to his conception of heaven—the "Celestial City," the "Heavenly City," the "New Jerusalem," the "Holy City," and the "City of God." Moreover, it was the city of trade, commerce, and property that helped undermine serfdom and that ushered in other freedoms in the process. Though industrialization posed a threat in the cities of Europe, more freedoms somehow emerged in cities, and more

---

[11] The word "freedom" is an abstraction that is symbolic, controversial, and fluctuating in its meanings. It embraces a variety of "freedoms from" and "freedoms to." Without elaborating on its complexities, I have used the word here in a circular sense in which man, given a tolerable environment, has tended to evolve institutions and devices that allow him greater social and economic mobility and a larger variety of personal options. The institutions he helps create in turn tend to fortify such options. The urban scene, I believe, has in the past provided this opportunity better than any other way of life that man has yet devised. The city is also a setting where he has been better able to acquire the knowledge essential to identify more electives, and where he is allowed to strive for their attainment free of unreasonable restraints.

freedoms survived in them. The story may, if given time, repeat itself even in the cankerous formations of the more recently industrialized areas. For despite its changes and challenges, the city still contains the raw ingredients of freedom. The city still harbors the hope, in an increasingly hazardous and complex society, that the social and economic fluidity which was its historic attribute can be maintained against the chaotic forces that challenge it. It is still the marketplace for goods and ideas, the locus of a contractual society, the mirror for emulation, the meeting place for diversities, the center of culture. In the European cities that once also felt the first shocks of industrialization, parliamentary government ultimately established its political validity, encrusted its precedents with a heavy layer of protective traditions, and constructed the essential devices for minimizing violent changes. Perhaps in the troubled cities of the developing world, the same values too may emerge and grow.

The swelling cities of the East may indeed be reliving some of the history of the Western cities. They have become the haven of the refugee, the hungry, the politically oppressed. The Filipino hinterlanders fleeing the Huks pour into Manila, the Hindus escaping the Moslems head into Old Delhi, and the victims of Chinese communism drift into Hong Kong. When his miserable two acres no longer yield enough grain for the Indian peasant, or the floods drown the Pakistani's meager crop, he moves toward the teeming city. As the desert wind blows over the drought-ridden land, the Arab whips his camel toward the bustling new human settlements.

But in too many of the developing cities, the older customs and institutions of value are weakening before the newer ones have taken root. The building of a stable life is thwarted by housing famine and the frustrations of crowded living. Unfortunately, those with the talent and vision to reform the social pattern are rare, and trained civil servants few. Hopes and fears for freedom and opportunity rise and fall with each crisis and with the disillusionments linked with it.

By 1950, one in every five of the world's people lived in cities of more than 20,000. With 50 to 60 million new mouths to feed annually, the push to the city gains impetus. In Asia, Africa, and Latin America, the total population is expected to increase by two-fifths in the fifteen years between 1961 and 1975, and urban populations are expected to double. Thus the urban housing stock must be increased four times in that period (without making allowance for dilapidation and decay).[12] The average income per person of only fifty cents a day in 90 percent of the world's countries has not kept the birth rate from rising. In fact, it is rising more sharply in the very areas that can least afford to accommodate more children. Yet for many, if not ultimately for most, the city is becoming the only alternative to hunger and despair.

With rates of urban growth in Asia 400 percent higher than in the West, and the movement to the cities only beginning, it is idle to speculate on what might have been the better life. The die has been cast. The irrepressible forces of urbanization are forging ahead, and in the long run there appears to be no other option. The question is only whether human endurance will persist in these settlements until better patterns emerge.

CONOR CRUISE O'BRIEN | CONTEMPORARY FORMS OF IMPERIALISM*

WE KNOW THAT when J. A. Hobson found the economic taproot of imperialism in the workings of the capitalist system at a given stage, several conditions applied which no longer apply today. Apart from the question of the validity of his economic analysis as applying to the conditions of his own day . . . and apart from the great technological and economic changes which the past sixty years have brought, there have also been *political* changes of such a character and on such a scale as to transform

---

[12] *The Role of Housing and Urban Development in National Development Programs, op. cit.,* p. 9. This figure includes relief of existing shortages.

* From *Studies on the Left,* Fall 1965.

the whole discussion. In Hobson's day—and Lenin's—there could be no doubt, on any side, about the relevance and usefulness of the term "imperialism." There were then British and French and Russian empires, openly labeled as such, and there were many men, and important men, who not merely defended but gloried in the existence of these empires. There were also influential men who openly preached the doctrine of America's imperial destiny. These men could properly be called "imperialists" and their doctrine "imperialism"; they and their increasingly vocal critics had at least these basic words and concepts in common. There was also something else in common: since all the powerful states of the early twentieth century— with the partial exception of a Russia in transition—were capitalist states, it was natural, and indeed inevitable, that contemporary imperialism should be discussed as a function or outgrowth of capitalism.

Two world wars and two major revolutions have changed that landscape out of recognition. The old empires seem to have disappeared; if they have not entirely disappeared, they have at least lost the name of empire. A new vocabulary has arisen— Commonwealth, Communaute, Union—"imperialist" is in popular present use solely as a term of abuse. Of the five great powers, recognized as such in the Charter of the United Nations by permanent seating on the Security Council, two now have Communist governments—a situation only flimsily disguised by the insertion of an American satellite delegation in China's place. None of the five great powers would admit to having today anything resembling an empire; all officially are against imperialism or deny its existence, although France's conversion from open imperial practice is so recent that the vocabulary of her spokesmen is still under repair. Imperialism, in the Hobsonian sense, can have no economic taproot in those powers which have ceased to be capitalist; as for the capitalist countries, these claim to have overcome the supposedly inbuilt Hobsonian compulsion and to have divested themselves of their empires and of any thought of acquiring empires.

Yet the term imperialism has not only survived the overt phenomena which it was used to designate in Hobson's day; it has acquired new life and is in far more frequent international use today than it was in the heyday of the empires. Why should this be? Is it, as some maintain, that the term has become purely emotive, of propaganda value only? Or has it still rational relevance, as a general descriptive term grouping sets of relations still existing, though officially unacknowledged, and continuing certain crucial patterns of the old imperial systems and ambitions? It is obvious that the most frequent uses of the term are operational, that is to say propagandist, and that it is thus used by both sides in the Cold War. The Communist side, or rather the Communist sides, have used it most persistently and aggressively, concentrating in recent years on "American imperialism" especially in Latin America, the Near East, Southeast Asia and the Congo. Western spokesmen have retorted by attacks on "Soviet imperialism" in Eastern Europe and "Chinese imperialism" in Tibet, Southeast Asia and the Indian border, and Chinese imperial ambitions towards Indonesia, Africa, etc. The peoples of the newly independent countries are warned from time to time, mainly by American writers and speakers, to be careful not to fall under the sway of a far more cruel form of imperialism than that which they have just shaken off. There has, however, been something halfhearted and ineffective about Western propaganda on these lines; it remains a *tu quoque* and an intellectual gimmick rather than a driving force as Communist anti-imperialism is. The peoples addressed—Africans, Asians, Latin Americans—find it impossible, on the basis of their historical experience, to believe in the sincerity of Western anti-imperialism, and many non-Communist Westerners also find such propaganda distasteful. Many Englishmen and Frenchmen dislike hearing Americans tell the peoples of Ghana or Guinea that Russian rule will be "even more oppressive" than English or French rule was. And many feel—though they do not say—that the rule of more advanced over less advanced people is part of the law of nature and that if the Russians and Chinese were genuinely imperialists, and only imperialists, it would be possible to reach agreement with them. At bottom the West objects to Communists not in so far as they may be imperialists, but in so far as they are revolutionaries.

Western propaganda on "Communist imperialism" lines also errs when it assumes that African and Asian governments necessarily shrink in horror from the thought of the domination of one people over another. Most of these governments are themselves the instruments of such rule over "minority" peoples —and most of them feel that unless they are ready when necessary to take repressive action against minorities, or against refractory elements among the minorities, their states will break up and collapse. Thus many of these states were sympathetic to the Chinese action in Tibet, when this action was presented to them in the light of bringing a dissident peripheral minority to heel—which is of course how the Chinese government envisaged the action. Again Asian and African governments are impressed when an Asian nation like China—or formerly Japan —shows the capacity to act as a great power acts, even in ways which would be stigmatized as imperialist if used by a Western power against Africans or Asians. In such contexts even left-wing African spokesmen are themselves liable to use the classic language of imperialism. Thus I have heard an African delegate, speaking against the inclusion of the question of Tibet on the agenda of the U.N. General Assembly in 1958, argue that the Chinese action was justifiable because Tibetan society was archaic, stagnant and monk-ridden, and the Chinese would bring roads, medicine and education. There was truth in much of what he said, but every argument he used could have been— and was—used to justify, say, Mussolini's conquest of Ethiopia. The man who spoke thus at the U.N. was the delegate of Ethiopia.

Not unnaturally such contradictions have enabled some Western and other spokesmen to pour scorn on the moral position of African and Asian governments, and to deny to these governments any moral right to challenge Western imperialism, or colonialism or the actions of white settler governments. It was the practice of Mr. Eric Louw, representing South Africa when that country still defended its practices in the U.N. General Assembly, to rattle the bones of all the minority skeletons in the U.N. cupboard—caste discrimination in India, oppression by Ethiopia of its Moslem subjects, by Sudan of its non-Moslem subjects and so on. Again there was truth in much of what he said, but he left his audience at best indifferent. Outside a few Western delegations, no one felt that the treatment of minorities in some independent African and Asian countries was seriously comparable to *apartheid*.

White domination over nonwhite has been after all an almost universally experienced reality. South Africa is a symbol of the continuance of this reality. It is not surprising that the non-white peoples, guilty though some of them are of particular and local acts of aggression, should resent the symbol of their universal bondage. In their reaction to pictures from South Africa or Dixie, the Moslem from Khartoum and his rebellious subject the pagan from Southern Sudan would be at one. It is quite true that the moral altitude from which African and Asian governments criticize the West is often less elevated than those governments assume; such governments are not wiser or nicer than other governments, only weaker, and therefore more limited in the scale of their depredations. But the consensus of non-white opinion which they reflect is important and it is this con-sensus, and not the morals of those through whom it finds expression, that Western policymakers should take into account. Western policy should—and hopefully must—ultimately be based on the values professed in the West, including that of con-sent of the governed, and not on, say, the example of Baghdad's treatment of the Kurds. Yet some Western commentators write as if the policies of Baghdad, Khartoum, etc., constitute a vindi-cation of Western imperialism.

In the propaganda battle over "imperialism" the West has been the losing side; the Western nations, and in particular the United States, are still widely regarded as the imperialists and have generally failed in their efforts to pin this label onto the Communist countries. Is this due to resentments arising from past history, including the deep resentments generated by white color-consciousness? Or has the fear of Western imperialism an objective referent in the present? When we are discussing the reactions of many thousands of people, repre-senting in some fashion hundreds of millions of others, the answer to the first question has necessarily to be a qualified one. On personal observation, however, I would say that the role of resentment of *past* wrongs is less than it is often represented to be, and in many of the countries concerned is no more than a latent factor, which in normal circumstances does not become manifest at all. No country is more militantly anti-imperialist in its language than Ghana, yet it is almost impossible to find a Ghanaian who has any really bitter memories of British rule; villagers everywhere respond with spontaneous friendliness to the sight of a white face; the products of the secondary schools and university who man the civil service, the embassies and the U.N. delegation are pro-British to a degree which seems to an Irishman even a little mawkish. It is true that the class in between villager and elite, the class of those whose education stopped at primary level, is a somewhat embittered body, as well as an important one, and not disposed to be sentimental about the benefits of British rule. The real bitterness however is directed against the Ghanaian elite, who have enjoyed secondary and higher education; the anti-Western attitudes of the "Standard VII" boys are principally directed, not so much against the West as such as against a native elite which happens to be, on the whole, pro-Western. A similar problem, though at present with greater dominance of pro-Western elites, prevails in Nigeria. Combinations of this kind, whether with a "Nigerian" or "Ghanaian" balance, are to be found throughout all those territories of the former British—and with some qualification French—empires which were not burdened with settlers from the metropolis. (The Belgian Congo, exposed within living memory to the most ferocious and unbridled form of colonial rapacity, is of course quite a different matter.) I find it hard to believe, therefore, that among most of the newly independent countries, resentment of *past* wrongs is a really live factor, actively and independently inspiring present choices. But past experience illuminates contemporary events. Most Algerians, for example, are far too pre-occupied with the pressing problems of the present to waste much time in brooding over the wrongs inflicted on them by the French. But when Algerians hear on the radio, from a Western source, that peasants in certain parts of Vietnam are being brought together in special villages for their protection against terrorists, it is inevitable that these Algerians should think of the French regroupment camps and of the realities which underlay the French army's claim that it was protecting villagers from terror. From this it is a short step to concluding that America's war in Vietnam, like France's in

Algeria, is in reality an imperialist war accompanied by mendacious slogans. As this is just what the Communist press and radio say it is, the net effect for so many people will be to strengthen confidence in the Communist picture of world events, while deepening skepticism about the picture presented by the Western media; this skepticism extends of course to stories of Soviet and Chinese imperialism. (Similarly, those who have lived under people like Trujillo or Batista are not likely to be roused to free world enthusiasm by news of the emergence of another anti-Communist strong man in, say, the Congo.) Algeria is, of course, an extreme example, but even those— like, say, the English-speaking West Africans—whose recent experience of colonial rule has been on the whole a benign one, are sensitized by their past history in such a way as to be repelled by much in the present conduct of the Western powers. Even the benevolent generations of British rulers carried with them their racial exclusiveness and assumptions of superiority, and even the most pro-Western Ghanaian or Nigerian is necessarily affected by corresponding doubts and suspicions—which normally he will seek to repress—about white attitudes toward nonwhite peoples. These doubts and suspicions can be fanned into hostility by certain news and above all news pictures. An African who has just seen pictures of white Americans using dogs and cattle prods against black men is not psychologically prepared to believe that the white Americans who land in Vietnam have come to help the yellow man. And the more closely he follows the news from Vietnam the less he will be disposed to accept the American official version.

One may note here, to the credit of the American system, how ill-adapted that system is, in certain respects, to the successful waging of a colonial-type war. The French in Algeria did not distribute to the world pictures of their harkis torturing prisoners; British reporters covering Mau Mau had plenty to say about Mau Mau atrocities but little or nothing about atrocities committed by the suppressors of Mau Mau. But American wire services do distribute to the world pictures of "Viet Cong suspects" being tortured by America's Vietnamese allies; American reporters tell of indiscriminate shooting, including the shooting of children, by American marines. Critics of American imperialism can buttress their case with abundant and horrifying detail supplied by impeccable American sources. No corresponding facilities are available to critics of Soviet or Chinese policies and activities.

It seems fair, then, to conclude that the hostility of the newly independent countries to Western imperialism derives not so much from past resentments as from the actual flow of world news, interpreted, as we all must interpret news—in the light of personal and community experience. That news, so interpreted, makes up a pattern in which the Western whites, who control almost all the physical resources of the non-Communist world, seek also with a high degree of success to control its nonwhite peoples, indirectly and by guile where possible, directly and by force where necessary. This is what is meant by "Western imperialism" today.

How far is this picture valid? Personally I believe that it is substantially accurate, and it is meaningful to speak of Western imperialism, in this sense, as one of the greatest and most dangerous forces in the world today. Those who would deny or minimize its existence assert, with some degree of truth, that the Hobsonian version of imperialism no longer applies if ever it did apply, and that there is no adequate economic motive for imperialist activities. Thus, if France, for example, has a powerful say in the political life of Upper Volta, this is not because she needs the resources or the market—both of them almost nonexistent—of that desolate and destitute country, but on the contrary, because France annually makes up the deficit in the Upper Volta budget. This might be defined as *un*economic imperialism. Such examples can easily be multiplied, by writers like Mr. Brian Crozier, to bring into ridicule the idea of economic imperialism and, implicitly, of *all* forms of Western imperialism. I have heard Barbara Ward explain to a Ghanaian audience that the advanced countries of the West have no longer any serious need either for the markets or the resources of the underdeveloped countries generally, and consequently have no economic need either to control or to develop these countries; without the underdeveloped countries, according to this thesis, the advanced countries will continue to progress while, without the advanced countries, the underdeveloped are doomed to continue to stagnate. (It is a measure of Barbara Ward's charm and powers of presentation that this bleak doctrine was received with loud applause by her Ghanaian audience—admittedly an "elite" one of university students.) The Ward thesis, at least as understood and here summarized by me, itself seems open to some question. I find it hard to believe that Britain is so indifferent to the resources of Kuwait, the United States to those of Venezuela, or Belgium to those of Katanga, as this thesis seems to suggest. Nor does the thesis seem to take sufficient account of the overseas interests of particular groups in the advanced countries. It is uneconomic for France to pay prices higher than world market prices for Ivory Coast *robusta* coffee, but this practice is highly economic for those Frenchmen who own Ivory Coast coffee plantations. Political leverage of interested groups (Standard Oil, United Fruit, etc.) has done much to create, through the mass media, the pattern of anti-Communist public opinion and, by now, anti-Communist *reflexes*. One may, however, agree with the Ward thesis to the extent that economic motives are not in *themselves* sufficient to account for a worldwide effort by the Western countries and especially by the United States to control the politics of the underdeveloped countries generally.

That such an effort exists, is, I think, undeniable. It is a declared goal of the United States, not merely to prevent Soviet and Chinese territorial expansion, but to check the spread of a political doctrine: communism. This cannot be done without close surveillance of the internal politics of all countries deemed vulnerable to communism—including all underdeveloped countries—without discreet guidance of these politics when necessary, without economic pressure and without in the penultimate resort intervention by all the methods practiced by all secret services including bribery, blackmail and political assassination. The Congo is an obvious case in point. I have myself heard a senior and responsible American official state that it was not America's responsibility to prevent the Congolese from massacring each other, but it *was* America's responsibility to keep communism out of the Congo. In practice, American officials, some employed by the C.I.A. and at least one by the United Nations, actively intervened in Congolese politics in order to bring about the downfall of Lumumba and the triumph of his enemies; his subsequent murder and the murder of his principal associates at the hands of these enemies were then regarded as an internal Congolese affair. Professor Paul W. Blackstock in *The Strategy of Subversion: Manipulating the politics of other nations* writes approvingly of the effectiveness of U.S. intervention in this period. C.I.A. intervention in the troubled Congo in support of Colonel Joseph Mobutu contributed materially to the stabilization of the fledgling native regime during the first year (1960–61) of independence. "Stabilization" here appears to be a technical term meaning American control. It should be noted, as demonstrating the formidable and unexpected political weapons which the United States can deploy in an anti-Communist effort, that although Mobutu was, as Andrew Tully states, "discovered" and backed by the C.I.A., it was actually from the United Nations—as has recently been shown by Catherine Hoskyns in *The Congo Since Independence*—that he got the money to pay his troops. The United Nations, on the authority of Andrew Cordier, also saw to it that the credit for raising this money went to Mobutu, and that Mobutu's superior, General Lundula, suspected of being loyal to Lumumba, was prevented, through U.N. control of the Congo's airports, from returning to the capital at the critical time.

The Congo in some ways is an extreme case, a *cas limite*, and the limit it stands for, in the eyes of many Africans and Asians, is the limit to their own freedom. From this example they see that if their government shows what are, in the eyes of U.S. officials, Communist tendencies, the diplomatic, political, secret service, and financial resources of the greatest of world powers may be turned against them and that a political receiver nominated by Western interests—a Tshombe—may be put in charge of their affairs. They know further that if they withstand the political shock—which few of them indeed feel strong enough to do—they may have to face actual military intervention, as those other *cas limites*, Santo Domingo and Vietnam, have demonstrated. If there are sizeable Western business interests in their territory they will know that their position in relation to these interests is less than that of a fully sovereign state, for their dealings with these interests will be among the criteria of their non-communism, that is to say, of their continued existence. But even if they have little or nothing, like many of the so-called French-speaking African territories, this does not exempt them from Western surveillance, for even these wastelands form part of that "reservoir of strategic space" which is Africa in the eyes of such competent Western observers as Professor Hans Morgenthau. The position of these countries, with backward economies, often dependent on the export of a single raw material, would be weak in any case in relation to the advanced countries, agreement of whose nationals sets the price of the commodities. When to these structural conditions of dependence is added the latent, and sometimes overt, tutelage implied in the doctrine of "containing communism" it is not surprising that many people in the poor countries should feel their present independence is little more than a façade, and that in reality they still form part of a sort of Western empire, which is not the less real, economically and politically, for having no legal existence. If the Communist Parties have taken up the slogan of "the struggle against neo-colonialism"—a word not of their coinage according to Professor I. I. Potekhin—it is that they see in this situation, and in the resentments generated by it, the point of departure for revolutionary change. In other words the application of the American policy of "containing communism" is regarded by Communists themselves as a principal generator of communism. This is of course especially so in those "end-games" where, as in Indo-China, the Congo and much of Latin America, the "containment" process, working by elimination, has thrown up, as "friends of the West" and holders of power, discredited and parasitic groups with little or no unpaid support within their own countries.

The policy of "containing communism," which is both the mainspring and the justification of contemporary Western forms of imperialism, has a number of points in common with Stalin's policies in postwar Europe. The anti-Communists, like Stalin, seem to envisage their policies as essentially defensive; like Stalin they prefer to work through stooges, reserving military action for the last resort; like Stalin they describe the state of affairs which results from their maneuvers as "freedom," and like Stalin they are in fact adept at the manufacture of satellite states. More adept than he; indeed, for every member of the United Nations which, in a critical vote, accepts the "whip" of the Soviet Union, there are at least five members which will follow the "whip" of the United States. In part as a result of this, and in part because of other pressures, the United Nations on most important matters and at every level—Security Council, Assembly and Secretariat—is preponderantly influenced by United States policy. The delegation seated as representing China is symbolic of this preponderant influence.

If indeed it is to remain the settled and official policy of the United States to prevent the spread of communism, the quasi-imperial involvement of the United States in the domestic affairs of every country in the "free world" becomes inevitable. There is no way of being sure of "stopping communism" without interfering, by force if necessary, in the internal affairs of every country in which communism may appear. What such interference means in the penultimate resort we have seen in the Congo. What it means in the last resort we are seeing in Vietnam. There seems to be no doubt that, left to itself, Vietnam would go Communist; in the effort to prevent this, the United States has taken France's place as imperial power in Southeast Asia; the shadowy governments in Saigon disguise this fact, by now, even less effectively than France's role was disguised by the Emperor Bao Dai. It seems clear that the policy of "containing communism" is likely to lead to other accretions of direct imperial responsibility—as distinct from indirect rule, as in the Congo—in other parts of the globe. And in an age of awakened nationalism, and of the existence of great powers outside the Western system, imperial responsibilities are likely to involve wider resentments and greater bloodshed and infinitely greater risks than they did in the nineteenth century.

On a recent television program we saw the President and the Secretary of State defending their Vietnam policy. They gave three reasons for continuing the war: prestige, honor— meaning the necessity to abide by pledges—and the defense of the freedom of South Vietnam. The first two are contingent, that is to say that they are reasons which can be invoked for persisting in *any* policy, however bad; both were invoked in defense of France's Algerian war policy, until the time came when they had to be dropped. The only *substantive* reason invoked—and that briefly and skimpily—was the so-called defense of freedom. But what meaning can be assigned to the defense of freedom in South Vietnam? It is obvious that the people of

South Vietnam do not enjoy freedom in any of the senses in which we so commonly understand the word; they are subject to the arbitrary will of juntas dependent on foreign military and economic support. "Freedom" here is a purely technical term, meaning the exclusion of Communists from power by force if necessary. Mr. James Reston, in a recent article in the *New York Times*, seemed puzzled by the failure of Asians to understand the fact that the U.S. championed their independence and nationalism. He himself failed to understand that the concepts of independence and nationalism are wholly vitiated by the qualifications which current U.S. policy attaches to them. In terms of that policy, independence must be non-Communist or it is not independence; nationalism must be non-Communist, or it is not nationalism. But what happens in a country where nationalists are Communists or pro-Communists, and where independence is thought of as being able to have one's own form of government, even if it should be a Communist form? What happens then is that an outside power, the United States, intervenes to impose its own doctrine of what independence and nationalism should constitute in the country concerned. This, it seems to me, constitutes the ideological mainspring of the most widespread form of contemporary "imperialism." The doctrine of the containment of communism is necessarily an imperialist doctrine.

Here are certain questions which I would like to have considered:

Is it really in the national interests of the United States to fight communism wherever it appears? If so, why?

Why should it be assumed that a state which becomes Communist as Yugoslavia did—i.e., without either Russian or Chinese intervention or active American opposition—should be any more hostile to the United States than Yugoslavia is?

Should not the emergence of a plurality of centers and forms of Communist doctrine and power lead to a radical re-examination of policies formed in the days when it was assumed that any new Communist territory represented an automatic extension of the monolithic power of the Kremlin?

Has anti-communism become so rooted in the American way of life that no American government can at present afford to allow any country which is at present non-Communist to become Communist?

If so, how is such an attitude likely to be affected by the deepening of the American involvement in the Vietnamese war? Is the doctrine of the necessity to fight communism likely to be hardened by this involvement—leading perhaps to other similar involvements elsewhere—or will the doctrine be brought into question, once the cost becomes more clear?

Granted that the foreign policies of the United States are increasingly challenged in academic or other intellectual circles, has this challenge now any effect, or is it likely to have any effect, on U.S. public opinion generally?

An outsider like myself sees something of the impact of present U.S. policies on the outside world. Only insiders . . . can come near to gauging the likelihood of a revision of these policies. That is why I should like to [hear the answers to] such questions as these. A great deal surely depends on the answers, for all of us.

FRANTZ FANON	VIOLENCE IN THE INTERNATIONAL CONTEXT*

WE HAVE POINTED OUT many times in the preceding pages that in underdeveloped regions the political leader is forever

* From *The Wretched of the Earth* by Frantz Fanon. Reprinted by permission of Grove Press, Inc. Copyright © 1963 by Presence Africaine.

calling on his people to fight: to fight against colonialism, to fight against poverty and underdevelopment, and to fight against sterile traditions. The vocabulary which he uses in his appeals is that of a chief of staff: "mass mobilization"; "agricultural front"; "fight against illiteracy"; "defeats we have undergone"; "victories won." The young independent nation evolves during the first years in an atmosphere of the battlefield, for the political leader of an underdeveloped country looks fearfully at the huge distance his country will have to cover. He calls to the people and says to them: "Let us gird up our loins and set to work," and the country, possessed by a kind of creative madness, throws itself into a gigantic and disproportionate effort. The program consists not only of climbing out of the morass but also of catching up with the other nations, using the only means at hand. They reason that if the European nations have reached that stage of development, it is on account of their efforts: "Let us therefore," they seem to say, "prove to ourselves and to the whole world that we are capable of the same achievements." This manner of setting out the problem of the evolution of underdeveloped countries seems to us to be neither correct nor reasonable.

The European states achieved national unity at a moment when the national middle classes had concentrated most of the wealth in their hands. Shopkeepers and artisans, clerks and bankers monopolized finance, trade and science in the national framework. The middle class was the most dynamic and prosperous of all classes. Its coming to power enabled it to undertake certain very important speculations: industrialization, the development of communications, and soon the search for outlets overseas.

In Europe, apart from certain slight differences (England, for example, was some way ahead), the various states were at a more or less uniform stage economically when they achieved national unity. There was no nation which by reason of the character of its development and evolution caused affront to the others.

Today, national independence and the growth of national feeling in underdeveloped regions take on totally new aspects. In these regions, with the exception of certain spectacular advances, the different countries show the same absence of infrastructure. The mass of the people struggle against the same poverty, flounder about making the same gestures and with their shrunken bellies outline what has been called the geography of hunger. It is an underdeveloped world, a world inhuman in its poverty; but also it is a world without doctors, without engineers and without administrators. Confronting this world, the European nations sprawl, ostentatiously opulent. This European opulence is literally scandalous, for it has been founded on slavery, it has been nourished with the blood of slaves and it comes directly from the soil and from the subsoil of that underdeveloped world. The well-being and the progress of Europe have been built up with the sweat and the dead bodies of Negroes, Arabs, Indians and the yellow races. We have decided not to overlook this any longer. When a colonialist country, embarrassed by the claims for independence made by a colony, proclaims to the nationalist leaders: "If you wish for independence, take it, and go back to the middle ages," the newly independent people tend to acquiesce and to accept the challenge; in fact you may see colonialism withdrawing its capital and its technicians and setting up around the young state the apparatus of economic pressure.[1] The apotheosis of

---

[1] In the present international context, capitalism does not merely operate an economic blockade against African or Asiatic colonies. The United States with its anti-Castro operations is opening a new chapter in the long story of man's toiling advance towards freedom. Latin America, made up of new independent countries which sit at the United Nations and raise the wind there, ought to be an object lesson for Africa. These former colonies since their liberation have suffered the brazen-faced rule of Western capitalism in terror and destitution.

The liberation of Africa and the growth of consciousness among mankind have made it possible for the Latin American peoples to break with the old merry-go-round of dictatorships where each succeeding regime exactly resembled the preceding one. Castro took over power in Cuba, and gave it to the people. This heresy is felt to be a national scourge by the Yankees, and the United States is now organizing counter-revolutionary brigades; it puts together a provisional government, burns the sugar-cane crops, and generally has decided to strangle the Cuban people mercilessly. But this will be difficult. The people of Cuba will suffer, but they will conquer. The Brazilian President Janio Quadros has just announced in a declaration of historic importance that his country will defend the Cuban Revolution by all means. Perhaps even the United States may draw back when faced with the declared will of the peoples. When that day comes, we'll hang out the flags, for it will be a decisive

independence is transformed into the curse of independence, and the colonial power through its immense resources of coercion condemns the young nation to regression. In plain words, the colonial power says: "Since you want independence, take it and starve." The nationalist leaders have no other choice but to turn to their people and ask from them a gigantic effort. A regime of austerity is imposed on these starving men; a disproportionate amount of work is required from their atrophied muscles. An autarkic regime is set up and each state, with the miserable resources it has in hand, tries to find an answer to the nation's great hunger and poverty. We see the mobilization of a people which toils to exhaustion in front of a suspicious and bloated Europe.

Other countries of the Third World refuse to undergo this ordeal and agree to get over it by accepting the conditions of the former guardian power. These countries use their strategic position—a position which accords them privileged treatment in the struggle between the two blocs—to conclude treaties and give undertakings. The former dominated country becomes an economically dependent country. The ex-colonial power, which has kept intact and sometimes even reinforced its colonialist trade channels, agrees to provision the budget of the independent nation by small injections. Thus we see that the accession to independence of the colonial countries places an important question before the world, for the national liberation of colonized countries unveils their true economic state and makes it seem even more unendurable. The fundamental duel which seemed to be that between colonialism and anticolonialism, and indeed between capitalism and socialism, is already losing some of its importance. What counts today, the question which is looming on the horizon, is the need for a redistribution of wealth. Humanity must reply to this question, or be shaken to pieces by it.

---

moment for the men and women of the whole world. The almighty dollar—which when all is said and done is only guaranteed by slaves scattered all over the globe, in the oil wells of the Middle East, the mines of Peru or of the Congo, and the United Fruit or Firestone plantations—will then cease to dominate with all its force these slaves which it has created and who continue, empty-headed and empty-bellied, to feed it from their substance.

It might have been generally thought that the time had come for the world, and particularly for the Third World, to choose between the capitalist and socialist systems. The underdeveloped countries, which have used the fierce competition which exists between the two systems in order to assure the triumph of their struggle for national liberation, should however refuse to become a factor in that competition. The Third World ought not to be content to define itself in the terms of values which have preceded it. On the contrary, the underdeveloped countries ought to do their utmost to find their own particular values and methods and a style which shall be peculiar to them. The concrete problem we find ourselves up against is not that of a choice, cost what it may, between socialism and capitalism as they have been defined by men of other continents and of other ages. Of course we know that the capitalist regime, in so far as it is a way of life, cannot leave us free to perform our work at home, nor our duty in the world. Capitalist exploitation and cartels and monopolies are the enemies of underdeveloped countries. On the other hand the choice of a socialist regime, a regime which is completely orientated toward the people as a whole and based on the principle that man is the most precious of all possessions, will allow us to go forward more quickly and more harmoniously, and thus make impossible that caricature of society where all economic and political power is held in the hands of a few who regard the nation as a whole with scorn and contempt.

But in order that this regime may work to good effect so that we can in every instance respect those principles which were our inspiration, we need something more than human output. Certain underdeveloped countries expend a huge amount of energy in this way. Men and women, young and old undertake enthusiastically what is in fact forced labor, and proclaim themselves the slaves of the nation. The gift of oneself, and the contempt for every preoccupation which is not in the common interest, bring into being a national morale which comforts the heart of man, gives him fresh confidence in the destiny of mankind and disarms the most reserved observers. But we cannot believe that such an effort can be kept up at the same frenzied pace for very long. These young countries have agreed to take up the challenge after the unconditional withdrawal of the ex-colonial countries. The country finds itself in the hands of new managers; but the fact is that everything needs to be reformed and everything thought out anew. In reality the colonial system was concerned with certain forms of wealth and certain resources only—precisely those which provisioned her own industries. Up to the present no serious effort had been made to estimate the riches of the soil or of mineral resources. Thus the young independent nation sees itself obliged to use the economic channels created by the colonial regime. It can, obviously, export to other countries and other currency areas, but the basis of its exports is not fundamentally modified. The colonial regime has carved out certain channels and they must be maintained or catastrophe will threaten. Perhaps it is necessary to begin everything all over again: to change the nature of the country's exports, and not simply their destination, to re-examine the soil and mineral resources, the rivers, and—why not?—the sun's productivity. Now, in order to do all this other things are needed over and above human output— capital of all kinds, technicians, engineers, skilled mechanics, and so on. Let's be frank: we do not believe that the colossal effort which the underdeveloped peoples are called upon to make by their leaders will give the desired results. If conditions of work are not modified, centuries will be needed to humanize this world which has been forced down to animal level by imperial powers.[2]

The truth is that we ought not to accept these conditions. We should flatly refuse the situation to which the Western countries wish to condemn us. Colonialism and imperialism have not paid their score when they withdraw their flags and their police forces from our territories. For centuries the capitalists have behaved in the underdeveloped world like nothing more than war criminals. Deportations, massacres, forced labor, and slavery have been the main methods used by capitalism to increase its wealth, its gold or diamond reserves, and to establish its

[2] Certain countries who have benefited by a large European settlement come to independence with houses and wide streets, and these tend to forget the poverty-stricken, starving hinterland. By the irony of fate, they give the impression by a kind of complicit silence that their towns are contemporaneous with independence.

power. Not long ago Nazism transformed the whole of Europe into a veritable colony. The governments of the various European nations called for reparations and demanded the restitution in kind and money of the wealth which had been stolen from them: cultural treasures, pictures, sculptures, and stained glass have been given back to their owners. There was only one slogan in the mouths of Europeans on the morrow of the 1945 V-day: "Germany must pay." Herr Adenauer, it must be said, at the opening of the Eichmann trial, and in the name of the German people, asked once more for forgiveness from the Jewish people. Herr Adenauer has renewed the promise of his people to go on paying to the state of Israel the enormous sums which are supposed to be compensation for the crimes of the Nazis.[3]

In the same way we may say that the imperialist states would make a great mistake and commit an unspeakable injustice if they contented themselves with withdrawing from our soil the military cohorts, and the administrative and managerial services whose function it was to discover the wealth of the country, to extract it and to send it off to the mother countries. We are not blinded by the moral reparation of national independence; nor are we fed by it. The wealth of the imperial countries is our wealth too. On the universal plane this affirmation, you may be sure, should on no account be taken to signify that we feel ourselves affected by the creations of Western arts or tech-

[3] It is true that Germany has not paid all her reparations. The indemnities imposed on the vanquished nation have not been claimed in full, for the injured nations have included Germany in their anti-Communist system of defense. This same preoccupation is the permanent motivation of the colonialist countries when they try to obtain from their former colonies, if not their inclusion in the Western system, at least military bases and enclaves. On the other hand they have decided unanimously to forget their demands for the sake of NATO strategy and to preserve the free world; and we have seen Germany receiving floods of dollars and machines. A Germany once more standing on its feet, strong and powerful, was a necessity for the Western camp. It was in the understood interests of so-called free Europe to have a prosperous and reconstructed Germany which would be capable of serving as a first rampart against the eventual Red hordes. Germany has made admirable use of the European crisis. At the same time the United States and other European states feel a legitimate bitterness when confronted with this Germany, yesterday at their feet, which today metes out to them cut-throat competition in the economic field.

niques. For in a very concrete way Europe has stuffed herself inordinately with the gold and raw materials of the colonial countries: Latin America, China and Africa. From all these continents, under whose eyes Europe today raises up her tower of opulence, there has flowed out for centuries toward that same Europe diamonds and oil, silk and cotton, wood and exotic products. Europe is literally the creation of the Third World. The wealth which smothers her is that which was stolen from the underdeveloped peoples. The ports of Holland, the docks of Bordeaux and Liverpool were specialized in the Negro slave trade, and owe their renown to millions of deported slaves. So when we hear the head of a European state declare with his hand on his heart that he must come to the help of the poor underdeveloped peoples, we do not tremble with gratitude. Quite the contrary; we say to ourselves: "It's a just reparation which will be paid to us." Nor will we acquiesce in the help for underdeveloped countries being a program of "sisters of charity." This help should be the ratification of a double realization: the realization by the colonized peoples that *it is their due,* and the realization by the capitalist powers that in fact *they must pay.*[4] For if, through lack of intelligence (we won't speak of lack of gratitude) the capitalist countries refuse to pay, then the relentless dialectic of their own system will smother them. It is a fact that young nations do not attract much private capital. There are many reasons which explain and render legitimate this reserve on the part of the monopolies. As soon as the capitalists know—and of course they are the first to know— that their government is getting ready to decolonize, they hasten to withdraw all their capital from the colony in question. The spectacular flight of capital is one of the most constant phenomena of decolonization.

[4] "To make a radical difference between the building up of socialism in Europe and our relations with the Third World (as if our only relations with it were external ones) is, whether we know it or not, to set the pace for the distribution of the colonial inheritance over and above the liberation of the underdeveloped countries. It is to wish to build up a luxury socialism upon the fruits of imperialist robbery—as if, inside the gang, the swag is more or less shared out equally, and even a little of it is given to the poor in the form of charity, since it's been forgotten that they were the people it was stolen from." Marcel Péju. "To die for De Gaulle?" Article appearing in *Temps Modernes,* no. 175–76, October-November 1960.

Private companies, when asked to invest in independent countries, lay down conditions which are shown in practice to be inacceptable or unrealizable. Faithful to the principle of immediate returns which is theirs as soon as they go "overseas," the capitalists are very chary concerning all long-term investments. They are unamenable and often openly hostile to the prospective programs of planning laid down by the young teams who form the new government. At a pinch they willingly agree to lend money to the young states, but only on condition that this money is used to buy manufactured products and machines: in other words, that it serves to keep the factories in the mother-country going.

In fact the cautiousness of the Western financial groups may be explained by their fear of taking any risk. They also demand political stability and a calm social climate which are impossible to obtain when account is taken of the appalling state of the population as a whole immediately after independence. Therefore, vainly looking for some guarantee which the former colony cannot give, they insist on garrisons being maintained or the inclusion of the young state in military or economic pacts. The private companies put pressure on their own governments to at least set up military bases in these countries for the purpose of assuring the protection of their interests. In the last resort these companies ask their government to guarantee the investments which they decide to make in such-and-such an underdeveloped region.

It happens that few countries fulfill the conditions demanded by the trusts and monopolies. Thus capital, failing to find a safe outlet, remains blocked in Europe, and is frozen. It is all the more frozen because the capitalists refuse to invest in their own countries. The returns in this case are in fact negligible and treasury control is the despair of even the boldest spirits.

In the long run the situation is catastrophic. Capital no longer circulates, or else its circulation is considerably diminished. In spite of the huge sums swallowed up by military budgets, international capitalism is in desperate straits.

But another danger threatens it as well. Insofar as the Third World is in fact abandoned and condemned to regression or at least to stagnation by the selfishness and wickedness of Western nations, the underdeveloped peoples will decide to continue their evolution inside a collective autarky. Thus the Western industries will quickly be deprived of their overseas markets. The machines will pile up their products in the warehouses and a merciless struggle will ensue on the European market between the trusts and the financial groups. The closing of factories, the paying off of workers and unemployment will force the European working-class to engage in an open struggle against the capitalist regime. Then the monopolies will realize that their true interests lie in giving aid to the underdeveloped countries—unstinted aid with not too many conditions. So we see that the young nations of the Third World are wrong in trying to make up to the capitalist countries. We are strong in our own right, and in the justice of our point of view. We ought on the contrary to emphasize and explain to the capitalist countries that the fundamental problem of our time is not the struggle between the socialist regime and them. The Cold War must be ended, for it leads nowhere. The plans for nuclearizing the world must stop, and large-scale investments and technical aid must be given to underdeveloped regions. The fate of the world depends on the answer that is given to this question.

Moreover, the capitalist regime must not try to enlist the aid of the socialist regime over "the fate of Europe" in face of the starving multitudes of colored peoples. The exploit of Colonel Gargarin doesn't seem to displease General de Gaulle, for is it not a triumph which brings honor to Europe? For some time past the statesmen of the capitalist countries have adopted an equivocal attitude towards the Soviet Union. After having united all their forces to abolish the socialist regime, they now realize that they'll have to reckon with it. So they look as pleasant as they can, they make all kinds of advances, and they remind the Soviet people the whole time that they "belong to Europe."

They will not manage to divide the progressive forces which mean to lead mankind toward happiness by brandishing the threat of a Third World which is rising like the tide to swallow up all Europe. The Third World does not mean to organize a great crusade of hunger against the whole of Europe. What it expects from those who for centuries have kept it in slavery is that they will help it to rehabilitate mankind, and make man victorious everywhere, once and for all. But it is clear that we are not so naive as to think that this will come about with the cooperation and the good will of the European governments. This huge task which consists of re-introducing mankind into the world, the whole of mankind, will be carried out with the indispensable help of the European peoples, who themselves must realize that in the past they have often joined the ranks of our common masters where colonial questions were concerned. To achieve this, the European peoples must first decide to wake up and shake themselves, use their brains, and stop playing the stupid game of the Sleeping Beauty.

EDMUNDO FLORES

LATIN AMERICA*

ALLIANCE

FOR REACTION

THE ALLIANCE FOR PROGRESS, born a little more than four years ago, has undergone an ugly transformation and has entered a "hard" stage peopled by characters out of the Pentagon, the CIA and the Marine Corps. The passwords now are military aid, counter-insurgency, civic action and armed intervention. The Brazilian coup and the occupation of Santo Domingo are the two better known—but by no means the only—incidents of this hard stage.

What is the rationale behind the return to direct intervention and U.S. military power? What are the differences, if any, between President Johnson's "Invade Thy Neighbor Policy" and Theodore Roosevelt's "Gunboat Diplomacy"? How will Latin America react this time?

In 1960, Cuba demonstrated only too clearly that the pressures for social and economic reform in Latin America were formidable. The defensive response of many frightened American nations was the Alliance for Progress. In ten years, with

* From *The Nation*, June 21, 1965.

the magic of 10 billion U.S. dollars, the alliance would streamline rigid social structures, revitalize economies and pave the way for political stability. The miracle of the Marshall Plan would be repeated in Latin America and Communist expansion would be contained once more. There need be no more Cubas in the Western hemisphere.

As originally envisaged at Punta del Este, the alliance was to achieve the rapid economic and social transformation of Latin America essentially by parliamentary, peaceful and gradual reforms. The key to the whole program was to create and maintain favorable incentives for foreign and domestic private investment. The monetary and fiscal systems of Latin America were to be improved along the lines of traditional banking orthodoxy. Efficient and equitable systems of land tenure were to be implanted through reforms which would encourage family farms. Effective systems of labor relations were to be institutionalized. Low-cost housing, educational programs and improvements of public health and sanitation were the main goals on the social-reform front. A general target was the annual increase of per capita income by 2.5 percent.

For the North American official mind the long-term, ideal socio-political model for all the lesser members of the Alliance was, of course, the United States—or, more accurately, the simplified, Sunday-supplement stereotype which plain Americans and the State Department take to be the essence of the United States: free elections, free enterprise, free trade, free press, consumer sovereignty, balanced budgets and the pursuit of happiness. However, no one suggested the outright adoption of this ambitious model. Instead, a more modest showcase was sought.

The first showcase was Puerto Rico. But though President Kennedy and his advisers seemed pleased with it, the Latin Americans were unambiguously upset by the colonial connotations which they, and many Puerto Ricans as well, associate with that island. North Americans finally caught on to the notion—though they did not understand it—that the prospect of having more Puerto Ricos in the hemisphere is as obnoxious to Latin Americans, of whatever ideology, class or income level, as the prospect of more Cubas is to the State Department. After Puerto Rico, therefore, Colombia became the showcase, but not for long either—not with the anarchy and violence of the last fifteen years. After its military coup, Brazil captured the model country award, though by the time this had happened the search had been abandoned and the initial hopes of the alliance had been replaced by a more "realistic" policy. By then, Teodoro Moscoso, the Puerto Rican bureaucrat who with some embarrassment had coordinated the initial stages of the Alliance, had been fired. Thomas C. Mann then had shouldered the burden of redirecting the Alliance toward the overt freezing of the status quo, even if this meant keeping more and more of the hemisphere under military control.

The Latin American oligarchies like the status quo. They are content with their lot and do not want change or development. They fear reform, revolution and Castro. Although in unguarded moments they perhaps envy the stability and progress of Mexico, they despise its non-aristocratic, *nouveau riche*, anticlerical ruling classes. Not surprisingly, therefore, during the formative stages of the alliance, the conservative Latin American governments disagreed with its goals and rhetoric. Loud opposition was voiced by governments, political parties and private-interest groups. However, as soon as the Latin Americans cut through the unfamiliar pieties and torrid slogans that the North Americans were using so freely, and grasped the essentially conservative character of the enterprise called the alliance, they gave their support. The Latins had been scared by the "revolution of rising expectations" because this vague cliché does not translate well into Spanish and carries connotations of *revolución* in its straightforward sense, not in its recent Madison Avenue usage. But once they realized that the North Americans were in no mood for change either, they promulgated with loud fanfare the legislation to start phony fiscal and land reforms—and to get dollar credits.

President Kennedy got from Congress funds to start operations and assembled a cumbersome international bureaucracy around the Organization of American States. The Inter-American Development Bank, capitalized at $850 million when it was founded in 1959, was put in charge of virtually all the finances of the alliance and brought onto its staff a few good economists from Latin America. The Committee of Nine, dubbed the "Nine Wise Men," developed into a sort of Cecil B. DeMille spectacular in which nine local talents were charged with advisory attributions and billed as Latin America's Brain Trust. Recently, when it became obvious that the alliance was on the verge of collapse, the Inter-American Committee ICAP, headed by the Colombian Carlos Sanz de Santa Maria, was improvised as an emergency booster to keep it alive until military reinforcements arrived.

The alliance was not designed to put into effect real, fundamental, irreversible reforms. Its purpose was precisely the opposite: to devise technological and administrative improvements as a means of avoiding drastic shake-ups. Insofar as the "reforms" of the alliance fulfilled these conditions, great efforts have been made to carry them out. Thus, President Belaúnde of Peru, an architect by profession, pushed for the construction of his pet project: a highway in the Amazon (instead of land reform); the Colombian government began to build dams (instead of land reform); land-reclamation projects were launched in several countries (instead of land reform); and the construction of low-rent public housing mushroomed.

The Inter-American Development Bank and other agencies provided credits and conventional technical assistance. The United States, the Economic Commission for Latin America, FAO, the foundations and many universities also engaged in research and technical assistance. Foreign experts could be seen everywhere. Some were concerned with fiscal policies, others with industrial and urban schemes. There were specialists on farming, seeds, birth control, 4-H Clubs and all the measures which, under different guises, are commonplace in the advanced countries. However, these techniques seemed singularly incapable of developing their own momentum in most of Latin America. Some built-in mechanism that operates wherever there is widespread poverty, hunger, unemployment, illiteracy, religious fanaticism and rigid social stratification seemed to reject innovation as rigorously as the human body rejects kidney transplants.

The foreign technicians and Peace Corps adolescents who were not corrupted and absorbed by the local elite or who were not immediately discouraged by the futility of their efforts gradually became aware of the enormous difficulties they were facing and realized the tragic inadequacy of their ethnocentric, feeble tools and incantations. Thus they came to understand something that many Latin American nationalists who are really interested in the development of their respective countries had known since the inception of the alliance: that La Alianza para el Progreso was another case of too little, too late and too damned superficial.

In the meantime, the economies continued to deteriorate. Inflation rose at staggering rates, food shortages and food imports increased, capital flight persisted, the exodus of peasants to the cities mounted, and the military share of the budgets kept growing. In Peru, Ecuador, Venezuela and Colombia landless peasants occupied haciendas and challenged the army. Sometimes they were killed but at other times were left alone. In the mines of Peru, Bolivia and Brazil miners went on strike and fought the army and the police. The plantations of tropical and equatorial Latin America were rocked by labor disputes. The men and women on the streets of Buenos Aires, Santiago and Rio looked shabbier every season. Prostitutes proliferated. University students—the only opposition not in jail or exile in the countries run by the military—went on strike, rioted and battled the police and the army practically everywhere.

After the Bay of Pigs, U.S. military activities in Latin America were greatly intensified. The Defense Department expressed strong support for the "Military Civic Action" concept defined as "the use of preponderantly indigenous military forces on projects useful to the local population at all levels in such fields as education, training, public works, agriculture. . . ." Civic action is "a weapon against Communist-inspired subversion . . . a technique of guerrilla warfare and counter-insurgency.[1] The proposed total Latin American military assistance program for 1964 amounted to $77,262,000.

[1] U.S. Department of Defense, *Armed Forces Information and Education: for Commanders,* "Civic Action: the Military Role in Nation Building," vol. III, No. 14 (January 15, 1964).

In June, 1963, Defense Secretary Robert McNamara asserted:

Until about 1960, military assistance programs for Latin America were oriented toward hemispheric defense. As it became clear that there was no threat of significant overt external aggression against Latin America, emphasis shifted to internal security capabilities for use against Communist-inspired subversion or overt aggression and to civic-action projects designed to promote stability and strengthen national economies.[2]

When Thomas C. Mann became the head of the alliance in 1964, he added to it this military dimension. All kinds of gimmicks were tried to improve the image of Latin American soldiers in the United States. College professors got grants to study their positive role in social innovation. The idiotic notion that the military is the only group on which the United States can rely because it is familiar with discipline and technology and is sincerely anti-Communist is being pushed in the mass media. *Time* recently called General Barrientos, the American Air Force-trained Bolivian usurper, "the Steve Canyon of the Andes."

Many Latin American officers are training in the United States. It is piously expected that through professional contacts with U.S. soldiers they will absorb apolitical attitudes and that as they become "more professional in outlook, they will by conviction and necessity eschew politics."[3] The obverse proposition—that increased contact may further politicize the U.S. military—should at least be considered.

Thus, the inadequacies of the alliance, the anticipation of a spreading revolutionary wave, and the recognized incapacity of the local elites to defend even their own interests, resulted in hurried attempts by the United States to increase the political influence of the military in their respective countries. More

[2] "Military Aid to Latin America in the U.S. Congress" by Michael J. Francis; *Journal of Inter-American Studies,* July, 1964.
[3] "The Military" by Lyle N. McAlister in *Continuity and Change in Latin America,* edited by J. J. Johnson, Stanford University Press.

ominously, it also brought the "no-nonsense" unilateral decision to intervene directly in order to avoid the threat of communism in any Latin American country. This attitude sooner or later would blast the inter-American system, but North Americans knew from experience that the OAS could be intimidated and bought when the need arose.

After the army, of course, the carpetbaggers would follow. The external expenditures for military aid and counter-insurgency would be neatly brought home again by private U.S. enterprise. "Freedom"—and United States corporations abroad —would be protected. The differences between this policy and "Gunboat Diplomacy" or "Dollar Diplomacy" are matters of style. After Santo Domingo, there is not much difference in the Latin American mind between Theodore Roosevelt, Woodrow Wilson or Johnson. At the receiving end, intervention is intervention is intervention.

The Brazilian coup was the biggest triumph for the "hard" policy. General Castello Branco received instant recognition, extravagant praise and quick alliance aid. Brazilian humor is famous. The U.S. Ambassador has been proposed as a candidate in the future Brazilian elections under the slogan: "Avoid Intermediaries: Lincoln Gordon for President."

If Castello Branco could cure the ills of Brazil with "unconditional" financial and technical aid from the U.S., then, perhaps, the "hard alliance" would find a way out. But his chances of success are negligible. It is more likely that as the pressures in favor of genuine radical reforms rise—and they will inexorably—local military repression and U.S. armed intervention will grow in scope and brutality. In addition to Brazil, many countries are under the tutelage of the alliance-Pentagon-CIA axis. Primarily, they are the fourteen countries that were corralled into the sad farce of giving retroactive legality in the OAS to the invasion of the Dominican Republic.

To believe that the pressures for reform in Latin America are created by Communist activities is childish. The turbulence that pervades the politics of most of the Latin American countries stems from the prevalence of ancient and rigid social conditions and institutions inimical to economic development and social change. As long as a handful of men own almost all the land, and a few foreign corporations control the mineral wealth, the public utilities and plantations, Latin America will be torn by violence and instability. The Communists are not responsible for these conditions; they only exploit them to their own advantage. Mr. Mann should have learned this basic lesson while he was Ambassador to Mexico.

Ironically, Juan Bosch is one of the few Latin Americans who understand and value the great democratic tradition which de Tocqueville admired; the tradition of which FDR and his New Deal form part. The way Juan Bosch has been treated and the clumsy invasion of the Dominican Republic have created more hatred toward the United States in Latin America than the combined anti-colonial propaganda of China and Russia.

B. CASES IN POINT

INTRODUCTION

WE HAVE CHOSEN to focus on the problems of poverty in one specific area of the world—Latin America—not only because Latin America has occupied an increasingly important place in the foreign policy considerations of the United States since the Good Neighbor Policy of Franklin D. Roosevelt, but primarily because Latin America seems at the present time to be the part of the world most agitated by the possibility of revolutionary movements.

In order to better understand the underdeveloped world the question is asked: What is it like to be poor—a most common condition for the vast majority—in a Latin American country? The following accounts of life and death among the poor in Latin America provide some answers to this question.

"Letter from Peru" by Norman Gall describes in realistic terms the conditions of poverty in one Latin American nation, by no means the poorest. Michael Maccoby focuses on a rural Mexican village and poignantly reveals the hope, despair, and conflict among the villagers. An increasingly significant phenomenon, as Abrams has pointed out (see pp. 285–295), is the growth of urban slums in underdeveloped nations; in "Latin American Shantytown," Sam Schulman offers a frightening view of life in Bogotá, Colombia. Eduardo Galeano, Latin American journalist, reports on his visit with the guerrillas in rural Guatemala. He describes them as "the first successful revolutionaries on the mainland of Latin America."

| NORMAN GALL | LETTER FROM PERU* |

The peasantry itself . . . cannot function independently in the political arena. It is deeply cleft into layers with sharply conflicting economic interests. It is the most numerous, but also the most scattered and backward section of the population. It is localized and limited, economically and psychologically. For these reasons the village has, in China as elsewhere, always been subject to the town. The peasantry has always been at the command of the urban class able to centralize, weld, control, whether in the economic process or in politics. Without the centripetal force of the city, around which the rural economy must inevitably revolve, the peasant is helpless, especially the poorest peasant, the most exploited and nearest to the soil. His own attempts to better his own lot, without the aid of or in defiance of the dominant city class, have almost invariably taken the form of isolated acts of violence without permanent issue.

—Harold R. Isaacs,
The Tragedy of the Chinese Revolution

TOWARD the end of Calle Recoleta in the old Inca capital of Cuzco in southern Peru, there is a whitewashed adobe building with cavernous doorway and sagging balcony, where Indians wait in the shadows outside the office of the Peasants' Federation of Cuzco. Late at night the balcony is packed with emaci-

* From *Commentary*, June 1964.

ated beings wrapped in worn and dusty ponchos, shod in sandals cut from old rubber tires. Some chew slowly on coca leaves and dehydrated potatoes; now and then a derby-hatted woman stirs from her sleep, unwraps an infant from her shawl to give it the breast. Little other noise or movement issues from the mass of stinking bodies parked on the balcony. Some dazed, frightened eyes stare into the dimly lit office of the peasant federation. It is hard to believe that these Indians are capable of revolution, that this building in this tired city of ancient stone, from which the Incas ruled half a continent, is the seat of a major Communist-led offensive which is pushing Peru toward a terrible confrontation with the cruelties of her past.

On the other side of the balcony is the office of the Cuzco Workers' Federation. Inside, Ernesto Quispeledesma, one of the young lawyers serving as "juridical advisers" to the *sindicato* is listening to three Indian peons who just walked twelve hours from a hacienda near the town of Urcos. Beneath a poster announcing a world youth meeting in Prague, a university student is writing a receipt for monthly payments (between twenty cents and two dollars per family) from a *personero* (headman) of another community. The news from Urcos is that eight peasants have been killed and twenty wounded at the Hacienda Ninabamba; there was a fight with the *hacendado* (planter), who had a machine gun and rifles in his house. "That is a new *sindicato* of ours," Quispeledesma told me. "We don't know what happened yet. I am going there tomorrow to find out."

The Hacienda Ninabamba is a small plantation of rich pampa lowland in the valley of the Vilcanota River. The owner, Miguel Luna, is in the class of large landholders forming a little over 1 percent of Peru's farmers and owning over 62 percent of its land. The hacienda system of agriculture has never been very productive in the Peruvian sierra and is now in a visible state of decline. Some of the *hacendados* have already abandoned their holdings to the Indians, and the average planter's dwelling resembles a run-down American Southern farmhouse of the turn of the century, with its homemade furniture, discolored wallpaper, and ancient photographs of stiffly posed ancestors. Many of the manorial families are represented now by only an aged couple and a few servants who look after their needs, their children having left to become merchants or government officials in Lima or Cuzco.

In the weeks before the clash at Ninabamba the peasants refused to do any work for the plantation and insisted on their right to the land they were farming; Miguel Luna, along with other *hacendados,* began arming to defend his property. Then an agitator named Cesar Galdos, cousin of the famous Trotskyite peasant leader Hugo Blanco, appeared on the farm, and leaflets of the Castro-sponsored *Movimiento de la Izquierda Revolucionaria* (MIR) were later found there. With the arrival of Galdos, the Indians demonstrated in front of the main house, declaring they would soon take over the land. On Christmas afternoon Luna's twenty-five-year-old son, educated at a Paris boarding school, got into a fight with two Indian youths and shot one of them in the foot with a pistol. The youths returned that night with several hundred Indians who assaulted the hacienda with clubs, crude farm implements, slingshots, sharpened wood poles, and a few knives. Luna, his son, and a friend opened fire with a light machine gun and rifles, and the Indians fled with terrified screams from the garden of the *hacendado*'s house, leaving behind some thirty casualties.

Lucio Quispe, twenty-nine, is a survivor of the massacre. A limp felt hat falls to his ears, framing the tension of his broad mouth and his small, moist eyes, shining with terror and injury. A brown poncho with faded red stripes covers his shoulders. His legs are bare beneath his knees, save for the rubber-tire sandals. *"Buenas tardes,"* he says, bowing timorously: this is virtually the only Spanish he knows. On his shoulder he carries a *chaquitaclla,* a digging stick with a footrest and an iron blade, with which he plows and cultivates his half-acre plot, while his young wife follows behind breaking the clods into small pieces with her hands. "We joined the *sindicato* to better our conditions," Lucio Quispe tells me in so many words. "Before we organized last March we had to work 150 days a year for the right to farm our land. We were paid a sol and a half [six cents] a day for our work. After we joined the *sindicato* our pay was raised to five and a half sols [twenty-two cents]." He lives in a crumbling, windowless adobe house, with a ladder leading to an upper room where he stores his corn. His family of four exists on a diet of potatoes and corn. To keep him warm on winter days in the field, where the temperature often drops to twenty degrees below zero, he drinks *aguardiente,* a sugar-based brew strong enough to light a kerosene stove. To forget his hunger and his troubles he chews coca leaf and a lime ball to produce cocaine as well as a gastric secretion to ease his hunger. "We don't know what to do with the Indians," said Julio Luna, brother of the Ninabamba *hacendado* and president of the *Sociedad Agropecuaria de Cuzco.* "They are animals. These Indians are good for nothing, not even for eating."

The degradation of the 6 million Quechua Indians, half of Peru's population, has passed through several stages. The Inca nobility governed them despotically but nevertheless allotted them enough fertile land, kept enough grain in reserve, and were humane enough as masters to maintain the Quechua population. During the two hundred years of Spanish rule that followed, Quechua numbers were to diminish by half. With the Spaniards came the *encomenderos,* the noblemen who were granted the labor of an Indian community in return for administering its land, and later the *corregidores,* minor judicial officials assigned to defend Indian legal rights. Many of the *encomenderos* and *corregidores* merely seized the Indian communal lands they were supposed to protect and sold the inhabitants into slave labor in the mines. The republican period (1824 to the present) freed the growing mestizo (half-breed) class from royal restrictions and they in turn seized whatever fertile Indian land they could get their hands on. Many Quechua communities were eventually driven from the river valleys to the mountain sides where the first Communist organizers found them about a decade ago.

Because of the continual stealing of Indian land through a variety of legal malpractices, the corruption of the traditional Spanish legal system, based on a civil code rather than precedent and trial by jury, reached an extreme in Peru. During the colonial period, according to anthropologist George Kubler, "The Indians were constantly wandering back and forth between the *repartimiento* [reservation] and the seat of their *Audiencia* [regional court] to secure legal papers, usually worthless, for which they were heavily charged by the swarms of parasite solicitors and scriveners who made their living in the Spanish cities from this occupation." Barratry among the Indians continues to thrive in Peru. As in colonial times, many of these lawsuits never reach trial because the judge or the lawyer or both wind up in the planter's pocket.

So far as local government is concerned, it is a matter of a few prominent families dividing up the jobs among their retainers. Last December Peru held its first municipal elections in forty years. Of 1,500 district (county) capitals, 1,200 lack aqueduct and sewage facilities and 725 lack roads to the outside world. The local judge, like the *corregidor* before him, is so badly paid that the judicial process has come to resemble an auction. And even with the new municipal elections, the Indians, who make up 95 percent of the Sierra countryside, cannot elect officials of their own because the literacy requirement prevents them from voting.

"When we go into town to see the mayor or the judge, we must wait for hours," said Horacio Quispe, the sixty-year-old head of the community of Acna. "We are told to clean the floors and toilets of the city hall and the priest's house and the stables behind them. Then we are told to go back to our village and come back the next day with lambs and pigs to offer as gifts. Then they will hear our case." The community of Acna, 12,000 feet high, is a confusion of stony patches of about a half-acre each, farmed at a sixty-degree incline for corn and onions and potatoes. In more fertile parts of the sierra, a peasant's holding often consists of one or two furrows.

The land hunger in the sierra, as well as the poverty, are comparable to the worst in Asia. Because of the extensive mountains, deserts, and jungles, only 1.2 percent of Peru is under cultivation, with 62 percent of the population farming it. Only 0.44 acres per capita are under cultivation in Peru, compared with 0.79 in India and 0.42 in China.

The formation of peasant *sindicatos* in the Andes dates back to 1952, when the Argentine buyers of the Hacienda Lauramarca decided to oust the 6,000 Indians living there and hire laborers in their place. Communist leaders organized a peasant union for defense of the land and stopped the eviction. Despite this, however, the Communist party in Cuzco remained a preserve of intellectuals allied with the small Workers' Federation and lacking any substantial following among the Quechua-speaking Indian masses. In fact, many of the Communists owned haciendas themselves, sent their children to Roman Catholic schools, and, as lawyers, built lucrative practices defending other planters in the courts. It has been the younger generation of revolutionary leaders who, since the mid-1950s, have developed the peasant federation movement—a feat that seems the more remarkable when one considers the immense cultural as well as physical boundaries which have kept these communities apart from the rest of the nation. If the older Communists still give strategic advice to the peasant movement, it is the young, Quechua-speaking lawyers and field organizers who, night after night, make their way on foot and horseback over treacherous mountain paths and the great expanses of the *altiplano* to isolated haciendas and Indian villages. Several such difficult journeys are necessary to break down the intense distrust of an Indian village toward outsiders, and several more to convince it that free land can be obtained merely by forceful demands. Many of the organizers themselves were born in Indian communities and are recent converts to mestizo culture. Some have been trained in Russia and Cuba and function as professional, subsidized agitators. They remain in close touch with the two hundred peasant unions belonging to the Cuzco federation through a system of couriers, who will walk one or two whole days from their community to bring an item of news to the Calle Recoleta headquarters. These Peruvian *sindicatos* now have an estimated membership of 250,000 made up of hacienda peons and members of isolated mountain communities. They were responsible for some 150 hacienda invasions in 1963 and twenty-five more in the first months of 1964. At least seventy-one people have died in the fighting.

The Peruvian sierra has its romantic *Fidelista* hero in Hugo Blanco, a twenty-nine-year-old agronomist who became a Trotskyite after studying at Argentina's Universidad de la Plata. In La Convencion Valley, Blanco and a few friends have developed Peru's most troublesome peasant federation. The valley is little more than a thickly forested ravine until it spreads out beyond the hamlet of Quillabamba—eighty miles from Cuzco—to merge hundreds of miles away with the great jungle forming Peru's indistinct frontier with Brazil. These fertile lands were grazed by cattle until the 1930s when an epidemic wiped out most of the cows and peasants, forcing the *hacendados* to switch to cash crops and to rent their land to tenants or *arrendires*. To get the land into production, the landlords obligated the *arrendires* to more labor than they could possibly provide, with the result that the *arrendires* sublet part of their lands to indentured peons, or *allegados,* who in turn might subdivide the land two or three times after that. All of which produced a grotesque confusion of land tenure, with the kulak-like *arrendires* exploiting the sub-tenants and strengthening their holdings through equity in capital improvements such as irrigation and coffee planting. Since 1958, with the assistance of Cuzco University students subsidized by the Communist-led Cuzco University Federation, Blanco's federation mobilized the *allegados* against the *hacendados* and *arrendires* and persuaded them to refuse to do their contracted work.

More violent tactics were not long in coming. On Christmas Day, 1962, a band of about two hundred peasants disarmed two policemen at Chaullay, near Quillabamba, and that night clashed with police reinforcements at Chaullay Bridge. Using machine guns the police killed thirty of the peasants. Meanwhile, three policemen were killed in two other attacks and Blanco was formally charged with their deaths.

After these incidents, Blanco and his companions withdrew deeper into the valley, his so-called guerrilla operations really a desperate flight from the police and army troops who were pouring into the area. He was finally captured last May in La Convencion Valley, and since then he has been in jail in the south coast city of Arequipa where, police say, he sees visitors, issues manifestoes, and directs key activities of his Revolutionary Workers' Party. In December he went on a hunger strike, and 5,000 of his followers marched on Cuzco, enforcing a general strike and destroying a bridge, telegraph lines, and train rails. Nevertheless, the government refuses either to try or to free him.

After Blanco's capture, the military junta, which had nullified the 1962 elections by a *coup d'état,* initiated a program of agrarian reform on two plantations in La Convencion Valley. One one hacienda, some 3,800 acres (for which the owner received $10,000) were distributed among 260 peasants. The plots consisted of eroded hillsides that might produce one crop every three or four years; the good pampa land, reserved for sugar cane, remained in the owner's possession and was farmed by hired labor from outside the valley. The *sindicato* leaders urged the peasants to refuse to pay for the land under the low-price, long-term plan of the government. Those who insisted on buying were taken from their homes, dressed up as women, and dragged through the streets of Quillabamba.

Revolutionary activity in the sierra is still limited by such primitive means of coercion and will remain a political rather than a military problem until the Indians get modern weapons. But this may happen sooner than expected. Last May, seven Peruvian youths, all sons of middle- or upper-class families, were killed or captured crossing the border from Bolivia. The police announced that they had been trained at Che Guevara's guerrilla warfare school in Minas del Frio, Cuba, and were carrying arms and money to assist Hugo Blanco. Some eighteen months earlier a Varig airliner, carrying a group of Cuban officials, had crashed en route to La Paz, Bolivia. A packet of documents found at the crash reportedly contained plans for revolutionary activities in the sierra to be carried out from the Cuban embassy in La Paz. Peru had already broken diplomatic relations with Havana in December 1960, following the discovery of records in the Lima embassy of payments to Peruvians to finance Communist activity and to provide favorable publicity for the Cuban Revolution. Luis de la Puente Uceda, head of the Castro-supported Movement of the Revolutionary Left, is reliably reported to have received at least $70,000 for trips to Cuba.

If Cuba is indeed supplying military assistance, the weapons have not appeared in the sierra—though police claim to have discovered several stores of them in the coastal cities. Some observers are convinced that Cuban weapons will not be used as long as the new government of Fernando Belaunde Terry remains in power. For Belaunde, a devout Catholic who is allied with the small Christian Democratic party of Lima intellectuals, won the Presidency with Communist support in 1963, and he still depends on that support today.

The immediate political danger posed by the Quechua uprising in Peru is that of a military coup which would again frustrate the movement to establish constitutional democracy in Peru. This movement is already split, largely because of bitter enmity between Belaunde and Victor Raul Haya de la Torre, though it should be said that Belaunde's hatred of Haya's American Popular Revolutionary Alliance (APRA) is shared by almost everyone else in Peruvian politics. It is this animosity which has led Belaunde—whose own Accion Popular Party is too small, amorphous, and *personalista* to run a strong national campaign—to accept the support of the disciplined Communist machine, just as, on the other side, it has led Haya to form an alliance with the oligarchical party of ex-dictator Manuel Odria, whose regime was responsible for the death and imprisonment of many *Apristas*. In last December's municipal elections, in which APRA was badly beaten, Peruvian voters were treated to the extraordinary spectacle of Odria's wife running as APRA candidate for mayor of Lima.

Thus the two main democratic factions are dependent on extremists of the left and right respectively and can agree on very little. (Rival proposals for agrarian reform legislation, for example, have been stalled for months in the Congress, which is controlled by the APRA-Odria coalition.) Following the Ninabamba slaughter, the APRA-Odria coalition voted a congressional censure of the Belaunde cabinet for failing to take action against the Communists. In February Belaunde finally declared martial law in Cuzco Department after eight thousand Indians invaded haciendas near the railroad town of Sicuani, and nineteen peasants were killed. If the disorders continue, as they probably will, the "soft on Communism" refrain is likely to produce another military coup in Peru. Short of a counter-coup uniting the peasants, their cousins in the slums of the coastal cities, the Communists, the progressive or "Nasserist" elements in the armed forces, and the Lima middle classes—all of whom support Belaunde—another military dictatorship would leave Peru that much more exposed to the tide of revolution that is slowly rising in the countryside.

Meanwhile, the Peruvian oligarchy bides its time behind the scenes. It continues to maintain its stranglehold upon the economy, as evidenced by the fact that one-tenth of 1 percent of the population still earns 20 percent of the national income (56 percent of the population earns less than $4.50 a month). The main instrument of the oligarchy's economic power is the banking system: five banks owned by a few families control three-fourths of Peru's commercial credit, roughly the same proportion of which goes to borrowers in the Lima area. Other domains of the Peruvian oligarchy, sometimes shared with U.S. corporations, are large-scale commercial agriculture, mining, cement and other construction materials, as well as the booming Lima real-estate market. The political power of these families has been demonstrated many times in the past. Their favored method is to create an artificial credit and food scarcity and then bribe a few generals to carry out a military coup. With the growth of a "Nasserist" spirit in the armed forces and of a substantial middle class in Lima, one of the big questions in Peruvian politics today is whether the oligarchy still has enough power to overthrow Belaunde's regime.

U.S. policy is caught between the peasants' claims to elementary justice and the Peruvian oligarchy's strong connections in American business and political circles. Since the 1952 revolution, the United States has paid more than $250 million to contain the threat of increasing Communist power in Bolivia and each year provides roughly one-third of Bolivia's annual budget. No such contribution has been made to Peru, which has had no revolution. So far the Alliance for Progress in the sierra, apart from the work of 150 Peace Corps Volunteers, has been limited to the Food for Peace plan and to programs of road building and technical aid to large cattle breeders, none of which can be said to have strengthened the government's position against the oligarchy.

In a recent interview Belaunde said that "we have made many requests for funds from the United States for loans to support our programs, but there are many studies and reports and discussions and, so far, very little real help." Belaunde's main proposal is for a $300 million "marginal highway" on the eastern slopes of the Andes, running through Colombia, Ecuador, Peru, and Bolivia. The highway is designed to give these countries a ground route to the east coast cities of Brazil and Argentina and to open up the *selva* or jungle area for colonization. According to Belaunde, "the only real agrarian reform possible in Peru must be carried out in the *selva,* east of the Andes, where there is much rich land. Elsewhere, there is practically none."

Meanwhile, the U.S. apparently has shelved Belaunde's very modest request for a $10 million loan to buy *"picos y palas"* (picks and shovels) to equip 144 tool-lending centers in the sierra. Indian agricultural tools are so primitive that the introduction of iron implements in sufficient quantity could by itself initiate a technological revolution in the sierra. According to Belaunde, the Export-Import Bank agreed to finance the purchase of road-building machinery, but not of agricultural tools which could be lost or stolen and did not constitute a good risk. On the other hand, the Peruvian government with its overstaffed, low-paid, underskilled, and often corrupt bureaucracy, has still to inspire confidence in its capacities, especially in view of the fact that it proposes to carry out fundamental social reforms while working a twenty-eight-hour week with two months' annual leave.

"Picos y palas" is an integral part of Belaunde's attempt to develop Peru through community work programs. "More than half of the populated parts of our national territory remain inaccessible," Belaunde wrote shortly before his 1963 election. "For this reason we think it necessary to turn our eyes to the towns and villages themselves. We must revive the unextinguished flame of the communal spirit, which continues bearing unexpected fruits in the heights of the Andes and the plains of the *selva.* We must promote this voluntary work, which is the way of humble and patriotic people, lacking money, of paying their tributary portion to the nation."

Invoking the communal traditions of the Inca empire, Belaunde's program may be all too romantic, but it is not much more so than the Alliance for Progress itself. At present the large U.S. AID mission in Peru, like many others in Latin

America, is bizarrely overstaffed in its comfortable Lima office and understaffed in the field. In Lima AID occupies several floors of a large office building, while it only has two representatives in the desperately backward Department of Cuzco. Thus, the Alliance for Progress both imitates and encourages the traditional overcentralization of Latin American governments. This is one of the reasons why the alliance has had a very limited effect in Peru, and would have had practically none at all but for the 450 Peace Corps Volunteers who work in the slums and countryside.

To be sure, the situation in the Peruvian sierra is so explosive that the mere presence of a *gringo* at the scene of a strike or demonstration can be an incitement to violence; consequently, American field personnel have frequently been withdrawn when an eruption has occurred in the sierra. However, Peru has entered a period in which the politics of extreme poverty—of insurrection with nothing to lose but miserable lives— are in the ascendancy. Electoral democracy, having fared so badly at the hands of the army and oligarchy, is in the Belaunde regime undergoing its final test as a viable political system for Peru.

The Andean highlands of southern Peru and Bolivia form a single geopolitical unit where 10 million people live in extreme poverty with few economic and social relations with the outside world. However, these relations are increasing with the penetrations of modern technology as well as of political currents such as the Alliance for Progress and the militant inspiration of the Communist-led peasant federations. Twelve years ago Bolivia had her peasant revolution, which brought little improvement. Peru, less purely Indian, appears to be in for a longer and less decisive class struggle carried on amid the tensions of a 3.4 percent annual rise in population and a historic national incapacity for political cooperation. Confronted by such realities as these, the alliance policy of sowing social reform and political democracy has begun to founder, and the Johnson Administration is backing away from President Kennedy's missionary commitment to the development of Latin America. But the problems of revolution and repression in Latin America, and of creating new markets for our mushrooming productive capacity, do not diminish because our initial solutions have not borne fruit. Nor can they be resolved by cutting back foreign aid and reverting to our hemispheric policies of the Republican 1920s and the Truman–Eisenhower postwar period. The United States has been irrevocably cast in the role of an international institution responsible in a great measure for the stability and progress of this hemisphere. We cannot pretend to remain merely a nation among the nations of America while our power and interests lie deeply embedded in the life of every republic and Latin America continues its deterioration into a continental slum. Not only in Peru, but increasingly throughout Hispanic America, the seed-bearers of revolution from the towns continue to sow the whirlwind in the countryside. The rapid organization of the Quechua Indians is merely one striking example of another "alliance for progress" in the Americas against which our own schemes for the guidance of history must either contend or risk being violently swept aside.

**MICHAEL
MACCOBY**

LOVE AND
AUTHORITY*

OVER HALF the people in the world live in peasant villages. Social scientists who have observed rural life in many of the developing nations report that peasants from Latin America, India, and the Near East seem more like one another in many ways than like their urban compatriots. In Mexico, the city-trained technician or agricultural worker who enters the peasant village feels himself almost as much a stranger as does the North American, and has as little understanding of the peasant character. Mexicans experience the same frustration and puzzlement when their plans for agricultural improvement or community

* From *Atlantic Monthly*, April 1964. Copyright © 1964 by The Atlantic Monthly Company, Boston, Massachusetts. Reprinted by permission.

development meet the solid wall of peasant indifference and distrust. The Mexicans are not alone; peasants everywhere distrust townspeople.

In the peasant village we have studied, many problems stem from the same factors that have plagued peasants in other countries and in other eras. His small plot of land—all he can physically handle with slow, unprofitable methods of farming—and his loss of profit to city buyers have determined the peasant's life for centuries. He may switch from a wooden to a steel plow, but this makes no essential difference in the forces that control his existence. Only in the United States has industrialized agriculture all but wiped out the peasant population.

Erich Fromm, who has worked in Mexico for thirteen years, teaching and training Mexican psychoanalysts, first began the study six years ago, with financial support from the Foundations Fund for Research in Psychiatry. He had noted that almost all the anthropological studies in Mexico focused on Indian communities, which constitute no more than 10 percent of the population and which reflect a history significantly different from that of the Spanish-speaking mestizo, the descendant of mixed Spanish and Indian ancestry. Dr. Fromm was particularly interested in studying a mestizo village which had once been a hacienda (a large, semifeudal plantation) to discover how the character of the peasant, formed by generations of semifeudal peonage, has changed since the Revolution of 1910, which apportioned lands to the ex-peons and for the first time gave them the opportunity to direct their own destinies.

Las Cuevas, the village chosen, has a population of 850, small enough so that we can study each individual intensively. It is picturesque, dominated by a stone aqueduct built in the seventeenth century and by the ruins of the hacienda building, burnt early in the Revolution. Some of the older men served in Emiliano Zapata's army, which was formed from this district. Others fought against him. Many wished only to be left in peace, like Don Mardonio, who says that when Zapata's men entered the village, he would dress in the white manta shirt and trousers of the revolutionary, and when the government men came, he would hurriedly change his clothes. Others hid in the mountains and barely managed to survive.

While the village is reminiscent of the past, there are many signs of change. Although some people live in huts of sticks and sweep floors of packed dirt, others have houses of adobe, brick, or cement, with large patios shaded by banana and avocado trees, with purple bougainvillaea on the yellow walls and wild poinsettias blooming in the winter. The streets are unpaved, but within the last five years the village through its own efforts raised enough money to install running water and electricity. Over half the households have radios, and there is a television set in the town hall and in the houses of a few rich peasants.

Surrounding the village are some of the most fertile fields in Mexico, planted mainly with sugarcane, and in the summer rainy season, rice. In the distance, mountains separate the village from Taxco and Acapulco to the west and Mexico City to the east.

Just as striking as the setting of village life are the human problems that mar it. Many people lack work and barely manage to subsist. Others do not take advantage of what they have. They plant their fields with crops that pay little, or they neglect their work. Twenty percent of the adult men are alcoholics, and another 20 percent are heavy drinkers who waste at least two days of work a month and money desperately needed by their families. Alcohol leads them to magnify quarrels and insults, and a friendly exchange in a canteen may end in a machete or pistol fight; a misinterpreted look can be the cause of murder.

There is little deep friendship among the villagers. Few feel trust or fellowship outside their own families. Unless a common enemy threatens the group, the villagers seldom join together for community projects. Although they are ashamed of it and wish to be thought modern, most of the villagers are superstitious, suspicious that some women are witches, and will blame a child's illness on the evil eye. Although they respect modern medicine, they still turn to traditional curers to treat illnesses that resist the doctor's treatment, especially those of psychosomatic origin.

The villagers are not blind to these problems, for their ideals constantly clash with reality. They know that they gained from the revolution. The land which was once part of the hacienda was parceled out to the villagers in *ejidos,* plots of rich land, averaging five acres in size, which belong to a man as long as he works them. *Ejido* land is meant to be inalienable and indivisible, to be passed on to a wife, son, or daughter. The *ejido* land symbolizes Zapata's ideals, which the villager willingly accepts. He is meant to be a free man and to work with his fellows cooperatively, in the spirit of the community. What keeps him from realizing this ideal? What are the roots of alcoholism, violence, and despair?

When Dr. Fromm and a group of his students, all Mexican psychiatrists, first entered the village, they told the leading men they wished to study just these problems, in the interest not only of this village but of other villages which suffered equally.

It is fair to ask why the villagers accepted the study and the many hours of answering personal questions, responding to inkblot and other projective tests. For most of them, such an abstract project made little sense, but they probably decided that the help promised—medical care and aid in working on the town plaza—were worth the bother; and in any event, they seemed to enjoy talking about themselves. The image of a new patron for the village fitted the dreams of many. But one leader, more intelligent and honest than most, had doubts. "I shall be frank," he told the group of investigators. "You say you are interested in helping us and in understanding us. I don't know what the others expect from you. But it has been my experience that when someone from the city comes to a peasant village, it is for one of two reasons. Either he wants to exploit us or he is interested in becoming senator or governor." The investigators told him there was some truth in what he said, but they asked him to give them a chance to prove that for once in his life, this reasoning could be wrong.

Our study has had three general aims: first, to describe the character of the villager, or the range of character types, in terms which, while not based on the value judgments of our own society, accurately portray his strengths and his weaknesses; second, to trace the major formative influences, the factors in his social and economic experience, in his beliefs, in his family background, which prove most pertinent to the molding of the villager's character; and finally, to determine whether violence, alcoholism, distrust of self, and lack of initiative are mainly his reactions to poverty and exploitation—expressions of anger and despair which would disappear if conditions changed —or whether they would persist even if the peasant saw before him the path to a better life.

The study is based on lengthy interviews, mainly given by Dr. Felipe Sanchez, a Mexican physician who has also treated the villagers' illnesses and delivered their babies for more than five years. Two anthropologists, Dr. Theodore Schwartz and his wife, Lola, lived in the village for a year, observing the people at work and at leisure. Besides investigation by interview and observation, new stimuli have been introduced: readings in good literature (the villagers particularly liked the peasant stories of Tolstoy, and *Grimm's Fairy Tales*), weekly movies followed by discussions, a library, and an agricultural club for boys.

Except in those indigenous communities where land and religion are unified in mystical observances and where the society is self-contained, the conditions of peasant life in Mexico do not encourage love of land and agricultural work. A Mexican villager sees nature symbolized by the hot sun that drains his energy, or the land that gives him little for his effort: five acres of sugarcane result in a year's profit of only $40. Despite his industry and initiative, a planting of better paying crops can be ruined by bad weather, insects, or disease, and even if he has the luck to escape nature's displeasure, the market may be saturated. Under these circumstances, many peasants look with envy at the factory workers, sheltered from the elements, with less backbreaking work and more security.

Despite the hardships, a few peasants express love for their work. Perhaps in these peasants love for the land is part of appreciation for the experience of creation, of nurturing a plant, animal, or child, of seeing labor bear fruit. But a carpenter or skilled mechanic might feel the same way. Possibly this reaction is characteristically Mexican.

As a part of their intensive interview, all of the villagers were asked for their concept of love. Their answers tell a great deal about their attitudes toward life. The villager whom I shall quote first is one of 70 *ejidatarios* (55 men and 15 women).

Doña Teresa, as I shall call her, is about fifty and has never attended school. She is unmarried but has a fifteen-year-old daughter, and she supports her younger sister who was left with two children by her husband. Doña Teresa's family is one of the oldest in the village; her ancestors worked in the hacienda. Although she does relatively little manual work on her own land, she runs a canteen and raises pigs and chickens profitably on her house site. She is passionate by nature, suspicious of outsiders, loyal and affectionate to her friends, violent and unforgiving to her enemies. She says:

> Love is very sacred, because without love there would not be the world we would have if we loved each other, because even though there is friendship, it is not enough. One must love. Beginning with love of parents, of sweethearts, love of a husband, love of children, love of a good friendship; even to raise an animal one must love. It is incomparable, because people even commit suicide if they do not know love. The love of a father is eternal. The love of friends one retains even when they are away. Love of God, one must have also, for God sends us love in the form of understanding.

Doña Teresa's answer is more detailed than those of many who share her attitude, but some 15 percent of the villagers answer in a similar way. What these villagers express in their concept of love is the knowledge that love is not a bewitchment or a sexual attraction, but a deeply rooted trait of character, a respect for someone or an interest that is always different, depending on the person or object loved, but always essentially the same.

Don Nicolas, a peasant of fifty-eight years, states the same idea more briefly: "Love is a force that makes a person seek the well-being of those he esteems." Don Fortunato, a young farmer aged twenty-seven, says, "There are many kinds of love, for a plant, for the land. First, there is love of God. Second, for a father or mother. Love is to love a woman, the love that one's sons grow and develop. One has many loves."

Many villagers without an active, loving orientation express concepts of love that nevertheless move the listener by their authenticity. Their thoughts are deeply felt, but they react with passivity or resignation to the hardships which have eroded confidence in their own powers. Instead of creating love, they wait to be loved, and they receive little from the land or from others who also feel their inability to give.

The concept of love most often stated by villagers reflects the feeling that all good things of life lie outside onself, beyond reach; one must await passively the experience of happiness or love, being grateful if it arrives but without power to keep it. For these receptive people, joy lasts only momentarily, if at all. It may remain no more than a dream, a promise that never materializes, but which soon sours into disillusion. Of course, these villagers are not so different from other people. Few in any society have developed an active loving orientation to others and to their work, or a sense of self not dependent on outside supports. But the villagers have more cause to lack hope than most people.

Some people with hoarding characters tend to apportion their love, like a limited supply of money, to those children who merit it by obedience and good behavior. Says Doña Soledad, "I cannot feel as much affection for a son who acts badly as I do for one who treats me well." In work as in love, the hoarding orientation implies storing one's forces, avoiding spending too much interest and energy. Such peasants make good store-keepers, and as farmers they are seldom lazy. They earn a better living than the poorest, but they stick to old methods and are suspicious of anything that demands a new burst of activity.

Why is it that some peasants are able to develop an active orientation to love and work, despite conditions that foster despair in others? Perhaps they were born with a stronger will to live, or they were fortunate to experience the loving care of parents who nurtured the force necessary for growth. A simple reason for the depth and beauty of the average Mexican peasant's concept of love, despite economic scarcity and lack of formal education, is that love is what interests him. What does he have to think about, other than his own feelings and those of his fellow villagers? The routinized work, unchanged for centuries, demands little thought or planning. It does not occur to him to start a new industry, partly because he lacks models and capital. In fact—and this is common to other peasant societies—he opposes projects initiated by any village entrepreneur. He believes the village's resources have been parceled out once and for all; a new use of them presages one person's gain at the cost of others.

Culturally, life is barren, without the traditions, legends, and rites of Indian communities. Television has arrived only recently. There are occasional movies or dances. Las Cuevas, which wishes to be progressive, has done away with *jaripeos*, local bull-fights. After work, some young men, the most productive, play basketball. The others hang around the plaza or the bars. Nothing in the experience of most villagers leads to thoughts of life outside, except as alien and dangerous. In these circumstances most minds are dulled; some people leave, and the best of those who remain refine the experiences that do come to them, by directing their intellect into familiar channels.

As in all societies, the peasant develops the kind of intelligence that fits his needs. And it is noteworthy that our tests do not measure the kind of intelligence the peasant most values. The peasant may learn to detect fine differences in the state of a plant, an animal, or the weather. He studies people, trying to understand what lies behind their gestures and expressions. He does not respond to words alone, because he knows words often hide feelings or are meant to be polite. He may formally agree with another person, even though he does not mean it, in order not to insult him, and he is surprised when the man from the city who accepted his polite assent to some project then reproaches him for lack of responsibility. The productive peasant has developed his mind not as a machine, finely tooled to solve abstract problems, but in order to stimulate life and growth in all that he respects.

Don Guadalupe, aged seventy-five, who has never been to a school, tells us how a father should treat his sons. "If the Architect of the universe sends you a son, tremble. You cannot know if his soul will be good or evil. All you can do is to be a loving father, protecting him until he reaches the age of twelve. From twelve until he is twenty, be his teacher. And from twenty on, be his friend."

Why so few villagers develop productive characters is a complex problem, similar in peasant communities everywhere. Among other reasons are economic factors and social and psychological forces. The most important is based on scarcity—

hunger, the vagaries of the market, lack of land and of the rational use of it. A few peasants by their industry have transcended these conditions, but many lack the hope or life force necessary to mature. As long as peasants are saddled with rudimentary methods of farming on small plots and remain subjugated to the cities, they will remain distrustful and fatalistic.

In the village today, despite the peasants' greatly improved conditions, the psychological attitudes of the peon persist. Peasants lacking faith in themselves still seek patrons with whom they act the part of humble supplicant. In fact, when the land was partitioned, some villagers refused to accept *ejidos,* because they feared that the old hacienda owner would return to punish them. The competitive and distrustful attitudes characteristic of all peasants were more deeply etched by the hacienda experience and persist even though they conflict with the revolutionary ideal of cooperation.

These social attitudes mirror family relationships in which bonds between brothers are weakened by the tie to parents. The parents, like the hacienda owners, demand strict obedience from children, although their treatment of infants who have not yet developed a strong sense of self is warm, giving, and undemanding, and mothers show a deep sense of responsibility for children combined with a willingness to sacrifice for their wellbeing. Their strictness is rooted in the idea, perhaps historically planted, that willfulness and independence are signs of *lo malo* ("badness") that must be eradicated. With this attitude parents probably saved their children from getting into trouble with the hacienda masters, but now it cripples the growth of self-reliance. It persists both because of its self-perpetuating effects and because peasant fathers and mothers imitate the child-rearing techniques of their parents.

After the age of six, when boys must work in the fields and girls in the household, the child is expected to obey without question. He is taught that what is right is what his parents consider right. He constantly feels guilt and seldom learns to distinguish between his own rational conscience and the fear that he will transgress a parental commandment. Since parents often punish but hardly ever reward, the child lacks a sense of doing anything worthwhile; it is enough to avoid trouble.

The chance that he might rebel against this irrational authority and band together with his peers, as children do in the United States and Western Europe, never materializes. Parents discourage play with other children. Furthermore, the society lacks models for fraternal cooperation. Even the games of children, unlike our games such as hide-and-seek and ring-a-levio, lack the symbolic acting out of the group banding together to home-free-all their comrades from the central authority. Rather, in their hide-and-seek, called "burnt leather," the boys run from the central person, who has the right to whip each child he catches with a leather belt. Until the study entered the village, the young boys had never played such cooperative games as baseball or soccer, although a group of young men have been playing basketball, which was introduced twenty years ago by a schoolteacher.

The feudal heritage weakens the peasant's self-reliance and undermines the moral supports of reliability, cooperation, and fellow feeling. Those who assume authority tend to fall into the irrational, exploitative pattern of the hacienda system, and many of the most able villagers, to escape being a target for hostility and distrust, refuse to accept elected positions of command. One villager elected to office fell ill and remained ill until another person was chosen to replace him. Often the official positions fall to weak figureheads who excite no one's suspicions. The villagers distrust the community leaders, suspecting that those who institute communal projects siphon off the profits into their own pockets, whereas if a man openly assumes the role of patron for gain, they are more likely to admire his virtues and flatter him, seeking his favor.

Anyone who tries, as we did, to introduce new projects into the village runs up against the peasant's attempt to place him in the category of either a hypocritical do-gooder or an openly exploitative but manageable patron. It is deceptively easy to fall into the role of patron, cushioned by the flattery of the village and by the feeling that only in this way can anything get done. We had the idea of helping the boys of the village to start an agricultural club. The aim of this club, founded by Dr. Schwartz, has been to teach the boys new methods of farming and animal-raising, to give them the opportunity of earning some money by their work, and to stimulate a sense of responsibility and an experience of cooperation with their peers.

Perhaps we made our first error by giving them too much to start with, including hybrid seed, corn, chickens, milk-producing goats, pigs, and a cow. Instead of assuming responsibility, the boys treated us as patrons to whom they must remain submissive, awaiting orders. When because of bad luck and our inexperience, animals fell ill or the crops yielded little, the boys became apathetic and despairing instead of working harder. A volunteer from the American Friends Service Committee moved into the village to supervise the boys, but they worked well only so long as he was there. If he left for a few days, animals went thirsty and the fields stayed untended.

After two years of little progress, we decided to try to analyze with the boys the attitudes and feelings which caused their lack of initiative. Together with Señor Antonio de la Torre, the volunteer from the AFSC, I began to meet with the boys for two hours a week for a kind of group psychotherapy centered around the problems of work. At first the boys blamed their neglect of the animals on lack of time and lack of knowledge, but they soon saw this as a rationalization for deeper problems, since they had plenty of time to play and they avoided learning what we were eager to teach them.

What blocked their energy and self-development was the same feudal pattern of behavior that keeps the village from progressing as much as it might. Each boy felt his only bond within the club was his tie with us, the patrons. Cooperation meant only that if he worked more, others would work less and cut into his reward. Despite a new system of profits based on individual work, the boys still saw their fellows as rivals who were trying to get the most out of the club with the least work. Even in our meetings, when one boy spoke to another, it was to accuse him, never to support him. When the boys spoke to me, their words were tinged with guilt, as though they feared that whatever they did, I would be dissatisfied.

During the first meetings most of the time passed in painful silence. Finally I asked them to say what was on their minds. No one would speak, until Candido, the bravest and most responsible, admitted that he had been thinking about going to a dance that night. But he was afraid to tell me, sure that I would be angry. I said that I did not want to schedule meetings that conflicted with dances and that they were free to go, but I asked that we talk some more at the next meeting about their fear of saying what was on their minds.

In what followed we discussed the ever-present guilt that each boy felt before his parents and any other authority. He had been taught that to anger the authority for whatever reason meant punishment. Therefore, with parents, with employers, or with us, it was better to remain silent, to do only what one was told to do, to avoid any initiative. I pointed out to them how this attitude was rooted in centuries of hacienda life and how as long as they kept it, they would remain peons in their souls and never be free men. By accepting the idea that the right thing to do depends on another's judgment, they could never develop their own sense of right, they could never be the masters of their own activity, and they would always be more interested in escaping punishment than in their work.

After this meeting there was a surge of initiative and responsibility, but when I asked the boys what had happened when Antonio left for a few days, they all turned their eyes sheepishly to the ground. "I heard that you did a good job by yourselves," I said. Yes, it had been true, but they were unable to give themselves credit. The other side of guilt about disobeying authority was the conviction that nothing they did could be praiseworthy, for no one had ever stimulated the sense of satisfaction in a job well done. Their only rewards resulted from obedience.

We tried to interest the fathers of the boys in the club so that when we left, there would be a continuing direction. The club had by now grown to the stature of a small business with valuable animals and some 350 chickens which produce 220 eggs a day. But the parents either lacked interest or felt that like every other cooperative enterprise begun in the village, this would fail. Naturally, this attitude, well known by the boys, weakened their confidence.

In a last attempt to enlist the support of the fathers and mothers, we called a meeting. When the parents heard about the difficulties the boys had in cooperating, and the losses due to negligence, they were all for giving up the club. One father said, "You should move the club to a village that will appreciate it."

"Why do you waste your time?" asked another. "These boys are not worth it." We assured the fathers that the boys had done a great deal, and that we would not leave until the club was financially solid, but privately we wondered how the club would carry on without help from the older generation and how the boys who were present at the meeting would react to their fathers' fatalism and lack of hope.

At our next reunion, I asked them what they had thought of the meeting. By this time the group of boys who came to these discussions had shrunk from twenty to a hard core of six of the older boys, who always came. One said that the meeting seemed fine. He was immediately challenged by the others. "What do you mean fine?" asked Cheque. "They have no interest in helping us, they think we are no good, and they want the club to end." Cheque and others realized that they could expect no support from their parents, and they decided that they could do without it. "Already we know more about chickens than they do," said one boy, "and we have learned how to market the eggs. Even if they were to help, they would only order us around and take the profits."

After this discussion the boys began for the first time to cooperate in setting a day in which each one took the others' animals to pasture. Together they built a roof for the corral in which their goats were quartered. They demanded that others cooperate or leave the club. Those of the older boys who had before shunned any leadership in order not to seem to put themselves ahead of others accepted the fact that if they did not lead, nothing would be done. They organized a dance to raise money; and taking advantage of the Mexican love of lotteries, they sold chances on a pig, realizing a greater profit than they would have made in the market. They began to think of new projects, such as fixing up a village bathhouse, long run-down by disuse, and charging a few cents for showers. They petitioned and received village approval for the project.

It is still too early to conclude that these changes in attitudes will last. These boys who are now fifteen and sixteen years old will soon leave the club, marry, and work for their own families. Then the test will be whether they maintain the fraternal ties of the club, based neither on family nor on personal advantage but on shared work and play. As adults, will they have both the interest and ability to help another generation of boys? As fathers, will they encourage their sons' independence?

The aim of this project was not to change the village but to see whether the young people on their own could respond to opportunity. It is interesting to note, although statistically speculative, that just as 15 to 20 percent of the adult population can be characterized as loving and productive, so five out of twenty of the boys have become responsible and cooperative. Perhaps our project has done little more than encourage the growth of those who with maturity might have developed anyway. But these boys are becoming different from the older peasants, who are still limited by the feeling that community progress is impossible and that love and interest are rooted only in the family and their own land. Unlike their fathers, the boys are learning that leadership does not invariably mean exploitation, that a man can work with another who is neither his patron nor his peon.

Fatalism, distrust, and hopelessness were born in the experience of the hacienda and reinforced by the scarcity of land and living, common to peasants everywhere. Since the revolution, some peasants have taken advantage of the greater opportunities. Others have fallen back into old ruts. Still others have left the village to work in the city or, under the bracero program, have traveled to the United States for a few months a year, where they earn more than they could make in the village. In the future, economic necessities will probably move more peasants from the villages into the cities. Industries will need more workers; good land is scarce, and the small holdings of the peasant are inefficient for a nation which must increase its food supply. Many of the young boys say they would go to the city if they could be assured of a good job, such as that of auto mechanic. A few aspire to be teachers, doctors, or engineers. But almost half of the others prefer to work in the fields, if they can make a living. To Aristeo's remark that when tilling the soil one is only burned by the sun, they answer that in an

auto-repair shop one cannot breathe. "Besides," says Candido,
"here in the country one can work with animals. And I like
to be in the hen house, because the chickens sing to me."

SAM
SCHULMAN

LATIN AMERICAN
SHANTYTOWN*

IN BRAZIL it is called *favella*; in Argentina, *banda de miseria*;
in Peru, *barriada*. In Colombia it is *tugurio*. But whatever the
name, its characteristics are the same: It is the rudest kind of
slum, clustering like a dirty beehive around the edges of any
principal city in Latin America.

In the past two decades poor rural people have flocked to
the cities, found no opportunities but stayed on in urban fringe
shantytowns, squatting squalidly upon the land. In modern
Caracas or cosmopolitan Lima, as in tens of other Latin-American cities, a glance at the surrounding hills is a view of misery
at its worst. Death is easy and often. Hunger and pain are
facts of everyday life.

Traditional living patterns undergo intense strain and often
give way in these slums. Living almost like animals, the *tugurio*'s
residents are overwhelmed by animality. Religion, social control, education, domestic life are warped and disfigured.

For more than nine months my wife and I studied and
worked in such a slum—the "Barrio of 65" ("the 65th Street
Neighborhood")—a hillside shanty settlement in Bogotá. The
barrio clings to the rounded knobs and slopes of the small foot-
hills at the base of the Andes along the eastern edge of the
city. A wide dirt path, an extension of Calle 65 (65th Street),

* From the *New York Times Magazine*, January 16, 1966. Copyright
© 1966 by the New York Times Company. Reprinted by permission.

winds through the area and gives it its name. There are about 250 individual dwelling units and about 1,200 residents.

Throughout Latin America, extensions of the central city have been traditional living areas for the poor. Squatting has always been an accepted mode of life, and even at the turn of the century, small isolated squatters' holdings began to spring up around Bogotá. With the beginning of national strife after the assassination of the Liberal Party leader, Jorge Eliecer Gaítan, in 1948, thousands ran for safety to Bogotá. The city could not absorb them. It had neither industry nor services to provide places for the illiterate and untrained country people.

They spilled over into the uninhabited or sparsely settled hills bordering Bogotá's poor sections and remained, building hovels. In the lower part of the Barrio of 65, property owners expanded their facilities, adding a few more rooms facing a courtyard, building additional shacks nearby, and renting these out for nominal fees to the newcomers. As the newcomers kept coming, spaces between shacks and more permanent dwellings were filled: a few more scraps of cardboard, a few more rolled-out oil cans, a few slabs of corrugated iron for rooms. These, too, were soon rented.

About four years ago, several of the tenants of the lower barrio, tired of paying rent, began an invasion of a large municipally held hill above them. With the settlement upon the hill a new phase of the barrio's growth began, and, month by month, a few more shacks crept upward. In 1966 they are still creeping.

And they are still creeping up most of the other hills bordering the poor areas of Bogotá. At present, one in every 10 residents of this city of more than 1.7 million lives in a hillside *tugurio*. Seven out of 10 urbanites in Colombia are poor, but the *tugurio* is the worst face of urban poverty.

There is no real water supply in this *tugurio*. Women and children fetch water in old oil or lard cans from a municipal hydrant at the base of a hill. Only a few homes have electricity— illegally secured by tapping the electric company's power line. A few houses have one- or two-burner bottled-gas stoves; most residents cook over small wood fires around each of which are placed three large stones supporting a cooking pot.

The barrio has about 20 latrines. A few belong to special families, and their doors are secured by padlocks. Others are not so exclusive; they belong to groups of people or to compounds. In every case, foul water carrying human excrement floats from under the privies and runs in black rivulets down paths of the barrio. Children play alongside and in the contaminated streams.

It is no surprise that endemic and epidemic diseases run rampant. Children are the chief victims. A measles outbreak may kill large numbers of youngsters. Infant diarrheas, upper respiratory infections, malnutrition also take a high toll.

Diets are typically protein-low, if not completely protein-absent. The average daily fare is built largely around potatoes, rice and a hot drink made from unrefined sugar. When it is possible—and it rarely is—a heavy soup is made from scraps of meat or fish that have been classified as unsalable in local food markets. Perhaps a chicken that has been carefully raised among the children and debris of the barrio is added.

Sheep, hogs, a few cows are seen, but they are usually raised for sale. A burro or two are the prized animals of only a few, and these are used to aid in the dull and heavy tasks associated with slum life—hauling water, firewood, or clothes to be laundered in a ravine a few blocks away.

Living space is extremely limited. In the lower area of the Barrio of 65 a family usually has a single room and a small lean-to for cooking. Houses of the upper barrio are larger. They, too, may consist of only a single room, or the space may be partitioned into several rooms of minimal dimensions. Most of the barrio's residents live close to one another. A child being spanked is heard by 50 neighbors. The total effect is that of masses of tightly packed shacks ringing small common patios. Here clothes are hung to dry, garbage is accumulated, a hog and some chickens are enclosed, and here the children pass most of their day.

A typical house has a low ceiling and a dirt floor. A rustic door or curtain at the entrance shields the residents from wind, rain and passersby. Windows are rare. In this dingy room, a family sleeps, dresses, eats and attends to its personal necessities. One or two narrow beds—usually handmade cots or their cheap, poorly made commercial equivalents—are placed against the walls. One bed is usually reserved for adults, who often sleep with the youngest child. Other children sometimes crowd five to a bed. More hardy youngsters roll up in blankets and sleep on the earth floor.

A wooden trunk, containing most of the family's possessions, is placed alongside a bed. Atop the trunk is the family's wash-basin. A chair or two and a small table may be wedged in among the other things. Clothes, especially "Sunday" clothes, are hung on the wall, the door, the headboard of a bed, or may dangle down from the ceiling. Beneath one of the beds is the dwellers' chamberpot. Profusely ornamenting the walls are re-ligious pictures and a photograph or two: the bride at marriage, the husband doing his stint in military service, the baptism or confirmation of a child.

This can be home for a dozen people. Privacy is unheard of, and all know the extreme intimacies of human contact. Only darkness hides the nakedness of this contact.

The home has no real facility for bathing. And washing is not a cherished custom. Faces and hands of children and adults may be cleaned, hair combed or brushed for receiving visitors, attending mass or going to the local church. But usually the living area smells heavily of continued, unwashed occupation, and is usually in disarray. The chamberpot often is not emptied after each use, but only when it is full. Then it is dumped into one of the few latrines, a drainage gutter or the paths that serve as streets in the barrio. Children grow up with the sounds of sleeping, eating, evacuation and sexual relations—of their own family, and their neighbors—in their ears.

In this setting, traditional norms of family life are challenged. Most of the barrio's residents still have their roots in the country. But Colombia's rural poor still retain their basic peasant dignity. There are free spaces and clean air beyond their shacks; there is a tiny garden growing products for home consumption; there is no sharp comparison between peasant life and the affluence of many others. Close by, perhaps, is the master's fine home, but it is a singular jewellike exception to those of his peasants. In the city, whole neighborhoods of fine homes and vast numbers of "better" people are only blocks away from the *tugurio*. There is no longer free space and tiny gardens. And the peasant's dignity is buried in urban poverty's abyss.

In such a setting, there is little feeling of community. True, when outside authorities seek to exert control within the barrio, residents may come together in common defense. But generally they are tied only by the bond of misery, and do not help each other.

Violence is common. A weekend seldom passes without some explosive episode. The men, whose chief recreation is playing a rustic pitch-and-toss game called *tejo* and drinking beer, may dispute a point and fall into a drunken fight with fists or knives. A backyard rivalry or sexually based competition among women may result in a stabbing. Habitually, men castigate both their women and their children by beating them, and a mother's reprimand to a child is often a hard slap or a switch across the face or bottom. Brutality is part of life, and is accepted.

Unemployment is another fact of life. Economic need is so great in the barrio that young people try to obtain jobs as soon as they can, if jobs are available. It is easiest for young girls to secure positions as beginners in domestic service: They earn between $3 and $4 a month, and are supplied uniforms, sleeping quarters and food. The relatively few men in the barrio are employed at simple tasks—when they can find work—such as gardening and construction.

But squatters, never an integrated part of the greater community of Bogotá, face the employment dilemma of most other deprived peoples: "Last to be hired, first to go." And unemployment has soared in the city. In late 1965 it amounted to almost 20 percent of the labor force. Those who have suffered most are the unskilled people of the *tugurios*. Mothers and children are often seen in better neighborhoods begging. Idleness, extreme poverty and need have forced some of the men to become petty sneak thieves; some of the women have turned to prostitution; many of the children have become street gamins.

Unemployment and disrupted family structures go hand in hand. More than half, perhaps as many as two-thirds, of the family units in the barrio are quasi families, lacking a permanent father. A few have no mother or father, and children live with grandparents, aunts, godparents or friends. Abandoned women with children are commonplace. A man feels little obligation to the woman he lives with and seldom participates in guiding the development of children. In an almost totally Roman Catholic country, people of the barrio do not have time, money, or ambition to indulge in the requisites of the church. A "free union," a condoned form of sexual alliance, is the dominant form of marriage in the slums. Partners are married as long as they wish to remain married.

There are, of course, some couples in the barrios who are both legally and religiously married, but they are rare exceptions. Their marriage is not seen as something "better." In the eyes of other residents, they have had "more luck," "more money" or "more pull."

Outside the barrio, however, a religious marriage is thought to have greater prestige and slum couples will invent such an event to keep from being humiliated. In a recent series of interviews, a field worker reviewed the details of their "marriage" with a pair from the barrio, speaking to each member individually. Both said they had been married in the church, but each gave the name of a different church and even a different date for the event.

But any man and woman who live together in the barrio are considered "married," and the woman is addressed as *"Señora."* It is also custom to call an unmarried mother by the same term: She is a *señora*, though she is single. Children born to any "married" couple will bear their father's surname; those born to a single woman will bear hers.

Barrio women have many children. Contraception, even the simplest kind, is not understood. It is not unusual for a married woman to have had 10 or 12 pregnancies. Many babies die at birth. But the death of a child is not a horrible event. There is grief, but also a feeling that the "tiny angel" goes directly to heaven. There is also the feeling the child is fortunate to meet God without having to endure the hardship of adult life. It is a rare family in the barrio that does not have one or more *angelitos.*

Even in homes where the husband or male partner is seldom

present, he is the undisputed source of authority. A husband's needs are met before those of any other member of the family. He eats first, and the best of what little there may be. Children do not disturb him when he is resting. Spending money for beer while his children beg for food is not considered wrong.

Even the health of others is subordinated to his needs. Children are not taken to the local clinic when they are ill because their mothers must spend most of their mornings preparing lunch for working husbands. It would have angered the men if lunch were not brought to the job on time. Women make long treks on foot or in overcrowded buses with freshly cooked food to keep their men in good spirits. A seriously ill child might die for lack of attention on one hand; a woman might face a beating, social castigation and possible desertion on the other.

All important decisions are made by men. The role of a woman is simply caretaker of the home and children. Children are brought up by their mothers and seldom have an adequate example of an adult male on which to orient their lives. When a man is not working, he spends his time with his cronies, not with his youngsters.

Some mothers will lock their children in shacks for hours on end while doing day work. The money earned is quickly given to the husband. One completely happy young man, living in his mother's house with his wife and child, felt extremely fortunate: his mother had a steady job and his wife worked several days a week. He did not work. He would periodically look for a job, but he was not driven to finding work. There was no need to do so while his women were employed.

Family life in a *tugurio* is based upon simple, uncluttered, primitive norms. It reflects the attitude of people who know and expect only harshness. Yet there are few ugly children. They are beautiful, with the smooth skins and large dark eyes of the Colombian mestizo; they are joyful, playing along the dirt paths and in the contaminated waters of the barrio. But life's harshness bends them. Women age while still young, and men are content to be brutes. The barrio, in the end, makes its people as ugly as itself. Families cannot help but mirror the harsh and ugly total social milieu that encompasses them.

Each year, the barrio forces itself more and more on its

residents. Few can leave, for there is really no place to go. Gradually fear of the "outside" develops.

In mid-1965 two families were offered the opportunity to leave and start new lives with adequate financial support from an agency of the municipal government. Both refused: the first, because the barrio had always been "home" and its members wanted their roots to be maintained; the second, because of intense fear of all the unknowns of an inimical big city.

The *tugurio* is a deep intellectual and spiritual crevice filled with constant misery and peopled with depressed and passive human lives. Escape is virtually impossible and, when a way out is allowed a select few, they do not understand. They suspect it, and remain in the depths. And the depths will remain for decades. The *tugurio* is firmly rooted in Colombian urban life.

There are some men—their numbers are small, but they are growing—of goodwill and insight who are profoundly disturbed, and passionately concerned wth the eradication of these sub-human clusters. Msgr. Ruben Isaza, Bishop Coadjutor of Bogotá, has called them "malignant tumors that have grown upon my city" and, along with others of his countrymen, is working for their displacement and for the betterment of the social and economic factors which have created them. There is much planning, and there are the beginnings of action programs. The Mayor of Bogotá is dedicated to a platform of slum clearance, and has given first priority to the *tugurios*. The Colombian Army has established labor battalions to help construct low-cost homes for *tugurio* inhabitants. The Alliance for Progress has given substantial sums—and will continue to give them—to assist the Colombian Government's urban resettlement agencies in the diminution of the *tugurios*. High-school and university students, religious groups, citizens' organizations, the major newspapers of Bogotá and other cities—all have voiced concern and are urging development programs to remedy a condition which they admit is abhorrent, dangerous and shameful to their national pride.

But the Colombian economy is too weak to support a full-scale "war against poverty." The fight against the *tugurios*, the scores of barrios like the Barrio of 65, moves at a slow pace, and the problem is large—growing a little bit larger every day.

WITH THE

EDUARDO
GALEANO

GUERRILLAS

IN GUATEMALA*

CÉSAR MONTES, the leader of one of the two principal guerrilla groups operating in the Guatemalan countryside, unfolded an Esso map of his country. He was standing in a jungle clearing. "See here?" he said. "This is where the guerrillas started, in the Sierra de las Minas. Later they spread to the north—to the Vera Paces, the Indian regions, and then into the lowlands— Rio Hondo, La Palma, San Cristóbal, Rosario, Gualán, San Agustín, and Teculután. For some time now we have also been operating in the western region, the most densely populated Indian areas. Half the people in Guatemala are Indians, and you can be sure they will play a decisive role in our revolution. But it is a slow and difficult job. We are faced with four centuries of distrust which the Indians have had for the whites and the mestizos." Montes proudly pointed out several Indian guerrillas in his encampment, and added that they were devoted Catholics.

It seemed fitting that Montes was using an Esso road map to explain the whereabouts of the Guatemalan guerrillas. Although he had personally learned the art of warfare by actual fighting, a number of other guerrilla leaders had been taught by U.S. Army officers. Luis Augusto Turcios, a former commander of Montes' FAR (*Fuerzas Armadas Revolucionarias*) who was recently killed in an automobile accident at the age of twenty-four, had been trained at the Army Ranger school at Fort Benning, Georgia. Yon Sosa, the commander of the other guerrilla group, MR-13, which controls part of Izabal in northeastern Guatemala, learned guerrilla warfare from U.S. instructors at Fort Gulick in the Panama Canal Zone.

But, of course, what the American military is trying to do is

* Translated by Bernardo García-Pandavenes. From *Ramparts*, September 1967.

not to train the guerrillas themselves, but the people trying to suppress them. Even more so than with other Latin American countries, the U.S. is quietly pouring arms, money and "advisors" into the anti-guerrilla effort in Guatemala. It is an involvement beginning to look ominously like the U.S. presence in South Vietnam in the years before American combat troops arrived there. The war is no longer just Guatemala's.

Just what the extent of American military involvement is, no one knows for sure. Many Guatemalan officers have been trained by the U.S. Army at bases in the Canal Zone and in the U.S. itself. But U.S. involvement is greater than this. The guerrillas themselves claimed at one time that one thousand members of the U.S. Special Forces were aiding the Guatemalan Army. This figure seems high, but the U.S. government has officially admitted the participation of men from the U.S. Eighth Special Forces group in the military training of Guatemalans.

A former Guatemalan Army sergeant told me about the courses in anti-guerrilla warfare he took from Special Forces instructors: "The classes were held at the 'La Cajeta' farm in Zacapa. We were there from May to October of last year. They told us that Cubans were heading the Guatemalan guerrillas. They taught us camouflage techniques, how to survive in the mountains, how to undo booby traps. As for prisoners, we were advised to do away with them whenever we were not able to take them with us."

General Robert W. Porter, Jr., commander of the U.S. Southern Army Command in Panama, told the House Committee on Foreign Affairs in April 1966 that the U.S. Army engineers and rangers were working on "civic action" programs in the border zone where troops from Guatemala and Honduras have been fighting guerrillas. The "civic action" consists mostly of distributing powdered milk, medicines and promises to villagers under guerrilla influence. "The guerrillas must first be close by before we even get water," a peasant from the Izabal region said to me. But from reports both by Guatemalans and American newspapermen, it appears that American military involvement in Guatemala consists of more than "civic action," and is roughly similar to what it was in South Vietnam during the years before

U.S. combat troops arrived there: the U.S. supplies many arms to the Guatemalan Army, American "advisors" accompany Army units on missions, and high-level advisors dispense their advice at offices in the headquarters of the various armed forces, the Ministry of Defense, and even the national police department. And on some occasions the U.S. appears to have dispensed more than advice. In an interview, Guatemalan Vice President Don Clemente Marroquín Rojas told me that one time a squadron of U.S. planes flown by U.S. pilots took off from Panama, made a napalm bombing raid on a suspected guerrilla camp on a Guatemalan mountainside and returned to Panama without even landing in Guatemala. It is obvious that the U.S. considers Guatemala a test case for the survival of guerrilla movements in Latin America, and that it is not willing to risk another Cuba.

The forces of Yon Sosa and César Montes have squabbled fiercely over doctrinal differences, but now seem on their way to a united front. Besides their war against the Guatemalan Army, the two guerrilla movements have something else in common: many of their members and leaders are very young. Montes is twenty-five. One of his deputies, nicknamed Manzana (which means apple in Spanish—he got the name for having a red face) is only twenty and has been with the guerrillas since he was seventeen; two older deputies are only twenty-four.

The guerrillas have to be young to survive. Their life is grueling and they have to keep walking to retain their advantage of surprise and to avoid the regular-Army forces pursuing them. Often all they have to eat are boiled wild leaves with salt. They keep moving continuously, clearing their way through the wet jungle with machetes. "Our columns are extremely mobile," Montes says. "This is why the Army can never catch us, despite all the operations they have launched. We have several patrols operating in different parts of the country. They have not been able to capture any of our camps for a simple reason: we never set up fixed camps. Only a few of our food deposits have been discovered, but that is all. It is hard to walk so much, but you soon become used to it. Guerrillas have walked, for instance, from the Izabal Lake to San Agustín Acasaguastlán, which means you have to go across the highest peaks in Guatemala. We have been able to do that in twenty days, without stopping, going from six in the morning until sundown every day, just eating breakfast before leaving and supper before going to sleep." Most of his troops, Montes said, are farmers; a few are students.

César Montes himself is called El Chiris, a Guatemalan word meaning small child. Slightly built, he has features that seem almost delicate. "Don't ask me to look mean in a photograph because no one would be taken in," he laughingly told me. At the age of thirteen, he was expelled from a Catholic school, due to his fury over the CIA's coup against the leftist Arbenz regime. At eighteen he led student demonstrations and saw his fellow students shot dead before his eyes. At twenty he went to the mountains. By twenty-four he was leader of one of the most important guerrilla movements in Latin America.

In order to bring the local peasants over to their side, both groups of Guatemalan guerrillas use the method known as *propaganda armada* ("armed propaganda"). This, incidentally, is a method the Cuban guerrillas never practiced: guerrillas go into villages, occupy them for a few hours, explain to the peasants the principles behind their fight, and leave cell-like committees behind them. The guerrillas feel they can only succeed with the support of the peasants. "The peasants are the eyes and the ears of the guerrillas," says Yon Sosa of MR-13. "We are always kept informed about the enemy, and the enemy never finds out where we are. They would have to do away with the whole population to defeat us. But before that ever happens, we will have turned the enemy into dust." The guerrilla weapons I saw included .45 caliber Thompson machine guns, Belgian Brownings and other automatics of Swedish and German makes, Garand guns of World War II vintage, a few M-1s and some Colt .45s. "The Army claims it takes weapons from us quite often," César Montes said, "but they have never been able to show any of our weapons to be Cuban, Czech or Soviet. And they have never found any foreign soldiers in our ranks. Our weapons don't come from Cuba, but from the Guatemalan Army itself. We buy them. If they are capable of selling their country, why wouldn't the soldiers sell their weapons? And everyone knows where our money comes from: we collect ransoms from kidnapping big capitalists who have been exploiting Guatemalan workers for years. We always choose exploiters who are widely hated by everyone."

Montes was deeply scornful of the American "advisors" who are helping the Guatemalan Army in its anti-guerrilla operations. In a sophisticated way, he knows that they too have read Mao and Guevara: "They operate in a mechanical way. They have read in Mao's works that the guerrilla is to the people what the fish is to water, and they know that fish die when taken out of water. They really believe that they can do the same thing to us, that they can isolate us. And perhaps they can deceive part of the people part of the time, but not the whole time. The peasants need land but they don't have any. They need housing, but the government builds homes for military officers. You cannot stop the peasants from helping us when you don't give them the things that they need." Montes was holding Pope Paul VI's encyclical *Popularum Progressio*, from which he read at random: ". . . Farmers become aware that they are undeserving of poverty . . . the scandal of painful disparities . . ." he winked. "The Pope is more intelligent than the Guatemalan right. Read this over and you will see how clearly he explains the causes of violence."

Montes described to me how an American named Ronald Hornberger had once come to the guerrillas claiming to be a newspaperman. "He acted very confident; we talked with him in the mountains for a few days. He dropped names and addresses from the capital, but we double-checked within a few days and found that none of the people he had mentioned had ever heard of him. He also lied about the place he had supposedly left his luggage. He seemed to be interested only in the military aspects of our struggle and not at all in our political motivations. All his questions were of a highly specialized military nature. He was an ace in the handling of any weapon. He brought some military equipment which he said was a gift to us. We tried him and executed him. On his waist under the shirt he wore a fine nylon cord, the kind used by Green Berets for strangling."

The U.S. has given napalm bombs and other arms to Guatemalan troops, and sometimes crops and fields are razed in an effort to deprive the guerrillas of their food supply. As in Vietnam, this kind of action often results in the killing of innocent peasants, and the turning of more and more people against the regime. A guerrilla described to me how on the Alexandria Mountain near Río Hondo, he and a band of other guerrillas discovered the bodies of five peasants charred by napalm beyond recognition lying in the middle of a field.

If ever there was a country ripe for revolution, Guatemala is it. An article by Dan Kurzman in the *Washington Post* of March 13, 1966, refers to Guatemala as "a country that has made virtually no political, economic or social progress since the Communist-infiltrated government of President Jacobo Arbenz was overthrown in 1954." The article goes on to discuss the achievements of Castillo Armas, who was put into power in the place of Arbenz by a CIA coup in 1954: "Castillo Armas proved to be something less than a democratic crusader. Instead of pushing land reforms, he earned the indignation of many peasants by returning to the big landowners virtually all of the estimated 1.5 million acres expropriated by the Arbenz regime. . . . Guatemala has known little but stagnant dictatorship and corruption since 1954."

Take just one example of the tremendous gap between rich and poor in Guatemala: taxes. Any Economics 101 college student knows that progressive income taxes tend to reduce the gap between rich and poor, because the rich have to pay a somewhat higher proportion of taxes. Taxes on consumers, such as sales taxes, don't reduce the gap because they hit everyone equally. But out of the $119 million the Guatemalan government collects annually in tax revenues, *only 7 million comes from income or property taxes*, and that 7 million includes all the taxes paid by U.S. firms in Guatemala, like the United Fruit Company.

By every standard Guatemala's extreme poverty is appalling. Only 15 percent of the federal land is under cultivation. Only 750 tractors are in use in the entire country. The country is short one million housing units. In the province of Quiché, there is only one doctor per 120,000 people. A shortage of clinics, hospital beds and medicine extends throughout the entire country. But, ironically, Guatemala is one of the seven Latin American countries that is repeatedly praised by the State Department for having joined the U.S. in shipping medicine to South Vietnam. Out of every 10,000 children born alive, 1,200 die before the age of four. Most of the remainder are condemned to a life without schools, shoes, milk and toys. Seventy-five percent of the population is illiterate, shoeless, and gets less than one-third of the minimum daily food requirements. Three-quarters of the population earn twenty cents a day or less. A quart of milk costs two days of labor for the peasant of Alta Verapaz; three days of labor will pay for a pound of meat.

Guatemala's Army is probably the only one in the world which has one colonel for every thirty men. In many other ways as well, it is corrupt and inefficient, the officers more interested in their fat salaries and special vacations than in pursuing their duties. The morale of enlisted men—many of whom have been "shanghaied" while wandering drunkenly along a city street and enlisted against their will, like sailors in the old British navy—is appallingly low. When a private is killed in battle, his corpse is seldom returned to his relatives. Given these conditions, it is not surprising that the American military has taken such a strong interest in beefing up the Guatemalan Army's will and ability to resist the guerrillas.

Far from alleviating the misery and poverty of Guatemala, American involvement in that country has done much to cause it. Until 1944, Guatemala had been just another Central American "banana republic." It was ruled by the dictator Ubico, a pro-Nazi general, who looked out for the interests of North American corporations and the local oligarchy. But when he was overthrown by the 1944 popular revolution, a vigorous plan for widespread education was put into effect, and the Indians began to become politically conscious, farm workers and city workers started joining labor unions, and Guatemala seemed to be demonstrating that a Latin American country can, on its own accord, break away from backwardness and poverty. The Arbenz regime accelerated many of these reforms, and in the first months of 1954, more than 100,000 Guatemalan families had received new land under the agrarian reform law. Then Washington decided that the Arbenz regime was "Communist-infiltrated" and was setting a dangerous example, and the CIA started preparing an invasion against Guatemala, with the blessing of the OAS. Included among the indignant Latin American leaders who raised their hands to condemn the Arbenz regime at a special OAS conference were some of the bloodiest dictators in the history of the continent: Batista, Trujillo, Somoza, Pérez, Jiménez, Odría, Rojas, Pinilla and others.

Castillo Armas, a graduate of the U.S. Command and General Staff College at Fort Leavenworth, Kansas, invaded Guatemala with troops trained and paid by the United States. His invasion was supported by C-47 bombers piloted by the CIA. When he had taken over the country, Castillo Armas returned all the expropriated uncultivated land to the big landlords and gave away millions of acres of the country to an international oil cartel. The Guatemalan Oil Act was written in English and sent to the Guatemalan Congress in that language to be passed. One Congressman, who still had some sense of dignity left, requested that it be rendered into Spanish. Opposition newspapers which had operated freely under Arbenz were closed; democratic political leaders, students and labor union officers were sentenced to death, prison or exile. Finally Armas himself was assassinated. "It is a great loss to his own nation and for the whole free world," Eisenhower said. The forces of the right and of the Guatemalan military have been in control of the country most of the time ever since.

One day early in 1967, in an office in downtown Manhattan, blood rushed to the face of Abraham Weber as he shouted, "I am never going to allow a small Central American country to impose its will on an American company! Do you understand?" The person he was addressing was a Guatemalan, Carlos Rafael López Estrada, who had just resigned as the lawyer for the IRCA (International Railways of Central America). The IRCA used to belong to the United Fruit Company until a New York court applied the anti-trust law and forced United Fruit to get rid of it. The railway ended up in the hands of investors Abraham Weber and Louis Yaeger. Guatemala hasn't profited one centavo by the change. These foreign trains, the only ones the country has, look as if they were taken from a documentary on the Mexican Revolution of 1910: ancient and squeaky, practically useless, they render the poorest service imaginable. The IRCA doesn't pay taxes. Yet in Guatemala, even Indians who use carts to carry their produce to market and even bicycle owners must pay taxes. The railways do not even pay their own mailing expenses. The state no longer has the right to check the company's records. The IRCA statement that it is losing money is accepted as the truth. Weber's rage against López Estrada came because the lawyer had suggested a few discreet changes in the arrangement between the railway and the Guatemalan government, "to give the government the feeling that its sovereignty was recognized," as López Estrada put it to me.

American involvement in Guatemala since 1954 has not been restricted to exploiting the country's economy. Recent revelations have shown that the U.S. exercised a decisive hand in Guatemalan internal politics even after the CIA's 1954 coup. An article in the *Chicago Daily News* last December revealed that "the U.S. instigated and supported the 1963 coup by the Guatemalan military to overthrow the constitutionally elected President, Miguel Ydígoras Fuentes." The reason for American support of the coup, the newspaper said, was to forestall what was thought to be an imminent victory in the Guatemalan presidential election by Juan José Arévalo, who had been President from 1944 to 1950 and who, despite his non-Communist stance, was too far left for American comfort. The paper goes on to explain why the American-supported military coup led to some of Guatemala's problems today: "This is because it [the Guatemalan coup] was followed by a military dictatorship whose unpopularity helped a Castroite guerrilla movement to flourish."

The military regime which came to power after the 1963 coup finally did permit elections to be held early last year. But the middle-of-the-road government which was elected clearly depends on the Army for its existence. And the Army's behind-the-scenes influence shows who musters the real power.

In a recent pastoral letter, the Archbishop of Guatemala wrote about the "silence of cemeteries" being imposed upon his country. His reference was to the wave of right-wing terrorism which has swept through Guatemala unchecked for the past year. Newspapers provide their readers with daily accounts of corpses, mutilated or burned on the roadsides, or floating down the middle of the Motagua River, most of them forever unidentifiable. Fishing in the region of Gualán has stopped—far too many corpses have been found caught in the improvised dams the fishermen have built to catch fish. In Gualán itself, American military men frequently visit the home of Mariano Sánchez, the Guatemalan Army's local representative and the leader of the local terrorist gang which hunts down "Communists" with a fury reminiscent of the Indonesian massacres.

Under none of its former military dictatorships has Guatemala known a systematic terrorism like the one which has taken hold of the country under the present regime. Even members of the President's own party have been assassinated by right-wing armed gangs. These groups have close ties with the Army and enjoy its full protection.

A man I met in Guatemala City had received several warnings. He had been "advised" to leave the country. A friend of his had received a pathetic letter from the Mexican border: "They tortured me and I gave them your name. I know that you have nothing to do with it, but I had to tell them something, something . . . you can't begin to imagine. . . ." Another prisoner he knew had had his testicles crushed with a pair of pliers. The large majority of these so-called "Communists" are university professors whose sole crime consists in having participated in the reform governments of Arévalo and Arbenz. Or sometimes, they are relatives of government enemies. For instance, the brother of guerrilla commander César Montes, who lived a totally unpolitical life, was found dead, crushed by torture, three days after he was detained by the Army.

Mario Julio Ruano Pinzón, a former sergeant in the Guatemalan military police, told me his experience: he is the sole survivor of four soldiers who witnessed the machine-gun massacre of twenty-eight political and labor leaders a year ago in an Army warehouse. Three colonels were in charge of this job; one of them is now Minister of Defense, Colonel Arriaga Bosque. The soldiers had carried the bodies in bags, dripping in blood, to vehicles that took them to an airplane, from which the bodies were then dumped into the Pacific. Three of the soldiers later died. One was found stabbed to death in a boarding house, another was shot to death in a bar in Zacapa, the third was riddled with bullets in a bar behind the central station in Guatemala City. Julio Pinzón deserted. His photograph appeared in every newspaper. The Army is still looking for him.

Although the right-wing terrorist gangs officially operate without anyone's sanction, it is fairly clear that they represent the will of the Army. A *New York Times* story of July 14, 1967, under the headline "Guatemalan Rightists Outdo Reds in Terrorism," summed up the situation: "No amount of Army denial has been able to shake the conviction, widely held among most informed persons here, that most of the rightist, anti-Communist groups are, in fact, a creation of the Army and that many of their members are junior officers . . . these armed irregulars have been criticized for being so indiscriminate in their attacks that a large number of innocent persons, guilty perhaps of no more than leftist and liberal leanings, have been tortured, killed, or terrorized."

The terror goes on. Even in the center of the capital, men have been dragged from their homes or gunned down on the streets. Newspapers report six, seven cases each day.

A new law implies that no member of the security forces may be held responsible for a crime of homicide. Certain of the big landowners have been legally raised to the level of local political authorities, with full rights to bear weapons and to form their own private police forces. Vice President Marroquín Rojas justifies this measure because, "The landowners constitute the vital source of production."

There could be no more helpful aid than a government like this in making César Montes and Yon Sosa the first successful revolutionaries on the mainland of Latin America. What gives the Guatemalan situation a significance beyond that small country is that the Pentagon, as in the cases of other revolutions lately, is backing the wrong side. And as long as that way of thinking prevails in Washington, there are likely to be as many Guatemalas in Latin America as there will be Vietnams in Asia.

C. MEANS TO AN END

INTRODUCTION

THE UNITED STATES spends less than one-half of one percent of its gross national product on foreign economic aid and this percentage seems likely to decline. Few industrialized nations do much better. France leads the world with just over one percent. Although the authors in this section make clear that simply spending more money is not enough, no attempt to reduce poverty in the world can hope to be effective without money and considerable amounts of it. The following articles concentrate on what the United States can do in attacking world poverty, but it is obvious that one country alone cannot do the job. Sizable contributions must be forthcoming from the rest of the industrialized world, both capitalist and Communist. The problems of poverty in the world are huge and complex, and no complete solution exists. Yet these conditions must not stop Americans from thinking, arguing, writing, and making a beginning, however partial and limited.

William Appleman Williams begins a search for possible answers with the suggestion that the United States must change its political response to revolution in the underdeveloped world. By opposing revolutions, he suggests, we are inhibiting the economic and social change needed to eventually bring democracy and stability to these nations. *Revolution in the Revolution?* is designed by its French journalist-author, Régis Debray (at this writing on trial in Bolivia) to be a handbook for Latin American revolutionaries. One of the book's theses is that ideology develops along with a revolutionary movement and cannot be imported or imposed. The implications of this analysis for our relationship with developing nations is serious.

The pattern of United States foreign aid must be changed if it is to achieve its objectives. Michael Brower offers suggestions for reducing waste and using our resources more efficiently. Amitai Etzioni analyzes the importance of pluralism in United States relations with the rest of the world. Since the bi-polar world of the postwar years no longer exists, Etzioni argues that American foreign policy must change to deal effectively with this new situation. Robert Asher outlines a program designed to serve both the needs of the underdeveloped nations and our own long-range goals. He warns that the aspirations of the underdeveloped world, though not realizable today or tomorrow, cannot be postponed indefinitely. In the concluding selection, Barbara Ward soberly reminds the powerful Western nations of their responsibilities toward their own citizenry, those who have neither power nor plenty, and the peace of the world.

WILLIAM APPLEMAN WILLIAMS

THE WISDOM OF AN OPEN DOOR FOR REVOLUTION*

The tradition of all past generations weighs like an Alp upon the brain of the living.
                                                    Karl Marx

It is not my duty as a historian to predict the future, only to observe and interpret the past. But its lesson is clear enough; we have lived too long out of contact with reality, and now the time has come to rebuild our lives.

Callitrax, historian of Lys, in *The City and the Stars,* by Arthur C. Clarke

* From *The Tragedy of American Diplomacy* by William A. Williams, World Publishing Company. Copyright © 1959 by William A. Williams.

Yes, strictly speaking, the question is not how to get cured, but how to live.

Marlow to Stein, in *Lord Jim*,
by Joseph Conrad

FUTURE HISTORIANS are apt to conclude that America's "total diplomacy" of the Cold War was governed by the principle of the boomerang. For in little more than a decade, the United States found itself confronted by a reality that was almost the opposite of the world it had confidently expected to emerge as the product of its program and policies. The Soviet Union neither surrendered nor collapsed nor embarked upon an effort to remodel itself in the image of Western liberalism. Instead, it continued its economic development and began to evolve and structure a Russo-Marxian system designed to institutionalize and regularize the politics of mature industrialism.

Throughout the rest of the world, America was confronted by revolutions which looked elsewhere (and within themselves) for inspiration, help, and guidance. Even its conservative and liberal allies began to turn away from the example and the advice of the United States. At home, meanwhile, the spirit of the people, the substance and form of politics, and the functioning of the economy all denied that the diplomacy of the cold war could be defended on the grounds that it had at least improved the nature and the tone of life in America.

Perhaps the most hopeful sign was the existence of a general, though vague and unfocused, awareness that the program and policies of the past were insufficient unto the present and the future. But while a growing number of leaders recognized the fact of failure, and even specified numerous symptoms, almost none of them seemed to grasp the origins of the crisis. For that reason they did not offer much in the way of a new approach.

One of the most revealing examples of the underlying doubt and confusion, and consequent stress on symptoms, was provided by Harry Schwartz in the *New York Times* of April 6, 1958. Since Schwartz was the Russian expert of the *Times* (which had vigorously supported the Cold War from its inception), a scholar whose books had emphasized the harshness, brutality, and weaknesses of Soviet society, and a political reporter and commentator who had exhibited little patience with critics of American policy, his article was particularly significant. It amounted, in more ways than one, to an admission that the failure of American policy had become news fit to print.

With considerable astuteness, Schwartz itemized the illusions upon which American policy was founded. He gave priority to the idea that the Soviet Union "will collapse," pointing out that it "has clearly been at the base of our postwar containment policy." His judgment was simple: it "seems unrealistic." Next he referred to the accepted idea that the conflict between America and Russia "is one between our absolute good and their absolute evil." He admitted that description was misleading because, "despite its evils and its demands, Communist rule in the Soviet Union has brought major advances in industrialization, in education and in health protection." As for the Soviet people, "they have made enough progress since the worst years of Stalin's rule to believe that the future will bring still more progress and will be more tolerable than the past."

In response to such harsh verities, some American leaders grasped fervently for Henry Wallace's old argument that the best way for America to recover lost ground—and come out on top—was to export an enlightened and updated version of the New Deal to India and other underdeveloped areas of the world. While certainly the most relevant program offered by any segment of American leadership, that proposal was nevertheless the product of a rather sophisticated naiveté which assumed that technicians, surplus food, and American machinery would convert wrong-headed revolutionaries into fine, upstanding liberals who turned their backs on false Communist gods that failed.

Considered against the backdrop of American foreign policy since 1890, such a proposal seemed impressively progressive. But when judged against the world scene, the result was startling: American leaders had reopened the great debate of the mid-1940s a decade too late. For Schwartz and others proposed little more than a liberalized and more effective version of the traditional Open Door Policy. They advised being more generous in extending economic aid and more intelligent in building "adequate communities of interest with other free nations." But the issues were neither generosity nor intelligence. America had exhibited and dispersed great quantities of both commodities.

The trouble was of a wholly different order. All segments of American leadership still shared the traditional objective of the 1890s: Stabilize the world in a pro-American equilibrium. Yet that conception of what could and should be done was precisely the cause of the continuing crisis. The scene recalled Alice in Looking-Glass Land running as fast as she could to stay under the same tree—with the vital difference that she was not succeeding in her effort. This image helped dramatize the point that America was not the victim of a simple case of failure, but rather was plagued by the infinitely more subtle paradox of the failure of success.

Though ridiculed and condemned by many experts and commentators (who nevertheless followed its essentials in their own policy recommendations and actions), the Open Door Policy had provided the strategy and tactics that enabled the United States to establish a new and persuasive empire during the era when the colonial empires of the eighteenth and nineteenth centuries were dying and being given the *coup de grâce* by the twentieth century revolutions in economics and politics, in the relationship between the colored and the white peoples of the world, and of anticolonial nationalism. The very success of the Open Door Policy enabled America to exercise varying degrees of economic, political, and military influence and authority in the very countries that were driving the British, French, and Dutch back to Europe. Such power also carried with it the spirit of American idealism and the vision of a better life for foreign peoples. And in many specific cases these ideals had to some extent been realized in the process of American expansion.

But the triumph of the Open Door Policy was subject to the same process of cause and consequence—of change—which carried it to victory in fifty years. These results were inherent in the conception of the world which originally produced the policy and which translated it into concrete programs and actions. Central to the failure in success was the fact that the Open Door Policy defined America as an alien power in the eyes and the experience of most of the rest of the world. The Open Door Policy did not cease being a program of imperial expansion simply because it spurned territorial and administrative colonialism in favor of an empire of economics, ideology, and bases.

Attracted by its anticolonial character, foreign peoples initially welcomed it as a policy of assistance and friendship with no strings of absentee ownership attached. But within a generation they sensed that its minimum objective was to stabilize and freeze the status quo of Western supremacy and that its optimum goal was to institutionalize American expansion. At the end of a half-century they were rebelling against the subordination of their own cultural, political, and economic life that was implicit in, and was practiced under, the policy of open-door expansion. Hence it is clear that any effort to rehabilitate the Open Door Policy would only serve now to compound the existing failure and crisis—there are no better policies to accomplish the purpose. The goal of an open-door empire has been achieved. It is necessary to change the objective. First, because the traditional one is impossible to sustain and, second, because there are viable alternatives available to the opponents of America's open-door empire. If clung to much longer, the policy of open-door expansion will very probably end by producing either the literal isolation or the nuclear destruction of the United States.

Considerable intellectual and emotional discipline and courage are required if Americans are to change—not merely revise —their conception of themselves and the world. These demands and difficulties are dramatically illustrated by American policy during the Korean War.[1] Immediately after the North Korean forces crossed the 38th parallel, and the United States had committed its forces in the battle, Secretary of State Ache-

---

[1] This discussion of the Korean war draws principally upon the materials in *Military Situation in the Far East. Hearings Before the Armed Services Committee and the Foreign Relations Committee, U.S. Senate,* 82nd Cong., 1st Sess. (5 Vols., 1951); Truman's *Memoirs;* and C. Whitney, *MacArthur: His Rendezvous with History,* Knopf, New York, 1956; but also on J. W. Spanier, *The Truman-MacArthur Controversy and The Korean War,* Harvard University Press, Cambridge, 1959, and the materials in his fine bibliography.

son publicly defined American policy in unequivocal terms. The United States was fighting, so he declared, "solely for the purpose of restoring the Republic of Korea to its status prior to the invasion from the north." This was a straightforward indication that American leaders, at least at that time in that situation, had reached the point of modifying their traditional strategy of the Open Door Policy. The war was not to be used to extend the policy, as had been done—or attempted—in World Wars I and II.

Within three months, however, that apparent modification had gone the way of Wallace. It had been dismissed. President Truman approved military operations north of the 38th parallel on September 11, 1950, very probably on the assumption that General MacArthur's landing at Inchon, scheduled for September 15, would be a success. Orders translating the President's decision to MacArthur were sent on the day of the invasion. When his brilliant and difficult operation at Inchon did turn the tables on the North Koreans, MacArthur advised Secretary of Defense Marshall of his proposed directive to troops crossing the parallel. Marshall promptly ordered the general to withhold the document. "We desire that you proceed with your operations without any further explanation or announcement and let action determine the matter. Our government desires to avoid having to make an issue of the 38th parallel until we have accomplished our mission."

The mission, as Acheson later revealed, was to realize one of the earliest, turn-of-the-century objectives in the strategy of the Open Door Policy. Put simply, it was to free Korea of Russian as well as Japanese influence. World War II had accomplished the latter; the Korean conflict would finish the job. Under American leadership, the United Nations General Assembly on October 7, 1950, approved a resolution authorizing "all appropriate steps to be taken to ensure conditions of stability throughout Korea." As Ambassador Warren Austin explained in supporting the resolution, the United States considered "the political aspect of the problem identified with the 38th parallel" to be "a matter of major concern."

Secretary Acheson was later asked the key question during a congressional investigation:

Senator Harry Cain: What, may I ask, were our United States forces doing on the shores of the Yalu River last November if it was not in an attempt to crush the aggressor and to unify Korea by force?

Acheson: General MacArthur's military mission was to pursue them and round them up . . . and, as I said many times, we had the highest hopes that when you did that the whole of Korea would be united. . . .

Senator Cain: If, sir, the Red Chinese had not entered the war, and our allied forces would have rounded up all those who were a party to the aggression in Korea, we would then have unified Korea by force; would we not?

Acheson: Well, force would have been used to round up those people who were putting on the aggression . . . unifying . . . it would be through elections, and that sort of thing.

Force would have played a part. . . .

Finally, it is clear that the attitude toward China that was an inherent part of the open door outlook served in a real sense to subvert the effort to apply the strategy of the Open Door Policy to Korea. The United States assumed that it could unify Korea by force because it did not believe, despite many indications to the contrary, that the Chinese Communists would intervene. And the explanation of that belief resides in one of the classic axioms upon which the Open Door Policy was based; namely, that China and Russia were natural enemies, and that China would therefore align itself with the United States.

The power and the momentum of the traditional outlook as revealed in the Korean episode do not justify any optimism about the magnitude of the effort involved in changing such established assumptions and habits of thought. Yet it is wiser to employ such courage and discipline for living than for dying. There is, indeed, no courage or discipline involved in following failure down the trail to disaster. Tragedy is a tool for the living to gain wisdom, not a guide by which to live. Joseph Conrad's penetrating advice for getting to the heart of a fundamental issue is more fruitful: "The way is to the destructive element submit yourself, and with the exertion of your hands and feet in the water make the deep, deep sea keep you up."

Applied to the issue of America's conception of itself and the world, that insight suggests that the first step is to deny the validity of the crucial assumptions which provide the foundation for that *Weltanschauung*. Thus a radically different concept replaces the accepted thesis that America's freedom and prosperity depend upon the continued expansion of its economic and ideological system through the policy of the open door. Instead, it appears that America's political and economic well-being depend upon the rational and equitable use of its own human and material resources at home and in interdependent cooperation with *all* other peoples of the world. America can neither take its place in nor make its contribution to the world community until it believes and demonstrates that it can sustain prosperity and democracy without recourse to open-door imperial expansion. The central issue of the mid-twentieth century is how to sustain democracy and prosperity without imperial expansion and the conflicts it engenders. The reason is obvious: the sparks from those collisions now fall into a nuclear tinderbox. It is all very well to converse bravely, seriously, and learnedly about surviving such a holocaust, but that is like sitting around the evening fire talking about what to do in the morning after the horse has been stolen instead of discussing ways and means of barring the barn door that night.

It is true that there are no completely foolproof locks, but it does not follow from that quite mundane observation that the risks of using the ones we have are greater than the risks and costs of getting along without the horse—or of buying another one. Yet this is precisely what we are doing when we give up on disarmament on the grounds that it cannot be 100 percent guaranteed in advance, and turn instead to discussions of how to intimidate the Soviets with superweapons, or of how to rebuild the United States after a nuclear war.

One of the most disturbing features of international affairs between 1952 and 1962 was the extent to which it was the Russians, rather than the Americans, who sensed and appreciated this essential aspect of reality. For this is the real meaning of the Soviet doctrine of coexistence. They are proposing that the existing political and military balance be accepted as the foundation of world politics for an indefinite period. It is ironic, but in a deadly way, that it has been the United States and China which have refused to agree to this proposition.

The American nonrecognition of Mao Tse-tung's government has served in this sense to mask an unspoken entente between them on this crucial point of policy. There is not even any conscious thought—let alone any conspiracy—involved on the American side of this agreement. For that matter, American policy makers seem wholly deaf and unconscious to the point despite the very broad hints that have been shouted from the Kremlin. As far as Washington is concerned, it could in this respect be called the best-kept secret treaty in the nation's entire history. The only way that the United States can break free of this entangling alliance with the Red Chinese is by accepting the Soviet doctrine of coexistence.

Americans must do this, not only to make it possible to slow down the dangerous momentum of the Cold War toward thermonuclear war, not only to strengthen the advocates of coexistence in China, but even more in order that Americans themselves can apply their intelligence and humanitarianism to the very real and serious problems in the United States. This proposal has nothing to do with reviving and embracing either the theory or the practice of isolationism. There is no longer any question of whether or not we shall have relations with the rest of the world; there is the far more significant one of the kind of relations we shall have. That problem cannot be discussed intelligently to any relevant conclusions so long as it is defined in the narrow terms of the existing approach. We need to ask questions about the very *nature* of the traditional foreign policy of the United States, not questions concerning merely the *means* of putting it into operation. The right kind of questions are admittedly those that make us squirm. But isn't it time to find out whether we can still take that kind of question?

Isn't it time to stop defining trade as the control of markets for our surplus products and control of raw materials for our factories? Isn't it time to stop depending so narrowly—in our thinking as well as in our practice—upon an informal empire for our well-being and welfare?

Isn't it time to ask ourselves if we are really so unimaginative that we have to have a frontier in the form of an informal empire in order to have democracy and prosperity at home? Isn't it time to say that we can make American society function even better on the basis of equitable relationships with other people?

Isn't it time to stop defining trade as a weapon against other people with whom we have disagreements? Isn't it time to start thinking of trade as a means to moderate and alleviate those tensions—and to improve the life of the other people?

Isn't it time to stop trying to expand our exports on the grounds that such a campaign will make foreigners foot the bill for our military security? Isn't it time instead to concern ourselves with a concerted effort to halt and then cancel the armaments race?

Isn't it time to stop saying that all the evil in the world resides in the Soviet Union and other Communist countries? Isn't it time to admit that there is good as well as evil in those societies, and set about to help increase the amount of good?

Isn't it time to admit that our own intelligence reports mean that the Russians have been following a defensive policy in nuclear weapons? Isn't it time to take advantage of that attitude on their part, break out of our neurosis about a Pearl Harbor attack, and go on to negotiate an arms control measure?

Isn't it time to admit, in short, that we can avoid living with Communist countries only by embarking upon a program that will kill millions of human beings? Isn't it time, therefore, to evolve and adopt a program that will encourage and enable the Communist countries to move in the direction of their own utopian vision of the good society as we endeavor to move in accordance with our own ideals?

For beyond acceptance of coexistence, the United States must embark upon a patient and concerted effort to establish and maintain by continued negotiation and development a *modus vivendi* with the Soviet Union, the People's Republic of China, and their allies. To this effort, economic agreements, involving normal credits and loans and a continuing increase of trade in consumer items and goods needed for general economic development, are basic. Such an approach will facilitate two processes essential to continued peace. First, it will open the way for continued reform within Communist countries. That will make it easier, secondly, for the United States to allocate its aid and assistance to other nations through the appropriate agencies of the United Nations. Future requests to the United States for aid should be referred to such committees of the United Nations for mutual discussion and decision. If approved, such grants should be administered by the United Nations. For if America's objective is the improvement of life throughout the world, then there is no better way to speed that process. Such a policy would also strengthen America's own position. For it is true, as Thucydides is reputed to have remarked, that the greatest exercise of power lies in its restraint.

Once freed from its myopic concentration on the Cold War, the United States could come to grips with the central problem of reordering its own society so that it functions through such a balanced relationship with the rest of the world, and so that the labor and leisure of its own citizens are invested with creative meaning and purpose. A new debate over the first principles and practices of government and economics is long overdue, and a statement of a twentieth century political economy comparable to *The Federalist* papers would do more to enhance America's role in the world than any number of rockets and satellites. The configuration of the world of outer space will be decided on the cool green hills of earth long before the first colonizing spaceships blast free of the atmosphere.

Having structured a creative response to the issue of democracy and prosperity at home, the United States could again devote a greater share of its attention and energy to the world scene. Its revamped foreign policy would be geared to helping other peoples achieve their own aspirations in their own way. The essence of such a foreign policy would be an open door for revolutions. Having come to terms with themselves—having achieved maturity—Americans could exhibit the self-discipline necessary to let other peoples come to terms with themselves. Having realized that "self-righteousness is the hallmark of inner guilt," Americans would no longer find it necessary to embark upon crusades to save others.

In this fashion, and through a policy of an open door for revolutions, Americans would be able to cope with the many as yet unknown revolutions that are dependent upon peace for their conception and maturation. Only in this way can either the general or the specific tragedy of American diplomacy be transcended in a creative, peaceful manner. Otherwise the next Cuba may very well be the last. For unless the existing attitudes and policies are changed, another Cuba will clearly be dealt with through military intervention involving American troops. And that—even without direct Soviet or Chinese retaliation in kind—could insure the final catastrophe.

Of course, such an American intervention would have profound and reactionary consequences in Russia and China, and hence upon the relationship between them. The result would be a further acceleration of the already very serious momentum toward thermonuclear war. It would very probably, whatever the outcome of the specific intervention by the United States, produce an increasing loss of control on both sides.

The way to transcend tragedy is to reconcile the contrasting truths which define the tragedy. Left instead to run out the string of their own logic, as they were and did in Cuba, the clashing truths will sooner rather than later kindle a global nuclear fire. To transcend tragedy requires the nerve to fail. But a positive effort to transcend the Cold War would very probably carry the United States and the world on into an era of peace and creative human endeavor.

For the nerve to fail has nothing at all to do with blustering and self-righteous crusades up to or past the edge of violence. It is instead the kind of quiet confidence that comes with and from accepting limits, and a concurrent understanding that accepting limits does not mean the end of existence itself or of the possibility of a creative life. For Americans, the nerve to fail is in a real sense the nerve to say—and mean—that we no longer need what Turner called "the gate of escape" provided by the frontier. It is only in adolescence or senility that human beings manifest a compulsive drive to play to win. The one does not yet know, and the other has forgotten, that what counts is how the game is played. It would actually be pathetic rather than tragic if the United States jumped from childhood to old age without ever having matured. Yet that is precisely what it will do unless it sloughs off the ideology of the Open Door Policy and steps forth to open the door to the revolutions that can transform the material world and the quality of human relationships.

Perhaps it is by now apparent to the reader that there is a basic irony involved in this conception and interpretation of American foreign policy as tragedy. This irony arises from, and is in that sense caused by, the truth that this essay is in two respects written from a radical point of view.

First, it is radical in that it seeks to uncover, describe, and analyze the character and logic of American foreign policy since the 1890s. It is therefore critical in the intellectual sense of not being content with rhetoric and other appearances, and of seeking instead to establish by research and analysis a fuller, more accurate picture of reality.

Second, it is radical in that it concludes from the research and reflection, that American foreign policy must be changed fundamentally in order to sustain the wealth and welfare of the United States on into the future. This essay recommends that the frontier-expansionist explanation of American democracy and prosperity, and the strategy of the Open Door Policy, be abandoned on the grounds that neither any longer bears any significant relation to reality.

This essay also points toward a radical but non-Communist reconstruction of American society in domestic affairs. And it is at this point that the irony appears: there is at the present time no radicalism in the United States strong enough to win power, or even a very significant influence, through the processes of representative government—and this essay rests on the axiom of representative government. Hence, ironically, the radical analysis leads finally to a conservative conclusion. The well-being of the United States depends—*in the short-run but only in the short-run*—upon the extent to which calm and confident and enlightened conservatives can see and bring themselves to act upon the validity of a radical analysis. In a very real sense, therefore, democracy and prosperity depend upon whether the New Frontier is defined in practice to mean merely a vigorous reassertion of the ideology and the policies of the past or to mean an acceptance of limits upon America's freedom of action.

The issue can be stated as a very direct proposition. If the

United States cannot accept the existence of such limits without giving up democracy and cannot proceed to enhance and
extend democracy within such limits, then the traditional effort
to sustain democracy by expansion will lead to the destruction
of democracy.

<table>
<tr><td>RÉGIS
DEBRAY</td><td>EXCERPTS FROM

REVOLUTION IN

THE REVOLUTION?*</td></tr>
</table>

WE ARE NEVER completely contemporaneous with our present.
History advances in disguise; it appears on stage wearing the
mask of the preceding scene, and we tend to lose the meaning
of the play. Each time the curtain rises, continuity has to be
re-established. The blame, of course, is not history's, but lies in
our vision, encumbered with memory and images learned in
the past. We see the past superimposed on the present, even
when the present is a revolution.

The impact of the Cuban Revolution has been experienced
and pondered, principally in Latin America, by methods and
schemas already catalogued, enthroned, and consecrated by
history. This is why, in spite of all the commotion it has provoked, the shock has been softened. Today the tumult has died
down; Cuba's real significance and the scope of its lessons,
which had been overlooked before, are being discovered. A
new conception of guerrilla warfare is coming to light.

Among other things, Cuba remembered from the beginning
that the socialist revolution is the result of an armed struggle
against the armed power of the bourgeois state. This old
historic law, of a strategic nature if you like, was at first given

* From Ramparts, September 1967. The selections are from the
American edition of Revolution in the Revolution?, published by Monthly
Review Press. Translated by Bobbye Ortiz. Copyright © 1967 by Librai-
rie François Maspero; English translation copyright © 1967 by Monthly
Review Press. Reprinted by permission.

a known tactical content. One began by identifying the guerrilla struggle with insurrection because the archetype—1917— had taken this form, and because Lenin and later Stalin had developed several theoretical formulas based on it—formulas which have nothing to do with the present situation and which are periodically debated in vain, such as those which refer to conditions for the outbreak of an insurrection, meaning an immediate assault on the central power. But this disparity soon became evident. American guerrilla warfare was next virtually identified with Asian guerrilla warfare, since both are "irregular" wars of encirclement of cities from the countryside. This confusion is even more dangerous than the first.

The armed revolutionary struggle encounters specific conditions on each continent, in each country, but these are neither "natural" nor obvious. So true is this that in each case years of sacrifice are necessary in order to discover and acquire an awareness of them. The Russian Social Democrats instinctively thought in terms of repeating the Paris Commune in Petrograd; the Chinese Communists in terms of repeating the Russian October in the Canton of the twenties; and the Vietnamese comrades, a year after the foundation of their party, in terms of organizing insurrections of peasant soviets in the northern part of their country. It is now clear to us today that soviet-type insurrections could not triumph in prewar colonial Asia, but it was precisely here that the most genuine Communist activists had to begin their apprenticeship for victory.

One may well consider it a stroke of good luck that Fidel had not read the military writings of Mao Tse-tung before disembarking on the coast of Oriente: he could thus invent, on the spot and out of his own experience, principles of a military doctrine in conformity with the terrain. . . . But once again in Latin America, militants are reading Fidel's speeches and Che Guevara's writings with eyes that have already read Mao on the anti-Japanese war, Giap, and certain texts of Lenin—and they think they recognize the latter in the former. Classical visual superimposition, but dangerous, since the Latin American revolutionary war possesses highly special and profoundly distinct conditions of development, which can only be discovered through a particular experience. In that sense, all the theoretical works on people's war do as much harm as good. They have been called the grammar books of the war. But a foreign language is learned faster in a country where it must be spoken than at home studying a language manual. . . .

The Latin American revolution and its vanguard, the Cuban revolution, have . . . made a decisive contribution to international revolutionary experience . . .

Under certain conditions, the political and the military are not separate, but form one organic whole, consisting of the people's army, whose nucleus is the guerrilla army. The vanguard party can exist in the form of the guerrilla foco[1] itself. The guerrilla force is the party in embryo.

This is the staggering novelty introduced by the Cuban Revolution. . . .

Thus ends a divorce of several decades' duration between Marxist theory and revolutionary practice. As tentative and tenuous as the reconciliation may appear, it is the guerrilla movement—master of its own political leadership—that embodies it, this handful of men "with no other alternative but death or victory, at moments when death was a concept a thousand times more real, and victory a myth that only a revolutionary can dream of" (Che). These men may die, but others will replace them. Risks must be taken. The union of theory and practice is not an inevitability but a battle, and no battle is won in advance. If this union is not achieved there, it will not be achieved anywhere.

The guerrilla force, if it genuinely seeks total political warfare, cannot in the long run tolerate any fundamental duality of functions or powers. Che Guevara carries the idea of unity so far that he proposes that the military and political leaders who lead insurrectional struggles in America be "united, if possible, in one person." But whether it is an individual, as with Fidel, or collective, the important thing is that the leadership be homogeneous, political and military simultaneously. Career

---

[1] The Spanish word *foco* (French *foyer*) refers to a center of guerrilla operations rather than a military base in the usual sense. Since there is no exact English equivalent, the original Spanish word has been retained throughout.—Tr.

soldiers can, in the process of the people's war, become political leaders (Luis Turcios, for example, had he lived); militant political leaders can become military leaders, learning the
art of war by making it (Douglas Bravo, for example).

In any case, it is necessary that they be able to make it. *A
guerrilla force cannot develop on the military level if it does
not become a political vanguard.* As long as it does not work out
its own line, as long as it remains a pressure group or a device
for creating a political diversion, it is fruitlessly marking time,
however successful its partial actions may be. How can it take
the initiative? On what will it build its morale? Do we perhaps
believe that it will go "too far" if it is allowed to become the
catalyst for popular aspirations and energies, which will *ipso
facto* transform it into a directive force? Precisely because
it is a mass struggle—the most radical of all—the guerrilla
movement, if it is to triumph *militarily,* must *politically* as-
semble around it the majority of the exploited classes. Victory
is impossible without their active and organized participation,
since it is the general strike or generalized urban insurrection that will give the *coup de grâce* to the regime and will
defeat its final maneuvers—a last-minute *coup d'état,* a new
junta, elections—by extending the struggle throughout the country. But in order to reach that point, must there not be a long
and patient effort by the mountain forces to coordinate all forms
of struggle, eventually to coordinate action by the militia with
that of the regular forces, to coordinate rearguard sabotage by
the suburban guerrillas with operations carried out by the
principal guerrilla group? And, beyond the armed struggle,
must there not be an effort to play an ever larger role in the
country's civilian life? Whence the importance of a radio
transmitter at the disposition of the guerrilla forces. The radio
permits headquarters to establish daily contact with the population residing outside the zone of operations. Thus the latter
can receive political instructions and orientation which, as
military successes increase, find an ever-increasing echo. In
Cuba *Radio Rebelde,* which began transmitting in 1958, was
frequently utilized by Fidel, and confirmed the role of the Rebel
Army's General Staff as the directive force of the revolutionary
movement. Increasingly, everyone—from Catholics to Com-

munists—looked to the Sierra, tuned in to get reliable news, to know "what to do" and "where the action is." Clandestinity became public. As revolutionary methods and goals became more radical, so did the people. After Batista's flight, Fidel broadcast his denunciation of the maneuvers for a *coup d'état* in the capital, thus depriving the ruling class in a matter of minutes of its last card, and sealing the ultimate victory. Even before victory, the radio broke through government censorship on military operations, a censorship such as prevails today in all embattled countries. It is by means of radio that the guerrillas force the doors of truth and open them wide to the entire populace, especially if they follow the ethical precepts that guided *Radio Rebelde*—never broadcast inaccurate news, never conceal a defeat, never exaggerate a victory. In short, radio produces a qualitative change in the guerrilla movement. This explains the muffled or open resistance which certain party leaders offer today to the guerrilla movement's use of this propaganda medium.

Thus, in order for the small motor really to set the big motor of the masses into motion, without which its activity will remain limited, it must first be recognized by the masses as their only interpreter and guide, under penalty of dividing and weakening the people's strength. In order to bring about this recognition, the guerrillas must assume all the functions of political and military authority. Any guerrilla movement in Latin America that wishes to pursue the people's war to the end, transforming itself if necessary into a regular army and beginning a war of movement and positions, must become the unchallenged political vanguard, with the essential elements of its leadership being incorporated in the military command. . . .

We have only to observe the difficulties in which Algeria finds itself today, because of yesterday's division between the internal fighters and their government outside the country. There is no better example of the risks implicit in the separation of military and political functions when there is no Marxist vanguard party. Thus it is the revolutionary civil war that strengthens the historic agencies of the new society. Lenin, in his last notes, wrote that "the civil war has *welded* together the working class and the peasantry, and this is the *guarantee of an invincible strength*."[2]

In the mountains, then, workers, peasants, and intellectuals meet for the first time. Their integration is not so easy at the beginning. Just as there are divisions into classes elsewhere, groups can arise even in the midst of an encampment. The peasants, especially if they are of Indian origin, stay to themselves and speak their own language (Quechua or Cakchiquel) among themselves. The others, those who know how to write and speak well, spontaneously create their own circle. Mistrust, timidity, custom have to be gradually vanquished by means of untiring political work, in which the leaders set the example. These men all have something to learn from each other, beginning with their differences. Since they must all adapt themselves to the same conditions of life, and since they are all participating in the same undertaking, they adapt to each other. Slowly the shared existence, the combats, the hardships endured together, weld an alliance having the simple force of friendship. Furthermore the first law of guerrilla life is that no one survives it alone. The group's interest is the interest of each one, and vice versa. To live and conquer is to live and conquer all together. If a single combatant lags behind a marching column, it affects the speed and security of the entire column. In the rear is the enemy: impossible to leave the comrade behind or send him home. It is up to everyone, then, to share the burden, lighten his knapsack or cartridge-case, and help him all the way. Under these conditions class egoism does not long endure. Petty bourgeois psychology melts like snow under the summer sun, undermining the ideology of the same stratum. Where else could such an encounter, such an alliance, take place? By the same token, the only conceivable line for a guerrilla group to adopt is the "mass line"; it can live only with their support, in daily contact with them. Bureaucratic faintheartedness becomes irrelevant. Is this not the best education for a future socialist leader . . .? Revolutionaries make revolutionary civil wars; but to an even greater extent it is revolutionary civil war that makes revolutionaries.

[2] Draft of a speech (not delivered) for the Tenth Congress of Russian Soviets, December 1922. Lenin's emphasis.

Lenin wrote: "The civil war has educated and tempered (Denikin and the others are good *teachers*; they have taught well; *all our best militants have been in the army*)."[3]

The best teacher of Marxism-Leninism is the enemy, in face-to-face confrontation during the people's war. Study and apprenticeship are necessary but not decisive. There are no academy-trained cadres. One cannot claim to train revolutionary cadres in theoretical schools detached from instructional work and common combat experiences. To think otherwise would be justifiable naiveté in Western Europe; elsewhere it is unpardonable nonsense.

The guerrilla group's exercise of, or commitment to establish, a political leadership is even more clearly revealed when it organizes its first liberated zone. It then tries out and tests tomorrow's revolutionary measures (as on the Second Front in Oriente): agrarian reform, peasant congresses, levying of taxes, revolutionary tribunals, the discipline of collective life. The liberated zone becomes the prototype and the model for the future state, its administrators the models for future leaders of state. Who but a popular armed force can carry through such socialist "rehearsals"? . . .

Here the political word is abruptly made flesh. The revolutionary ideal emerges from the gray shadow of formula and acquires substance in the full light of day. This transubstantiation comes as a surprise, and when those who have experienced it want to describe it—in China, in Vietnam, in Cuba, in many places—they resort not to words but to exclamations:

> The renovating spirit, the longing for collective excellence, the awareness of a higher destiny are in full flower and can develop considerably further. We had heard of these things, which had a flavor of verbal abstraction, and we accepted their beautiful meaning, but now we are living it, we are experiencing it in every sense, and it is truly unique. We have seen its incredible development in this Sierra, which is our small universe. Here the word "people," which is so often utilized in a vague and confused sense, becomes a living, wonderful and dazzling reality. *Now* I know who the people are: I see them in that invincible force that surrounds us everywhere, I see them in the bands of 30 or 40 men, lighting their way

3 *Ibid.* Lenin's emphasis.

with lanterns, who descend the muddy slopes at two or three in the morning, with 30 kilos on their backs, in order to supply us with food. Who has organized them so wonderfully? Where did they acquire so much ability, astuteness, courage, self-sacrifice? No one knows! It is almost a mystery! They organize themselves all alone, spontaneously! When weary animals drop to the ground, unable to go further, men appear from all directions and carry the goods. Force cannot defeat them. It would be necessary to kill them all, to the last peasant, and that is impossible; this, the dictatorship cannot do; the people are aware of it and are daily more aware of their own growing strength.[4]

All these factors, operating together, gave shape to a strange band which was made to appear picturesque by certain photographs and which, because of our stupidity, impressed us only through the attire and long beards of its members. These are the militants of our time, not martyrs, not functionaries, but fighters. Neither creatures of an apparatus nor potentates: at this stage, they themselves are the apparatus. Aggressive men, especially in retreat. Resolute and responsible, each of them knowing the meaning and goal of this armed class struggle through its leaders, fighters like themselves whom they see daily carrying the same packs on their backs, suffering the same blistered feet and the same thirst during a march. The blasé will smile at this vision à la Rousseau. We need not point out here that it is not love of nature nor the pursuit of happiness which brought them to the mountain, but the awareness of a historic necessity. Power is seized and held in the capital, but the road that leads the exploited to it must pass through the countryside. Need we recall that war and military discipline are characterized by rigors unknown to the *Social Contract*? This is even truer for guerrilla armies than for regular armies. Today some of these groups have disappeared before assuming a vanguard role, having retreated or suffered liquidation. In a struggle

[4] From Fidel Castro's last letter to Frank País, written in the Sierra Maestra, July 21, 1957. The same wonderment is expressed today in the letters of Turcios, Douglas Bravo, Camilo Torres, and others. Of course this does not mean that it is easy to obtain peasant support immediately; but when it is obtained, it performs wonders. Fidel wrote the letter after eight months in the Sierra and after having escaped betrayal by several peasants.

of this kind, which involves such grave risks and is still only in the process of taking its first faltering steps, such defeats are normal. Other groups, the most important ones operating in countries whose history proves their importance for all Latin America—Venezuela, Guatemala, Colombia—have established themselves and are moving ahead. It is there, in such countries as these, that history is on the march today. Tomorrow other countries will join and supersede them in the vanguard role.

Has it been noted that nearly all of these guerrilla movements neither have nor want political commissars? The majority of the fighters come from Communist ranks. These are the first socialist guerrilla forces that have not adopted the system of political commissars, a system which does not appear to correspond to the Latin American reality.

If what we have said makes any sense at all, this absence of specialists in political affairs has the effect of sanctioning the absence of specialists in military affairs. The people's army is its own political authority. The *guerrilleros* play both roles, indivisibly. Its commanders are political instructors for the fighters, its political instructors are its commanders.

MICHAEL F. BROWER

U.S. AID*

PRESCRIPTION

FOR CHANGE

Author's note: For lack of time to make all the necessary changes, I have permitted use of this article without revision. If written today, it would be even more critical of United States development aid which has declined to little more than one quarter of one percent of a larger GNP, while defense is up to forty times as much. But also, I would place today relatively more emphasis than I did on other measures to promote development, including world commodity agreements, preferential treatment for imports from developing countries, multi-lateral in place of bi-lateral aid, and develop-

* From *The Correspondent*, No. 35, Autumn 1965. Copyright © 1965. All rights reserved. The Council for Correspondence, Inc.

ment of human resources and of institutions of teaching and research to nurture and retain them. And I would urge greater support for healthy, development oriented, nationalism and regionalism, even when it conflicts with United States commercial, economic, political, and military interests and objectives.

ALTHOUGH OUR IGNORANCE is still monumental, we have learned a great deal over the past fifteen years about promoting economic development. We now know that the transfer of Western industrial "know-how" through technical assistance programs, although important, is a slow and difficult process and by no means all that is required. Also vitally important are education and training of the human resources of the poor countries and careful national planning, or at the very least, a budgeting process which sets relative national priorities. Moreover, a serious effort should be made to administer these plans and priorities effectively in order to attain maximum practicable rates of growth and to avoid squandering scarce resources on the production or importation of luxury goods demanded by small but very rich elites.

We are also slowly learning the lesson long taught by Latin American economists, that many of the poor countries are losing more foreign exchange through declining world prices of their commodity exports than they are gaining in foreign aid and investment. Although supports can be placed under the prices of a few basic commodities, this can be only a partial and temporary solution. Needed are diversification and expansion of the exports of the poor countries, which must have freer access to the markets of the rich countries and perhaps even some form of preferential treatment for a time.[1] But this will take many years or even decades. In the meantime, to promote this diversification, and development itself, most of the developing countries will require considerable foreign aid.

And finally we have learned, or, as Teodoro Moscoso [former coordinator for the Alliance for Progress] points out, under President Kennedy we had apparently learned, that revolutionary reforms in land holdings, taxation, credit institutions, edu-

[1] See the articles by Isaiah Frank and John A. Pincus in the January 1964 *Foreign Affairs.*

cation, and housing are necessary in many countries, especially in Latin America, both as prerequisites for development and as essentials for the promotion of more just societies.[2] It is with regard to these last two items on the agenda for development, foreign assistance and internal revolutionary reforms, that United States policy is today most vulnerable to criticism.

The Present Aid Program

There is widespread misunderstanding and exaggeration in this country about just how much assistance our government is making available specifically to promote economic development. For the fiscal year 1965, the Congress appropriated funds totalling about $3.6 billion for this purpose, including $510 million for the Alliance for Progress, $980 million for the development loans and technical assistance to other parts of the world, and $104 million for the Peace Corps. To this we can add about $1.46 billion out of the total Food for Peace shipments under P.L. 480. Actually only about two-thirds of this food goes to support economic development, while one-third goes into straight consumption, helping to feed people who would not otherwise eat as much but who make no additional contribution to the growth and development of their economy.[3]

Administrative costs and miscellaneous small programs added

[2] For Moscoso, see *The Correspondent*, No. 35, Autumn 1965. For coverage of many issues of development, with statements from opposing viewpoints on each issue included, see *Leading Issues in Development Economics*, edited by Gerald M. Meier, Oxford University Press, 1964.

[3] P. N. Rosenstein-Rodan, "International Aid for Underdeveloped Countries," *The Review of Economics and Statistics*, May, 1961, p. 110. These food shipments are also overvalued in that the government totals them at current world market prices; yet it is clear that the world price would be driven down substantially if a sizable part of them were actually sold for hard currencies. Finally, when calculating the burden of the foreign aid programs to U. S. taxpayers, these government food shipments should probably not be counted at all. They are financed, not through foreign aid appropriations, but through the Department of Agriculture as support for American farmers, and shipping them abroad costs us less than storing them for even a few more months. See John A. Pincus, "The Cost of Foreign Aid," *The Review of Economics and Statistics*, November 1963, pp. 360–67.

$73 million more, for a total U.S. bilateral development assistance program of about $3.1 billion in fiscal year 1965. Adding about $500 million for U.S. development aid through multilateral channels brings the overall total to $3.6 billion. This represents only a little over one-half of one percent of our Gross National Product (GNP) for the year. Or subtracting the Food for Peace program, which is paid for by our domestic agricultural support programs, the burden was only one-third of one percent of our GNP.

Although President Johnson requested for fiscal year 1966 an increase of about $140 million for all of these programs together, he did not make a strong fight for it. At this writing, the Congress is completing its annual cutting ritual, and most of this increase, as expected, has been denied. The result will be assistance at about the 1965 level, but costing a smaller percentage of our GNP, which is growing at 5 to 6 percent each year.

Not included here are a number of other programs which are sometimes called "foreign aid"—the military assistance program ($1 billion in 1965 and going up), which ships arms to such countries as Korea, Taiwan, Pakistan and India (until the war broke out), and mainly South Vietnam; the "Supporting Assistance" and "Contingency" funds ($400 million and $100 million respectively in 1965), which support budget deficits in these and other countries whose governments the State and Defense Departments wish to support for short-range reasons of "security and stability"; and the Export-Import Bank, whose loans are usually at or near commercial terms and are designed primarily to promote American exports. Although small portions of the above programs may at times contribute to development, it is impossible to estimate the actual share, and it is difficult to avoid the conclusion that sometimes our military aid programs have a strongly negative impact on economic development.

Alternative Goals

It is impossible to make any precise estimate of how much aid the developing countries can wisely use in their race to raise income levels before being swamped with rising populations.[4] If it is real self-sustaining growth we want, our aid must be used not just for the temporary alleviation of hunger, but in support of internal changes which will bring about, among other things, a rise over the years in the net internal savings rate from present low levels of 5 to 9 percent of GNP up to 12 or 15 percent or above. But raising the savings rate is difficult in countries where the vast majority of people must consume virtually their entire income just to stay alive, and it requires a host of interacting reforms and initiatives in most poor countries, plus a certain amount of time. In those countries making such efforts, a great deal of foreign assistance can probably be put to productive use. Moreover, if the aid is not forthcoming, the alternatives will usually be either stagnation or near stagnation, or (as in China) the use of highly coercive policies by a dictatorial government determined to avoid stagnation by raising all of the necessary capital internally. Thus, within limits, foreign capital assistance can provide an alternative for dictatorial government coercion.

Estimates of the total amount of assistance needed depend on assumptions about how many countries will be making the kind of internal effort which justifies a major external assistance program. The whole non-Communist underdeveloped world has a combined total GNP of perhaps $225 billion—although this is a very rough estimate. If all these nations were to begin

[4] Certainly most of these countries should make a parallel effort to cut their birth rates through family planning, and the U.S. and the U.N. should offer every possible assistance. With populations growing at 2 to 3 percent in most of the poor countries, and up to and even over 4 percent in some Latin American countries, the problem is so serious that some authors have argued for first making an all-out effort to curb the population explosion while postponing a major push for economic development for a decade or more. But we will probably not get significant cuts in birth rates until enough parents are somehow motivated to limit the size of their families. And this may depend upon a further decrease in infant mortality rates, so that children under six can be expected to live, and on enough changes in the environment to offer hope that two or three children can lead a better life than six or eight. And both of these changes depend upon achieving some degree of continuing economic development. Moreover, even if population control *can* be achieved before development (and it may turn out to be possible), postponing development for a decade or two dooms hundreds of millions of people to life on the edge of subsistence followed by early death.

making the internal efforts needed to grow (with sufficient outside aid) at an average rate of 5 percent a year—the goal set down some years ago by the U.N. General Assembly—then the total capital needed by all of them might be around $34 billion per year.[5] If we make a further rough estimate that the present net savings in all of these countries averages 8 percent of their GNP,[6] or a total of $18 billion a year, then to fill the maximum present capital gap would require $16 billion in foreign capital each year.

Even if by some miracle the present less than $3 billion in private foreign net investment could be quickly raised to $4 billion per year, a gap of $12 billion would still remain to be filled with governmental assistance. As the richest of the industrialized countries, with something like 60 percent of their total income, the U.S. should certainly provide the lion's share of this aid. If we paid a straight 60 percent, the cost would be $7.2 billion per year. Or if we followed the progressive principle we practice in our domestic income tax, based on the concept that the greater a man's (or a country's) income, the greater proportionately the ability to pay, then our share would perhaps be 65 or 75 percent—which would mean $7.8 or $9.0 billion per year.

This is clearly more capital than is presently needed. By no means are all of the poor countries now ready or willing or able to make the reforms and serious efforts required before they can usefully invest enough foreign and domestic funds to begin rapid growth. But those that are—and this probably includes such large countries as Nigeria, Venezuela, Brazil, Chile, and prewar (and hopefully postwar) India and Pakistan —may now or soon be able to grow for a time at rates well above 5 percent, and they should not have their own efforts limited, as has sometimes been true in the past, by an arbitrary

[5] Several dollars of new investment are needed to produce each dollar of increased annual output. The present estimate assumes a marginal capital-output ratio (dollars of new capital needed to produce a single dollar of new annual output) of 3.0. This is the figure most widely assumed by development economists. The actual amount required varies between countries and among alternative kinds of investments.

[6] For estimates of net savings ratios by country and region and for discussions of capital-output ratios, see the article by Rosenstein-Rodan and also pp. 90–125 of the book edited by Meier, both cited above.

ceiling on the availability of foreign assistance. Perhaps a good temporary objective for U.S. development assistance should be one percent of our GNP, the target level set by the U.N. General Assembly several years ago. Since the U.S. GNP will be over $690 billion in the fiscal year 1966, this ratio would mean that President Johnson should have asked Congress for about $6.9 billion, or almost twice what he did request. Even the staid World Bank recently termed total world aid "wholly inadequate" and called for an extra $3 to $4 billion per year, or about 50 percent more than present world aid.

Another way to see this ratio between the developing countries' needs and our contribution is to note that for 1966 the President asked Congress for only $580 million for the Alliance for Progress. This was just slightly over half of the $1.1 billion annual average which the U.S. pledged for the decade at Punta del Este in 1961. It is true that several of the Latin American countries have done little except make paper plans towards fulfilling their own pledges of reform under the alliance agreements, and in most cases they should not be rewarded for continued inaction and subservience to reactionary feudal elements. But those governments making serious efforts should be supported to their full ability to use foreign assistance constructively. For its part the American government should obtain from Congress and have on hand a clear margin of extra funds —several hundred million dollars—to demonstrate our eagerness to support further constructive efforts.

In the debate about whether or not the American people can afford such levels of development assistance (and it is of course a matter for debate and individual judgment), such facts as the following should be kept in mind: our economy is adding each year around $40 billion in new national product, resulting in a federal tax take of $7 to $10 billion more each year. Our military budget is running over seven times as much as this proposed foreign assistance budget, and we are also spending almost that amount each year to put men on the moon and for other space ventures.

Since most of the developing countries are already very deeply in debt and heavily saddled with the burden of paying back existing loans, the type and terms of our assistance are as important as the amount. In Latin America the situation has gone so far, AID Administrator David Bell told Congress in 1965, that on the average "the debt-service burden is already the equivalent of one-half of the gross capital inflow." Clearly what is needed are more straight grants, or grant-like, long-term, low-interest-rate loans. Bell and his staff recognize this and have been moving for some time towards such "soft" term loans. But they need further support in the face of opposition from some Congressmen who do not understand why all loans should not be at or near standard hard commercial terms. Nor should all our loans go to support the specific, easily identifiable and glamorous projects which Congress tends to favor. In many countries equal or greater returns can be obtained through general program loans that pay for groups of smaller projects or for the imports of spare parts and raw materials needed to put existing industrial plants to work at full capacity.

Waste, Inefficiency, and Corruption

Such an expanded program of development assistance as I propose would, of course, be subject to an attack—even more vigorous than at present—on the familiar grounds of causing waste and corruption in the countries receiving aid. The answer is that of course there will be waste, inefficiency, and corruption in the uses of foreign assistance, as indeed there will be in almost any kind of serious effort to stimulate rapid growth. A look at our own experience—widely believed to have been successful—might be instructive.

In the 1820s and 30s, our state and local governments rushed to subsidize the building first of canals and then of railroads. Many of these were in badly chosen locations; many never paid for themselves; many were not even completed. And many states soon found themselves overextended in bonds sold (many of them abroad) to subsidize these "internal improvements." This was further aggravated by the fact that the people of that "irresponsible underdeveloped country" often refused to tax themselves to pay even the interest, let alone the principle, on these bonds. At least nine states defaulted on millions of dollars worth of bonds, causing considerable resentment among Englishmen—many of whom were bondholders—toward Americans whom they regarded collectively as a negligent and irresponsible people.[7]

In the decade after the Civil War a similar cycle was repeated in the Southern states, and construction was also begun on transcontinental railroads heavily subsidized by federal bonds and land grants. Such subsidies opened up the new country well before it would have been done by unassisted private enterprise, but a good deal of waste and widespread corruption of our state and national legislatures was dealt into the bargain.

Nor are such shortcomings completely behind us. Big business today is far from immune to waste and inefficiency—or to dishonesty, if the recent indictments for price-fixing are any indication. As for political corruption, Congress is evidently much more honest today than in 1873 when a member declared that "the House of Representatives was like an auction room where more valuable considerations were disposed of under the speaker's hammer than in any other place on earth";[8] but it is still difficult to extol the honesty of our state legislatures.

Waste and corruption are probably the inevitable concomitants of rapid growth, and perhaps especially so with regard to funds flowing in from abroad. Therefore the major goal of our assistance program should not be to minimize waste and corruption, for this would result in abolishing the program completely. Of course, some effort should be made to hold down the number of unproductive projects we assist and the amount of aid sticking to the hands it passes through. But an assistance program which concentrates on these goals, taking few risks and trying to be sure that every project is a safe bet, while it may make few "mistakes," will be too cautious and too slow and will inevitably be passing up too many projects and programs which would in fact bear fruit. And that is the greatest waste of all.

[7] See Leland H. Jenks, *The Migration of British Capital to 1875*, Thomas Nelson and Sons, Ltd., London; as reprinted by Knopf in 1963, esp. p. 104.

[8] Richard Hofstadter, *The American Political Tradition*, Vintage Books, New York, 1948, p. 170. For a recent scathing indictment of one present state legislature, see Senator Paul Simon, "The Illinois Legislature: A Study in Corruption," *Harper's*, September 1964.

There are in fact two kinds of waste we can no longer afford. The first is wasted time. We are a rich nation with resources to burn on thousands of items and programs, large and small, important and unimportant, public and private. Yet in the greatest human project of all time our efforts are half-hearted and lagging, and we are wasting precious time. We should be making an all-out effort to build a world of greater economic opportunity and human freedom, of greater dignity, hope, and justice. We should be doing this in part because it is the right thing to do, in keeping with our deepest religious and ethical ideals, in part because it is in our economic self-interest, and, if for no other reason, because it is in our long-range political self-interest. Simply put, the kind of world we would be trying to promote with such an assistance program is a world in which our American ideas and ideals—and indeed we Americans our-selves—would have the best chance of surviving. This is be-cause it would be a world in which there would be the best chance of limiting violence, maintaining peace, and promoting governments based on the consent of the governed.

Due to the population explosion, the revolution in weaponry, and the continuing technological shrinkage and tying together of the world, we have little time left in which to make this effort succeed. If population densities continue to increase with-out greater parallel increases in resources and in life hopes, the present rate of violence outbreak in—and over—the poorer countries will not merely continue, it will multiply. And sooner or later the rich nuclear countries will find themselves involved in a conflict which they cannot control and which may then expand to engulf much of the earth. Our political interest in helping the developing countries exists independently of com-munism, which should not be made the central explanation for our efforts. However, the existence of idealized communism as an alternative model and the concrete efforts of the Soviet and Chinese parties to organize these societies intensifies the dangers and shortens the time we have available in which to reduce the great poverty and injustice on which both commu-nism and violence thrive.

The other kind of waste we cannot afford is the squandering and subverting of our development resources on reactionary regimes which do not begin making the basic reforms necessary for the achievement of sustained growth and a more nearly just distribution of the good things in life. This problem is especially prevalent in Latin America, where wealth, income, political power, and in general a man's life chances are largely tied to the still-feudal distribution of land ownership, and where the rich people often pay very little—if any—taxes.[9]

Our aid around the world, and especially in Latin America under the Alliance for Progress, should be largely limited to those countries which are making real strides toward achieving the kind of nonviolent social revolution which these conditions demand, even though some of our own citizens and corporations may suffer losses through land and tax reforms. Those governments which are not making significant starts on the reform road should be pressured, cajoled, and in essence bribed with the bait of large foreign assistance funds to alleviate the pain involved.[10] For, as Vice-President Humphrey told Fordham University seniors in 1965, "if peaceful revolution is impossible, violent revolution is inevitable." And when revolutions do come, it will be a tragedy if once again they find our government supporting reactionary regimes, as happened in Cuba,

[9] See the articles by Thomas Carroll in Albert O. Hirschman, ed., *Latin American Issues, Essays and Comments* (Twentieth Century Fund, 1961) and in John J. TePaske and Sydney N. Fisher, eds., *Explosive Forces in Latin America* (Ohio State University Press, 1964). Carroll points out that in Guatemala 516 farmers (0.15 percent) control 41 percent of the agricultural land, in Ecuador 705 (0.17 percent) control 37 percent of the farm land, and in Nicaragua 362 owners control one-third of the land. And on the average in Latin America a decade ago some 10 percent of the owners held 90 percent of the farm land. This is especially serious in countries where land is, or provides, the main source of wealth and income, and therefore of political power. On taxes, Colombia's former President Alberto Lleras Camargo wrote in the October 1963 *Foreign Affairs* that rates were low, evasion widespread, and "not a single Latin American, whether of high standing or of the underworld, has ever been imprisoned for not paying his taxes or for sending in a fraudulent income tax report."

[10] This is difficult to accomplish under any circumstances, but especially when aid is being granted on a bilateral basis. More of our aid should be channeled through various multilateral institutions, and the pressures for reform in Latin America could best be exerted by a collective institution, with strong backing from this country, which would in fact carry out the policies jointly agreed upon at Punta del Este.

Vietnam and the Dominican Republic. Aid to such governments undermines the forces of reform within the country receiving the aid and in other countries as well. As Senator Morse said over a year ago, after President Johnson had resumed aid to the Dominican regime which overthrew democratically elected Juan Bosch:

> Until the United States unequivocally aligns itself with those democratic elements which are trying to bring about peaceful revolution in the social and economic spheres, the Alliance for Progress will be a pious exhortation rather than an instrument for dramatic change. Our "aid as usual" policy toward the Dominican Republic, Guatemala, Honduras, and Ecuador is the greatest single threat today to the success of the alliance.

Thus, as Teodoro Moscoso argues,[11] it is time for a divorcement of funds for short-range military and diplomatic objectives—for buying votes in the O.A.S. or the U.N., if that really is necessary, or for shoring up incompetent governments, which we surely do much too often—from other funds clearly appropriated and reserved for the promotion of social and economic reform and development. Pessimists argue that development assistance is really less popular in Congress and would suffer if split off from military aid. Perhaps this would happen, at least in the short run. But perhaps not. One positive indication is that Senator Morse was defeated almost ten to one (78 to 8) in his attempt to cut $100 million from the 1966 authorization for the Alliance for Progress. If that great persuader President Johnson and his top advisers could be convinced that we must once again begin to support rather than block social revolutions in the developing world, and if he could himself be persuaded to explain the program of development assistance to the American people in terms of its basic long-range purposes— *not* the short-term containment of communism through temporarily propping up unjust reactionary regimes—I believe that they would give it the kind of support it must have to succeed in time. But who will convince the President and his conservative State Department?

[11] *Correspondent,* Autumn 1965.

AMERICA IN A PLURALISTIC WORLD*

AMITAI
ETZIONI

THE FUTURE HISTORIAN,[1] writing about our decade with the wisdom of hindsight, may assert that few members of the 1964 Administration realized, or at least publicly acknowledged, the full political significance of two events that occurred in 1963. The installation of the "hot line" and the signing of the Test Ban Treaty, although of limited significance in themselves, marked (he will write) the end of the age of bloc-politics and the beginning of the "pluralistic" period.

The "hot line," a communication link between the White House and the Kremlin, was widely acclaimed for its function of averting accidental war. But almost no one saw in 1963 that it could also be used to disown an action of one's allies at a moment's notice. The USSR could instantly inform the United States that it did not approve, let us say, of a new Chinese attack on India. The same line could be used by the United States to disassociate itself from any rash move on the part of France, Germany, or any other ally. No wonder that requests from NATO allies to have a "hookup" with the line were politely, but firmly, turned down.

Similarly, the main significance of the treaty for partial cessation of thermonuclear tests is not the reduction of fallout or the limited damper it puts on American and Soviet development of nuclear weapons (which continues in laboratories, simulation computers and underground testing), but the fact that it was an attempt of the two nuclear giants to prevent the birth of more nuclear dwarfs, and to slow the growth of those already born.

* From *The Crossroad Papers*, edited by Hans J. Morgenthau. Copyright © 1965 by W. W. Norton & Company, Inc. Reprinted by permission.

[1] The thesis of this article is elaborated in my *Winning Without War*, Doubleday, New York, 1964.

The reason why the full potential of these two preliminary steps was not exploited, nor even fully understood, even after the 1963 *détente* in Soviet-American relations, is a familiar one. In 1964, the Administration is trying to solve 1954's problems —and it viewed 1968 in terms of 1948. More specifically, our foreign policy was and is still formulated in terms of a duopolistic strategy, based on the assumption of a bipolar concentration of world power (East and West), with other countries in a residual category ("nonaligned"). The main objective of our policy is still to contain Communist expansionism, in the hope that the frustration produced by Western countermoves, combined with internal pressures, will produce a "mellowing" or even disintegration of the Communist system. These changes in Communism are to be encouraged politically by a united Western counterbloc—and militarily by a combination of a nuclear deterrent, conventional forces, and the newly added subconventional (or "counter-guerilla" and "counter-insurrectionist") forces. The global distribution of power, according to this strategy, can be stabilized through a nuclear balance of terror, with the two giants in a stalemate, neither able to break the other. Moreover, policies of gradual expansion and roll-back cannot be vigorously followed because of the fear of triggering a nuclear war.

The dialogue in Washington is largely limited to variations on this theme; some insist that we need more missiles, others that we have more than enough. Some feel that there is room for some arms-control measures, others doubt that very much. Some still look for an opportunity for a military victory; others believe that such a concept, in the age of big bombs on a small planet, cannot even be defined. But, as a whole, a duopolistic, (two-bloc) balance of power (or stalemate) represents both a widely held political forecast and the prevailing strategy; East and West are still the key concepts of most Washington thinking.

But, in fact, every single component of this formula has changed since it was enunciated in the late forties. The technology of weapons puts at the command of both sides a military power that surpasses all imagination and which, in the long run, cannot possibly be held in check—the most carefully designed, closely guarded system has an occasional breakdown. The probability of a breakdown of the nuclear balance of terror might be small, but the magnitude of disaster that would occur is so large that the system simply cannot be lived with in the long run. Hence, the strategic question is how much longer the United States (and the U.S.S.R.) can prudently delay serious attempts at arms reduction and strengthening of global institutions?

While there is considerable disagreement among Kremlinologists *as to what degree the U.S.S.R. has mellowed,* there is little doubt that profound changes have taken place both domestically and in its foreign policy. The West must now answer the question: what will it offer to the U.S.S.R. when it has mellowed "enough," what strategy will replace containment when there is nothing left to contain but the drive of those who have vested interests in this position? What conditions do we require the U.S.S.R. to meet before it will be found to be as fully eligible for membership in the international community as, let us say, France?

Equally important as the changes within the Soviet Union have been changes in the blocs. They were never as integrated and united as we liked to believe. The history of NATO is one of crises and unfulfilled commitments, and the Sino-Soviet conflict has a longer history than we at first realized. As long as our European allies and the Asian allies of the U.S.S.R. were weak, there was the kind of unity that results from a single center of hegemony in each bloc (though the extent of our hegemony never remotely approached that of the Soviet Union). In both alliances, however, this kind of hegemony is gone forever. Washington likes to put all the blame for the crisis of the Western alliance on one man, but we should note that the French nuclear force was initiated before de Gaulle returned to power and will very likely outlive him. Also, while Germany is at the moment our favorite ally on the continent, the day is just around the corner when it will have both the power and the desire to pursue a more independent foreign policy. The Sino-Soviet conflict will surely have its ups and downs, but there will never again be a united Communist bloc as there was in the early fifties.

We must, then, face the fact that the world of the seventies will have several centers of power, not two. These will not be equal in magnitude; the United States and the U.S.S.R. will probably continue to stand out as nuclear giants. Nor will all the blocs treat all the others as equally remote. But matters concerning world order will no longer be decided in two capitals; the trend is back to a period of five or more big powers, and several emerging ones. This promises more maneuverability, and complicates the considerations of each power. It is an especially unhappy change for the two superpowers, who ran the show from the late forties to the late fifties.

What might United States policy be when Washington finally sees that no mixed-crew ships, tariff cuts, or summit meetings of Western heads of state will patch up the alliance? What will follow a fuller recognition of the dangers of nuclear war, the limits of arms control, and the fact that the East is also deeply divided? The answer cannot be readily given in terms of forecasting history. But, if we write an "optimistic scenario" assuming a better United States–U.S.S.R. understanding, we can foresee the development of a new American strategy for the pluralistic world, following the precedents of the "hot line" and the 1963 Test Ban Treaty. I like to call it the "strategy of competition"; the rest of this article is devoted to outlining assumptions on which the strategy is based.

Replacing the current bipolar strategy with a strategy of competition would promote forces, inside Communist as well as non-Communist countries, that are committed to a world of peaceful competition. Under this strategy, Communist countries need not be expected to refrain from advancing the values they believe in, so long as they limit the means employed to nonlethal ones. The West, too, is not committed to a static concept of peaceful coexistence, but is free to promote progressive, democratic forces, likewise through nonlethal means.

The strategy assumes that differences of belief and interest between the United States and the U.S.S.R. cannot be resolved. But it also assumes that it is not essential to resolve these differences; what is needed are effective limitations on their expression, so as to avoid escalation to the level of armed conflict of the confrontations that will continue to occur.

The new strategy assumes that competition is desirable, because it tends to bind the competitors to one set of institutions within which the competition is conducted, and to advance the values in the name of which the competition is conducted, for example, development. It is assumed that the long-run stabilization of the world order requires a re-allocation of global wealth in favor of the "have not" countries, and that interbloc competition is a most effective propelling power toward such re-allocation.

Similarly, the evolution of global institutions essential for the long-run solution of our international problems is accelerated by the quest of both sides to develop machinery to formulate the rules of the competition and to enforce them. In short, dynamic peaceful competition is very much preferable to static peaceful coexistence.

While the long-run aim of the strategy of competition is world peace through world law, the strategy itself is within the realm of power politics, like the bipolar strategy it seeks to replace. Both aim at improving the standing of the United States in the global content, *and* at the evolution of systems which will protect the American and other peoples from nuclear war. These objectives, we believe, can be "harmonized" with those of other big powers, since (1) some dangers are universal (especially nuclear annihilation); (2) some are shared by the United States and the U.S.S.R. but not by other powers, especially the challenge to their bloc status by their respective allies, which leads the two powers to formulate arrangements to their advantage in terms of universal values and institutions (for example, the ban on nuclear testing); and (3) the criteria for scoring points in the areas in which there is a direct contest between the United States and the U.S.S.R. (for example, which is developing "better"—India or China?). There is no sign that the stock of prizes to compete over in the third world will be exhausted by the time the contenders tire of the competition.

More specifically, the following assumptions are involved in a strategy of competition:

1. *The U.S.S.R. and the Soviet-led Communist camp are viewed as permanent members of the international community.* That is, despite crises in agriculture, a deficit in its foreign trade with non-Communist countries, and other difficulties, it is not

expected that the Soviet regime will collapse under its own weight, or under the pressures the West can bring to bear by withholding trade, through the Voice of America, and the like. Secondly, it is assumed that it is morally unacceptable and militarily ill-advised to try to break the U.S.S.R. by military power, which would involve American initiation of a nuclear war. Third, it is assumed that the U.S.S.R. either has mellowed enough or might mellow enough in the foreseeable future, particularly if encouraged by Western efforts, to continue to liberalize internally and to follow a foreign policy compatible with the standards of a stable, peaceful world community.

It is not assumed that the U.S.S.R. has lost its global ambitions or messianic urges, but rather that developments in the technology of weapons have brought the U.S.S.R. to realize that military advances are exceedingly dangerous. There are signs that the Russian people are growing increasingly tired of life in a garrison, and that the government is interested in shifting resources to raise the standard of living even further. The acceptance of the impossibility of massive military gains, and a desire for the reduction of international tensions necessary for domestic improvements, might lead the Soviets to be genuinely interested in limiting their expansion efforts to non-military means. We cannot rely on the word of the Soviet, or anybody else, for such a limitation; but we *can* follow a strategy that will test these assumptions without undue risk, and we *can* build forces that would encourage developments and institutions that would discourage tendencies toward regression.

Peaceful competition is preferred over peaceful coexistence precisely because we assume that the Soviet Union and its followers are not free from global ambitions, and that seeking to block all expressions of such ambitions by a rigid duopoly makes global accommodation unduly difficult. We will surely benefit from insisting that every power can appeal to all people— including those who live behind the Iron Curtain—through aid, trade, and communication of ideas, as long as no violence is used and no instigation to violence is involved. We have no reason to fear such a contest with the U.S.S.R., and the U.S.S.R. might be more ready to accept this kind of limitation of the contest than a total and global status quo.

2. *Assumptions about Communist China and the Chinese-led camp.* Ostracizing China encourages aggressive forces inside China, leaves it few options to alliance with Russia except isolation, and makes most worldwide arms control and reduction schemes unworkable. Gradual engagement of China in the world community, through opening the routes to travel, trade in nonstrategic materials, membership in the U.N., etc., might keep China from re-consolidating its relations with the U.S.S.R. and bring closer domestic liberalization and mellowing of its foreign policy. Internal collapse of the regime cannot be counted upon, and military moves against China might result in a war with the U.S.S.R., just as a Soviet attack on France would bring us into a war with Russia.

As long as the U.S.S.R. is not involved, China is a weak power *vis-à-vis* the United States. Hence it cannot, or could not in the foreseeable future, follow a highly aggressive foreign policy which the U.S.S.R. does not approve. Despite bellicose talk, China did not invade Taiwan, come openly and massively to the aid of the Vietcong (on the scale of United States assistance to the Vietnamese government), or drive deep into India. At least half a generation will pass before China—without massive help from the outside—will have the industrial base for an expansionist foreign policy, backed up by large-scale production of nuclear bombs and missiles (a few bombs do not make a nuclear power). This period should be used to bring China at least as much into the international community as Russia is today.

There is much to be gained from encouraging the entrance of China into the global competition with the United States and the U.S.S.R. We should not insist, in the rigid bipolar tradition in which our policy was formulated, that whoever is not with us is with Russia. Nor can we refuse to see that—as in other polycentric situations—whoever is competing with my foremost rival, is helping me, whether he knows and likes it or not. Absurd as it may sound to the present generation of American strategists, Communist China is rendering great services to the United States in this way. Gradually introducing China into the world community would increase these services. To illustrate, a Communist China in the U.N. would either require the two leading Communist countries to agree upon positions, which they have found rather difficult, or regularly to vote differently, demonstrating the Communist split on the most conspicuous public stage in the world, as well as splitting the Communist and pro-Communist vote.

3. *Assumptions about France and other Western allies.* The United States will always have a special affinity with countries that share its Christian, democratic, social-welfare tradition, no matter what their foreign policy. But the expectation that the retirement of one man could re-establish United States hegemony in the Western alliance and heal its cleavages is difficult to substantiate. The French nuclear force is not likely to melt away or be given up. While France is likely to be weakened in the succession crisis that will follow de Gaulle's departure, future leaders of France will find it difficult to renounce the image of glory as a world power that has been revived by the general. France must be viewed as a permanently independent power.

Britain has much to gain from playing the role of the great international mediator, and she is likely to continue to move slowly in a more independent direction—as already indicated by her trade with Cuba despite a "Western" blockade, and by her support of a "soft" line in the disarmament negotiations in Laos and in Berlin. It cannot be assumed that Britain, in or out of Europe, will serve much longer as an American anchor.

West Germany, at the moment the European backbone of NATO and the hub of American efforts to re-establish its hegemony in the Western alliance, might become the next black sheep of the alliance. It is growing in economic and military power and is increasingly intent on using it to bring about "reunification." This goal, which was until recently a slogan to which politicians paid lip service, might tomorrow be the motive for a deal with Russia, a military move against the East German government, or both.

In short, the alliance—drawn up in the days of a much more direct Soviet threat in Europe, a much greater credibility of the American protection, and a much weaker Europe—is becoming ever weaker. No "Grand Designs" will reverse this trend; one does not paste together fifteen nations into a federation to suit the latest designs of the State Department.

The United States reaction until now has been to invest more and more in stillborn efforts to patch up the alliance and delay the initiation of policies that would take cognizance of the pluralistic trend of the world. Recognition that the wheels of history cannot be turned back would bring to a halt the training and arming of Europeans with nuclear arms, which undermines the 1963–64 Soviet-American *détente* and provides additional power to Germany. Measures such as the internationalization of the routes leading to West Berlin, recognition of the border between Poland and West Germany and some arms-control scheme in the area might yield considerable Soviet concessions in exchange. We should no longer delay considering these steps out of fear that they will hinder the patching-up of an alliance that is anyhow in serious disarray.

4. *The emerging pluralistic world deeply affects our assumptions about the United Nations.* The U.N. was to be an instrument of the world community. In effect, it served for years as an instrument of Western foreign policy, as the West commanded an almost automatic majority for its resolutions. But the U.N. has changed; now the representatives of the southern hemisphere—Latin America, Africa, and Asia—can outvote the northern ones any day of the week. Since, for reasons of their own, many of these countries tend to favor better United States-U.S.S.R. relations and the strengthening of the U.N., a new role for it is evolving. The U.N. can no longer be used in the narrow service of Western interests, but it *can* function as the institution which develops the rules and the machinery to limit the global competition to nonlethal means and to provide opportunities for the peaceful settlement of disputes.

As long as there are nation states, it is unreasonable to expect them to regard the U.N. as something above and beyond power politics and national interests. But national interests are not eternal; they change with time and circumstance. An increasing number of the smaller powers are coming to identify their interests with the strengthening of the U.N. and of the world community and institutional network of which it is the center.

We often voice support for a gradual increase in the functions and power of the U.N. There is no reason we should not pursue this policy more vigorously in the new age. Negotiating outside and around the U.N. not only weakens it, but makes us more sensitive to our real and pseudo allies in NATO and less responsive to third countries and other blocs. Working through the U.N. makes our policy more truly global, in line with our duties as a world leader. This is a mantle that was thrust upon us, but by now we should be getting ready to wear it with fewer sighs and groans.

The suggested change in United States foreign policy can be translated into a myriad of policy shifts and adaptations. Few of these policy recommendations are new; some are known as steps that have been rejected in the past—for example, trade with Communist China—because they did not fit into the bipolar framework. These proposals ought to be re-examined now, in the light of the new strategic outlook. There are other measures that we have advanced but that the U.S.S.R. has flatly rejected in the past; some of these might be much more acceptable in the context of a new policy. Policies tried unsuccessfully in the past might prove more effective in the coming years, either because they fit better into a pluralistic than a bipolar world (for example, settlement of the Berlin issue), or because the solutions were advanced only halfheartedly in the past (for example, various arms-reduction measures). All these varied proposals have often been discussed and cannot be reviewed within the limits of the space available here, nor is it necessary to do so. Those who can make the transition from outmoded conceptions molded in the forties to a strategy of competition taking into account current realities will readily see the specific policy suggestions that follow. Those who rigidly adhere to obsolete conceptions can hardly be expected to support such proposals. Now, more than ever, foreign-policy debate focuses on the strategic outlook. It is no longer a question of a specific adaptation or adjustment. A strategy based on a bipolar world is defunct in a world that is becoming pluralistic. The advancement of freedom and justice and the achievement of a durable peace call for a strategy of peaceful competition which will be both conducted in the framework of global institutions, and seek to advance their evolution.

ROBERT E.
ASHER

THE UNITED STATES AND DEVELOPING NATIONS*

The Progressive Shattering of Illusions

THE REVOLUTION of rising expectations—alleged to be sweeping relentlessly across Asia, Africa, and Latin America—turned out on closer inspection to be barely perceptible in many parts of the world. The less-developed countries were not a homogeneous group, equally ready for independence, equally determined to modernize, equally eager for foreign aid, or equally capable of using it.

They were not uniformly poor. The extremes of wealth and poverty within less-developed countries proved greater than the gap between average income levels in less-developed and highly developed countries. Privileged classes refused to yield up their privileges, pay taxes, and behave responsibly. The new bureaucrats, uncertain of their future and determined to make hay while the sun shone, were not unanimously averse to storing some of the hay in Swiss banks.

Less-developed countries did not see the Soviet threat in the same ominous light that we saw it. Military aid, instead of strengthening the forces of the free world vis-à-vis the Communist world, permitted some of the recipients to gird themselves for attacks on their neighbors. Traditional rivalries were sharpened and, within aided countries, the internal distribution of political power was modified in favor of the military at the expense of civilian authority. Juntas and military dictatorships may thus have been encouraged.

On the civilian side, the mere revelation of more efficient and scientific ways of raising food and producing goods did not lead

* From *The Crossroad Papers,* edited by Hans J. Morgenthau. Copyright © 1965 by W. W. Norton & Company, Inc. Reprinted by permission.

to their adoption. Technicians became frustrated by deep-rooted social and institutional barriers of which they had been only dimly aware.

The emergence of the Soviet bloc as a source of foreign aid in the mid-1950s increased the bargaining power and orneriness of the less-developed countries. Those that were chafing under Western restrictions could buy leeway by threatening to switch their patronage.

Pioneering in new and complex fields, United States leadership and United States administration were sometimes less than brilliant and not every failure was the fault of the foreigners. Before long, most Americans knew (or thought they knew) of some disastrous project somewhere, some implausible investment, some administrative hanky-panky.

Officially, the standard response was to minimize the defects, to paper over the cracks, and to make fresh investments in order to save those already made. Inability to confess error made it hard to benefit from experience. Almost nowhere could the situation be brought under control and the United States seemed incapable of withdrawing from a country in orderly fashion before getting kicked out. When it tried, as in the Aswan Dam case, it acted so clumsily that the results were worse than letting ill-enough alone.

The United States was necessarily intervening in the affairs of other countries, but seemingly in a misdirected, unbalanced way. It preserved indefensible Maginot lines between aid and trade and between economics and politics. It tended to think of intervention in the domestic political affairs of the countries receiving aid as wrong in principle and unnecessary in practice. Democracy was believed to be a kind of natural state that would be attained in other countries, too, once the obstacles were removed and levels of living began to improve. Democratic governments would pursue peaceful foreign policies and live harmoniously with other self-respecting nations.

Events in Brazil, Cambodia, the Congo, Cyprus, Ghana, Haiti, Indonesia, Korea, Laos, Panama, Pakistan, Peru, Turkey, Vietnam, and elsewhere disillusioned many. The disenchantment came, moreover, during a decade in which the richest country in the world was faced at home with a slow rate of economic growth, a high rate of unemployment, a balance-of-payments crisis, and growing tension over the solution of its own minority problems. Sustained and generous efforts to relieve hardship abroad in the absence of a thriving economy at home, and in the face of repeated rebuffs from recipients, became exceedingly difficult. . . .

Nature of the Development Process

Revolutions are by definition disorderly affairs. A supposedly law-abiding country like the United States, witnessing the culmination of a hundred-year struggle to liberate its own colored minority, should not be dismayed by the untidy, drawn-out course of events elsewhere. Excesses will continue to occur and opportunities will be missed. Unreasonable demands will be made and reasonable people—hearing them from the comfortable vantage point of a home in the suburbs or a seat in Congress—will be shocked.

What I have said about revolutions in general applies to the ebb and flow of the specific revolution politely called development. Development involves the top-to-bottom transformation of whole societies. It means fundamental changes in traditional values, motivations, institutions, and patterns of behavior. It normally requires inspired leadership and a redistribution of political power. It has economic, psychological, and sociological, as well as political aspects. At best, it will be an erratic, two-steps-forward, one-step-backward, one-step-sideways movement. It is a long-term job for which there are as yet no blueprints and few generally accepted guidelines. Nevertheless, the United States response must be more mature than "Stop the world, I want to get off."

Development, we now know, depends primarily on the will and capacity of the people of the developing country far more than on natural resources or imported supplies. The wish to develop, unfortunately, is more widespread than the will to develop, and we know relatively little about how to translate the wish into the will.

Development is a process rather than an end. Our aim should be to facilitate the unfolding of the process to the point where the local population will not only be desirous but capable of improving its lot, will have some confidence in its ability to do so, and will be earning enough foreign exchange to pay for its growing volume of imports without special subventions from abroad. Gross national product, per capita income, and other economic indexes in the developing country should move upward, but salvation does not lie in increasing these to the highest degree. The larger pie must have more to it than a strengthened upper crust.

A decent sharing of the increased wealth; the elimination of discrimination based on race, color, or creed; higher literacy rates; improved educational facilities; broader and better-informed participation in political life; and efficient and humane administration—these, too, are vitally important.

There is no assurance that economic growth will be accompanied by desirable social and political changes or vice versa. Nor is it certain that self-governing, self-sustaining peoples will be prepared to live harmoniously with either their neighbors or the United States. It merely seems more likely than that frustrated, insecure, starving populations will do so.

Outside aid strategically applied can ease the transitional period. The type of aid and the spirit in which it is offered are important, but the fact that it takes more than money to launch the development process does not mean that money is unimportant.

The nature of the development cycle is such that the balance-of-payments deficit of the developing country swells before it shrinks. At the very early stages of development, as explained in the *Report of the Council of Economic Advisers,* technical assistance may be the nation's principal need. As the country acquires the skills and institutions enabling it to help itself, however, its capacity to invest is likely to grow more rapidly than its ability to save. Moreover, for some time at least, it must obtain from abroad the great bulk of the manufactured and semi-manufactured goods that it uses in establishing new industries and raising incomes. Consequently, its requirements for imports rise rapidly.

India is a prime example of this stage of development. It is strategically located, has the largest population of any nation in the non-Communist world, and is making impressive progress without sacrificing its democratic institutions. But it is critically short of foreign exchange. India consequently serves as a dramatic reminder of the perils of assuming that money doesn't really matter. Greece, on the other hand, provides evidence that the need for extraordinary assistance does not last indefinitely, and that major beneficiaries of foreign aid can and do become self-supporting.

The prospects for an early decline in total requirements for extraordinary assistance are slim indeed, but every success story will inspire some of the stragglers. It is not unreasonable, therefore, to envisage a gradual reduction in the number of recipients and a gradual increase in the number of contributors.

Where is the money to come from? It is ironic that when defense expenditures were mounting and disarmament seemed decades away, there was much talk about devoting a portion of the savings from disarmament to development. Now that defense expenditures may actually be leveling off, however, "realism" has taken over and aid appropriations are shrinking.

United States Interest in International Development

In domestic affairs, the politician who subordinates the concerns of his constituency to the welfare of the nation as a whole is hailed as a statesman. In foreign affairs, however, the man who fails to put the domestic welfare first—ahead of the welfare of the world as a whole—risks being called a traitor. Foreign policy, therefore, tends to be justified at home on the ground that it serves the national interest in a fairly immediate and tangible fashion. This very justification makes it suspect abroad. Why, it may then be asked, should others honor us or be grateful to us for pursuing an essentially selfish course of action? Yet, so ingrained is nationalism and so muddled the state of the world today, that altruism is almost equally suspect.

The nations of the world have had very little experience in looking at their problems from a truly international viewpoint and seeking accommodation on the basis of the welfare of all. Meanwhile, each country must convince itself that a proposed activity serves its national interest.

The national interests of the United States and the developing countries are not identical and there is little point in pretending that they are. They do overlap, though, in ways that permit both sides to benefit, each in its own way, from the type of relationship that has been evolving. . . .

Co-existence with totalitarian regimes will, I hope, always be difficult for the United States. Our objective must therefore be to keep the alternative of non-totalitarian paths to development open for as long as possible to as many as possible. Our values cannot be imposed on others or imparted on a take-it-or-leave-it basis. Continuous contact and adaptation are necessary if the values of a free society are to have relevance and appeal in the new nations. Their political and economic systems will never become carbon copies of ours, but we can live with a wide range of non-totalitarian, or decreasingly totalitarian, political and economic systems.

The conventional economic arguments for United States participation in the development process are valid though overworked. We are, of course, helped by having foreign markets for our products, and rich countries make better markets than poor countries. We can use imports from many sources, and the sources should be reasonably secure and stable. The developing countries are in truth the economic "new frontier." But the United States can maintain full employment and a high standard of living at home with a very low level of imports and exports, if it chooses to do so. Should it?

Arnold Toynbee has described the impulse to protect wealth, if one has it, as one of the natural human impulses. "It is not particularly sinful, but it automatically brings a penalty with it that is out of proportion to its sinfulness. This penalty is isolation. It is a fearful thing to be isolated from the majority of one's fellow-creatures, and this will continue to be the social and moral price of wealth so long as poverty continues to be the normal condition of the World's ordinary men and women."[1]

Participation in international development programs is a way of breaking out of the isolation in which we would otherwise be dwelling. Such participation helps us to live at peace with ourselves as well as with others.

[1] Arnold J. Toynbee, *America and the World Revolution,* Oxford University Press, 1962, p. 101.

Moral arguments have gone out of fashion and humanitarianism does not occupy a prominent place in international relations. Nevertheless, it is not contrary to the national interest to follow the dictates of our conscience. The inequality that exists between nations, the grinding poverty that permeates so many nations, is no longer tolerable within the borders of a modern, progressive nation–state. This inequality is corrected within a country like the United States or Great Britain by continuous transfers of wealth from the richer citizens to the poorer citizens and from the richer areas to the poorer ones. The world, it has been said, has become too small for fellow-feeling between man and man to stop at political frontiers.[2]

In addition to the moral and economic arguments, important military and political considerations could be mentioned. Even the most convincing presentation of the American interest in promoting development offers little guidance regarding the proper geographic and financial scope and operational techniques of the effort. The situation confronting the United States in Vietnam as this chapter is being written illustrates the unpalatable alternatives we are doomed from time to time to face.

Agenda for the Future

If we are clear enough about the nature of the revolution in which, willy-nilly, we are participating, we should be able to develop an agenda for the future based on a viable blend of long-term and short-term considerations.

The immediate job appears to be to take stock of our situation, to prevent further backsliding, to make sure that we use the full arsenal of instruments at our disposal, yet also to realize that our influence is limited. The next item of business is to make the necessary resources available to the less-developed countries with maximum incentives to use them productively, while minimizing the usual strains between donor and recipient.

Military aid cannot be dispensed with—Communist China's probes into India show why—but making the appropriations directly to the Department of Defense should, without divorcing military aid from other instruments of American policy,

[2] "The Vienna Declaration on Cooperation for Development," Theodor Körner Foundation, July 1962, para. 2.

enable the Agency for International Development (AID) to concentrate more exclusively on international development.

The United States is not obligated to help nations that do not want American help or have no interest in helping themselves. We can probably afford to be more hard-boiled than we have been in choosing and retaining clients. Nor, now that we are no longer the sole source of aid, need we supply every kind of assistance sought. There are surely some things that we do better than others do them, and some that it is more in our interest to do. These priority tasks will suffer so long as we allow ourselves to be diverted into providing an almost infinite range of services. Development assistance, moreover, can be harmful as well as helpful, and will be if it enables receivers to postpone for too long painful adjustments that they will sooner or later have to make.

There is no merit in stoically bearing burdens that others may be induced to share. A more rational division of labor is needed between bilateral and multilateral programs (that is, between United States, British, or French national agencies and United Nations, Inter-American, and European-Economic-Community agencies). Elsewhere I have suggested some guidelines for the expansion of multilateral efforts.[3]

The kind of policing of foreign aid engaged in by the General Accounting Office, with its periodic revelations about roads and airports that serve no visible economic purpose, is utterly inappropriate to anything as sensitive as the development effort. American ingenuity is capable of devising less heavy-handed methods of safeguarding the integrity of its bilateral programs.

In any event, we cannot vest the entire responsibility for promoting development in a handful of public agencies. A total effort requires total involvement. It has become platitudinous to call for greatly enlarged roles for private business, for trade union and professional groups, for women's organizations, universities, foundations, municipalities, etc., but it is no less necessary because it is platitudinous. Research on the interrelations of economic, social, and political development must also be

[3] Robert E. Asher, "Multilateral Versus Bilateral Aid: An Old Controversy Revisited," *International Organization,* Autumn, 1962, Brookings Reprint No. 66.

stepped up and provision made for incorporating research findings into operational activities at the earliest possible date.

Fostering the development of democratic institutions is a top priority field for both research and action. The Communists have a vast network of cultural societies, friendship clubs, political parties, and student groups; democrats appear unnecessarily squeamish about communicating their ideology and maintaining intimate contacts with kindred souls in other lands.

A new look at the methods of financing development is needed. One of the entrenched myths of the postwar era is that loans have character-building virtues lacked by grants. It is perfectly feasible to design a grant program that includes disciplinary features analogous to those alleged to be inherent in the loan process, but does not make comparable demands on the limited foreign-exchange earnings of the developing country.

Moreover, the balance-of-payments deficit that developing countries normally encounter need not be met entirely with loans and grants. Aid is not nobler than trade and there is much to be said for amending the ground rules governing the conduct of international trade so that more of the foreign-exchange requirements of the developing countries can be earned through international trade. The ardent desire of the developing countries for such amendments was amply demonstrated at the United Nations Conference on Trade and Development in Geneva during the spring of 1964.

The present international monetary arrangements also need attention. The development of Puerto Rico has not been hampered by periodic foreign-exchange crises, and bolder attempts might be made to build international institutions to the point where other underdeveloped areas can obtain comparable freedom. A small step in the right direction was taken in 1963 when the International Monetary Fund created a new "facility" for helping member countries that experience temporary declines in export earnings due to circumstances beyond their control.

We would be missing the boat completely if we thought of either the long-range or the short-range tasks primarily as challenges to our technical ingenuity. We can do all the right things with respect to monetary policy, trade, aid, and military support, and still stumble badly because of faulty political attitudes. Failure to appreciate the intensity of opposition in the less-developed world to the South African policy of apartheid, to the policies of Portugal in Angola and Mozambique, or to nuclear testing in the Sahara, will cost us dearly.

At the same time, we must devise more effective ways of enlisting the collaboration of developing countries in safeguarding human rights within the lands that they themselves control. The Charter of the United Nations calls not only for the maintenance of international peace and security and the promotion of higher standards of living. It demands with equal eloquence the promotion of "universal respect for, and observance of, human rights and fundamental freedoms for all."

Great powers have the capacity to inspire as well as to intimidate. The successful prosecution of our war against poverty and prejudice at home will provide a better climate for its successful prosecution abroad. The struggle of American minority groups for integration has its counterpart in the struggle of the less-developed countries for integration in the nascent world community. There is one important difference, however. The less-developed countries are not minority groups. They contain an overwhelming proportion of mankind. Their aspirations, though not necessarily realizable today or tomorrow, cannot for a century be gainsaid.

BARBARA WARD | THE RESPONSIBILITY OF POWER*

... THE UNIVERSALIST DREAM was not mistaken. Indeed the most powerful and effective forces of our time—our science and our technology—have realized it. What was false was to assume that there could be some easy, automatic self-regulating

* From *Nationalism and Ideology* by Barbara Ward. Copyright © 1966 by W. W. Norton & Company, Inc. Reprinted by permission.

method of achieving the profound readjustments in political loyalty, economic function, and philosophical meaning which the new society demands. What is really so curious about both versions of the liberal society—capitalist or Communist—is how little thought they give to the hard realities of international order, how much they assume that interstate relations will solve themselves and worldwide markets run of their own accord. The capitalist virtually says everything will be all right so long as you keep government out, the Communist if you bring government in. But the amount of sheer hard realistic thought on either side has been minimal, the wash of ideology and feckless optimism phenomenal. It is time for this to stop—on both sides. No *automatic* forces are going to build at the needed, worldwide level a decent political system, a functioning international economy, or a basis of reconciling and uplifting purpose. These needs simply have to be moved from the twilight zone of our thinking and given the priority, the urgency, and the attention we give day by day to national interests many of which, because of their international implications, we are virtually powerless to solve single-handed. At least we have to recognize where the priorities really lie and give up the assumption that some hidden hand will after all pull a rabbit of world order out of our planet's present largely unwearable hat.

Where does realistic thinking begin? Surely in those areas in which relevant concrete achievement is already an historical fact. What men have achieved once, they can achieve again, and orderly political institutions, functioning markets, and sustaining beliefs *have* already organized and vitalized very large areas of the earth's surface supporting very large numbers of the earth's population. If communications no faster than relays of horses and messengers could help to hold together the Chinese quarter of the human race, supersonic jets and images and voices bounced off space satellites should, technically, do the larger job more easily. True, the vast Chinese empire was a despotism, and this historical route to unity must be counted closed. No *one* center of power will conquer the world into unity. Today conquest means annihilation. We have to plan for a plural world with a number of power centers. In fact, at its appropriate level, the nation, in spite of the fantastic variations in its size and coherence—from 600,000 people in Gabon to 800 million in China—will almost certainly be a lasting, constituent element in any worldwide supranational system. But it will not be an ultimate element. After all, we are used to diffuse loyalties. A sense of the clan survives in Scotland. The sense of being Scottish survives in Britain. The sense of being British is very likely to survive in a European union. So will the sense of being French. Anyone who knows France finds incomprehensible the fear that such a land could in any real sense be submerged. It is far more likely to give all its neighbors, like its Africans, a Gallic tinge. And Europe in turn will have a sense of itself in any intercontinental association. No unity in the world will make Latin and "Anglo-Saxon" America alike. Anyway, who wants them to be? A world of interchangeable men and women is precisely the Orwellian nightmare of 1984.

The issue is function, not standardization. It is a sound principle of human order that social tasks should be left at the simplest and most human level at which they can be adequately performed—beginning with the family. Everyone understands the sense of a hierarchy of responsibility *inside* the nation. The central government does not overlay, just for the fun of it, the responsibilities that can best be carried by cities and counties or, in a federation, by the constituent states. But owing to the fixation of men's minds on *national* sovereignty, the top of the world's political pyramid is not there. We recognize authority and hierarchy up through all the levels of political, economic, and social need. Then, when at the highest level we reach the ultimate issues of survival itself, we recognize none. There is simply a blank arena, filled with the pressures and counter-pressures of irresponsible power. No one can call this reason. It represents a total failure of imagination and rationality.

It is not even as though the powers which would have, of necessity, to be exercised at a world level need be very extensive. Over much of the earth's surface federations as large as the United States or the Soviet Union have resources and scope enough to meet most of their citizens' needs and satisfy most of their aspirations. If similar federal structures could be established in other continents—Europe, Africa, Latin America, the Indian sub-continent—the underpinning of world order at subsidiary levels would be much more stable. Nor is this an entirely empty hope. Today, with some genuine enthusiasm and also with the hypocritical tribute vice pays to virtue, movements have started in most of these areas to edge toward greater unity, even if elderly and flamboyant anachronisms like General de Gaulle stand in the way.

At the world level, the political task lies almost solely in preventing war. Of course this fact also makes the range of tasks the most difficult, the most sensitive, the most frenzied of all for here national pride, illusions of grandeur, the pretensions of prestige, and all the paranoid follies of which man is capable rush to the protection of interests which may in themselves be perfectly legitimate but which can be neither realized nor mediated in the middle of the surrounding hysteria.

Yet within states methods of dealing with the most passionate conflicts of interest have been worked out. The rule of law, protected by an impartial police force and exercised through law courts, through rules of equity, through mediation, conciliation, and arbitration has brought the violent self-assertion of individual citizens, of groups, corporations, and subsidiary authorities under reasonable control. General Motors, whose corporate income is larger than that of a quarter of the world's nation-states, does not thunder "My interests, right or wrong" and hire thugs to settle the matter by violence. For all its power, its imagination is tamed by the acceptance of the need for legal settlement. Governments could be as peace-loving—and indeed as prosperous—were it not for the disastrous conviction loose in the world that the hierarchy of responsibility ends at the level of national sovereignty. Below may be law. All above is force.

Admittedly, we have made a first timid step toward the acceptance of worldwide law. The United Nations exists above all to provide alternatives to violence. Its meetings and corridors provide the informal venue for national leaders in search of compromise. Its debates attempt to build up a world consensus with enough moral force to deter aggressors. On a few occasions it has actually been able to act in a full governmental fashion—imposing solutions, as in Katanga, or policing areas of danger, in Cyprus, in the Gaza Strip, along the cease-fire line in Kashmir. These are not negligible achievements. If its intervention could be extended to such areas as Southeast Asia, the use of purely American power to deter Chinese "adventurism" could be withdrawn. If our eyes were not all but blinded by nationalist myopia, we would see in both the achievements and the possible extensions of the United Nations police power the most hopeful growing points of a world in which nuclear annihilation could cease to be, as it is now, a near certainty.

But the United Nations is still no more than a mock version of the kind of central power the world needs if it is to survive. Great states retain all but absolute sovereignty through the veto. All states tend to see the organization as a forum for maneuver and pressure on others rather than as an august symbol of the authority all accept. Nor will much difference be made by changes, however rational and desirable, in its machinery. Weighted voting, majority decisions, the abolition of the veto all no doubt make sense in rational terms, but they amount to very little unless a profound change occurs in the attitudes of the governments themselves. A Great Power does not cease to be a Great Power if the veto goes. Its simple scale of might is a veto since no outside force can exercise coercion without unleashing total war. The change has to come from a conversion, a new realism, a rational conviction that once the bomb is invented, only a world with peaceful means of settling disputes has any hope of avoiding ultimate incineration. And as every drunk, every addict, every paranoid will tell you, many prefer the disease to the cure.

It is for this reason that, at this stage of human development, a special responsibility seems to lie on the greatest power in history, the United States. It is, in some ways, the least trammeled with age-long memories of separate grandeur. It came to birth and then it came of age in a world already tilted toward universal solutions. It has kept, under its Americanism, a wider sense of the family of man. For this reason alone, American vision and American prodding helped to create whatever international institutions now exist. Moreover, America is already in a sense a plural world. It has had to absorb the nationalities of the world. It struggles bravely with the more difficult task of absorbing the races, too. It knows that diversity will remain the rule of any human society and in its complex but open federal system, it has given pluralism a working political form.

The degree to which this inheritance fits the United States to pioneer the new tasks of world order can best be illustrated by comparing with it the other great federal community of the modern age—Soviet Russia. There both history and ideology have so far reinforced the closed society. Tsarist Russia never made the break to liberal institutions, and the Marxist illusion that the state would wither away—which would doubtless have been proved an illusion anywhere—came straight up against one of the oldest, toughest, most encrusted traditions of holy despotism in the world. To expect such a state to take a lead in building the institutions of an open world would be to strain hopefulness too far. The miracle is that the monolith will sit down in the United Nations' plural community, put itself in a position to be judged by its neighbors, dourly defend itself, when outnumbered, with the veto, and on occasion even participate in a vote, a policy, or a decision. Statesmen from open societies tend to forget how extraordinary it is that Russia participates at all. Some of the liberal and universalist content of Marxism has after all survived in the despotic Russian container. The language of freedom and popular democracy—like the mask of virtue—may begin as hypocrisy. It could end as truth—whereas there is no "give" in the language of blood and soil and frenzied national paranoia. Hitler's reaction to the plural society of the League of Nations was to march Germany out.

Nonetheless the world of voting, of lobbying, of open decisions openly arrived at is not Russia's present, natural, comfortable environment. The lead in pushing, prodding, persuading, and guiding the nations toward the acceptance of minimal but essential world authority in the cause of peace can come only from the United States. True, it should be supported by every democracy with a comparable tradition of the open society. Nowhere perhaps does General de Gaulle's reactionary nationalism show itself more ominously than in his readiness to compete with Russia in limiting even the most modest extensions of United Nations responsibility.

And few contemporary hardenings of the nationalist position

are more tragic than that of India in its dispute with Pakistan. If the nation of Ashoka, Gandhi, and Nehru, if the great plural democracy of Asia cannot find ways to mediate a solution on the basis of the generosity, conciliation, and peaceful settlement it successfully and rightly claimed and exercised in 1947, then the ultimate chances of the rule of law, not force, in Asia seem remote indeed. India could be, as it were, as much the democratic pole of the vast Asian community as the United States has become in the Western world. But if self-righteous nationalism takes over and reliance on force becomes the rule, it is difficult to see victory in Asia for any but the most powerful community—which will be not the Indians but the Chinese.

There is a further reason for America's primacy in the tasks of peace. Peace does not consist only in the absence of conflict. It also entails some abatement in the causes of conflict. In fact, one can argue that if a man gives up his "right" to settle his grievances by private force, he may reasonably ask his government to see that they do not become too intolerable. The societies where civil peace reigns are not on the whole the most neglected, the most poverty-stricken, the most disillusioned. Violence breaks out in Watts, not Westchester County. The whole world has now passed beyond the phase of ignorant, passive, resigned destitution. Propaganda and communication have seen to it that everywhere, in Adlai Stevenson's celebrated phrase, the "revolution of rising expectations" works like a leaven. And in this worldwide society, the contrast between Watts and Westchester does not seem too far-fetched.

In 1965, the combined incomes of the white wealthy postcolonial North Atlantic nations who make up some 20 percent of the world's peoples, passed the million million dollar mark—which is about 70 percent of the world's income. Latin America subsists on an annual income of $60 billion—a sum the United States *adds* to its income in eighteen months. Africa's income is half as small again. These are the contrasts. Put into concrete terms, they mean half the expectation of life, five or six times the infant mortality, a fraction of the literacy, diets without protein, rural slums without work, city slums without drains or water. The gap between the nations to the north of the Tropic of Cancer and the rest of the world is fully as wide as the gap between nineteenth century tycoons and the raw, bewildered migrants huddling on Ellis Island.

Yet the gap, domestically, has been diminished. Larger shares in the national wealth through higher wages and "fringe benefits," transfers from rich to poor by taxation to increase education, health, and skills—these measures have transformed the migrants into citizens and turned the masses into the vast consuming market of the modern economy.

In the international economy, measures to give the developing continents more steady prices for their exports and to open up Western markets to their goods would, in a similar way, increase the "wages" they earn for their services in the world market. And sustained technical and capital assistance, increasing skills and health, providing infrastructure and building up the technological base of the modern economy would, like taxation at home, help to create peoples better able to help themselves.

All this we know. We have accurate estimates from such impartial bodies as the World Bank to show that at this moment the poor nations could absorb roughly another $4 billion a year in constructive investment. But ever since the flow of Western capital reached $9 billion in 1961, there it has stuck. Meanwhile Western income has grown by another $150 billion. The proportion of aid to national income is, therefore, falling while expectations continue to rise.

In all this the United States occupies a special position. It accounts for three-quarters of the increase in Atlantic income and it started the sixties from a national income base of nearly $600 billion. If it set the precedent of devoting to aid one percent of income, the sum would still only represent a quarter of its *annual* growth in wealth. In short, the sum itself would not be noticed. The burdens are political, not economic. Disappointments go all the way from Kashmir to Latin America's propensity for inflation. At home, they include "a weariness with well doing" that fails to produce immediate and spectacular results. So, at the moment, the wealthiest people in human history appear to be in a phase of disillusion about the consequences of generosity. Just so did Victorian duchesses speak of the "bad poor" who put coals in the bath. And if there is no drive in America to put life, drive, and enthusiasm back into the concept of international aid, no other nation is likely to shoulder the task.

At a factual level, the arguments against this attitude can only be made country by country, case by case. There are hundreds of success stories to set against the grisly examples of failure. How many people, for instance, know of the help given by the World Bank and the British Government to transform the long contested "White Highlands" in Kenya into an area of settled African farming? How many people know that the controversial Volta hydroelectric scheme was completed a year ahead of time and at a cost of $15 million less than the contract price? Who knows that in the rear of the Vietnam fighting, the first dams of the Mekong River scheme have actually been built? Who knows about Pakistan's agricultural breakthrough on the basis of tube wells? Of Central America's successful experiment in a common market? Of Africa's fantastic drive for education? Of the recent ending of aid to Taiwan and Greece? Of Mexico's surge to modernity? The failures hit the headlines. The successes are regarded as routine.

If anyone had looked at the British economy between 1800 and 1850—as it looked to Dickens or the "dismal scientists"— he might well have concluded that the whole experiment was destined to fail. The developing "South" is similarly entering on the fifty-year cycle of "breakthrough" to modernity. The first stages always look a mess. But it is unreasonable, it is folly to condemn on ten years' evidence an experiment which must, of necessity, take four or five decades to complete.

Today the issue is above all one of keeping faith. Better shares and progressive taxation helped to raise up the poor and create the modern market *inside* domestic society. We have to believe that similar policies, conducted as steadily, will have the same economic effect in the world at large—and will in addition profoundly influence political attitudes by ending the picture of wealthy white colonialists exploiting the "helpless" peoples of the developing world. Such a change is not a matter of policy or machinery. These are largely available. The World Bank, the International Development Authority, the International Monetary Fund, the United Nations Special Fund—all these organizations contain enough skilled and experienced men to run the economic organs of a world authority. The sums involved are relatively puny—some $12 billion a year compared with the $120 billion the developed world, capitalist and Communist together, spend on a system of armed security which threatens them both with extinction. Even as an insurance, it is not expensive. As the only means available to counter the grievances which lead to war, it looks positively cheap.

But it has little appeal. It inspires little enthusiasm and devotion. And the reason is simple. It lies in that lifeless zone beyond the thoughts of national voters and beyond the direct responsibility of national governments. Policies which are reasonable for Appalachia or Tyneside stop dead at the seashore. The reasons have nothing to do with culture or economic necessity or facts of any kind. They are simply rooted in the nonworking of human imagination, responsibility, and generosity once the blinkers of nationalism go on. Today faith, not fact, is what cripples our programs, closes our pockets, and dries up our hearts.

Contributors

CHARLES ABRAMS, Chairman of the City Planning Department of Columbia University, was formerly an adviser to the United Nations and the Agency for International Development. His books include *Forbidden Neighbors* and *The City is the Frontier*.

ROBERT E. ASHER, a former Special Assistant to the Assistant Secretary of State for Economic Affairs, is an international relations specialist with the Brookings Institution.

ALAN BATCHELDER, Assistant Professor of Economics at Kenyon College, is the author of *The Economics of Poverty* and a contributor to the *American Economic Review*.

ARTHUR I. BLAUSTEIN is Director of Inter-Agency Coordination and Inter-Governmental Affairs for the Northeast Region of the United States Office of Economic Opportunity.

EMILE BENOIT is Professor of International Business at the Columbia School of Business and School of International Affairs. He is co-author with Kenneth Boulding of *Disarmament and the Economy*.

MICHAEL F. BROWER is a faculty member of the Sloan School of Industrial Management at M.I.T. He was on the editorial board of the *Correspondent*, for which he wrote frequently.

HARRY M. CAUDILL, an attorney in Whitesburg, Kentucky, is author of *Night Comes to the Cumberlands*. He has spent six years in the Kentucky House of Representatives working for progressive legislation.

JOSEPH S. CLARK is the senior U.S. Senator from Pennsylvania and one of the Senate's foremost spokesmen for progressive legislation. He is the author of two books, *The Senate Establishment* and *Congress: The Sapless Branch*.

KENNETH B. CLARK, Professor of Psychology at City College of the City University of New York, is the author of *Prejudice and Your Child* and *Dark Ghetto: Dilemmas of Social Power*.

RICHARD A. CLOWARD is Professor of Social Work at the New York School of Social Work, Columbia University, and co-author of *Delinquency and Opportunity* with Lloyd E. Ohlin.

O. EDMUND CLUBB, who was a specialist on Asia in the State Department for two decades, is a lecturer at Columbia and New York Universities. He is a frequent contributor to periodicals on Asian affairs.

ROBERT COLES, research psychiatrist at the Harvard University Health Services, is a consultant to the Southern Regional Council and a member of the National Advisory Committee on farm labor. He has written numerous articles on the problems of desegregation and on the lives of migrant farm workers.

RÉGIS DEBRAY is a French journalist whose *Revolution in the Revolution?* is designed as a handbook for Latin American revolutionaries.

AMITAI ETZIONI, Associate Professor of Sociology and a research associate of the Institute of War and Peace Studies at Columbia University, is the author of *The Hard Way to Peace* and *Winning without War*.

FRANTZ FANON was the leading spokesman of the Algerian revolution. The late psychiatrist's book, *The Wretched of the Earth*, is a manifesto calling for the use of absolute violence against colonial oppressors.

EDMUNDO FLORES, Professor of Agricultural Economics at the National University of Mexico, is a frequent adviser to the United Nations on matters of land reform and economic development.

J. WILLIAM FULBRIGHT, Democrat from Arkansas, is Chairman of the Senate Foreign Relations Committee. He has written *Old Myths and New Realities* and *The Arrogance of Power*.

EDUARDO GALEANO is in charge of publications at the Universidad de la Republica in Montevideo. His latest collection of short stories is on the best-seller list in Uruguay. He has travelled extensively for UNESCO and was the editor of *Epoca,* a now defunct Montevideon daily newspaper.

NORMAN GALL is a reporter on the San Juan *Star* and a regular contributor to periodicals on Latin American affairs.

PAUL GOODMAN, poet, playwright, therapist, and social critic, is a fellow of the Institute for Policy Studies in Washington, D.C. His books include *Growing up Absurd, The Community of Scholars,* and *Compulsory Mis-Education*.

MICHAEL HARRINGTON, National Chairman of the League for Industrial Democracy, is the author of the widely acclaimed *The*

Other America, and a contributing editor to *Dissent* and *New America.*

ROBERT L. HEILBRONER is Professor of Economics at the New School for Social Research. His first book, *The Worldly Philosophers,* has become a standard introduction to economic history throughout the United States.

PAUL JACOBS is on the staff of the Center for the Study of Democratic Institutions. He is co-editor with Saul Landau of *The New Radicals,* and author of *Prelude to Riot.*

CHARLES C. KILLINGSWORTH is Professor of Labor and Industrial Relations at Michigan State University. He has served as a labor dispute arbitrator and a consultant to both labor and industry.

MARTIN LUTHER KING, JR., clergyman, civil rights leader, and winner of the Nobel Peace Prize, headed the Southern Christian Leadership Conference. His books include *Why We Can't Wait, Stride toward Freedom,* and *Where Do We Go from Here?*

OSCAR LEWIS is Professor of Anthropology at the University of Illinois. Among his books on the culture of poverty are *Five Families, The Children of Sánchez,* and *La Vida.*

BERNARD E. LOSHBOUGH is executive director for ACTION-Housing, Inc., in Pittsburgh, Pennsylvania.

MICHAEL MACCOBY, psychoanalyst, teaches at the National University in Mexico City. He is working with Erich Fromm on *Las Cuevas,* a study of a Mexican village.

CONOR CRUISE O'BRIEN, Albert Schweitzer Professor of the Humanities at New York University, is author of *To Katanga and Back* and *Writers and Politics.* In 1960–61 he represented the United Nations in the Congo.

ARTHUR PEARL, Professor in the Division of Psychological Service, School of Education, University of Oregon, is co-author with Frank Riessman of *New Careers for the Poor.*

FRANCES FOX PIVEN is Assistant Professor of Social Work at the New York School of Social Work, Columbia University.

THOMAS PYNCHON is the author of the highly praised novels *"V"* and *The Crying of Lot 49.*

FRANK RIESSMAN, Professor of Educational Sociology at New York University, wrote *The Culturally Deprived Child* and co-authored *New Careers for the Poor* with Arthur Pearl.

SAM SCHULMAN is a sociologist and former visiting graduate professor at the National University in Bogotá, where he was on an extended visit to Colombia made possible by a Ford Foundation grant.

STAN STEINER is a poet and novelist with a special interest in the Southwest. Among his writings are *The Last Horse* and a children's book on the Navajo.

BARBARA WARD (Lady Jackson) is a frequent contributor to *The Economist* of London. Her books include *India and the West* and *The Rich Nations and the Poor*.

WILLIAM APPLEMAN WILLIAMS is Professor of History at the University of Wisconsin. Among his most important books are *The Shaping of American Diplomacy: 1781–1947*. *The Contours of American History*, and *The Tragedy of American Diplomacy*.

ROGER R. WOOCK, who teaches at Hunter College, has been a consultant to the Office of Economic Opportunity and the National Teacher Corps. He is on the editorial board of the quarterly journal, *Urban Education*.

Index

WESTMAR COLLEGE LIBRARY